FIFTH EDITION

THE HUMAN VENTURE

A Global History to 1500

VOLUME I

Anthony Esler

College of William and Mary

Pearson
Education

Upper Saddle River, New Jersey 07458

A Cip catalog record for this book can be obtained from the Library of Congress.

F or my father, Jamie Arthur Esler,
who wrote the history of the world
on one page many years ago.

Editorial Director: *Charlyce Jones Owen*
Senior Acquisition Editor: *Charles Cavaliere*
Associate Editor: *Emsal Hason*
Senior Managing Editor: *Jan Stephan*
Production Liaison: *Fran Russello*
Project Manager: *Patty Donovan/Pine Tree Composition*
Prepress and Manufacturing Buyer: *Tricia Kenny*
Art Director: *Jayne Conte*
Cover Designer: *Kiwi Design*
Cover Art: Encounter Between Solomon and the Queen of Sheba (c) Archivo Iconografico, S. A./Corbis
Director, Image Resource Center: *Melinda Lee Reo*
Manager, Rights & Permissions: *Zina Arabia*
Interior Image Specialist: *Beth Boyd-Brenzel*
Cover Image Specialist: *Karen Sanatar*
Image Permission Coordinator: *Fran Toepher*
Photo Researcher: *Kathy Ringrose*
Marketing Manager: *Claire Bitting*

This book was set in 10/12 Times by Pine Tree Composition, Inc.
and was printed and bound by Courier Companies, Inc.
The cover was printed by Courier Companies, Inc.

© 2004, 2000, 1996, 1992, 1986 by Pearson Education, Inc.
Upper Saddle River, New Jersey 07458

Printed in the United States of America
7 8 9 10 V092 16 15 14

ISBN 0-13-183546-7

Pearson Education Ltd., *London*
Pearson Education Australia Pty. Limited, *Sydney*
Pearson Education Singapore, Pte. Ltd.
Pearson Education North Asia Ltd., *Hong Kong*
Pearson Education Canada, Ltd., *Toronto*
Pearson Educación de Mexico, S.A. de C.V.
Pearson Education—Japan, *Tokyo*
Pearson Education Malaysia, Pte. Ltd.
Pearson Education, *Upper Saddle River, New Jersey*

CONTENTS

Chapter 10 Domes and Minarets: the Spread of Islam (600–1300) 250

Chapter 11 Merchants and Missionaries of the Indies: India and Southeast Asia (600–1500) 271

Chapter 14   Toward a Larger World: From the Bantu Migrations to the Mongol Empire 500 B.C.E.–C.E. 1500   334

PREFACE

Prefaces are always challenging, and the prefaces to this book seem to get more challenging with each new edition. For a preface is at least in part a look ahead. And in the opening years of the twenty-first century, the global prospect before us looks less predictable than ever.

This fifth edition of *The Human Venture*, like its predecessors, attempts to provide a historical background to the changing world of today. Like earlier editions, this one tries to offer a genuinely global perspective, rather than a European history with add-ons about other cultures. It still aims at the broadest possible coverage—coverage of women as well as of men, of preurban as well as of urban-imperial peoples, of culture as well as of politics. It still tries to humanize the past with emphasis on the historical roles of individual human beings, from ancient emperors to laboring peasants. And this particular version of our global past still builds on a strong narrative line that reflects the nature of history as the author sees it—as a story going somewhere, obscure though that somewhere may still be to the principal historical actors—us.

A major goal of this new edition has been to adapt the book more closely to the requirements of classroom teaching and learning. The number of chapters, for instance, has been reduced from fifty to thirty—roughly the number of weeks in many academic years. This change, I hasten to add, has been largely accomplished by combining chapters, not by cutting! All chapters have again been revised, and each now has a new theme-setting "Glance Ahead" opener and a substantially updated bibliography.

There are also some new maps, some new pictures, and a new emphasis on the "Voices from the Past" boxes—one for each chapter now. The "Overviews" introducing each of the six large sections into which the book is divided have also been revised, and a new big-picture time line appended to each. And the book as a whole has been redesigned in a "trade-book" format that I hope will be easier for the reader to hold while absorbing the carefully digested insights of twenty-five centuries of historians from many times and lands.

Once more, I have included the odd anecdote and I hope some new insights picked up during the three months or more I spend overseas each year. Several weeks each on the upper Amazon, across the Outback and the Top End of Australia, in the Northwest Frontier Province of Pakistan, and among the ethnic minority villages of western China have certainly added to my respect for the indigenous peoples of the world. And annual visits to familiar neighborhoods in favorite European cities serve as a healthy reminder that the peoples of the developed world have a lot to teach each other too.

A key function of the preface, finally, remains to express proper gratitude to the many people without whom there would be no book at all. Here a primary debt must be to Charles Cavaliere, the new Prentice Hall history editor, for injecting a surge of youthful dynamism into this particular venture into the human past. Many thanks also to Emsal Hasan and Patty Donovan for getting me through the hard part—finishing—and to Adrienne Paul for handling every unlikely request of mine effectively and expeditiously.

Without the shared insights and shrewd criticisms of scholarly readers, of course, a synthesis as broad as this would be impossible. My thanks, then, to Kenneth Wilburn, East Carolina University; Louis McDermott, California Maritime Academy; Trevor Getz, University of New Orleans; Robert Garfield, DePaul University; and Pamela McVay, Ursuline College.

Thanks for past critical readings should also go to Akanmu G. Adebayo, Kennesaw State University; Alana Cain Scott, Morehead State University; Elizabeth C. George, Southern Illinois University; Farid Mahdavi-Izadi, San Diego State University; Linda L. Taber, Wayne State University; Joe Gowaskie, Rider College; John Voll, University of New Hampshire; Penny S. Gold, Knox College; Walter S. Hanchett, SUNY/Cortland; Donald L. Layton, Indiana State University; Melvin E. Page, Murray State University; Susan Fitzpatrick, Lindenwood College; Curtis Anderson, Oakland Community College; Dorothy Zeisler-Vralsted, University of Wisconsin, La Crosse; Ed Balog and James Hood, Lindenwood College; James Weland and Nancy R. Northrup, Bentley College; Thomas Anderson, Eastern Connecticut State University; Howard A. Barnes, Winston Salem University; Olwyn M. Blouet, Virginia State University; Robert Garfield, De Paul University; W. Scott Jessee, Appalachian State University; Gerald Newman, Kent State University; and John A. Phillips, University of California-Riverside.

Thanks again to scholars who have patiently labored to educate me over the years, including Marjorie W. Bingham of Women in World Area Studies; Mario D. Mazzarella and the Department of History at Christopher Newport College; J. F. Watts and the faculty of the trailblazing World Civilization course at City College of New York; Richard Snyder, William Pemberton, and the landmark World History program at the University of Wisconsin, La Crosse; and Bill Alexander, Cassandra Newby, and Jeanne Zeidler of Hampton University.

As always, my thanks must go to friends and colleagues here at William and Mary, who do their best to correct the sweeping generalizations I bring to the acid test of their expertise. For many years of help, my thanks to Ismail Abdalla, Berhanu Abegaz, Jim Axtell, Craig Canning, John Carroll, Ed Crapol, Judy Ewell, A. Z. Freeman, Phil Funigiello, Dale Hoak, Ward Jones, Kris Lane, Gil McArthur, Jim McCord, Leisa Meyer, Ed Pratt, Abdul Karim Rafeq, Ernie Schwintzer, John Selby, Tom Sheppard, Rich Sigwalt, George Strong, Cam Walker, and Jim Whittenburg.

For introductions to some fascinating corners of the world, my thanks to Steve and Peggy Brush, for Peru when things were much too exciting to be saddled with a guest as well; to Professor Dong Leshan, of the Chinese Academy of Social Sciences; to Chris Drake, for showing me how to look at the African land; to Carol Clemeau Esler, for all the village-level sojourns in Europe; to Marcia Davidson Field, for her insights into Latin America over many years; to Richard Goff, for caustic comments and sage council along the Atlantic; to Professor Isaria N. Kimambo, of the University of Dar es Salaam, for insights into African historiography; to Ross Kreamer for Java, Sumatra, and Vietnam; to Chris Mullen Kreamer, for sharing her remarkable "African destiny"; to Steve and Ann Marlowe, for expat Europe and much more; to Don Meyer, for Benares, the Ganges, and the border roads of India; to Ernie Schwintzer and Alice Davenport for Jakarta in tense times; and to Jerry Weiner, for running a tight ship from Abidjan to Zanzibar.

And thanks again to Cam Walker, who keeps coming up with amazing places we haven't ever been—two different versions of Shangri-la so far!—but never lets anything get in the way of that evening trip to the corner café.

Anthony Esler

PREFACE

Anthony Esler has taught history at the College of William and Mary in Williamsburg, Virginia, for most of his sixty-odd years. But he has also lived in many parts of the United States, accumulated several years of living and travel in Europe, and visited every inhabited continent several times. He spends a minimum of three months overseas each year, sampling the wine, exploring the streets and the ruins, and checking to see if the rainforests are still there. Esler's books reflect his enthusiasms. These include a fascination with generational conflict nurtured in the streets of the sixties, a passion for story-telling, and a preference for panoramic "big picture" history—like *The Human Venture*.

Esler on the road to the ruins of Tsaparang in western Tibet.

INTRODUCTION

VENTURE INTO HISTORY

AN UNDERTAKING OF UNCERTAIN OUTCOME

HISTORY AND CIVILIZATION

FROM ROME TO MACHU PICCHU

An Undertaking of Uncertain Outcome

History does not happen—it is made by human beings. It is made by people of differing opinions, of varied degrees of knowledge and control, of more or less good will. It is the work of all the peoples of this world, down all the human centuries. History is, has been, and will continue to be the common venture of us all.

The word *venture* derives from an old word for *adventure*—and history is surely that.

It is too easy in writing (or reading) a textbook to lose sight of the great adventure that is the human story. The long wanderings of our prehistoric predecessors over land and sea, peopling the continents, are epics of adventure that will never be written. The struggles of our ancestors with each other, sometimes savage and often tragic, are nonetheless tales of human heroism too. Even the silent inner struggles of the poet, the philosopher, or the prophet may be great adventures of the human spirit.

Nor are all the historic adventurers famous names in history books. The cabin boy who signed on to sail with Ferdinand Magellan and returned alive—one of seventeen to do so, the first human beings to circumnavigate the globe—was as much an adventurer as Magellan himself, whose bones whitened on a far Pacific shore. The peasant girl who never traveled ten miles from her medieval village but heard the voices of angels in the church bells ringing was as much an adventurer of the spirit as Joan of Arc, who rallied armies and left her name to history.

We are all of us part of the human venture. Bantus trekking across Africa, Amerindians descending the length of the Americas, builders of the ancient cultures of Egypt or India or China—we are all adventurers in history. The future may well look upon our highways and skyscrapers, our tumultuously expanding global computer network, our miles-high jets and rockets drifting among the stars, and see all of us today as a race of heroes.

A *venture*, according to *Webster's* dictionary, is "an undertaking involving chance, risk, or danger," an attempt fraught with "peril" and "jeopardy." We may be spared the great plagues, the long hungers, the slowly descending ice that pressed inexorably upon our ancestors. But the threats of sudden economic collapse, of faiths and ideologies in conflict, of wars open and secret are with us as much today as they ever were. And overpopulation, poverty, and famine, pollution, dwindling resources, and climatic change may be even more dangerous.

Webster's further defines a venture as "an undertaking of uncertain outcome." Here, too, history clearly qualifies. Even the most clearsighted historian would hesitate to say much about where we are all going—let alone whether we will ever get there.

There have been those who thought they saw the outcome. Chinese scholars saw history following a pattern of endless cycles. Medieval Christians and medieval Muslims sought meaning in history as the will of God. Enlightenment philosophers and the ideologues of the last two centuries have offered various versions of the gospel of progress as the road to utopia. But we do not know that any of these patterns imposed upon the human story accurately describes the primary direction in which history is moving. We do not know for certain that history is moving in any particular direction at all!

What does seem evident from the historical record is that we are trying. The outcome may be unsure, but human beings have been laboring for many centuries to give direction to the human story. In this sense, at least, our human venture into history is a purposeful one. We may frequently be blind to our true destination. We may often be operating at vigorous crosspurposes with one another, one nation or one people against another. We may fail of our endeavors; some of the most promising historic drives have broken down in the end, collapsing from internal rot or overwhelmed by external enemies. But they have been conscious drives. Launched in the names of whatever false gods or faltering causes, group follies or individual egotism, every great movement, every great civilization has nonetheless been, at least in significant part, a deliberate effort to impose human will upon the world.

HISTORY AND CIVILIZATION

The perilous course of human history is thus something more than an adventure. It is a great commitment.

To our ancestors several centuries ago, the word *venture* could mean simply an investment, a risking of capital in hopes of a golden return. The human venture into history may also be seen as such an investment—a commitment of energy, purpose, and generations of human lives to the great undertaking called civilization.

Civilization as it is usually defined began more than five thousand years ago in western Asia and northeastern Africa. From these beginnings in the river valleys of Mesopotamia and Egypt, this form of human society has since spread around the earth.

Definitions of the term *civilization* have varied down the centuries. One view, which goes back to ancient Greece and probably still farther back in China, would define civilizations like their own as "the higher culture," to be contrasted with the primitive ways of peasants, savage peoples, and other barbarians. The opposite approach, also of ancient lineage, would apply the term to virtually any society, with special emphasis on preurban peoples, whose ways of life are seen as every bit as complex and subtle, considerably more in synch with the natural world, and perhaps possessing ancient wisdom lost to the city-based cultures. Here, the word *civilization* will be used, along with more neutral terms like *urban* or *urban-imperial,* to mean a style of human life rooted in the city and larger political units, and in the material and cultural forms that historically have tended to go with these political structures.

The pattern has looked much the same everywhere and ever since. Civilization means cities and larger states, centralized and bureaucratic governments, classes and castes, technological advance and the growth of trade, the magical craft of writing, and increasingly sophisticated arts and sciences, religions, and philosophies. Not all of these are found in all cases, but the overall picture is similar and clearly recognizable wherever it appears.

Civilizations make possible larger and more complex human endeavors than could be undertaken by less developed societies. The larger resources and shared assumptions of a great civilization make possible great buildings, marvelous engineering works, and the integration of large numbers of people into a single system of administration and law. Civilization produces elaborate systems of thought, art of unexcelled subtlety and grandeur, and longer, healthier, less circumscribed lives for millions of people. Major civilizations, in short, substantially enhance the human capacity for achieving human goals.

Yet there are those who regard this entire enterprise as pointless, illusory, or even downright dangerous, and their objections are not to be lightly dismissed by the serious student of history.

As far back as ancient times, for instance, some students of the human past saw civilization as a pointless trajectory of rise and fall. Rome and Babylon, mighty once, are ruins today. What purpose, then, in laboring to build anew, if such desolation is the end of all constructive labor?

Others have pointed out that great crimes have been committed in the name of civilization. Narrow definitions of good and evil have led highly civilized peoples to deal savagely with others whose definitions differed from their own. Medieval Christian and Muslim societies, for all the glory of their cathedrals and mosques, fought each other for centuries in bloody crusades and *jihads.* Twentieth-century industrial civilization, while providing more material goods and human freedom to more people than ever before in human history, also invented total war and totalitarian tyranny, generated widespread economic exploitation, and did unprecedented damage to our natural environment.

Heavy charges, then, may be laid against the human enterprise we call civilization.

Perhaps the best response to all these criticisms lies in the historical record itself—in the long record of human commitment to the rearing of complex and far-reaching civilized societies. At least as striking as the pattern of rise and fall in the history of cultures is the eternal recurrence of the drive to build and build again, to raise civilization once more from its own ruins. Among the earliest styles of life, both hunting and gathering and pastoral nomadism are rapidly nearing extinction today. Even the self-supporting agricultural village is undergoing rapid assimilation into an urban-dominated order as peoples the world around rush to join the latest wave of civilized societies, those built on the culture of the machine.

On the whole, then, human beings seem to value what more sizable and complex societies can give them more than they fear the abuses of power that go with civilization. Preurban Germans and Mongols fought to get into ancient Rome and Han China, and village people the world around continue to flood into the cities of the developed world today.

From Rome to Machu Picchu

In this book, then, the mainstream of history will thus be the story of the city builders, the empire builders. The peoples who undertook the greatest of human enterprises appeared in all corners of the earth, on almost every habitable continent. Isolated at first, they slowly expanded the areas of their domination at the expense of their neighbors who did not know how to build great walls or make the magic signs that spoke on stone or clay or paper. By C.E. 1500, as we shall see, the tide was turning decisively against other forms of the human venture. At the beginning of modern history, the road was open to the final victory of the city-based civilizations.

Victory justifies much, and history, as we are often told, is always written by the winners. But there is more than simply victory to justify our focus on what this book sees as the great enterprise of civilization building. The builders of great civilizations have, after all, been constructing something of value.

The ruins of vanished civilizations strew the earth—evidence not so much of the inevitability of human failure as of the grandeur of the great enterprise at its best. The lengthening shadows of the Roman Colosseum, once the tourists have gone and the little old lady who feeds the cats is alone among the looming arches and the empty seats where crowds once cheered or turned thumbs down, remind us of the achievements of vanished Western empires. Chinese archaeologists are still exhuming the buried army of Huangdi, thousands of life-size statues of men, horses, even chariots that tell us much about that driven man and the laboring generations who built the Great Wall of China. The glooms and glimmers of St. Peter's in Rome, aglow with marble and pigment and bronze—room after room, acre after acre of art—remind us at every visit of what splendid things the European spirit has been capable. The towering Khmer temples of Angkor in Cambodia, the mysterious African ruins of Great Zimbabwe, and the roofless stone city of Machu Picchu, heaved high on a mountain peak above the Peruvian jungles, stir feelings of awe and wonder in even the most jaded tourist.

Socrates and Muhammad speaking in their market squares, Christ and Buddha wandering the dusty roads of Galilee or the banks of the Ganges, Confucius preaching common decency to a war-torn world—all had, at one level, a single message. It was the message of all the storytellers and praise singers, the shapers and singers of dreams, who have immortalized human heroism and human love, great leaders and great souls. It was a word the preachers and the poets shared: We can do better. We can be more.

With all the crimes and follies of past ventures into civilization on our consciences, we are thinkers, doers, builders. And the great enterprise continues. If the past is any guide at all to what lies ahead, we will probably go on constructing ever more elaborate attempts at civilization, as we have done for more than fifty centuries. The good society may still elude us, but we will not stop trying.

The crimes and follies, the labors, exploits, and achievements of first fifty centuries of human civilization are the subject of the first volume of this book.

CHAPTER 1

THE WORLD BEFORE HISTORY
Stone Age People

(5,000,000–3500 B.C.E.)

A Glance Ahead: History Builds on Prehistory

The hairy, beetle-browed cavemen and cavewomen you see in museum dioramas usually don't look as if they would rate very high on anybody's scale of civilization. In fact, however, prehistoric people played an essential and immensely innovative role in world history. It took millions of years of prehistoric biological development and cultural evolution to lay the foundations for the few thousand years of city-based history we have enjoyed thus far.

It was our prehistoric ancestors who discovered such basic skills as walking on two legs and manipulating things with their hands. It was they who learned how to make tools, how to herd animals and cultivate the soil, how to settle in villages and develop even more skills there. They explored the first forms of artistic expression and formulated some basic religious ideas. And they migrated restlessly around the globe, until all the habitable continents and countless islands had their scattered settlements of hominids.

And then, at the end of this long, slow progression, prehistoric humanity raised the walls and gates of the first cities and walked through them into history.

The Prehistoric World

Beginnings

Perhaps the most familiar version of the beginning of human life on earth is that given in the Judeo-Christian Old Testament:

> But there went up a mist from the earth, and watered the whole face of the ground
>
> And the Lord God formed man of the dust of the ground, and breathed into his nostrils the breath of life; and man became a living soul.[1]

And more familiar still:

> So God created man in his own image, in the image of God created he him: male and female created he them.[2]

One of the most vivid modern Western representations of the creation is surely the series of pictures painted by Michelangelo on the ceiling of the Sistine Chapel in the Vatican at Rome. Thousands of tourists daily crane their necks to gaze up at the magnificently muscled, hugely bearded figure of Jehovah dividing light from darkness with a gesture, rolling the sun and the moon into being, extending his powerful right hand to bestow upon Adam the ultimate gift of life.

An African version of the creation says that Doondari made humankind out of the "five elements"—fire, water, air, iron, and stone. The oldest of all creation stories, that of the "Memnite theology" carved in stone at Memphis on the Nile almost five thousand years ago, calls the creator Ptah and says that he made the first sentient beings with weapons in their hands! Down the centuries and around the world, "first things" have thus been matters of profound concern for many peoples.

---

[1]*Genesis 2:6–7*

[2]*Genesis 1:27*

Our own modern version of the beginnings of things is as exotic as any, though it seems (to many of us, at least) rather more likely to be true.

Setting the Stage

In the beginning, modern science tells us, the solid earth beneath our feet was not solid at all, but a ring of glowing, superheated gases swirling around the searing core of our sun. There was a cooling and a condensing, and where only the gaseous outreach of a spinning star had been, there were separate whirling chunks of slowly cooling matter. Several billions of years in the future people would call these "planets."

The cooling and settling continued, with dramatic changes in what became our world. This third planet out from the sun cooled and hardened on the surface, though the core has remained molten and seething. Water spread over much of the globe, and an atmosphere that we would find breathable slowly formed to a height of several miles above the surface. In this strange world of exploding volcanoes, flickering lightning, and bombarding cosmic rays, matter miraculously quickened into life in the primal seas.

From single-celled bacteria and "blue-greens" to shapeless jellies and shelled creatures in the sea, from shellfish to insects, from backboned fish to reptiles, birds, and beasts, animal life evolved. Vegetable life developed also over the uncountable hundreds of millions of years, from moss and horsetails to conifers and broad-leafed trees, from ferns to fruits and flowers. Long before the first identifiable hominid squinted into the sun, our Eden was prepared.

Change continued in the world around us even after the human race had begun to take shape. Shifts in the surface structures of the earth caused "continental drift" as the continental masses drifted slowly apart. The oceans grew and shrank, rose and fell. The climate changed drastically from one geological epoch to the next, caking the northern zone with ice, turning forests into grasslands, grasslands into deserts. Nevertheless, by the time history began, a recognizable geography had taken shape. Since, with some continuing changes, this was to be the stage for all our subsequent adventures, we should survey it briefly before going on to the actors and the story.

More than two thirds of the earth—the oceans, seas, lakes, and rivers of the world—was covered with water. The large expanses of dry land that protruded from this world-ocean formed seven continents. One of these, Antarctica, the frozen land around the South Pole, was all but uninhabitable. Of the other six, two were actually a single land mass, the great world island of Eurasia, divided for historical reasons into Europe in the west and the far larger expanse of Asia to the east. South of Europe, Africa, the largest continent after Asia, stretched southward across the equator and on toward the southern pole.

The other three continents lay farther away, cut off by seas and oceans from Eurasia and Africa. Australia lay at the far edge of Southeast Asia, in the western Pacific. North and South America, linked by the narrow isthmus of Central America, were isolated even more thoroughly from the rest of the world by the ocean barriers of the Atlantic and the Pacific.

Each of these continental land masses, and many of the islands that lay between them, had a range of climate and topography that provided a great variety of environments for human beings. These varying niches would in turn foster a variety of styles of life and help shape a number of historic societies.

Ecology and History

The twentieth century just past developed a strong awareness of the ecological dimensions of human society. Ecologists focus on the interrelatedness of all species of living things with each other and with the rest of their material environment. Historians have begun to find this approach useful too, especially in their attempts to understand the "big picture" of human life on earth.

Ecologists look upon all plants and animals—including people—as parts of chains, webs, cycles, interlocking niches, and other patterns of relationship. Our place in this

---

PROBING THE PAST

The excitement of digging up the past is vividly illustrated by this first-hand account of the 1974 discovery by paleo-anthropologist Donald Johanson and his colleague Tom Gray of the skeleton of a pre-human hominid, Lucy, believed to have lived three and a half million years ago.

What problems of identifying such bones are indicated by Gray's remarks? What can you deduce about the particular importance of the find from Johanson's thoughts? Maitland Edey, Johanson's co-author, is a distinguished writer on scientific subjects for nonscientific readers. What do you think he may have contributed to this dramatic account? (Assume Johanson and Gray did not happen to have a tape recorder running when they made their discovery.)

"The gully in question was just over the crest of the rise where he had been working all morning. . . . But as we turned to leave, I noticed something lying on the ground partway up the slope.
"That's a bit of a hominid arm," I said.
"Can't be. It's too small. Has to be a monkey of some kind."
We knelt to examine it.
"Much too small," said Gray again.
I shook my head. "Hominid."
"What makes you so sure?" he said.
"That piece right next to your hand. That's hominid too."
"Jesus Christ," said Gray. He picked it up. It was the back of a small skull. A few feet away was part of a femur: a thighbone. "Jesus Christ," he said again. We stood up, and began to see other bits of bone on the slope: a couple of vertebrae, part of a pelvis—all of them hominid. An unbelievable, impermissible thought flickered through my mind. Suppose all these fitted together. Could they be parts of a single, extremely primitive skeleton? No such skeleton had ever been found—anywhere.
"Look at that," said Gray. "Ribs."
A single individual?
"I can't believe it," I said. "I just can't believe it."
"By God, you'd better believe it!" shouted Gray. "Here it is. Right here!" His voice went up into a howl, I joined him. In that 110-degree heat we began jumping up and down. With nobody to share our feelings, we hugged each other, sweaty and smelly, howling and hugging in the heat-shimmering gravel, the small brown remains of what now seemed almost certain to be parts of a single hominid skeleton lying all around us."

Donald Johanson and Maitland Edey. *Lucy: The Beginnings of Humankind* (New York: Warner Books, 1981), pp. 16–17.

complex tangle of mutual dependency and interaction has undoubtedly had its impact, both on our development as a species and on the histories of the tribes, peoples, and other subdivisions into which we have divided ourselves.

As we will see, various of our prehuman ancestors evolved first in dense forests, moved on to open grasslands, and still later found themselves living in the shadows of ice-age glaciers. Each of these ecological niches had its impact on the way these ancestral prehumans lived, on their biological evolution, and on the course of prehistory. The first great change in the lifeways of prehistoric peoples—the shift from food gathering and hunting to settled agriculture—would come where it did because of a climate conducive to particularly valuable grains.

A similar level of significant interaction between peoples and their environments will be detected as we move on into history itself. Climatic change can drive peasants to rebellion and topple emperors who are seen as having lost the favor of the gods. The sedentary, agricultural settlements of people who lived on fertile soil; the hardy, nomadic lives of herders on sparse grasslands; the venturesome, violent, or mercantile societies of island or seacoast peoples all reflect the responses of a single species to a wide range of environmental niches.

Ecological interaction, however, is a two-way street. Throughout our span, humans and prehumans have been part of the ecological environment of other creatures too. As early predators, we played our part in the extinction of entire species. Most recently, technological exploitation of our world on a scale undreamed of before has apparently threatened to exhaust basic resources, polluted our living space, punched holes in our protective atmosphere, and generally shaken up the network of ecological linkages that have been shaping our world throughout its history.

Many factors, of course, have had a hand in shaping human cultures in history. For the time being, the fact of regional and cultural differences and the fact that geography and ecology helped determine them need only be noted here. There were, however, many ways in which our common humanity also determined our destiny as a species on this planet. It is to the emergence of that common human nature that we must now turn.

HUMAN DEVELOPMENT

The Bone Hunters

Almost all we know about the earliest stages of human life on earth has been uncovered during the last century and a half. The first Neanderthal bones clearly identified as belonging to prehistoric "cave men" were found by workers building a railway in the Neander Valley of Germany in 1856. Since then, archaeologists, anthropologists, and other professional "bone hunters" have dug up whole races of our human and prehuman ancestors. They have also stirred up considerable controversy in so doing.

Their discoveries have pushed the human story back far into the prehistoric past. In Olduvai Gorge in Tanzania, East Africa, Mary and Louis Leakey uncovered the skull that established the African origins of the human species. The skeleton of Don Johanson's "Lucy," found scattered over a hillside in Ethiopia, pushed prehuman origins back several million years. Hominid or humanlike bones from more recent times include those of the

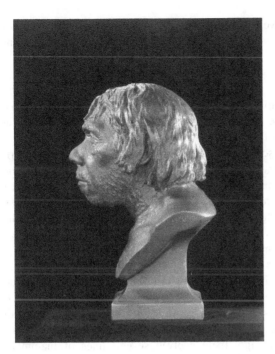

Neanderthal Man—as reconstructed from bone fragments by a modern researcher—squints into an uncertain future. Some authorities now suspect that the Neanderthal subdivision of the hominid family did not die out before breeding with <u>Homo</u> <u>sapiens</u> <u>sapiens.</u> Modern people may thus carry some of the genes of this long-vanished race. (American Museum of Natural History)

Cro-Magnon and Neanderthal types first found in France and Germany and their kin Peking Man and Java Man discovered at the other end of Eurasia. With many of these finds, rude stone tools and later pots, pictures, and bits of clothing have been unearthed.

Experts in many fields have contributed to our understanding of these remains. Geologists and laboratory scientists have learned to date the finds by analyzing the rock strata in which they are found or by carbon dating, which measures the dwindling carbon radiation of the finds themselves. Biologists link the surviving bits of bone to ourselves by comparing anatomical structures, blood groups, and chromosome patterns. Ethologists and anthropologists make more controversial comparisons with the behavior of other animals and of surviving food-gathering peoples like the Khoi-San of Africa or the Australian Aborigines.

Though they usually consist only of bones and stones, these discoveries have sometimes been much more sensational. The famous "Ice Man," an intact human corpse discovered frozen in the Alpine ice in 1991, came complete with deerskin coat, fur hat, stone dagger, bow and arrows, and a crude copper ax. Scientific theories can also be astonishing. Comparisons of genetic material from contemporary humans around the world, for instance, have led some scientists to claim that all of us can trace our ancestry to an "African Eve." This single early hominid—if the theory proves correct—lived in Africa 200,000 years ago.

The experts have come up with many such theories to explain the connections between these prehistoric remains, and between prehistoric people and ourselves. The pattern of evolutionary development favored by most scientists is outlined very generally in the next section. But how many earlier human-related species there were, how they related to each other, whether we have a "family tree" or a confusing evolutionary bush with many branches rather than a single central stem—all these questions await final answers.

Biological Evolution

A few simple numbers may help to put the story that begins here in at least rough chronological perspective. Dates have that value, at least, in history. And these dates are easy enough to remember, since all of them begin with five.

What is usually taught in school as modern history—from the world of Christopher Columbus and Leonardo da Vinci, Babur the Great and Suleiman the Magnificent, to the present age of Einstein and atomic power—covers a span of some five hundred years. The entire history of civilized humanity, from the first clay cities in ancient Sumer to the present, goes back more than five thousand years. The prehistoric line of human evolutionary development extends at least five million years into the past. It is this immense span of time with which we shall be primarily concerned in the present chapter.

Our most ancient detectable ancestors actually go considerably farther back than that. Scarcely recognizable as our kin to any but the informed scientific imagination, these small, furry creatures had huge nocturnal eyes and long tails. They balanced on high branches and snatched at insects in the primeval rain forests of the earliest age of mammals, not long after the passing of the dinosaurs. From these *prosimian* ancestors who lived tens of millions of years ago, there evolved several lines of mammals called *primates:* lemurs and their kin, Old and New World monkeys, and apes, the family to which the human race belongs. Among these ancient apes—whose other descendants today include orangutans, chimpanzees, and gorillas—there emerged as long as five million years ago the line of development known as *hominids,* of which the humans of our own time are the only surviving descendants.

Over this vast tract of time, from the first prosimian to the most developed hominid, the ancestors of humanity changed both biologically and culturally. These changes first enabled them to survive and then gave them increasing mastery of their environment. For biological evolution, a few paragraphs will suffice; for the story of our cultural evolution, the rest of the chapter will be required.

The biological changes over tens of millions of years were certainly striking. The eyes of that first tree dweller, for instance, evolved dramatically, developing both stereoscopic (depth) vision and color sightedness, very useful capacities for leaping from branch to branch or distinguishing brightly colored fruit from the green canopy that was the prosimian's world.

When our progenitors abandoned the shrinking primeval forest for the open grasslands five million years ago, more changes followed. Their legs and feet changed to permit erect bipedal walking on the African savannas. This in turn freed the hands for carrying game and foraged nuts and berries back to the family circle. The hands developed too, producing the most efficient opposable thumb for fine manipulation of any primate's. Most important, the hominid brain grew, doubling and tripling in size and evolving a neural capacity that gave human beings their most valuable biological advantage: the capacity to go beyond biology to culture.

Down the long evolutionary road, a number of hominid species developed, flourished for a time, and then died out. The earliest Australopithecines, of three and a half million years ago, were perhaps four feet tall and had brains about a third the size of a modern human's. Hominids of the Neanderthal line, who appeared perhaps 125,000 years ago, were close enough to ourselves, it is sometimes said, to pass for modern people in a crowd today.

These species left their bones on the African grasslands, in the caves of North China, or among the glaciers of ice-age Europe. But those hominids who survived were making delicate stone tools, burying their dead with ceremony, and decorating the walls of their caves with paintings of the animals they hunted as the last glaciers withdrew to the north. These survivors, who emerged approximately thirty-five thousand years ago, were the Cro-Magnon people, a subspecies of the hominid family called *Homo sapiens sapiens* ("wise people"). They were in fact the last of the hominid line. Biologically, they were indistinguishable from ourselves.

The Prehistoric Migrations

While it evolved physically, the human race was also spreading to almost every corner of the earth.

The earliest hominid species first evolved toward humanity in southern and eastern Africa. Fossil bones going back several million years testify to our long residence on that continent; the chromosomes in our DNA suggest all of us can trace our ancestry to a single "African Eve" in prehistoric times. And then, perhaps half a million years ago, human beings began to move northward. Both the motive for this greatest of human migrations and the means to make these journeys were provided by the most disturbing natural phenomenon of the period: the ice ages.

A rather modest drop in average temperatures in the Northern Hemisphere—no more than a few degrees—was enough to prevent the winter's snows from melting the following summer, so that next winter's snows piled on top of them. By 500,000 B.C.E. the ice stood thick over northern Europe and had intruded deep into North America. In time, however— forty thousand to sixty thousand years—the cooling trend reversed itself, and warmer weather pushed the edge of the ice cap back into the Arctic. This advance and retreat of the ice took place several times over the last half million years of the Old Stone Age.

The descent and withdrawal of the glacier turned Europe and other parts of the Northern Hemisphere from relatively barren areas to well-watered comparatively lush forests and grasslands, the latter especially capable of supporting deer, bison, hairy elephants, and other large game for hominid hunters. The freezing over of the north had a second great effect, however; by locking up a significant percentage of the earth's surface water in colossal ice sheets, the glaciers lowered the level of the world's oceans, creating temporary land bridges between large land areas that were otherwise cut off from each other by sea.

Perhaps two million years ago, then, our hominid forebears moved north out of Africa and up through the Near East into Eurasia. From the Near East, some drifted west into Europe, others eastward across Asia. A skull recently found in China indicates that our ancestors reached East Asia two hundred thousand years ago.

Migration beyond the Old World—Africa, Europe, and Asia—had to wait for the land bridges. Between 70,000 and 40,000 B.C.E., however, human beings reached Australia, going most of the way by land and improvising some sort of boats for perhaps only fifty miles or so. Between 40,000 and 20,000 B.C.E., other groups of humans followed their prey across another land bridge at what is today the Bering Strait to the Americas. Cana-

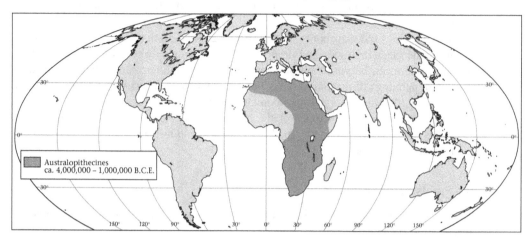

Australopithecines
ca. 4,000,000 – 1,000,000 B.C.E.

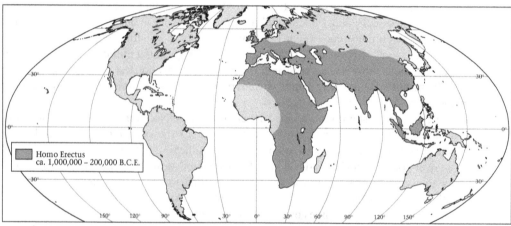

Homo Erectus
ca. 1,000,000 – 200,000 B.C.E.

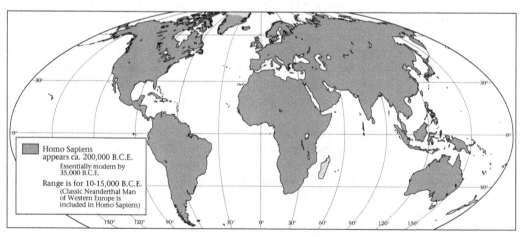

Homo Sapiens
appears ca. 200,000 B.C.E.
Essentially modern by
35,000 B.C.E.

Range is for 10-15,000 B.C.E.
(Classic Neanderthal Man
of Western Europe is
included in Homo Sapiens)

dian glaciation may have held them up for a considerable time, but once a corridor had opened southward, hunting and gathering humanity flooded south to feed upon whole new species of food plants and game. In a short time, perhaps no more than a few thousand years, the human race had colonized North and South America too.

The great migrations were neither as purposive nor as direct as this schematic account may sound. Quite likely, humans advanced and retreated as the glaciers did, hunting and gathering in the shadow of the ice. Whole branches of the evolving half-human race were caught in culs-de-sac and became extinct, along with the plants and animals they fed on. Others adapted to new conditions and drifted on, reacting to shifts in climate and vegetation, following the herds.

We should not imagine anything like the picturesque migrations of historic nomads, whole tribes and peoples trundling across the steppes with beasts and baggage. It might take a tiny hunting band several lifetimes to decide to move on to the next valley. But then, even at an average pace of no more than ten miles a generation, it would have taken early hominids only fifteen thousand years to travel from East Africa to North China.[3] Even with endless back-tracking and aimless wandering—since after all they had no plans for reaching North China, or anywhere else in particular—it is not surprising that our prehistoric ancestors were able to spread around the world in half a million years.

The Human Races

Closely related to these primal folk wanderings is another often-noticed aspect of our humanness: the racial differences that distinguish some groups of human beings from others.

They are very modest differences. No human type differs as strikingly from another as a St. Bernard does from a Chihuahua, or a tiger from an alley cat. But there are detectable physical differences among the three major racial groups—caucasoid, mongoloid, and negroid—and among such surviving racial remnants as the bushmanoid and pygmoid peoples of Africa and the australoids who were the original inhabitants of Australia. And these differences do go back to the great migrations of prehistoric times.

Racial differences seem to have evolved like other human adaptations, in order that subdivisions of the species might survive under the drastically differing conditions humanity encountered in various parts of the world. For instance, Eskimos tended toward stocky builds, which retain body heat in the arctic cold. Equatorial peoples developed high concentrations of skin-darkening melanin, which protect them from the sun's heat.

We thus became hardy and versatile animals indeed. Some of us developed immunities to the ever-present infectious parasites of tropical rain forests. Others built lungs capable of breathing the thin air of the Andes and the Himalayas. We have adapted physically as well as culturally to deserts where only a few spiny growths of vegetation and a handful of insects and reptiles can survive, and to arctic wastelands where houses must be built of snow and the sun does not rise above the horizon for half the year. We have learned to live in a wider range of physical environments than any other species on the face of the planet—and some of this versatility is due to racial variations.

Two or three other points should be briefly made about the racial diversity that is part of our heritage from prehistory.

---

[3]Richard E. Leakey and Roger Lewin, *Origins* (New York: E. P. Dutton, 1977), pp. 120–121.

First and most important, we are in fact not many but one single human race. Only one branch of the hominid line has survived—*Homo sapiens sapiens*—and we are all members of that species. Beneath all minor differences of lip thickness, inner eyefold, texture of hair, skin pigmentation, and proportion of leg length to length of trunk, we remain one breeding group, one people biologically.

Second, the various subdivisions of the species we have come to call *races* have historically become inextricably mixed almost everywhere—with generally excellent results. The exchange of cultural know-how that comes with the mixing of peoples made the polyglot, often turbulent Near East perhaps the most culturally productive corner of the globe. The historic isolation of a place such as Australia, by contrast, produced little in the way of social change and cultural development.

Finally, it scarcely needs to be mentioned that no one of the world's peoples has shown any intrinsic superiority to any other. There have been barbarians of every color, and enviable civilizations have been built by people of all racial stocks. In the end, it is the course of cultural evolution that distinguishes one people from another historically—not biological evolution. And it is to that cultural evolution that we must turn now.

PALEOLITHIC HUNTERS AND GATHERERS

The Foraging Band

In terms of cultural development, the evolving lifeways of the species, almost all of this first five million years is called the *Paleolithic period,* or Old Stone Age. This was the period when our human and prehuman ancestors survived by hunting and gathering with stone tools and weapons.

Like their prehuman ancestors, early hominids were both vegetarian and carnivorous. They were gatherers of nuts, roots, berries, and other vegetable food. They were also hunters of all sorts and sizes of game—from the huge, hairy mammoth and vast herds of deer to a wide range of smaller animals, birds, and fish. Their style of living and the whole course of their cultural evolution were significantly shaped by this fundamental activity of prehistoric people: the collection of sufficient food to keep them alive.

Humans seem to have learned quite far back that survival is a cooperative venture. Food gathering alone, the collection of primarily vegetable food, can be undertaken on an individual basis. Hunting, however, particularly the hunting of large animals, is practiced most efficiently by groups working in close cooperation. Prehistoric hominids, like wolves or lions, worked together to pull down animals as large as the giant sloth or the elephant-sized mammoth. Almost uniquely even among hunting animals, furthermore, hominids seem to have shared their food on a regular basis, dividing up game and vegetable food among all the members of the group.

From very early times, then, human beings were social animals, living and working together in the tight-knit community of a band of hunters and gatherers. In prehistoric times, as among Pygmies, Bushmen, or Eskimos today, a typical band probably numbered five or six nuclear families—no more than two or three dozen individuals altogether. These small groups developed some ingenious hunting techniques, inventing pits and other traps or using brush fires to drive whole herds of game over cliffs or into swamps where they might be easily killed. At certain seasons of the year, when major herds were due in the neighborhood, a number of such bands, adding up to several hundred hunters, might come together for a large-scale cooperative hunting expedition and a great gorge afterward.

The technology that accompanied this social evolution—and made much of it possible—included a large "kit" of tools and weapons. Rudely split rocks were apparently being used for cutting and scraping by prehuman creatures a couple of million years ago. During the hundreds of thousands of years that followed, hand axes and knives, scrapers and spears, and finally spear-throwers and bows and arrows were chipped out of flint or carved from wood all over Africa, Europe, and Asia. Long after Europeans with more complex metallurgical skills had landed in the New World, stone arrowheads, some exquisitely shaped, were still serving American Indians as well as they had all our ancestors.

Fire, clothing, and rude shelters also appeared well before history began. Our forebears met the millennial cold of recurring ages of ice, first by wrapping themselves in animal hides, then by sewing the hides into sleeves and pantlegs, coats and hoods. They took shelter in caves and under rocky outcroppings, then in tents and shelters made primarily of bone. They tamed fire perhaps half a million years ago, first using it where they found it, then learning to kindle it through friction. The warm yellow-orange flame, used for both heating and cooking, became the center of the developing group life of the prehistoric band.

It was a simple society, rude and dangerous. For several millions of years, from the African savannas to glacier-prone Eurasia, this was the lifestyle of all our ancestors. Around such fires, it has been suggested, the monkey jabber of earlier hominids may have become speech as hunters and gatherers laid plans for the next day's labors or tried to explain more clearly than grunts and gestures could about the one that got away.

Social relations within the hunter-gatherer community may also be deduced from what we know about surviving preagricultural peoples and from some basic facts of all human life. Thus it has been suggested that these small prehistoric bands, like hunter-gatherer societies of our own time, were probably roughly egalitarian. They had little of the division into castes and classes, the powerful sense of hierarchy that was to come with organization into larger social units.

Like foraging peoples still surviving in deserts and rain forests from Africa to Australia, prehistoric hominids probably recognized degrees of family kinship. They perhaps shared the meat of a large kill on the basis of elaborate social categories of their own, as hunting peoples still do. But in groups as small as two or three dozen, possessing so little in the way of material things, class divisions on the basis of power or wealth seem exceedingly unlikely.

Stone Age Women

Sexual distinctions probably did exist among our earlier prehistoric ancestors; but there is no reason to assume that prehistoric sex roles resembled those of any particular historic people, including our own. The female half of the human race has played many roles in a wide variety of societies down the centuries. This is quite likely to have been true in prehistoric times also.

There is some general agreement that among Stone Age hunter-gatherers, as among such peoples today, women were almost always the gatherers. Whereas hunting might involve more teamwork, gathering probably provided a more reliable source of food most of

A Venus figurine, found in Austria, of the sort that made earlier researchers see these cult objects as fertility symbols. What reasons can you think of for the omission of the individualizing face entirely? (Museum of Natural History, Vienna)

the time. Fruit, berries, nuts, roots, grubs, and shellfish were more stable and dependable sources of nutriment than the large or middle-sized game that might or might not show up at the water hole. Except in the depths of winter, then, Stone Age women—again, like hunter-gatherer women today—probably brought in most of the Paleolithic family's steady diet.

A few more generalizations may be risked about the role of women in prehistoric societies—some obvious, some rather more debatable. Women were, of course, the producers of new Paleolithic people and therefore essential to the survival of the band, indeed of the species. In addition, it seems likely that roughly monogamous pair bonding—close personal and social relations between individual men and women that provided a stable environment for rearing children—goes far back into our human and prehuman past. Women may also have been early recognized as custodians of the camp, the band's home base, while men and boys predominated in the hunting terrain.

Overall, women probably enjoyed more freedom and more influence in hunting and gathering societies than they often have in later civilizations. In surviving food-gathering cultures, at least, domestic chores and child-rearing duties are more equally shared between women and men. Within the band, women as foragers often have as much mobility and initiative as the male hunters do.

It is also possible, finally, that women were considered to have mysterious powers, perhaps on the order of those attributed to witches, prophetesses, and priestesses in later times. Almost all the sculptured figures that survive from Paleolithic times—the so-called Venus figurines—are of women. The figurines are by no means all of pregnant women, as was once thought, but range from virginal maidens to full-breasted mothers and withered crones.[4] Why these tiny figures were carved we do not know, but cult or religious purposes seem likely. In any event, these carved figures do seem to reflect the crucial place of women in the Stone Age world.

Beginnings of Religion and Art

If it is difficult to reconstruct the social life of the Old Stone Age, it would seem downright foolhardy to try to guess what went on inside the skulls of our hominid ancestors. Yet even here we can do some conjecturing, at least about our more recent forebears of later Paleolithic times.

There is at least some evidence that some sort of supernatural belief—the seeds of religion—existed as far back as 100,000 B.C.E. At that time prehistoric hunters appear to have set up the skulls of cave bears, early humans' fiercest challengers for the rock shelters they both needed, as though to worship these huge rivals. By 50,000 B.C.E., Neanderthal people were burying their dead with a care and ceremony that points to a belief in some sort of life after death. Corpses were painted with red ocher, positioned carefully with the knees drawn up, provided with flint weapons, and in one famous case—at Shanidar in Iraq—strewn with fresh flowers from the surrounding hills. Finally, Cro-Magnon cave paintings of game animals indicate the possibility, by 30,000 B.C.E., of magical rites aimed at controlling the game supply. It is about this time also that the Venus

The Ring of Brodgar, an impressive stone circle dating back to stone-age times, still looms over the heather of the Orkney Islands, off the northern coast of Scotland. Stone pit-houses and burial places reveal a thriving community who gathered here for ceremonies we can only guess at. Have you heard of megalithic monuments like this elsewhere in the world? (Anthony Esler)

---

[4]Patricia C. Rice, "Prehistoric Venuses: Symbols of Motherhood or Womanhood?" *Journal of Anthropological Research,* 37 (1981), 402–414.

figurines appear, quite possibly indicating not only respect for womanhood but special reverence for female divinities.

Bear skulls and burial customs, hunting rites, and rude statuettes are clues rather than proof. Still, they point to religion as one of the earliest detectable achievements of human abstract thought.

There is no question, however, about the early emergence of another basic impulse toward higher cultural expression: the invention of art.

As we noted previously, Cro-Magnon people—our own direct forebears—seem to have been the inventors of the arts. They engraved recognizable animals on bone. They produced the small stone Venus figures, rudely made, armless, but clearly representational and clearly intended to be feminine. Prehistoric musical instruments have been discovered, including bone drums, rattles, whistles, pipes, and "bull roarers." Still used by Aboriginal Australians on ceremonial occasions, bull roarers are attached to a string and swung around the head to produce a terrifying booming sound.

The most celebrated examples of prehistoric art are the paintings of bulls, bison, deer, horses, and other animals on the walls of caves. The most famous of them, including the dazzling painted caves at Lascaux in southern France, have been closed to the hordes of visitors whose very breath damaged pigments tens of thousands of years old. But you can go into the dark, cold caverns at nearby Les Eyzies for a glimpse of the leaping animals that filled the imaginations—and the lives—of Europe's prehistoric hunters. Thousands of miles to the south, you can see other prehistoric creatures, including some very realistic red giraffes, marching around the walls of caves in the sunny Motopo hills of southern Zimbabwe.

These prehistoric cave paintings have been interpreted in a number of ways: as hunting-cult ritual objects, as tribal totems, and even as art for art's sake. Whatever the artists' motive for making them, these naturalistic renderings of the game animals that were life itself to our ancestors certainly reveal a startling level of artistic skill.

What totems these people believed in, what taboos they practiced must remain largely objects of speculation. But we know from their graves that they talked seriously about life and death around their glowing fires. We know that bone music echoed from those painted caves tens of thousands of years before civilization as we know it was born.

NEOLITHIC FARMERS

The Discovery of Agriculture

Group life, rudimentary technology, and the beginnings of high culture thus flourished by the end of the Paleolithic period, or Old Stone Age, the immensely long period of human development that began several million years in the past and ended no more than twelve thousand years ago. The *Neolithic period* or New Stone Age was the age of the Agricultural Revolution, the final link in the long chain of cultural evolution that led to history proper.

The common designation of the period from 10,000 to perhaps 3500 B.C.E. as the New Stone Age refers to the new, ever more expertly crafted stone implement produced during this period. Metalworking remained undiscovered, but the polished stone tools and weapons of these last centuries of prehistory are a notable step beyond the flaked flints of earlier generations, and many steps beyond the split pebbles of our earliest precursors. The great event of the Neolithic period, however, was not the advance in stoneworking but a much more fundamental step forward in the material culture of the human race: the discovery of agriculture.

The original Agricultural Revolution was in fact the climax of prehistory—and the essential foundation upon which civilization itself would be built.

This great change from the moving life of hunting and gathering to the settled life of the farmer may have been made independently in a number of places, including several parts of Eurasia, West Africa, and Mesoamerica, but it was in the Near East that the best documented and historically most significant shift from following game to growing crops came first. It was a crucial change in the life of the race. Nothing as sweeping would occur again until the Industrial Revolution of the last two centuries.

Because the Agricultural Revolution was primarily a change in human methods of exploiting vegetable food, it is likely that this breakthrough was the work of women. As the primary gatherers of vegetable food, women would have been most likely to understand the cycle of growth, to see how human ingenuity might seize control of this natural cycle from seed to edible plant. Thus an annual visit to harvest wild grain could lead to watering, weeding, and finally scattering of seeds, perhaps in a religious ceremony to encourage a bumper crop the following year.

A number of explanations have been offered for this basic shift from hunting and gathering to agriculture. One likely cause may have been the simple exhaustion of game animals in a particular region, forcing humanity to seek other means of subsistence. Another primary cause may have been the development of new wild grains in warmer postglacial times, enabling people to settle down and live off these cereals and the animals who fed on them without having to do much cultivation at all. Recent archaeological finds do in fact reveal such transitional phases between food gathering and food producing. Thus Old Stone Age Russian hunters built semipermanent shelters of mammoth bone twenty thousand years ago, and the Natufian food-gathering people of what is today Israel lived in rude stone huts thirteen thousand years back.

Perhaps the earliest fully agricultural societies emerged east of the Mediterranean Sea in what is today Turkey. There climatic conditions favored particularly nutricious grain—einkorn and emmer wheat—which could, in turn, support a growing human population. The same grains could feed grazing animals, such as cattle, sheep, and later horses, which would provide food, clothing, and fellow laborers for the peoples who built early villages, towns, and cities.

On such foundations, then, the first agricultural villages rose in the Near East twelve thousand years ago.

Crops and Flocks

Agriculture most likely began with the simple practice of harvesting edible grains found growing wild, part of the normal food-gathering procedures of Old Stone Age people. Alert gatherers might sometimes encourage the ripening of the crop by extra care—for instance, by watering plants at the end of a dry summer. But the great break-through came when bands of *Homo sapiens sapiens* learned to plant some of the grain in order to guarantee a harvest the following year. Wherever this occurred—with wheat and barley in the Near East, millet in North China, corn in Central America—the wandering days of the hunting band were numbered and a new way of life was set in train.

Global Distribution of Hominids and Homo Sapiens

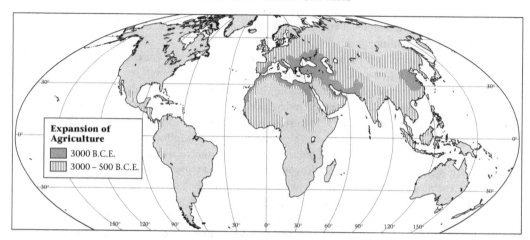

Expansion of
Agriculture

3000 B.C.E.

3000 – 500 B.C.E.

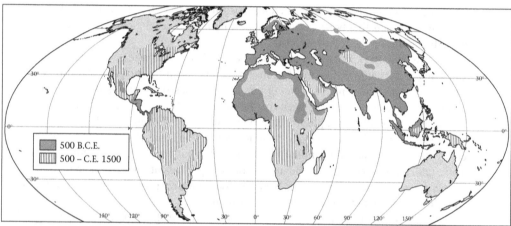

500 B.C.E.

500 – C.E. 1500

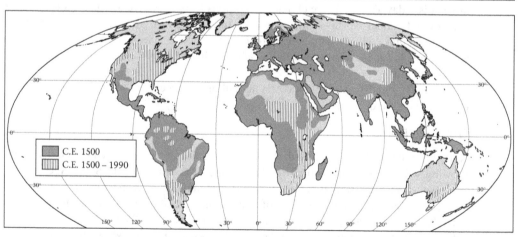

C.E. 1500

C.E. 1500 – 1990

Besides the growing of crops, another important aspect of the Agricultural Revolution was the domestication of animals. Again, transition stages have been hypothesized, including perhaps the herding and riding of reindeer, a comparatively docile game animal that is both ridden and herded in northern Asia today. From this success, Neolithic people could have moved naturally to herding other animals or to keeping them in pens and enclosed fields. Cattle, sheep, goats, and pigs were early domesticated in this way, horses only much later.

For some early peoples, the herding of animals became the center of their posthunting cultures. These peoples became pastoralists rather than cultivators of the soil. They did not settle, but followed their herds of deer, cattle, or horses from summer to winter pasturage, sometimes migrating across hundreds of miles of savanna, steppe, or even less attractive desert land in search of water and grass. Pastoral peoples remained closer to the lives of the hunting ancestors than farmers did. In historical times, at least, nomadic pastoralists came to covet the material goods accumulating among more settled peoples, with sometimes violent results.

Life thus grew in complexity as the Neolithic centuries rolled on. The settled agricultural peoples of the Near East, like their fellows in many parts of the globe, learned to cultivate their crops with care, to weed and irrigate, to use the manure produced by their stock to fertilize their croplands. They discovered how to breed stock for meat or for strength, how to use milk, milk products, and other animal and vegetable products seldom utilized by their hunting-and-gathering predecessors. First in the rain-watered hills, then in the river valleys that provided the most fertile land, these prehistoric farmers reaped a greater bounty than nature had normally provided for their Paleolithic ancestors.

Above, all, they grew in numbers. Farming was hard work, probably more demanding than hunting and gathering had been. But agriculture had the great advantage of feeding many more people from the same tract of land than could be fed by hunting and gathering. One estimate suggests that whereas the foraging economy could support one person per square kilometer, even primitive farming could feed fifty persons from a single square kilometer. From this population growth came the Neolithic agricultural village and—in time—the city, the political state, and all their history.

Life in the Neolithic Village

Prehistoric handicraft technology also improved significantly during the New Stone Age. As we noted previously, Neolithic people learned to make polished stone tools and weapons that eclipsed even the most impressive chipped flints of their forebears. They also developed such basic agricultural equipment as a simple stick plow, pulled first by a man and later by an animal, and a flint-bladed sickle with which they harvested grain.

Other crafts were probably the work of women. In their hands, the loosely woven net gave rise to baskets for carrying and storing and then to the weaving of cloth. Neolithic clothing progressed from animal hides to woven fabrics, first of all wool from the backs of newly domesticated sheep. The complex technology of ceramics—pots for storage, cooking, and other purposes—also simplified the lives of prehistoric peoples, and was probably also developed by women. And there is increasing evidence of trade, or perhaps of ritual exchanges of gifts, between one agricultural community and another.

Most striking, the New Stone Age produced the Neolithic village, and with it a revolution in the ways of life of the race.

About ten thousand years ago the caves and tent shelters of roving hunters were replaced by permanent collections of huts. These were simple structures, usually made of sun-dried mud, clay brick, or stone. You can visit a Stone Age village at Skara Brae in the Orkney Islands north of Scotland. Walking among the now roofless stone huts, you will find each equipped with a central cooking area, roughly partitioned sleeping spaces, and even stone shelves. Fish hooks and stone-edged scythes give clues to an economy that still included fishing even while the people learned to plant and harvest grain.

Class distinctions were probably still modest in the Neolithic period, but gender roles remained clearly defined. As in preurban cultures in historic times, women were primarily responsible for the raising of the children. In settled New Stone Age communities, however, they probably had more of them and devoted more time to child care. Farming required more hands than food gathering, and laborers lost to the contagious diseases that came with settled living had to be replaced.

Like their Paleolithic foremothers, some Neolithic women may also have been believed to possess supernatural powers. Women shamans have often served as channels or mediums in preurban societies, bringing the voices of the gods or of the dead to rapt audiences. From Neolithic times also come mysterious wall paintings showing women disguised as giant birds performing funeral rites.

Alternate Lifestyles

The human venture into history has taken many forms. Its most amazing enterprise, as we shall see, has been the series of essays in civilization that began in various parts of the world more than five thousand years ago. But 99 percent of the human story thus far was played out before civilization began. And even during the historical period, most of the world remained in the hands of people who were neither literate nor urban, who did not build states or litter the earth with massive ruins, people who, though they lived in historic times, lived pretty much as their prehistoric ancestors had.

Some of this continuing precivilized majority of the human race were village agriculturalists, living in many ways as Neolithic farmers did. Some would become pastoralists, nomads following their herds of sheep or cattle in an unending search for grass and water. Some would remain hunters and gatherers, living off game and fish, fruits, roots, and vegetables, as their Paleolithic forebears did before civilization began.

Climate and geography tended to determine the distribution of these basic styles of life—agricultural, pastoral, hunter-gatherer—around the globe during the first three thousand years of history. Thus, cultivators of such cereal crops as maize, wheat, millet, and rice were concentrated in the world's temperate zones. They flourished across central Eurasia—in Europe, the Middle East, China, and India—and in the middle parts of the Americas, from the southern reaches of North America to the northern highlands of South America. The cultivation of root crops, such as yams and manioc, was most common in the tropics, including the rain forests of South America, Central Africa, and Southeast Asia. In all these areas, agricultural villages were scattered over the land. But it was only in the temperate grain-growing regions that urban power centers eventually emerged.

Pastoral nomads wandered the steppes of Eurasia and the savannas of Africa. Their flocks of sheep and cattle were here one month and gone the next. In their journeyings they not infrequently brushed—often violently—against the new city-based civilizations of the Old World.

Finally, surviving hunter-gatherers were increasingly limited to the northern and southern extremities of the world's landmasses and the most arid corners of the earth. Hunting tribes as vigorous as their ice-age ancestors still stalked deer and other large game in the arctic regions of both the Old and New Worlds. Thinning populations of hunters and gatherers scraped a living out of much smaller game and meager vegetation in the desiccated southern reaches of South America and Africa and in Australia. Living thus primarily on the last frontiers, far from the fertile temperate zones, primordial hunters and food gatherers were unlikely to have any knowledge that such a thing as civilization existed in the world.

THE TRANSITION TO CIVILIZATION

The First Civilizations

For a period as long as all recorded history since, the agricultural village was the most complex form of human social organization, and the chiefdom and the primitive monarchy the most elaborate political structure. Then, sometime around 3500 B.C.E., small segments of the human family stumbled into a new and even more elaborate way of life. This new stage of human group life was achieved in the city-states and empires of ancient times. It is frequently described as the birth of civilization.

As noted in the Introduction to this volume, the term *civilization* has had a number of meanings. The definition employed here is essentially a technical one, like such descriptive terms as *food-gathering band* or *agricultural village*. Civilization is a complex amalgam of centralized government, expanded economic and technological capacities, and more elaborate social and cultural structures. Monument building, metal working, and writing are identifiable elements in some (though not all) civilizations.

Like the Neolithic village, cities and empires emerged in different places over a span of several thousand years. Beginning not much more than five thousand years ago, civilization appeared first in Mesopotamia, Egypt, northern India, and northeastern China. Later still, urban life and imperial structures evolved in Europe, parts of Africa and the Americas, Southeast Asia, Japan, and elsewhere.

These unprecedented developments in the cultural evolution of the race have been explained in a number of ways. Some attribute the rise of larger political units to climatic change; the gradual drying out of marshes along major rivers left firm but extremely fertile land capable of supporting much larger populations. Others describe the early states as "hydraulic empires," emphasizing the need for a central political authority to tame great rivers such as the Nile, the Tigris and Euphrates, the Indus, and the Huanghe (Yellow River) of China.[5] Imperial power, according to this view, was needed to maintain the elaborate systems of dams, canals, and rules for water use that were necessary if agriculture was to realize its immense productive potential along these waterways. Still others see the expansion of political power as fundamentally a matter of greed for dominion, wealth, and glory leading to military conquest. Certainly "conquest empires" arose in many parts of the world as a result of self-aggrandizing wars—the winners absorbing the lands of the losers in larger and larger imperial domains.

---

[5]Karl A. Wittfogel, *Oriental Despotism* (New Haven, Conn.: Yale University Press, 1957).

As noted previously, not all civilizations exhibit all these features. But all reveal a scale and complexity that distinguish them from hunter-gatherer bands, pastoral nomads, or agricultural villages. *Civilization* may be hard to define, but you will know one when you see one—whether it is in ancient Egypt or ancient Greece, China before Confucius, or pre-Columbian Mexico.

Monarchy, Hierarchy, and Patriarchy

Three organizational principles dominated most early civilizations. We may call them monarchy, hierarchy, and patriarchy.

Monarchy was a form of government in which political power was exercised by monarchs—kings, queens, emperors, or other powerful individual rulers. Monarchs passed on their power through hereditary succession, so that a single family might govern for generations, even centuries. Almost everywhere monarchs ruled in close alliance with gods and the priests who tended them. This divinely sanctioned political authority was commonly exercised through proliferating bodies of officials. These early scribal bureaucrats collected royal taxes, administered royal justice, kept the irrigation ditches in repair or the armies in the field, and ruled in the sovereign's name as far as his cohorts could reach or his justice prevail.

The society over which monarchs ruled was increasingly organized according to the principle of *hierarchy.* Society was divided up into groups based on the function they performed, on the prestige they enjoyed, or simply on how many material things they possessed. Those with highly valued functions, traditional prestige, or material wealth were ranked higher than other people. Thus, a priest, an aristocratic landowner, or a wealthy merchant would outrank an artisan, a peasant, or a slave in the new social hierarchy. This system of classes, castes, or social orders, which originated at the beginning of our history, is with us still today.

The term *patriarchy* refers to a family structure in which husbands and fathers exercise authority over other members. In a more general sense, patriarchy means male dominance of society as a whole. As we will see, women have always played a variety of roles in civilized societies. Nevertheless, it does seem to be true that the rough gender equality of food-gathering bands faded in early villages and cities. Men emerged as heads of the family, plowers of fields, soldiers, priests. Women were increasingly identified with household responsibilities and child rearing, with the "private sphere" of life, while men dominated the "public sphere"—the palace, the temple, and the battlefield.[6]

Economics, Technology, Culture

Crucial economic and cultural changes also characterized early civilizations. The city emerged as a uniquely powerful economic unit, the home of vast public buildings, specialized crafts, organized systems of religion, and elaborate fine arts.

The economic foundations of city-based civilizations that emerged about 3500 B.C.E. were broader and more complex than at any earlier stage. Urban centers were the focus of economic innovation as well as political development during the first two or three millennia of civilization—the Bronze and Iron Ages. It was in the cities that metallurgy and other advanced crafts developed, and from these centers of wealth and population that

---

[6]On this complex subject, see Gerda Lerner, *The Creation of Patriarchy* (New York: Oxford University Press, 1986).

long-distance trade reached out to similar urban areas, some of them hundreds of miles away. The hinterland, by contrast, was typically composed of agricultural villages much like those of Neolithic times, though their methods of cultivation were now more efficient and they were now firmly integrated into the larger city-centered economic unit.

In the earliest historic centuries, ancient artisans—builders, carvers of stone, workers in precious metals—joined painters, poets, philosophers, and prophets of many faiths in producing a high culture that still has the power to amaze and move us today. Vast structures such as the pyramids of Egypt or Mexico, the palace at Knossos, and the white temples on the Athenian Acropolis still draw tourists in the thousands. Jades and bronzes from the earliest periods of Chinese history have been treasured by collectors for hundreds of years.

Literature was highly developed as an art form long before any of our modern languages even existed. Early systems of writing, including Mesopotamian cuneiform, Egyptian hieroglyphics, Indian Sanskrit, Chinese characters, the Phoenician alphabet, and the Greek and Roman scripts derived from it, made it possible to preserve at least some of the wisdom and belief, the legend and poetry, of these dawn ages of human civilization.

SUMMARY

The human venture actually began several million years before history did. Humankind passed through a complex development long before city life, civilization—and with them, history—finally emerged. Crucial aspects of these first five million years included evolution, migration, and racial differentiation. The human species evolved biologically from prehuman forms to *Homo sapiens sapiens,* its present incarnation. At the same time, humankind evolved culturally, adapting to its changing environment with an ingenious series of technological and social inventions. During prehistoric times also, human beings migrated from their original home in Africa to all the other habitable continents: Europe and Asia, the Americas, and Australia. Racial differences developed as additional biological adaptations to these varied habitats.

The first stage of human cultural evolution was the Paleolithic or Old Stone Age, the hunting and gathering phase of human cultural evolution, which began several million years ago. The Paleolithic era brought such fundamental discoveries as fire, clothing, basic techniques of hunting game and gathering vegetable food, and the simple social organization of the hunting band. Women played an important role in Old Stone Age society. Forms of art and religious beliefs also took shape, probably toward the end of this period.

The second stage of human social development was the Neolithic agricultural phase, which began twelve thousand years ago. Having perhaps exhausted the game in a given area, some humans settled down to cultivate crops and domesticate animals. Over a few thousand years their stone tools improved drastically, and they learned to make textiles and pottery. They also lived a more settled life in small villages, with women, the probable discoverers of agriculture, playing an important part.

A third stage of human social evolution—and the beginning of civilization—was reached when villages evolved into cities. This happened for the first time more than five thousand years ago, around 3500 B.C.E. in the Middle East. The same transition occurred over the next two or three thousand years elsewhere in Eurasia, in northern Africa, and in Middle and South America. The more complex urban-imperial cultures that resulted were distinguished by such skills and trends as city- and empire-building, metal-working, monumental architecture, literacy, bureaucratic centralized government, class structure, and a tendency toward patriarchy. The unfolding of this final stage over the past fifty-five hundred years will be the central concern of this book.

Suggested Reading

Bettinger, P. L. *Hunter-Gatherers*. New York: Plenum Press, 1991. Contributions of archaeology and biology to our understanding of early human society.

Bogucki, P. *The Origins of Human Society*. Oxford: Blackwell, 1999. Argues that individual ambitions and decisions by prehistoric hominids led to the emergence of elites and social inequalities.

Borenhult, G., ed. *The First Humans*. San Francisco: Harper, 1993. Authoritative coverage of the Old Stone Age. See also the archaeological perspectives in P. Mellars, ed., *The Emergence of Modern Humans* (Ithaca, N.Y.: Cornell University Press, 1990), and essays in G. L. Isaac's *The Archaeology of Human Origins* (New York: Cambridge University Press, 1989).

Chambers, F.M., ed. *Climate Change and Human Impact on the Landscape*. London: Chapman and Hall, 1993. Studies of the complex relationship between humans and their environment.

Clive, G. *Timewalkers: The Prehistory of Global Colonization*. Cambridge, Mass.: Harvard, 1994. Valuable account of prehistoric human migration.

Diamond, J. *Guns, Germs, and Steel: The Fates of Human Societies*. New York: W. W. Norton, 1997. Widely discussed analysis, focusing on material environment as the key force shaping civilizations.

Ehrenberg, M. *Women in Prehistory*. Norman: University of Oklahoma Press, 1989. Women in prehistoric Europe. See also J. M. Gero and M. W. Conkey, eds., *Engendering Archaeology: Women and Prehistory* (Oxford: Blackwell, 1991), for papers on women in preurban societies in both the Old and New Worlds, and F. Dahlberg, ed., *Woman, the Gatherer* (New Haven, Conn.: Yale University Press, 1983), for essays on women in Paleolithic times.

Goudsblom, J. *Fire and Civilization*. London: Allen Lane, 1992. Emphasizes the contribution made by human control of a single basic force—fire—to the emergence of more complex societies.

Henry, D. O. *From Foraging to Agriculture: The Levant at the End of the Iron Age*. Philadelphia: University of Pennsylvania Press, 1989. A detailed study of the first such transition. See also B. Bender, *Farming in Prehistory: From Hunter-Gatherer to Food Producer* (London: J. Baker, 1975).

Johanson, D., and M. Edey. *Lucy: The Beginnings of Humankind*. New York: Warner Books, 1981. Highly readable account of an important discovery. See also D. Johanson, D. L. Johanson, and B. Edgar, *Ancestors: In Search of Human Origins* (New York: Villard Books, 1994).

Lerner, G. *The Creation of Patriarchy*. New York: Oxford University Press, 1986. A classic on the interaction of class and gender in the shaping of early society.

Lewis, M. W., and K. E. Wigan. *The Myth of Continents: A Critique of Metageography*. Berkeley: University of California Press, 1997. Explores the degree to which the six habitable continents are defined more by history and historians than by clear geographical boundaries.

Melko, M., and L. R. Scott. *The Boundaries of Civilizations in Space and Time*. Lanham, Md.: University Press of America, 1987. The concept of "civilization" defined by historians, social scientists, philosophers, and others. See also R. J. Wenke, *Patterns in Prehistory*, 3rd ed. (New York: Oxford University Press, 1990).

Simmons, I. G. *Changing the Face of the Earth: Culture, Environment, and History*. Oxford: Blackwell, 1989. Human impact on the world we live in.

 Please refer to the document CD-ROM for primary sources related to this chapter.

OVERVIEW I

ANCIENT CIVILIZATIONS

(3500–200 B.C.E.)

....

Civilization was born not once, but many times. Each of the earth's historic regions has in fact produced its own ancient civilizations, its own historic beginnings around the world.

Mostly in the fertile river valleys of the north temperate zone, elaborate structures of stone and wood and clay heaved up above the surrounding landscape. There were towers and labyrinthine palaces, massive city walls, and tangled warrens of city streets. And scuttling through those urban mazes were human beings with heads full of new questions and new ambitions. Living together in large numbers now, challenging and stimulating each other, some among them at least began to wonder how to build a better brick—how to get a larger share of the irrigated fields beyond the gates—and what to do about the new town rising only a few miles away.

Sometimes the wider goals and ambitions of which humans were now capable led them to attack their neighbors, forging large states and empires in the process. Sometimes the whole urban-imperial venture failed, falling before alien invaders or through the follies of their own builders.

But once they had invented civilization, humans never abandoned it for long. Sooner or later the glimmer of ambition would flicker once more across the faces of human beings. And then the walls would rise again, the labyrinths and towers.

An early cluster of the city-based societies we call civilizations emerged near the point where the continents of Europe, Asia, and Africa come together. These three linked continents are often referred to as the Old World, thus contrasting it with the New World of the Americas. The region where these three giant land masses join around the eastern end of the Mediterranean Sea became the cultural crossroads of this half of the inhabited world. Here four early centers of civilization emerged, interacting with and influencing each other in many ways. These were the ancient Mesopotamian peoples, the Egyptians, the Hebrews, and—just across a corner of the Mediterranean—the ancient Greeks.

Other city-based civilizations also emerged in ancient times in both the Old and the New Worlds. But isolation rather than interaction defined most of these more far-flung experiments in living beyond the agricultural village. Almost all the ancient civilizations of India and China, Mexico and Peru thus developed without guides or models, uninfluenced by either the developed peoples of the continental crossroads or by each other.

There were many differences among both groups of early civilizations. Some were essentially differences of style, in ways of achieving a common end. It is easy to distinguish between Greek temples and Indian *stupas* or shrines, between the two dozen letters of the Greek alphabet and the thousands of characters of written Chinese. But the differences are essentially stylistic ones: religious centers and written languages are common among civilized peoples.

There were more fundamental differences as well, of course. The small, squabbling, determinedly independent city-states of Greece, for instance, would seem to contrast fundamentally with the vast, relatively centralized empire of China. Here and there, high civilizations even emerged without benefit of key elements in the standard definition of a civilization. Neither the Olmecs nor the Chavín developed the art of writing, for example, and the pharaohs of Old Kingdom Egypt raised their awesome pyramids without having yet discovered the wheel.

Similarities, however, undoubtedly outweigh the differences among these ancient civilizations. A wander through their ruins reveals something of what all urban-imperial peoples were capable of doing. In a world where most human beings still lived in the one-room huts of tiny agricultural villages or in the tents of nomadic herders, such monumental achievements as the Egyptian pyramids or the Athenian Acropolis, the cities of Harappan India or the Great Wall of China clearly represented a major change in the lifeways of the human race.

Whether they raised their first walls and towers in the close-clustering crossroads of the Old World or at the farther reaches of the Old and New Worlds, these ancient peoples had taken a decisive step. It was the step that took the human race from preurban living to urban civilization, from prehistory into history.

ANCIENT CIVILIZATIONS

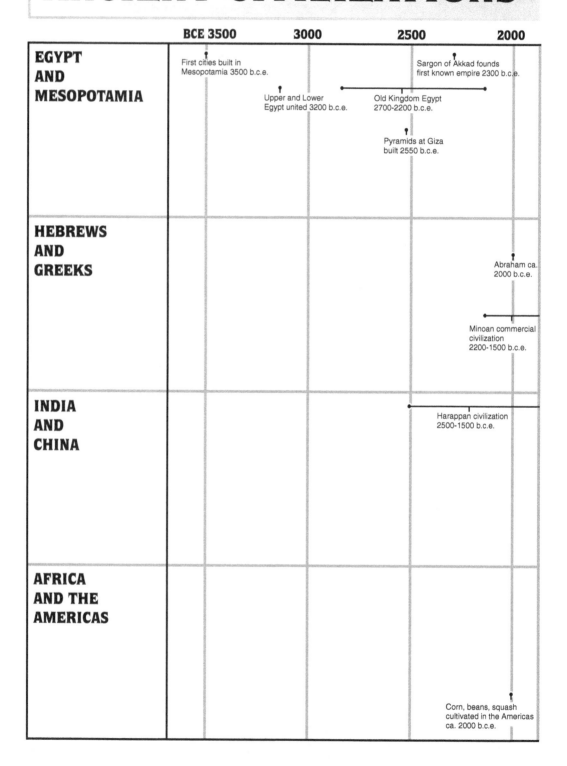

	BCE 3500	3000	2500	2000
EGYPT AND MESOPOTAMIA	First cities built in Mesopotamia 3500 b.c.e.	Upper and Lower Egypt united 3200 b.c.e.	Old Kingdom Egypt 2700-2200 b.c.e. / Pyramids at Giza built 2550 b.c.e.	Sargon of Akkad founds first known empire 2300 b.c.e.
HEBREWS AND GREEKS				Abraham ca. 2000 b.c.e. / Minoan commercial civilization 2200-1500 b.c.e.
INDIA AND CHINA			Harappan civilization 2500-1500 b.c.e.	
AFRICA AND THE AMERICAS				Corn, beans, squash cultivated in the Americas ca. 2000 b.c.e.

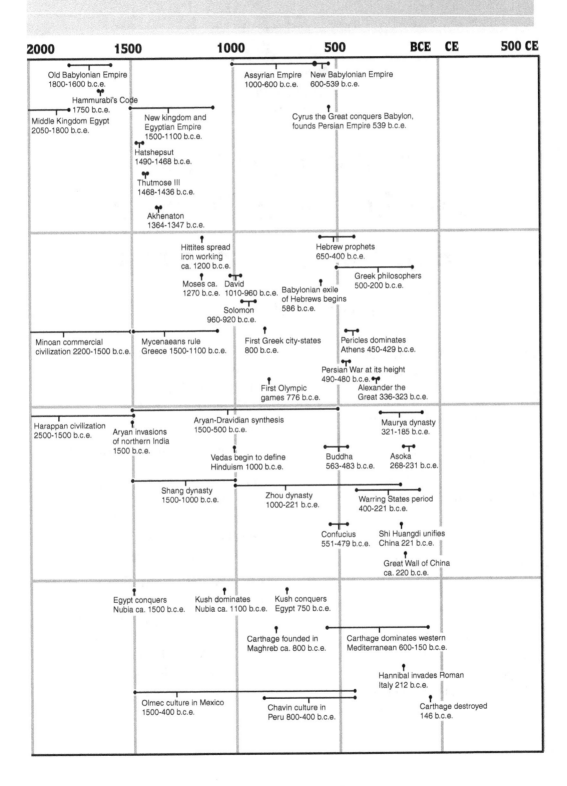

2000	1500	1000	500	BCE	CE	500 CE

Old Babylonian Empire
1800-1600 b.c.e.

Hammurabi's Code
1750 b.c.e.

Middle Kingdom Egypt
2050-1800 b.c.e.

New kingdom and
Egyptian Empire
1500-1100 b.c.e.

Hatshepsut
1490-1468 b.c.e.

Thutmose III
1468-1436 b.c.e.

Akhenaton
1364-1347 b.c.e.

Assyrian Empire   New Babylonian Empire
1000-600 b.c.e.   600-539 b.c.e.

Cyrus the Great conquers Babylon,
founds Persian Empire 539 b.c.e.

Hittites spread
iron working
ca. 1200 b.c.e.

Moses ca.   David
1270 b.c.e. 1010-960 b.c.e.

Solomon
960-920 b.c.e.

Hebrew prophets
650-400 b.c.e.

Greek philosophers
500-200 b.c.e.

Babylonian exile
of Hebrews begins
586 b.c.e.

Minoan commercial
civilization 2200-1500 b.c.e.

Mycenaeans rule
Greece 1500-1100 b.c.e.

First Greek city-states
800 b.c.e.

Pericles dominates
Athens 450-429 b.c.e.

Persian War at its height
490-480 b.c.e.

First Olympic
games 776 b.c.e.

Alexander the
Great 336-323 b.c.e.

Harappan civilization
2500-1500 b.c.e.

Aryan invasions
of northern India
1500 b.c.e.

Aryan-Dravidian synthesis
1500-500 b.c.e.

Vedas begin to define
Hinduism 1000 b.c.e.

Buddha
563-483 b.c.e.

Maurya dynasty
321-185 b.c.e.

Asoka
268-231 b.c.e.

Shang dynasty
1500-1000 b.c.e.

Zhou dynasty
1000-221 b.c.e.

Warring States period
400-221 b.c.e.

Confucius
551-479 b.c.e.

Shi Huangdi unifies
China 221 b.c.e.

Great Wall of China
ca. 220 b.c.e.

Egypt conquers
Nubia ca. 1500 b.c.e.

Kush dominates
Nubia ca. 1100 b.c.e.

Kush conquers
Egypt 750 b.c.e.

Carthage founded in
Maghreb ca. 800 b.c.e.

Carthage dominates western
Mediterranean 600-150 b.c.e.

Hannibal invades Roman
Italy 212 b.c.e.

Olmec culture in Mexico
1500-400 b.c.e.

Chavin culture in
Peru 800-400 b.c.e.

Carthage destroyed
146 b.c.e.

CHAPTER 2

Pyramid Tombs
and Ziggurat Temples
Egypt and Mesopotamia

(3500–100 B.C.E.)

A Glance Ahead: The First Cities, the First Nation

The range of ancient civilizations mentioned in the Overview spans three thousand years and much of the globe. Two of the most intriguing, however, have a special interest for us moderns, with our passion for priority, our enthusiasm for being first. As far as we know, the city-states of Mesopotamia, in what is today Iraq, were the first real cities built anywhere. And the kingdom of Egypt winding down the Nile—ancient Egypt of the pharaohs—was probably the first real country in history.

These patterns of political organization laid down by ancient Near Easterners and North Africans would play a crucial part in the future history of humankind.

Civilization emerged in cities. It spread across the earth in the larger and more complex units we call variously countries, nations, kingdoms, and republics. All these primary political units, furthermore, were capable of conquering their neighbors and creating even larger polities called empires. In the following pages, we will see these patterns emerging over and over as humankind discovers these basic forms of political organization thousands of years ago.

The Cities of Mesopotamia

A Land between Two Rivers

Nobody, of course, ever set out to build the first civilizations. They happened, like the growth of families or feuds between clans, like droughts or animal migrations or somebody learning from somebody else a better way to weave cloth or chip stone.

Gods demanded houses and servants, just as the heads of powerful families did, so temples and their attendant priesthoods emerged. Vendettas against neighbors or stock rustling raids threw up war leaders, and war leaders became hereditary rulers. Villages absorbed neighboring villages, and then a victorious local warlord threw a wall around them all, and a city emerged. People started counting their animals and making marks on clay to remind themselves how many there were, and writing was born.

Thousands of years in the future, learned people would look back and call it the birth of civilization.[1] They would tick off the elements of the new lifestyle: "urbanization . . . political institutions . . . organized religious beliefs . . . job specialization . . . social ranking . . . visual arts . . . a network of public works . . ." and of course "writing." But we do not need to postulate any conscious drive toward civilization-building to admire the remarkable consequences of these lives lived long ago.

We will begin this look at the oldest civilizations with the cities of ancient Mesopotamia. The first of these cities probably emerged a few brief centuries before the pharaohs united Egypt into the beginnings of a nation. This initial breakthrough into urban living came in the middle of the fourth millennium B.C.E. in Sumeria, in the southeastern corner of what is today Iraq.

Mesopotamia means "Between the Rivers" in Greek, and "Land of the Two Rivers" is as adequate a label as we are likely to get for a place where so many political states have come and gone. Geographically speaking, it is the swath of alluvial plain and patches of

---

[1]See Gregory G. Guzman, "A Working Definition of the Term 'Civilization' " in the *World History Bulletin*, Volume 7, No. 1 (1991) for a handy summary.

bordering hills that run northwestward along the banks of the Tigris and Euphrates rivers from the head of the Persian Gulf to the edge of the Anatolian uplands of modern Turkey. It is an arid region now. Where the land once blew golden with grain in the palm-lined fields along the ancient canals, the earth cracks in the sun today or smoulders with the ruins of recent wars. Where the cities of Mesopotamia once stood, shapeless mounds called *tells* remain, from which the archaeologist's spade can bring forth no more than a rough sense of the shape and scale of the achievement of these first builders.

Over a span of some three thousand years, from perhaps 3500 to 539 B.C.E., the center of Mesopotamian civilization moved slowly up the two rivers. Cities and empires first emerged in Sumeria, or Sumer, in the marshy delta at the head of the Persian Gulf. Civi-

ANCIENT CIVILIZATIONS OF EURASIA, 3500–1500 B.C.E.

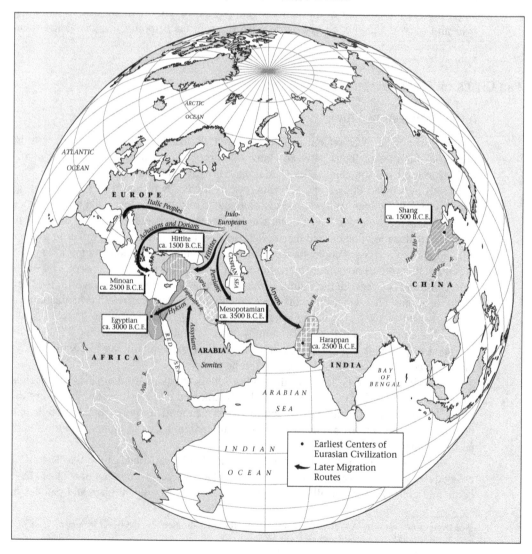

lization flourished next in Akkadian Babylon, farther up the rivers, and came to a violent climax in the northwest, in Assyria, during the first millennium B.C.E.

Irrigation, Building, Bronze Age Crafts

It may have been the gradual drying out of the sea-covered delta at the mouths of the two rivers, producing marshy but highly fertile land, that first drew Neolithic farmers. They came down from the rain-watered hills, where they had already learned to cultivate the land, pasture animals, and live in villages, into Sumer. We do not really know. A pre-Sumerian people were there already; they have left us only a few stone tools and some non-Sumerian names on the land. We do know that during the fourth millennium before Christ, two groups met and merged along the lower Tigris and Euphrates. There was a Sumerian-speaking people from somewhere to the north, perhaps around the Caspian Sea, and the first of many waves of people who spoke Semitic languages, drifting in from Syria or Arabia to the west. From the fertile fusion of these two groups, a vastly productive little society emerged as early as 3500 B.C.E.

The members of this society built reed huts in the marshes of a sort that may still be seen in the delta of southern Iraq today. They hunted birds and speared fish from graceful canoes with high prows and sterns that glided through the marsh grass with scarcely a ripple. But they were farmers as well as hunters and gatherers, and the rich alluvial soil favored agriculture. Out of the reeds and the mud of the delta, then, the ancient Sumerians built over centuries a small prototype of all the larger civilizations that would follow.

Their first great discovery was how to tame the erratic rivers of Mesopotamia. The sluggish Euphrates and the faster-moving Tigris crested late for planting. They frequently brought unmanageable quantities of rain water and melting snow down from the northern mountains to flood the land and sweep away homes and topsoil. Only with discipline and ingenuity did the Sumerians learn the proper combination of dikes, canals, and irrigation ditches for turning destructive floods into a source of ever more complex life.

By so doing they were able to raise enough food to support much larger populations than had been possible in the Neolithic villages of earlier times. The Sumerians grew barley as the staple grain of the south; wheat would flourish later, in northern Mesopotamia. They cultivated the date palm for fruit and for palm wine. They grew onions and garlic and garnished meals of unleavened barley bread with the oil of the sesame seed. Sumerian shepherds watched flocks of sheep and goats, from whose wool and hair clothing was made. They learned to use oxen to pull their plows, and patient donkeys became their primary beasts of burden. Only later, when Mesopotamian kings went forth to make war upon their neighbors, were camels and horses brought home from foreign parts and domesticated along the two rivers.

The Sumerians and their successors in the Land of the Two Rivers developed many crafts with great skill—textiles, pottery, and stone carving, the smelting of copper and the alloying of bronze. They even invented that archetype of human ingenuity, the wheel—solid and spoked—and the carts and wagons that went with it. Theirs is the first form of writing to come down to us. But their most important invention was the Mesopotamian city itself. The city became the center of this first of civilizations. And urban complexes, whatever their shortcomings as living spaces, have been the center of civilized society ever since.

The City and the City-State

Walls, high and thick, pierced with monumental gateways, were the most prominent feature of Mesopotamian cities. Within the walls the typical large town was divided into four quarters by main streets that entered the city through four main gates, one in the middle of each wall. The developing power structure of the city and the city-state was architecturally embodied in the king's palace, the temples of the gods, and the large houses of the leading citizens. Palaces and houses tended to be built around a succession of courtyards, meandering labyrinths of cool, thick-walled rooms, some of which were elaborately decorated with painting or colored tiles. Temples were characterized most strikingly by *ziggurats*—pyramidal, terraced towers visible from far beyond the city walls. The streets were mostly narrow and winding, crowded with shopkeepers and artisans, jostling slaves and citizens, priests in fluted skirts, and the majestic sedan chairs of the wealthy.

These first cities already contained a clear aristocracy and a detectable middle class. Handicraft industries, including the manufacture of textiles and metalwork in copper and bronze, produced a middle class of skilled artisans. Other bourgeois citizens included the merchants, especially the most wealthy among them, and the long-distance traders, whose caravans transported raw materials and luxury goods from one city to another. Above this stratum was a thin layer of aristocrats, royal officials, members of the royal family, and perhaps the chief priests of the major temples.

Few of the people who worked the fields outside the walls of these urban complexes were free peasants. Some were tenant farmers, holding their land in return for payment in kind to an absentee landlord who lived in the city. Others were serfs or even slaves, working the large tracts owned by the royal family and the chief gods of the city-state. All were subject to the rules laid down and the authority wielded by the officials who supervised the elaborate irrigation system that made the life of the city-state possible.

The developed irrigation systems of these first Mesopotamian hydraulic empires involved massive dikes and levees that protected the croplands of large parts of the valley from the often destructive annual floods. Canals carried the runoff water, ditches distributed it to individual fields, and everywhere the *shaduf*—a long pivoted pole with a weight at one end and a bucket of some sort at the other—lifted the water from larger channels into the furrows where the seeds were planted. Levees had to be constantly strengthened, canals and ditches redredged to prevent silting up, and large-scale drainage efforts made in the south to slow the salinization of the soil by the salt water of the Persian Gulf. Elaborate regulations, rigid authority, and a good deal of cooperation were necessary if such elaborate group labors were to be successful.

If class distinctions were much clearer in these early civilizations, gender differences seem to have been considerably more complicated. There is no denying the generally patriarchal tone of society and the state. Rulers, officials, priests, merchants, and heads of families were normally male. In the warlike Assyrian society described below, respectable women were veiled, prevented from owning property, married off by their fathers to establish business alliances, and could be sold into slavery and savagely punished for sexual offenses.

On the other hand, many Mesopotamian women did work outside the confines of the family as weavers, pottery makers, and even farm workers and manual laborers. In Sumer and Babylon, women could own property, sign legal contracts, and engage in business themselves. It is a complex picture, as gender relations will prove to be down the centuries.

The Palace and the Temple

The central institutions of Sumerian society were the monarchies and the cults of the gods.

The temple came first. The pyramidal ziggurats and broad temple complexes of the gods and goddesses—Anu and Enlil, Enki and Ninhursag and Innana (the last known later as Ishtar)—dominated the skyline of the Sumerian city. Each city had its own patron among the heavenly assembly, who was believed to bring rising rivers and rich harvests, to keep the barbarian from the gate, and to maintain order in the land.

Elaborate priesthoods served the major deities. Reverent hands dressed the cult statues daily, wafted food before their nostrils to feed them, played music to delight their ears. City dwellers could see their gods through the open doors of temple courtyards, dim and awesome in their niches. On great festival days such as the New Year, the gods and goddesses

---

PROBING THE PAST

This letter from an Assyrian courtier to Assurbanipal (668 – 627 B.C.E.) was written with a very practical purpose having little to do with historical interpretation. Yet his petition does offer an excellent brief summary of what good government and good times meant in ancient Mesopotamia.

What sanction for Assurbanipal's rule is stressed? What political and economic benefits has his rule conferred on his people? How does this courtier describe the "good life" for Mesopotamian women? Would a woman have agreed?

"To the king, my lord (Assurbanipal), from your servant Adad-šumi-usur:

Good health to Your Majesty! May the gods Nabû and Marduk give many, many blessings to Your Majesty.

When Aššur, the king of the gods, designated Your Majesty to rule Assyria as king, and when the gods Samaš and Adad confirmed by reliable oracles that Your Majesty should rule as king over all the countries, the great gods of the entire cosmos brought about during the reign of Your Majesty a happy rule with days and years in which law and order prevail: there are copious rains, abundant flooding of the rivers, favorable prices, and reconciliation of the gods; there is much piety and the temples of the gods are well provided. Old men dance with joy, young men sing happy songs, women and young girls happily learn to do what women do; they go into confinement and bring forth boys and girls, and the births are easy.

Why, then, since Your Majesty has pardoned persons condemned to death for their crimes, and has released those who for many years had been imprisoned, and since . . . the hungry have been sated with food . . . and those who had been destitute have been clad in sumptuous garments—why then should I and my son Arad-Gula, among all those happy people, remain restless and in low spirits? Only recently has Your Majesty shown his love for Nineveh by telling the prominent citizens: "Bring me your sons, they shall become servants at my court!" If this son of mine, Arad-Gula, could become a servant at the court of Your Majesty, serving together with these same people, then we too would be as happy as all other people are; we would dance and bless Your Majesty."

A. Leo Oppenheim, ed. and trans., *Letters from Mesopotamia* (Chicago and London: University of Chicago Press, 1967), pp. 149–150.

of the land of the Two Rivers, gorgeously robed, their dark saucer-like eyes staring, were carried up the avenue in procession above the heads of their reveling worshipers.

Veneration of the gods predated the birth of the city: the power of the king grew more slowly in Sumer. Initially, the growing city was probably ruled by a city governor and war leader called the *ensi,* who governed in conjunction with an assembly of the city's free adult male citizens. As war leader, however, the *ensi* accumulated emergency powers that he did not surrender. He thus emerged in time as a hereditary monarch, still general in wartime but responsible also for maintaining the irrigation system, regulating prices and wages, and implementing other welfare measures. The assemblies—no doubt legacies from earlier, smaller-scale social organizations—faded, and the power of the kings grew. By the days of the Assyrian hegemony, the king had absorbed many religious functions, and the power of the palace clearly exceeded that of the temples of even the most ancient gods.

MESOPOTAMIAN EMPIRES

Impediments to Empire

Beyond the city-states of early times, the most common larger form of political organization was the empire. Empires were most often created when one people conquered others, absorbing them into a single larger political unit ruled by foreigners.

Successful efforts at empire-building in the Tigris-Euphrates valley occurred less than half a dozen times over a period of nearly three thousand years. There was the Sumerian Empire of Sargon of Akkad in the twenty-third century B.C.E. There was the Old Babylonian Empire founded by Hammurabi in the eighteenth century before Christ. There was the fierce Assyrian predominance of the eighth and seventh centuries B.C.E. and the short-lived New Babylonian Kingdom of the sixth century B.C.E. After that, Cyrus the Persian swept down from the mountains, and Mesopotamia found unity at last—as a satrapy or province of the Persian Empire.

Many factors militated against unification in the Land of the Two Rivers during the three thousand years between the rise of the first Sumerian cities and the final fall of Babylon in the days of Belshazzar. Most obviously, the rich valley lay open to nomadic incursion from east, west, and north. Barbaric invaders such as the Akkadians, Gudians, Kassites, and Persians might in time be civilized by the enduring culture of Sumer. Nonetheless, such onslaughts from the deserts or the mountains repeatedly frustrated the best efforts of a Sargon or a Hammurabi to impose a single imperium on Mesopotamia.

A second challenge to larger unity was the appearance of a fragmented feudal order in much of Mesopotamia. As in medieval Europe many centuries later, feudalism in the Near East meant the division of a large measure of power among a landowning aristocracy. Such a divided socioeconomic structure evidently did not make for political unity.

A third force was what has been called *petty-statism*—a tendency of the region to break up into a number of middle-sized states, each enjoying local hegemony but none strong enough to overpower the others and impose a larger order on all of Mesopotamia.

A final roadblock to political unity was polarization. When one of the feuding Mesopotamian city-states did grow powerful enough to reach for supremacy, it was repeatedly confronted by the rise of a great rival. Polarization could clearly be as powerful an obstacle as barbarian invasions, feudalization, or petty-statism to unification in the Land of the Two Rivers.

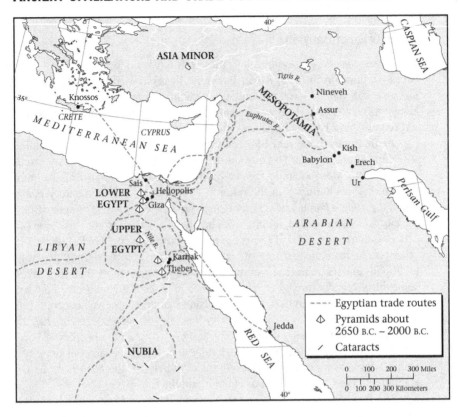

When unity did come, albeit temporarily, it came as centralized political authority has normally come to disunited peoples. It was imposed by blood and violence and attended with toppling walls and corpses steaming in the roadways, with kings struck down and gods carried off into exile. Yet such a larger order, however imposed, could bring with it a better life for all the divided peoples of the wide valley.

Sargon of Akkad

The most celebrated of Sumerian kings was Sargon of Akkad, who founded a dynasty around 2300 B.C.E. that governed much of Mesopotamia for almost a hundred years.

Having begun his career as a Semitic royal official of one of the lesser Sumerian city-states, Sargon replaced his royal master on the throne, overthrew the mighty dynasty of neighboring Uruk, and subsequently conquered most of the Tigris and Euphrates valley. He garrisoned his conquests with Akkadian troops and built himself a new capital, the rich and powerful city of Agade. His son and grandson ruled after him. But volcanic ash from an eruption may have brought drought to the region. And then the violent Gutians swept down from the neighboring hills to destroy the city and its imperial Mesopotamian domain. The powerful bronze head traditionally identified as Sargon shows a strong, curly-bearded face with heavy lips and a hawklike nose—the face of the world's first empire builder.

Perhaps the most famous of all attempts at Mesopotamian unity, however, was that of Hammurabi, the law-giver of Babylon.

Hammurabi of Babylon

Few cities outside of Sodom and Gomorrah have enjoyed a worse—or a more glamorous—reputation in history than Babylon. To persecuted early Christians, Rome of the Caesars was Babylon reborn, and the Antichrist himself was known as the Whore of Babylon. New York, Hollywood, and other modern metropolises famed for wealth and wickedness have been dubbed new Babylons in their turn.

At first glance, the real Babylon scarcely seems to deserve its reputation for wealth, worldliness, and power. The city on the Euphrates enjoyed only two periods of genuine supremacy in Mesopotamia: the period of the old Babylonian Empire, roughly 1800 to 1600 B.C.E., beginning with the reign of Hammurabi, and the century beginning around 600 B.C.E., when Nebuchadnezzar created the New Babylonian Empire. But the wealth of the city was never denied, and its size and physical splendor grew over the centuries.

Hammurabi (c. 1792–1750 B.C.E.) was born King of Babylon, the sixth in a line of otherwise undistinguished Amorite rulers of that city. He apparently governed his modest metropolis and its hinterland—at that time a city-state no more than fifty miles across—for some thirty years before he seized his chance to make Babylon great in the land. Then, late in his reign, he seems to have parlayed a combination of shrewd statecraft, brilliant timing, and military force into a far wider power than any of his predecessors had enjoyed. For a brief time, he and his heirs held supreme authority over all the peoples of Mesopotamia.

The reputation of Hammurabi as a ruler in peace, however, considerably outshines his claim to fame as an empire builder. In the chronicles of the Near East, he lived on not as Hammurabi the Conqueror but as Hammurabi the Lawgiver.

The three hundred Sumerian and Akkadian laws of *Hammurabi's Code* cover a wide range of civil and criminal matters, from land law and business law to regulation of family relations, from personal injury to military service, from witchcraft to taxes. Many of the principles promulgated in the code seem harsh to the modern reader. The principle of an eye for an eye, a life for a life, is here commonly invoked, centuries before Moses. Mutilation and death are repeatedly prescribed as fair and fitting punishments. And a clear sense of social hierarchy is reflected throughout; there is one law for slaves, another for their masters.

Yet the Code of Hammurabi does reveal a society with a highly developed belief in social justice. Even harsh punishment imposed by the state may be seen as an advance over the random retaliation of feuding clans that it replaced. And if the life of the slave is not rated as high in shekels of compensation as the life of a freeman, by the same token a nobleman may be punished more rigorously for the same offense than his social inferiors. Perhaps most important, there is a clear conviction that might does not make right, that the law has a fundamental obligation to protect the weak from the strong. It was not the worst foundation for this early attempt at a larger social order, which reached beyond the city-state to govern a whole people.

When the great king died, his heirs could not hold what he had won. New waves of preurban peoples appeared at the gates, most formidably the Kassites from the east, and within a century and a half, the brief Babylonian unification of Mesopotamia had crumbled away.

The next unifiers of the valley of the Tigris and Euphrates emerged still farther to the north, in the region that came to be known as Assyria.

Assyrian warriors in combat, vividly depicted on the walls of the royal palace at Nineveh. Charging troops, slaughtered foes, and severed heads all reflect the ferocity of the Assyrian war machine. (Erich Lessing/Art Resource)

The Assyrian Warfare State

The world has seen more than its share of frightfulness over the fifty-five hundred years since civilization was born in ancient Sumer. But the Assyrians were among the most savage of civilized peoples, even by modern standards of violence.

The source of the endless brutal military campaigns that are the very texture of Assyrian history has been sought in various aspects of this last great Mesopotamian culture.

One approach is simply to point out that geographically, Assyria was highly vulnerable, more open even than southern Mesopotamia to foreign invasion. The Assyrians may thus have treated their foes more savagely than usual in order to replace nonexistent natural frontiers with a wall of fear. There may also have been, at the royal palace and among the priesthood of their chief god, Assur, a sense of imperial and religious duty to impose and reimpose order on the chaos of the Near East in the second and first millennia B.C.E. There was, in addition, almost certainly a normal human lust for something for nothing, for the loot and tribute that made wars a paying proposition for the powerful Assyrian military machine. There may well have been, finally, more subtle economic motives at work. Some historians have detected behind Assyrian imperialism the need for copper and stone and timber, or the desire to control trade routes.

For whatever reason, the story of the rise and fall of the Assyrians is a story of almost unending war.

According to their own records, at least, they began to win wars with the barbarians in the fourteenth century B.C.E., during the Babylonian dark age that followed the decline of the heirs of Hammurabi. By the latter part of the eighth century, they were incorporating their victims into a large and growing empire. In the seventh century, under Sennacherib and Assurbanipal, Assyrian power overwhelmed Egypt and most of Mesopotamia. In the reign of the redoubtable Assurbanipal, Assyria thus stood briefly as master of the band of civilized states that ran from the Nile to the Persian Gulf.

Everywhere they went, they brought devastation. "I built a pillar over against his city gate," reported a ninth-century Assyrian ruler, "and I flayed all his chief men . . . and I covered the pillar with their skins. . . ."[2] Whole populations were deported, cities leveled, their gods—and sometimes their citizens—given over to the flames. And the tribute of a terrorized world rolled in.

But the lust for loot and victory of even the most martial people may be sated in time. Sennacherib built an aqueduct that pleased him perhaps as much as the looting of the land of the Hebrews.

It was perhaps a softening. And it brought its reward. Chaos closed over the Assyrian Empire in the last years of the seventh century. In 612 B.C.E., an allied force of Chaldeans from Babylon and Medes from the eastern mountains broke into the heart of Assyria, ringed Nineveh, and crushed it.

The punishment imposed upon the erstwhile terror of the world was as thorough as any inflicted by the Assyrians in their pride. Mighty Nineveh was leveled so efficiently that when the Greek general Xenophon passed that way two centuries later, no one could even identify the site for him.

Nebuchadnezzar and the New Babylonian Empire

The New Babylonian Empire, which briefly succeeded Assyrian power in Mesopotamia, was very much the creation of one man: Nebuchadnezzar II (605–562 B.C.E.), notorious in Bible history as the Chaldean ruler who carried off the Hebrews into their Babylonian captivity. Nebuchadnezzar was a conqueror and an empire builder in the by now time-honored Mesopotamian tradition. Seven years after the fall of Nineveh, while still crown prince of Babylon, he commanded the Babylonian army that crushed the forces of the Egyptian pharaoh at Carchemish in 605 B.C.E. As king, he led repeated expeditions down into Palestine, destroying Jerusalem, and carrying much of the population of Judea off into exile. At its brief height, the New Babylonian empire of the sixth century rivaled its Assyrian predecessor in size and splendor, governing once more from a single center all the land from the Persian Gulf to the Mediterranean.

Nebuchadnezzar built more than a mighty empire, however. He was celebrated in antiquity not as the man who took torch and crowbar to Solomon's Temple but as the rebuilder of the city of Babylon.

Just as Hammurabi was before him at Babylon, Nebuchadnezzar II was a great builder of canals and caravan roads, temples and palaces. He raised huge new crenellated walls around his capital, eleven miles long and so wide that a chariot could turn around on

---

[2]Samuel Noah Kramer, *Cradle of Civilization* (New York: Time-Life Books, 1967), p. 58.

the roadway that ran along the top. He opened the broad Processional Way through the heart of the city to the famous Ishtar Gate. He built the Hanging Gardens of Babylon—a towering ziggurat featuring terraces planted with trees and exotic plants—to please his Median wife, who missed the hills of her mountainous home.

But the Babylon of Nebuchadnezzar was a brief, final flowering. Its conqueror was one of history's great empire builders—Cyrus the Great. This half-barbarian king, called Cyrus the Shepherd by his Persian and Median troops, had already overrun all the kingdoms of the north and east, from rich Lydia on the Mediterranean to the far frontiers of India. Then in 539 B.C.E., he turned his leather-clad horsemen toward the richest plum of all—Babylon.

He found the ancient city ripe for the plucking. Nebuchadnezzar's successors had not ruled well, and there were powerful men within the walls who felt that their interests would be better served by a change of dynasty than by a protracted struggle with as famous a soldier as Cyrus the Persian. Cyrus's troops, with the help of a quisling governor, entered the city without resistance. And his victory marked the beginning of a new era in the Near East.

Just a caravan journey to the west, meanwhile, another remarkable center of civilization had been keeping pace with developments in Mesopotamia. This was the ancient African civilization of Egypt, to which we now turn.

THE PYRAMID AGE IN EGYPT

The Gift of the Nile

Civilization apparently emerged a few centuries later in the Nile valley than it did on the banks of the Tigris and the Euphrates, perhaps around 3200 B.C.E. But the Egyptians very quickly moved ahead of their neighbors beyond the Arabian Desert, in one area at least. Egypt early developed a powerful centralized government, whereas Mesopotamia remained a land of city-states and short-lived empires throughout its long history. Egypt thus enjoyed a high degree of unity, stability, and cultural continuity through much of its three thousand years of independent life.

As is so frequently the case, the course of Egyptian historical development was in large part set by the geographical framework within which Egypt evolved. "Egypt," reported the ancient Greek historian Herodotus, "is the gift of the Nile." The river was clearly central to the daily life of the Egyptians. The heart of the land was that part of the river from the first cataract at Aswan to the fan-shaped delta where it flowed into the Mediterranean. (The Nile, incidentally, flows northward to the Mediterranean, so that *Upper* Egypt is in the south, *Lower* Egypt in the north.) The river winds six hundred miles from the cataracts to the delta, gouging out a valley that is seldom more than a few miles wide. Only over the last hundred miles or so does the valley open up into the flat, triangular delta spread along the sea. The traditional "two lands" of Egypt were defined by this difference: Upper Egypt, with its sacred city at Thebes, covered most of the river valley; Lower Egypt, with its even more ancient capital at Memphis, comprised mostly the delta.

The great river's annual rise and fall were crucial for the life of Egypt. The Nile has its sources far to the south, in the mountains of Ethiopia and the lake country of equatorial Africa. Each year spring rains in these far-off regions sent high water surging north across the Sudan and the lands of ancient Nubia, thrashing through the cataracts, and rolling on at a more majestic pace through the sandstone- and limestone-walled valley of Upper

Egypt. Here the rising waters overflowed their banks and deposited over the narrow valley a layer of rich black mud, alluvium picked up along all the hundreds of miles from central Africa. It was this rich gift of fertile soil and life-giving water that enabled the Nile valley to bloom and made Egypt the most favored land in the ancient world.

Egypt and Africa

The African location of Egypt brought the kingdom of the Nile more than fertile soil, however. Some cultural influences also flowed north from inner Africa into Egypt.

As we will see, scholars have long seen Mesopotamian influences at work in Egyptian civilization. More recently, historians like Cheikh Anta Diop have urged the importance of African influences on the shaping of Egyptian culture. Evidence of inner African influence on the emerging Egyptian kingdom includes political, social, and cultural similarities.

Culturally, Egyptians shared both myths and individual gods—including an important jackal-headed god of the dead—with other African peoples. Among similar artifacts, you can see wooden headrests like those used in ancient Egypt still in use in parts of rural Africa today. Social customs common to this ancient civilization and later African cultures include circumcision and totemic animals symbolizing a clan or people. There are also parallels between Egyptian and other African languages.

Similar political patterns also suggest closer ties than was once thought between Egypt and the rest of Africa. Matrilineal descent—the inheritance of property and power through the female side of the family—was common in Africa and crucial in Egypt, where even pharaohs often married their sisters to guarantee their hereditary power over the land. Specific forms and rituals of divine kingship also link the pharaohs with kings and chiefs from farther south.

We will see later contacts, often initiated by the Egyptians, in later centuries. For now, it will suffice to plant the kingdom of the pharaohs firmly in African soil before going on to survey Egypt's own development and its key role in the history of the Near East and the Eastern Mediterranean.

The Pharaohs Unify the Land

Perhaps as early as the fifth millennium B.C.E., the hunters and nomadic pastoralists who had gravitated to the well-watered river valley had discovered the agricultural potential of the endlessly replenished black earth along the Nile. Like their Neolithic fellows farther east, they settled into agricultural villages. There were differences, of course. The cereal on which Egyptian agriculture was based was wheat instead of barley, and the Egyptians grew flax for clothing instead of depending on sheep's wool. Like preurban peoples in many places, the Egyptians organized themselves into clans having animal totems, such as the crocodile or the hippopotamus. They probably worshiped these animals as well, since many of the gods of later Egyptian times were depicted with animal heads on their otherwise anthropomorphic—human-headed—bodies.

Along the Nile, as along the Tigris and Euphrates, it took slow centuries and many generations for village life to evolve into something more complex. Nevertheless, the outlines of a distinctly Egyptian culture were clear before the Old Kingdom ever began.

Sometime between 3500 and 3000 B.C.E., cooperative economic effort appeared as the Egyptians began to try to control the great river with dikes and catch basins. Copper was used more widely. The population grew. There was, however, less of the bustling urban life that had flourished in early Sumeria. Nor did trade play such an important part in Egypt; the Nile valley was so nearly self-sufficient that there was apparently little felt need for exotic foreign imports.

There were some influences from outside, even this early. Mesopotamian-style cylinder seals have been found in Egypt. Sumerian pictograms appear among the earliest Egyptian hieroglyphics. But there was one great difference: Because there was less urban commercial culture in Egypt, the city-state also failed to appear. Instead, Egypt seems to have moved relatively early directly into the centralized monarchical state.

There was one intermediate stage, however. After the villages along the river, there were the two lands of Upper and Lower Egypt. We do not know a great deal about these two lands before they became one. We know that the vulture of the goddess Nekhbet was sacred in Upper Egypt, the cobra of Wadjet in Lower Egypt. We know that the kings of the upper valley wore a white crown, the kings of the delta a red one. And we know that their two peoples fought each other.

We do not need to follow the struggle of the cobra and the vulture, the white crown and the red. After generations, maybe centuries, the warriors of Upper Egypt fought their way northward from inner Africa to the Mediterranean. A new capital was founded at Memphis, and the crowns of Upper and Lower Egypt were combined into the double crown of the pharaohs. By 3000 B.C.E., Egypt stood as a united land.

The Old Kingdom: The Pyramid Builders

Old Kingdom Egypt—the stable, monumentally impressive first period of Egyptian history—was not a large nation by today's standards. It covered about the same area that Mesopotamia did—approximately ten thousand square miles. But in 3000 B.C.E. there was no nation in the world as large or half as centralized.

There was resistance, of course. Egyptians of the valley and Egyptians of the delta did not lose a sense of their differentness. The pharaoh was always officially "the King of Upper and Lower Egypt," "the Lord of the Two Ladies" (the vulture and the cobra), and as such was crowned and symbolically buried in each of the two lands. There were separate treasuries for the two halves of his kingdom and much duplication of officials.

More challenging still to the fundamental unity of the state was the tendency toward fragmentation embodied in the *nomes,* the provinces of pharaonic Egypt. Independent totemic tribes or clans prior to unification, the nomes could become centers of disunity under ambitious governors.

To hold the nation together, the early pharaohs, like the princes of Mesopotamia, forged a powerful alliance with the temples and the priests. Mesopotamian kings ruled as stewards or bailiffs of the gods; the pharaohs claimed that they themselves were incarnations of divinity.

Pharaoh was believed to be the son of the sun god Re. The reigning pharaoh was also Horus the sky god, symbolized by the falcon. On his death, "the falcon flew to the horizon," and the dead pharaoh became Osiris, king of the underworld. "What is the king of Upper and Lower Egypt?" a statesman of a later dynasty rhetorically inquired. "He is a god by whose dealings one lives, the father and mother of all men, alone by himself, without an equal."[3]

---

[3]Milton Covensky, *The Ancient Near Eastern Tradition* (New York: Harper & Row, 1966), p. 51.

Above all, he was "the good god." Every year he performed religious ceremonies that guaranteed the rising of the river. He and his officials ruled the land in the spirit of *Ma'at,* a combination of truth, justice, and order that was for the Egyptians the highest of virtues. In the underworld, the souls of the dead were weighed against *Ma'at.* In this world, pharaoh himself was its living embodiment and the guarantee that the land would be ruled in its spirit.

To carry out the will of the god-king, the Egyptians developed an elaborate administrative system as early as the Old Kingdom. The chief administrative officer under the pharaoh was the vizier, whose roles included chief judge, superintendent of public works, and general right hand to the king. Under the vizier an impressive array of bureaus emerged, including the treasuries, the ministry of agriculture, the officials in charge of the irrigation system, and a secretariat that piled up an immense volume of public records.

There was also a provincial administration charged with governing the nomes. The rulers of these provinces, the *nomarchs,* exercised considerable local authority. In particular, they controlled the local militia, the source of most of the military strength of the kings of Upper and Lower Egypt.

The body of the Egyptian bureaucracy—and subsequently the top spots as well—was staffed by scribes, the masters of the sacred art of writing. If the records they left behind are any indication, Egyptian scribes were busy bureaucrats. They conducted censuses of land and people, estimated the size of the harvest, and collected taxes in kind. They supervised the vital irrigation system, organized the care and feeding of the pharaohs and the building of the royal tombs. Next to the divinity of pharaoh himself, these scribal administrators were the glue that held ancient Egypt together in a genuine national state built many centuries before its time.

Old Kingdom Egypt was a thoroughly ordered state. Society was organized hierarchically, as it would be almost everywhere in the increasingly complex cultures of the civilized world. Peasant farmers were the backbone of the nation—and the bottom of the social pyramid. Many of them were serfs on royal or noble lands, required to labor on building projects as well as to till the soil. Above these peasant *fellahin* were the royal officials, the priesthoods of the temples, the nobles, the princes, and the incarnate god upon the throne.

This hierarchy was symbolized most massively by the pyramid tombs of the pharaohs of the famous fourth dynasty—the dynasty of Khufu (known to Western history as Cheops), builder of the great pyramid at Giza, ca. 2550 B.C.E. Today the tombs of the pharaohs loom in splendid isolation above the sands. Originally the royal pyramids of Khufu, Khafre, Menkaure, and the rest stood not alone but as centers of ordered necropolises, cities of the dead. Each pyramid was surrounded by the smaller pyramids of queens and princes of the blood and by row after row of the flat-roofed *mastaba* tombs of high officials. The total effect of these ranks of tombs laid out along straight-ruled streets must have been somberly impressive. It expressed to perfection the order of the living state. In death as in life, the "good god" ruled, and his people slept around him.

The Middle Kingdom: A Bridge between Two Worlds

The Middle Kingdom and the intermediate periods before and after it may be seen as a historic transition, a bridge between two worlds. During these half-dozen centuries Egypt moved from the self-contained, intensely conservative land of the pyramid builders to the more dynamic—and more turbulent—New Kingdom. Therefore, this entire period, from the collapse of the Old Kingdom around 2200 B.C.E. to the emergence of the New Kingdom about 1550, will be considered here as a whole.

The initial phase of this great transition is what historians have called the First Intermediate. We do not know what triggered this great disruption. There may have been a series of low Niles, or a succession of weak rulers. There was clearly a good deal of political turbulence, particularly among the nomarchs. There was famine in the land of the bountiful Nile, and marauding desert bedouin appeared in the delta. The poor cried out for justice—so the scribes lamented—and all Egyptians longed for a return to the immemorial order of past centuries.

What they got was not a return to the past but a dynamic new direction in national life. Ambitious dynasts from the new city of Thebes in Upper Egypt wrested the kingdom from the last royal house to rule in Memphis. During the twentieth and nineteenth centuries before Christ, the powerful twelfth dynasty restored prosperity and order along the Nile.

The Middle Kingdom thus inaugurated brought what seems to many historians a new concern for the governed on the part of twelfth-dynasty pharaohs. Contemporary scribes talked of a new sense of civic responsibility among the governed themselves during this briefest of the three Egyptian kingdoms.

But the most striking new dimension was the outward reach of the pharaohs of the twelfth dynasty. Trade expanded rapidly in the prosperous new era. Egyptian merchants traded with Palestine and Syria, satellite civilizations of ancient Mesopotamia, and even sailed to Minoan Crete, the island kingdom where the first European civilization was just emerging. Egyptian arms pushed south along the Nile into Nubia, the land of the nearest black African people, and on into the Sudan.

Thus for the first time Egypt became involved on a large scale with the busy life of the Near East and north-eastern Africa. From Middle Kingdom days on, the pharaohs were to play a key role in the history of both Africa and the Near East.

Contact with the outside world could flow two ways, however. The dynasties that followed the twelfth seem to have produced less capable rulers. Tendencies toward dissolution of the union, no longer restrained by a firm hand, reasserted themselves. And covetous strangers from overseas, attracted by the wealth and increasingly visible weakness of Egypt at the end of the Middle Kingdom, began to appear once more in the delta.

Shortly before 1700 B.C.E.—in the middle of the Second Intermediate—the gathering storm burst over Egypt in what ancient Egyptians regarded as their greatest catastrophe: the invasion of the Hyksos.

The priest Manetho described the onslaught of this mysterious Semitic-speaking people as "a blast of God." The seizure of power by the Hyksos may not have been quite that dramatic. The Hyksos influx was part of a general reshuffling of nomadic peoples during the second millennium B.C.E., to be discussed in the next chapter. These folk migrations were slow infiltrations as often as they were invasions. The invaders of Egypt actually spent several generations settling in the delta. Once they had seized power from the enfeebled pharaohs of the Second Intermediate, the Hyksos found nobles and nomarchs quite willing to collaborate with their leadership.

As often happens when a less sophisticated people overpowers a more developed culture, the newcomers soon became culturally assimilated, taking the names of the people they ruled, worshiping their gods, following all the traditional royal rites to the letter. For a century, perhaps a century and a half, they remained the predominant force in the Egypt of the Second Intermediate.

Governing the delta, dominating the valley, the Hyksos were also responsible for some valuable innovations. The use of bronze instead of the softer copper became widespread at this time. New weapons of war invented on the distant steppes were probably introduced by the intruders—notably the two-wheeled horse-drawn war chariot.

Then, as had happened twice already in Egyptian history, a powerful force surged out of the south to restore the direction of that history to Egyptian hands once more.

THE EGYPTIAN EMPIRE

The New Kingdom: The Turn toward Empire

The spearhead of this northward drive was the princely house of Thebes and its current head, Ahmose I, founder of the eighteenth and most powerful of Egyptian dynasties. His father and his brother had rallied noble opposition to the Hyksos before him. Around 1550 B.C.E., Ahmose led an army up the Nile, mastered the delta, captured the Hyksos capital, and harried the foreigner out of the land. He even pursued the Hyksos into Palestine, where they were conspiring with local chieftains for help, and destroyed their base there.

Returning to Egypt, the liberator crushed rebellions by some of the nobility and the Nubian princes who had collaborated with the Hyksos. He heaped the loot of all his victories at the feet of Amon, the sun god of Thebes. The priesthood of Amon thus became the most powerful in Egypt, and Thebes the new capital.

Thebes and the Theban princes were now at the head of an Egypt cleansed of foreign power. Egyptians had also had a taste of foreign conquest themselves, and of the loot and tribute that flowed from it. It was a heady experience, and it was to sweep Egypt into its last great age, the *New Kingdom* and the *Empire* (1550–1100 B.C.E.), when for four centuries Egyptian power would dominate the civilized peoples of the ancient Near East.

Queen Hatshepsut and Thutmose the Conqueror

The kings and queens of the New Kingdom seem to stand out in bold relief against the background of the centuries. These rulers of the last half of the second millennium B.C.E. were shapers of the history of their times. They also vividly illustrate those times, in all their strange ambitions and exotic grandeur. It will therefore be in order to slow the pace now and look into a royal lifetime or two as it was lived thirty-five hundred years ago.

Lying across the river from Thebes, the mortuary temple of Pharaoh Hatshepsut (ca. 1490–1468 B.C.E.)—wide and many-pillared, the cliffs of Deir el-Bahari looming dramatically behind it—is one of the most splendid sights in Egypt. And Hatshepsut was unique among pharaohs. She was a woman.

There were other powerful queens in Egypt, especially during the eighteenth dynasty. But Hatshepsut governed the land, not as pharaoh's wife, but as sole ruler.

The daughter of one pharaoh and the widow of another, she began her reign as regent for the male heir to the throne. Soon, however, she went beyond this quite legal role. Unprecedentedly, she declared herself the child of Re and the god's designated ruler, had herself crowned with the double crown, and seated herself on the golden throne of the pharaohs.

Hatshepsut's most lifelike surviving statue shows an attractive, slightly built woman wearing the clothing and headdress of the king of Upper and Lower Egypt. She is known to have surrounded herself with brilliant and ambitious advisors, and to have lavished wealth on the powerful priesthood of Amon at Thebes. She trumpeted her deeds from temple wall and obelisk in true pharaonic fashion. It was a bravura performance, and we would like to know more about it.

The reign of Hatshepsut, however, is more than a startling historical anomaly. It illustrates a crucial aspect of New Kingdom history: the commercial development and widespread prosperity that made this one of the most pleasant times in Egypt's long history.

Under Hatshepsut, as under other pharaohs, high-prowed "Byblos travelers" plowed the gentle swells of the Mediterranean north to the cities of Phoenicia and beyond, while tinkling Egyptian caravans followed the great military roads north and east to Mesopotamia. Nubia and Sinai poured their copper and gold into the coffers of Egypt. Hatshepsut's most renowned commercial venture, however, was the expedition she dispatched down the Red Sea to the Terraces of Incense, the legendary land of Punt, where the natives had beards like Egyptian gods and lived in grass houses built on pilings. The Egyptian fleet returned laden with ebony and ivory, perfumes and spices, apes, monkeys, leopard skins, slaves, and thirty-one live myrrh trees, which were ceremoniously replanted in front of the queen's temple at Deir el-Bahari.

She was a great ruler. But greatness sometimes kindles greatness in its rivals, and Hatshepsut had a great rival indeed. Prince Thutmose, the royal heir she had supplanted, grew into a restless young man. He was a skilled archer and charioteer, the darling of the militaristic elements among the aristocracy who longed for a more aggressive foreign policy. Thutmose himself seems to have chafed in his powerful aunt's leading strings, and to have resented the ambitious "new men" with whom she filled her court.

And then one year, as our meager records run, the young man had become Pharaoh Thutmose III, the new king of the two lands, and was preparing his chariots for war. Hatshepsut simply disappears from the records, and presumably from this world. It has been suggested—though there is no firm evidence—that the great queen did not "go gently into that good night."

Thutmose III (ca. 1468–1436 B.C.E.) the "Napoleon of Egypt," embodied another and even more typical aspect of the history of the imperial New Kingdom: the unending military campaigns that fill the annals of the epoch. Thutmose himself fought seventeen campaigns, and he did more than anyone else to establish the bounds and form of Egypt's New Kingdom empire. From his time on, the pharaoh as god was complemented, if not replaced, by the pharaoh as hero and empire builder in the minds of the Egyptians.

Thutmose III was a short, thick-chested, bull-necked man with a large nose and immense physical strength and courage. His famous victories—the siege of Megiddo, the battle of Kadesh, the crossing of the Euphrates into the lands of the Mitanni—and the defeated princes who groveled in the dust before him to "beg breath for their nostrils" are long forgotten. But he did construct a genuine empire for Egypt that stretched over much of the ancient Fertile Crescent, from the Euphrates to the fourth cataract of the Nile. "I let you trample down the far corners of the lands," chanted the great god Amon on the granite of Karnak, "the circle of the ocean was caught in your fist."[4]

There was more to it, of course, than the favor of the gods. The soldiers of Thutmose III, battle-hardened veterans after a few campaigns, were equipped with the latest swords, bows, and armor of the late Bronze Age and led by the light, beautifully constructed chariots that

---

[4]George Steindorff and Keith C. Seele, *When Egypt Ruled the East* (Chicago: University of Chicago Press, 1957), p. 55; Pierre Montet, *Lives of the Pharaohs* (Cleveland, Ohio: World, 1968), p. 102.

the Hyksos had bequeathed to Egypt. Thutmose carefully established garrison towns, local governors, and a sophisticated system of puppet kings to control what he had conquered.

Thutmose III raised obelisks as far south as the fourth cataract to thunder his imperial greatness to the world. They still stand today—in Rome, Istanbul, London, and New York's Central Park—loot for later empires larger by far than his.

Akhenaton, the Heretic Pharaoh

Perhaps the most fascinating of all the New Kingdom pharaohs was Akhenaton (ca. 1364–1347 B.C.E.), described by later scholars as the heretic pharaoh, a religious visionary, or the doom of his dynasty. Akhenaton was in fact everything to intrigue the historian—and the romancer. He was abnormally ugly, but he had a beautiful wife, the swan-necked Nefertiti. He loved his family and his own version of religious truth. His unique contribution to Egyptian history consisted in his effort to impose monotheism upon the people of the Nile valley thirteen and a half centuries before Christ.

The son of one of the later pharaohs of the famous eighteenth dynasty, the prince apparently became fascinated in his youth with one of the smaller solar cults, the worship of Aton, the sun disk itself. This fascination led the grown man to change his own name from Amenhotep IV (Amon Is Satisfied) to Akhenaton (Spirit of Aton). It drove him to move the capital of Egypt from Thebes, the stronghold of the priesthood of Amon, to a new city

The heretic pharaoh Akhenaton, prophet of a lost religion. From the grotesquely exaggerated features and the encumbering royal regalia, an intensely human face looks out upon the world. (Hirmer Fotoarchiv)

that he reared in the wilderness halfway between Thebes and Memphis, a city he christened Akhetaton ("Horizon of Aton"). His zealous faith, finally, apparently led him to launch a campaign to destroy all the other cults and replace them with the worship of the one true god, Aton the sun disk, throughout Egypt.

In this fantastic venture, Akhenaton shook up Egypt as it had not been shaken since the days of the Hyksos. The great Aton was represented not in human form, like the other gods, but simply by the solar disk. Rays spread down from it, and at the ends of the rays there were hands. Temples of Aton were built without roofs, so that the worshiper might commune directly with the god and feel in return the light and heat of the great creative force sailing majestically through the sky above. An Atonist hymn sometimes attributed to Akhenaton himself declares the glory of the one god, "beautiful, great, dazzling, and exalted over every land."[5]

The new city dedicated to the one god rose in a few years beneath the cliffs along the river near the present-day village of El-Amarna—hence the label Amarna Period for the whole unlikely adventure. Temples and palaces, fine homes for high officials, pleasure gardens and lovely courtyards grew up at the new cult center. Akhenaton may have been a fanatic, but there is an idyllic quality to those years at Horizon of Aton, cut off from the world and the gathering storm, that can scarcely fail to charm.

But it was not possible to transform the faiths of two thousand years in a single generation, and it took no more than the premature death of the pharaoh to destroy his new religion. The authority of the old cults was restored soon after Akhenaton's passing. Horizon of Aton was abandoned to the lizard and the jackal, and Akhenaton's very name was chiseled from the monuments and obliterated from the king list, as though he had never been. His youthful heir, Tutankhamun, returned to the faith of his ancestors and became a worshiper of Amon.

Final Glories and a Long Decline

Egypt had powerful pharaohs and pleasant times to come. But the empire grew harder to hold as its enemies grew more numerous and powerful. Despite intermittent high points, then, the last centuries of ancient Egypt are a story of long decline.

Pharaohs like Ramses II fought the Hittites to a standstill and watched the short-lived Hittite Empire crumble while life went on along the Nile. They repelled the attacks of the Sea People (the biblical Philistines), the greatest plague to descend upon the delta since the Hyksos. They built great temples and huge statues of themselves, and perhaps made Egyptians of the twelfth century B.C.E. think that the eternal life of Egypt would never end.

Royal women and women of the priestly classes achieved great wealth and power during this last millenium of Egyptian history. Pharaoh's daughters became chief priests of Amon at Karnak and de facto rulers of Upper Egypt. Their wealth and the battalions of administrators who served under them were proverbial.

But weak kings, overmighty priests, and continuing waves of invaders undermined the state. During the thousand years that followed the end of the New Kingdom in the eleventh century, Theban priests, Libyan mercenaries, Nubian kings, Assyrians, Persians, Macedonians, and Romans ruled Egypt in turn. The notorious Cleopatra, who welcomed Julius Caesar to Egypt, was as much Macedonian as she was Egyptian, and the most famous Egyptian city of her day was the thoroughly hellenized metropolis of Alexandria. The Egypt of the Pyramid Age and the Empire had long since passed into history.

---

[5]Steindorff and Seele, *When Egypt Ruled the East*, p. 214.

Rich and Poor, Men and Women

The lives of ancient Egyptians, like those of many other peoples, depended very largely on their place in the social hierarchy. We have many pictures of Egyptian *fellahin* hard at work in the fields, following a light plow or scattering seed in the furrows, harvesting wheat and barley, herding cattle in the delta, or fishing in the Nile. There was steady work also on the dikes and channels and basins that controlled the river, as well as compulsory labor on the tombs, temples, palaces, and public building projects of the pharaohs. But these projects depended for their success more on plenty of time and careful planning than on the flogged and sweated labor of the Hollywood epics. What records we have indicate a less than onerous work schedule: two four-hour work stints daily with a long noon siesta in between.

The condition of women was equally ambiguous among the Egyptians. Poor women worked as hard as their husbands, grinding grain at home and gleaning in the fields, with minimal time off to bear children. On the other hand, in contrast with many societies, Egyptians seem to have welcomed daughters as enthusiastically as they did sons.

The Greek historian Herodotus was struck by the freedom of Egyptian women to work and move freely in society. "The Egyptians," he wrote, "in their manners and customs, seem to have reversed the ordinary practices of mankind. For instance, women attend market and are employed in trade, while men stay at home and do the weaving."[6] A woman was allowed to go into business for herself if she could demonstrate that she had had three children and could read and write. Among the professions filled by women were midwifery, mourning, dancing, music, some important priesthoods and—Herodotus to the contrary—weaving. The women of the royal harem in fact ran the state cloth manufactures and oversaw women weavers in the temples. Women are also recorded as running wig shops, dining halls, and other establishments.

As noted previously, Egypt was a matrilineal society from top to bottom. All property was inherited in the female line. Even pharaoh frequently had to marry a sister in order to be sure of the crown. The leverage this gave the Egyptian woman must have been considerable.

The pictures we have of Egyptians at feasts seem to reveal a convivial people. They sat on reed mats with finger bowls and jars of wine at hand, while servants bore the festival meats around. The company was cheerfully mixed, men and women sitting easily together, crowned alike with garlands and entertained by the music of lutes and tambourines.

THE WISDOM OF THE FIRST CIVILIZATIONS

Writing, Learning, and Literature

Writing is one of the most important of the skills that would distinguish the peoples within the walls from many of their neighbors. Both the Egyptians and the Mesopotamian peoples developed forms of writing, though their approaches differed significantly from one another.

The true inventors of writing were probably the nameless precursors of the Sumerians in the marshy delta of the two rivers. Sometime during the later fourth millennium B.C.E., however, Sumerian scribes were making lists of goods and produce, flocks and harvested grain. They did so by scratching crude *pictograms* (pictorial representations) of the items in question on a small clay tablet with a reed stylus. The strokes of the triangular reed came to

---

[6]B. Waterson, *Women in Ancient Egypt* (New York: St. Martin's Press, 1991), p. 25.

be known as *cuneiform* (wedge-shaped) script. Over the centuries these signs began to be used simply to represent the *sound* of the names of the original articles. Several of these sound-symbols or *phonograms,* could then be combined to represent other words. The result was an exceedingly complicated system of writing that combined pictograms and phonograms and required a long course of specialized training in the scribal schools.

Only professional scribes could read in ancient Mesopotamia, and the only "libraries"—collections of classic texts—were in the scribal schools and perhaps the temples. Such science and philosophy as there was is frequently closer to folk sayings and fortune-telling than to the complex systematic thought of later ages. Nevertheless, the Mesopotamians left some mathematical insights and astronomical observations that still impress us. They based their number system on six rather than on ten; to them we owe the sixty-minute hour and the division of the circle into 360 degrees. The Babylonians charted the movements of the planets and predicted eclipses of the sun and the moon. Their knowledge of the night skies was so celebrated, in fact, that the word *Chaldean* became a synonym for *astronomer* in the ancient world.

The most famous literary product of ancient Mesopotamia is the *Epic of Gilgamesh,* the half-legendary Sumerian king who is sometimes called the Mesopotamian Hercules. The surviving fragments of this long poem tell how Gilgamesh and his friend Enkiddu, the wild man of the desert, killed the monster Huwawa and the Wild Bull of Heaven; how Gilgamesh scorned the advances of the goddess Ishtar; how he lost the faithful Enkiddu; and how he set out on his last and greatest adventure, the search for eternal life. His dreamlike journey to the twilight realm of Utnapishtim, sole survivor of the great flood that once destroyed humankind, climaxes with his discovery—and loss—of the plant that confers everlasting life, and with his final realization that death is the appointed end of every human life—even the life of a hero.

Among the Egyptians, as among the Mesopotamians, the discovery of the art of writing began quite literally as picture writing, as cuneiform had. But whereas the Mesopotamians soon reduced their little pictures to a collection of quick strokes of the stylus, the official Egyptian hieroglyphic writing never completely abandoned the pictographic element. In the hands of conservative Egyptians literacy remained to a considerable degree "picture writing" from one end of Egyptian history to the other.

Carved on stone monuments, this ancient priestly and official writing looked extremely impressive. But it proved a bit cumbersome for busy scribes scrawling with reed pens on papyrus, the paper Egyptians made from the pith of the papyrus stem found along the Nile. As a working script, therefore, hieroglyphic writing evolved over centuries into a cursive script called *hieratic,* which looked more like modern Arabic than like pictograms.

Egyptian observation of nature could be remarkably precise also. This was certainly the case in astronomy, one of the fields of scientific inquiry in which they were most successful. They divided the night sky into separate constellations, compiled detailed records of the nightly positions of some heavenly bodies, and constructed on this basis a calendar that is remarkably close to the solar one in use today. They used mathematics in a practical way as well, to survey and reestablish boundary lines after the annual inundation had washed out line markers up and down the Nile. They used measurement and calculation for architecture and engineering, for predicting harvests and totaling royal tax receipts.

Egyptian medicine, which enjoyed great renown among other ancient peoples, also operated on the basis of experience and rules of thumb—plus a sizable dollop of magic. Nevertheless, Egyptian doctors did show genuine clinical concern with symptoms, diagnosis, and treatment. And some of the prescribed remedies include drugs, such as castor oil, that may even have done the patient some good.

Over the thirty-odd centuries of ancient Egypt, writing became a craft and a career ladder for government or temple scribes, a device for communicating at a distance and for keeping records. Like most early written languages, however, it was not originally intended as an instrument for literary expression.

Egyptian literature includes hymns such as Akhenaton's song of praise to the sun and epic accounts of the victories of Thutmose III, which have the qualities of religious and patriotic literature from many times and lands. We have poetry too, especially from the New Kingdom, sad poems on the brevity of human life and happy poems of love. Perhaps the most impressive literary products of ancient Egypt, however, were to be found in the philosophical "wisdom literature" and the lively prose of Egyptian stories and tales.

Wisdom literature, common throughout the ancient Near East, includes collections of proverbs like those attributed to Solomon in the Old Testament. Here they are attributed to sages and pharaohs. These "instructions" urge youth to obey and respect their elders and betters and to sing the praises of old ways and ancient institutions.

If the Egyptians loved anything more than a good maxim for life, it was a good story. The most famous tale by far is the Middle Kingdom *Story of Sinuhe,* a first-person account of a noble Egyptian who, having been exiled from his native land, fights his way to fame and fortune among the bedouin of Syria. Yet Sinuhe's greatest joy—and no doubt the profoundest satisfaction of his readers—comes when he is summoned home to Egypt in his declining years by pharaoh himself. Egyptians loved to hear about wanderings in distant lands, but in the end they couldn't imagine anyone being happy far from the sound of the wind in the reeds along the Nile.

The Arts: Gold and Lapis Lazuli, Obelisks and Pyramids

The Mesopotamian palaces and temples that have been excavated from the mounded earth have a simplicity of design and detail that could have produced an effect of monumental grandeur above the arid plain. Palaces, like private homes, were constructed around a series of courtyards. Monumental gateways, square towers, and crenellated walls provided some exterior variety, and glazed tile and wall paintings of animals and men enlivened cool, dim interiors. In Babylonian and Assyrian times, sculptured columns, stone reliefs on walls, and huge human-headed bulls and other creatures added an air of imperial magnificence to the Mesopotamian palace.

The temple, however, was the Mesopotamian city's dominant feature. The most striking element in the temple complex was the pyramidal terraced tower, or ziggurat. Wide stairways, much like those of the later pyramid temples of the Mayans and the Aztecs, led to the flat top of the ziggurat, where a special shrine to the god or goddess stood. A simple, open structure, it was nonetheless god's house to the ancient Mesopotamians.

The sculpture of ancient Mesopotamia does not catch the modern imagination as immediately as that of some other cultures. Yet there is a convincing vitality in the smooth round face of a five-thousand-year-old Sumerian woman, bright-eyed and smiling still, her simple gown cut to leave the right arm and shoulder free for work. A rare wall painting of Assyrian officials brings these civilized savages to life, with their looped gold earrings, their black hair and beards oiled and dressed in ringlets. There is even a tense realism in the famous Lion Hunt Frieze: the horse of Assurbanipal charging with mouth open and tendons taut, and the dying lioness, arrows buried half their length in its flanks, dragging paralyzed hindquarters behind it, yet rearing up to roar in final defiance at the king of kings.

The cylinder seal, the most distinctive of Mesopotamian art forms, was carved in intaglio on a small stone cylinder, then rolled over soft clay to leave a unique identifying mark on anything from a merchant's goods to a private letter. On these carved seals, animals, gods, and men mingle freely with symbolic objects, the owner's name in cuneiform script, and other sculptured space fillers. The endless ingenuity of the carvers as they fill these tiny friezes with gracefully balanced figures rearing up, wrestling, sometimes seeming almost to dance across the clay, can stir the sense of beauty in the observer still.

The same may be said of the gold of Ur. A treasure trove of necklaces, helmets, cups, and other artifacts exhumed from royal tombs, they are all as directly accessible to us in their intricate beauty as anything from Cartier's or Tiffany's. The smooth golden sheen of a bull's head or a dagger blade plays beautifully against the beard or the hilt, made of the blue stone called lapis lazuli of which Mesopotamians were so fond. The monumental power of the vastly winged, human-headed bulls that once guarded the palace of Khorasabad still stops museum visitors in their tracks and draws their eyes inevitably upward.

The Egyptians were even greater builders than the Mesopotamian peoples—and they built in stone.

It is the immense age and the colossal size of the Old Kingdom pyramids that have awed posterity. The forty-five hundred years and the two and half million cubic yards of solid stone in the great pyramid of Khufu add up to one of the most awesome of human engineering feats. Many of the gigantic masonry blocks had to be quarried at Aswan, five hundred miles up the Nile, floated down the river, and moved by sledge, levers, ropes, and straining human muscle across the desert and up immense temporary earthen ramps to their places in the rising structure. And all this without benefit of the wheel!

Obelisks were another Egyptian architectural specialty. These tall, thinly tapering stone spires cut in a single block sometimes stood almost a hundred feet high. Their hieroglyphic inscriptions described the achievements of the pharaohs who erected them, as the gold that gilded their pointed tips proclaimed the glory of Hatshepsut or Thutmose III.

Temples to the gods also challenged the Egyptians to build greatly. Hordes of tourists gape daily at the eighty-foot columns at Karnak, raised by the celebrated New Kingdom warrior Ramses II, elaborately carved with hieroglyphics, and crowned with the characteristic papyrus-bud capitals of ancient Egypt. The facade of the temple at Abu Simbel, carved out of the living rock of the cliffs along the Nile, was flanked by four sixty-five-foot-tall statues of the powerful New Kingdom pharaoh Ramses seated on his throne.

The gold of King Tut's tomb—the famous tomb of Tutankhamun, discovered practically intact in 1922—has shown us how dazzling the luxury art of the Egyptians could be. The golden sarcophagus of King Tut has symbolized the splendor of the pharaohs to generations of museum goers, though Tutankhamun himself, Akhenaton's unhappy successor, was a pharaoh of no particular distinction.

The conservative genius of the Egyptians is nowhere better revealed than in their representations of the human figure in paint and stone. In bas-relief sculpture and wall painting, the famous Egyptian "canon" included such exotic requirements as representing the head and limbs in profile while showing the eyes, shoulders, and torso in a full-face view. The pharaoh, of course, was always to be painted or sculpted several times the size of his servants, soldiers, or defeated foes.

The softer, more human style of the Amarna period, which was centered in Akhenaton's new city dedicated to Aton, depicted that unfortunate pharaoh not as the wide-shouldered, lean-hipped superman of yore but as the pot-bellied, long-headed, downright ugly figure he apparently was. The Amarna style also gave us the long-necked beauty of his queen, Nefertiti, much as she must have been in life, and painted their small daughters playing in their gardens, large-eyed and oddly sweet despite their shaved heads and thin, gracefully posed limbs.

Polytheistic Religions

The sources of religion have been sought in many places. Among them surely are the need our ancestors felt for supernatural help to ensure a supply of game, growing herds, rich harvest. Other sources no doubt include the desire of people for divine support when they deal with life transitions such as birth, initiation, and death and with such special afflictions as war, pestilence, famine, and oppression.

But a developed religion seems to require more than these. It requires an encounter with the numinous. The word comes from the Latin *numen,* meaning divine power. A numinous experience is defined by students of the history and nature of religion as a sense of the presence of something "wholly other," something totally different in kind from all the material realities of everyday living. One may have a sudden sense of the presence of divine power in nature itself—in running water, the whispering leaves of a giant tree, the knee-buckling immensity of the sky above. It may come in the lifting of the sun's disk above the horizon, in a circle of standing stones, in a carven idol, in an icon or a crucifix.

At this deepest level of experience, the origin of all religious belief is the same. As far as we can tell, the meditating Hindu, the Muslim Sufi, and the Christian saint all experience much the same thing at this transcendent moment: In their own minds, at least, they are all in the presence of the Lord.

To express the inexpressible, religious leaders have had to turn to metaphor. They have tried to say what that awesome encounter with the numinous was *like* in the everyday material world the prophet and his people all know. Inevitably, however, this expedient has brought religious discourse from the level of the universal down to the historically conditioned realities of a particular time and place. God is white and male in a white man's world; Shiva is a high-caste Indian; the sun god rides across the sky in a chariot in ancient Greece and sails down a celestial Nile in the mind of the Egyptian.

The peoples of ancient Sumeria, Babylonia, and Assyria, like most peoples in most times and places, were believers in polytheism—the existence of many gods and goddesses. They felt themselves to be surrounded by spiritual presences. There were gods and goddesses associated with practically everything—gods of earth and sky, storm and bountiful harvest, brick mold and irrigation ditch. Most of these divinities were thoroughly anthropomorphic; they were depicted in sculpture as awesome figures with the long hair and square-cut beards of many Mesopotamian peoples and with the saucer-sized eyes that make them instantly recognizable in any museum.

In early Sumer the chief divinities in the numerous pantheon included Anu, the lord of heaven; Enlil, the water god; the earth mother, Ninhursag; the gods of the sun and moon, Utu and Sin; and the powerful goddess of love, Ishtar. Other leading divinities emerged over the centuries, notably Marduk, the chief god of imperial Babylon, and Assur, the sun god of the Assyrians.

Around these many divinities elaborate rites grew up. The great gods were believed to dwell within the ritually crafted and consecrated cult statues that the priests tended so

Isis on the left and Osiris on the right watch the weighing of a princess's heart against the symbol of Ma'at. This picture of a judgment in the underworld is from a New Kingdom papyrus copy of the Book of the Dead that was buried with a royal mummy. (Funerary Papyrus of the Princess Entiuny [ca. 1025 B.C.E.]. From the tomb of Queen Meryet-Amun at Deir el-Bahari, Thebes. The Metropolitan Museum of Art, Museum Excavations, 1928–1929, and Rogers Fund, 1930)

carefully in the temples. Around these figures a year-round succession of ceremonies, processions, sacred drama and other liturgical observances developed. Mythologies, sacred texts, and theological literature added to the richness of Mesopotamian religion.

There were also subtle changes in the religious conceptions held by the Mesopotamians over the three thousand years of their history. In the earliest times, gods and goddesses were conceived of as "indwelling wills and powers," divine presences *within* the natural forces, crops, and flocks necessary for human survival.[7] These early divinities embodied the mysterious power that made the barley grow or the palm produce plentiful clusters of dates.

By the time of Sargon of Akkad, however, a political metaphor is increasingly used to describe the reality of the divine. Gods are *rulers* of humanity. They protect the citizens of a particular city-state, or they lead the people to imperial conquest of their neighbors. And as the monarchy grew among the Mesopotamians, so a single god came to be honored as the king of the divine assembly, just as the *ensi* governed on earth.

During the last Mesopotamian centuries, divinities seemed more and more like parents. The gods became as concerned about the behavior and the well-being of their worshipers as parents are for their children. In hard times, it was comforting to know that higher powers cared.

Toward the very last, in the days of the Assyrian terror and of unchecked barbarian incursions, religion seems to have degenerated into the rankest superstition. There was "a

---

[7]Thorkild Jacobsen, *The Treasures of Darkness: A History of Mesopotamian Religion* (New Haven, Conn.: Yale University Press, 1976), p. 21.

coarsening and barbarization of the idea of divinity . . . witchcraft and sorcery were suspected everywhere; demons and evil spirits threatened unceasingly."[8] In the worst of times, perhaps, it was hard to believe that there *were* any higher powers.

The Egyptians had the reputation of being the most religious and other-worldly of peoples. It is easy for moderns to imagine the Egyptians as a darkly superstitious race who worshiped monstrous animal-headed gods and were obsessed with mummies and tombs, with death and what comes after it. In fact, as we have seen, most Egyptians seem to have been thoroughly materialistic about most things, to have loved gardens and children and the hot African sun. But like their Near Eastern neighbors, they did worship many gods, some of whom retained more than a trace of their animal origins. And of all the earlier civilizations, the Egyptians seem to have been the most concerned with the universal fact of death and the dream of life eternal.

More than two thousand gods were worshiped by the people who lived along the Nile. The chief of these was always a god of the sun—first Re, the sun god of Memphis, later Amon of Thebes. There were other widely worshiped divinities, including Horus the sky god, represented as a falcon; Thoth the ibis-headed god of wisdom and of scribes; Hathor the cow, the Egyptian goddess of beauty; and Anubis the jackal-headed god of the tomb.

The Quest for Immortality

The most popular of Egyptian myths—particularly from the Middle Kingdom onward—was the sacred story of Isis the merciful and her husband Osiris, the god who rose from the dead. Many an Egyptian mother told her children how Osiris, son of the sky and the earth, married his sister Isis and ruled over all the gods, until their jealous brother Set murdered Osiris, tore him to pieces, and scattered the dismembered divinity up and down the land. But the story had a happy ending. Before mother put out the lamp she would tell how Isis, grieving but determined, hunted over the world to recover her husband's body and bring it back to life, perhaps with a touch of the *ankh,* the looped cross that Egyptian mothers wore as amulets round their necks. Osiris lived still, as king of the underworld, with the loyal and compassionate Isis at his right hand. Egyptians fully expected to meet the divine pair when they too passed to the land of silence.

Mummification was a fine art in ancient Egypt. The corpse was washed with expensive oils, debrained through the nostrils, eviscerated through an incision in the abdomen, and dried for some weeks in a packing of natron, a crystalline substance with a special capacity to absorb moisture. It was then massaged and washed again, stuffed with amulets, more natron, and sometimes sand, sawdust, or other filling, wrapped carefully in endless strips of white linen, and returned at last to the mourning relatives for burial.

The spiritual parts, meanwhile, were believed to be undergoing their own transition from this life to the next.

To guide the soul through the underworld to its final judgment, the survivors inserted a collection of spells and ritual responses in the sarcophagus before interment. This so-called *Book of the Dead* depicts many aspects of the afterlife, climaxing in the final weighing of the soul against the principle of righteousness, *Ma'at.* This last judgment took place in the Hall of the Double Law under the eyes of twelve sceptered gods. The ape of Thoth crouched on the balance beam, jackal-headed Anubis adjusted the scale, and the hideous Devourer of

---

[8]Ibid.

the Dead crouched below, crocodile jaws agape for the soul found wanting. The soul that had not sinned against the gods, however, became "an Osiris," was led into the presence of the great king of the underworld, and was received into the company of the immortals.

SUMMARY

Civilization was born fifty-five centuries ago around the eastern end of the Mediterranean Sea, in Mesopotamia and Egypt. It produced a growing network of cities in the Near East, the first real nation in Egypt, a number of small empires, and two of history's most impressive cultures.

Mesopotamia—present-day Iraq—was the site of the first urban imperial culture. Mesopotamian peoples built elaborate irrigation works and walled cities in the valley of the Tigris and Euphrates rivers. They also developed the city-state, a polity centered on the new urban complex but including the hinterland of villages around it. These city-states were dominated by priests in early times, later by kings.

Though normally divided into separate city-states, ancient Mesopotamia also produced several early empires. The earliest such empire was that of the Sumerian ruler Sargon of Akkad in the twenty-third century B.C.E. The most famous was that of Hammurabi the Lawgiver of Babylon, founder of the Old Babylonian Empire in the eighteenth and seventeenth centuries B.C.E. The most oppressive was the Assyrian Empire (eighth and seventh centuries); the most admired in antiquity was the short-lived new Babylonian Empire of Nebuchadnezzar in the sixth century.

Egyptian civilization developed along the fertile banks of the Nile. Separate kingdoms first took shape in Upper and Lower Egypt but were unified by the first pharaohs around 3000 B.C.E. The Old Kingdom, or Pyramid Age (twenty-seventh to twenty-second centuries B.C.E.), was an extremely stable, strongly conservative society held together by pharaohs who were believed to be divine and by a busy scribal bureaucracy. The Middle Kingdom that followed (twentieth to eighteenth centuries B.C.E.) witnessed a transition to a more dynamic culture that interacted commercially and militarily with the rest of the Middle East.

The New Kingdom (sixteenth to twelfth centuries B.C.E.) saw the pharaohs of the powerful eighteenth dynasty building a large and impressive Egyptian Empire. Under Hatshepsut, the only female pharaoh, Egypt grew rich in trade. The successful general Thutmose III and his successors conquered most of the crescent from Nubia around through Palestine to Mesopotamia. And Pharaoh Akhenaton, a religious zealot, attempted to impose a monotheistic religion on the nation, though his unique cult only lasted Akhenaton's lifetime.

From about 1100 B.C.E. on, Egypt underwent a long decline. During this period the ancient land was frequently ruled by foreigners, and after the first century B.C.E. it disappeared into the vastly larger empire of the Romans.

Both Egypt and Mesopotamia were rooted in the polytheistic religion most common everywhere in the ancient world. Mesopotamians developed the first writing, cuneiform, and were skilled at astronomy and mathematics. They built truncated pyramidal temples called ziggurats and carved stone cylinder seals with which they left their mark on clay.

The Egyptians produced the best-known early form of writing, the system of pictograms known as hieroglyphics. They erected massive pillared temples to their animal-headed gods, proclaimed their pharaohs' achievements on gold-tipped obelisks, and left as their most famous monuments the huge pyramid tombs of the Old Kingdom.

Suggested Reading

Bottéro, J. *Religion in Ancient Mesopotamia.* trans. T. L. Fagan. Chicago: University of Chicago Press, 2001. Scholarly study of early polytheism.

Clayton, P. A. *Chronicle of the Pharaohs.* New York: Thames and Hudson, 1994. Narrative of reigns and dynasties.

Crawford, H. E. W. *Sumer and the Sumerians.* New York: Cambridge University Press, 1991. Good overview, with helpful illustrations.

Diakonoff, H. E. W., ed. *Early Antiquity.* Chicago: University of Chicago Press, 1991. Essays on early civilizations from Sumer to China.

Diop, C. A. *The African Origin of Civilization: Myth or Reality?* trans. Mercer Cook. New York: Lawrence Hill, 1974. Provocative study, including discussion of the influence of other African cultures on Egyptian civilization. More recent is M. Bernal's widely discussed multivolume study, *Black Athena: The Afroasiatic Roots of Classical Civilization* (New Brunswick, N.J.: Rutgers University Press, 1987–1991), which also emphasizes the African roots of Egyptian civilization.

El Mahdy, C. *The World of the Pharaohs.* New York: Thames and Hudson, 1990. Illustrated guide to ancient Egypt.

Kubba, S. A. A. *Mesopotamian Architecture and Town Planning.* Oxford: B. A. R., 1987. Agricultural villages evolve toward cities.

Lepre, J. P. *The Egyptian Pyramids.* Jefferson, N.C.: McFarland, 1990. Solid introduction to the tombs of the pharaohs. See also A. R. David, *The Pyramid Builders of Ancient Egypt* (London: Routledge and Kegan Paul, 1986), which focuses on "pharaoh's workforce," the people who physically built these monuments.

Moorey, P. R. S. *Ancient Mesopotamian Materials and Industries.* New York: Clarendon Press, 1994. Scholarly examination of archaeological evidence.

Potts, D. T. *Mesopotamian Civilization: The Material Foundation.* Ithaca, N.Y.: Cornell University Press, 1997. Valuable overview of material culture, drawing also on the cuneiform record.

Redford, D. B. *Egypt, Canaan, and Israel in Ancient Times.* Princeton, N.J.: Princeton University Press, 1992. A scholarly, sometimes provocative study. For an introduction to disputes over the chronology of the ancient history of the region, see P. James, *Centuries of Darkness: A Challenge to the Conventional Chronology of Old World Archaeology* (New Brunswick, N.J.: Rutgers University Press, 1993).

Redman, C. W. *Human Impact on Ancient Environments.* Phoenix: University of Arizona Press, 1999. Examines the ways in which ancient peoples impacted the world they lived in.

Robins, G. *The Art of Ancient Egypt.* Cambridge, Mass.: Harvard University Press, 1997. Brief but scholarly overview.

———. *Women in Ancient Egypt.* Cambridge, Mass.: Harvard University Press, 1993. Scholarly discussion illustrated by well-chosen art. A good introduction to the subject is B. Waterson, *Women in Ancient Egypt* (New York: St. Martin's Press. 1991).

Saggs, H. W. F. *Babylonians.* Norman: University of Oklahoma Press, 1995. Society in the ancient Mesopotamian city-state.

Silver, M. *Economic Structures in the Ancient Near East.* Totowa, N.J.: Barnes & Noble, 1985. Uses modern economic theory applied to Mesopotamian clay tablets to explain the economic organization of the region.

Simpson, W. K., ed. *The Literature of Ancient Egypt: An Anthology of Stories, Instructions, and Poetry.* Includes examples of all of the literary forms.

Spenser, A. J. *The Rise of Civilization in the Nile Valley.* London: British Museum Press, 1993.

Taylor, J. H. *Death and the Afterlife in Ancient Egypt.* Chicago: University of Chicago Press, 2001. Explorations of immortality as this ancient African people understood it.

Walker, C. B. F. *Reading the Past: Writing from Cuneiform to the Alphabet.* London: British Museum, 1990. Stimulating introduction to early forms of writing.

CHAPTER 3

PROPHETS AND PHILOSOPHERS
The Hebrews and the Greeks

(1500–200 B.C.E.)

A Glance Ahead: Small Peoples with Large Ideas

While Mesopotamian peoples raised their walled cities and Egyptians built mightily along the Nile, others also brought remarkable contributions to the new style of life called civilization. Among these, two other peoples from the eastern end of the Mediterranean, the Hebrews and the Greeks, generated a dazzling range of new ideas. Their religious, moral, philosophic, and artistic insights would provide the intellectual underpinnings for many future societies—including our own.

Neither of these two small peoples, the ancient Greeks and Hebrews, conquered many of their neighbors or built great empires. In time, both were scattered across the world. Greek ships still plow the seas and oceans of the globe, while descendants of the ancient Hebrews have settled into many lands down the centuries. But in the *Torah* and the rest of the *Old Testament,* in the philosophy of Plato and Aristotle and the art of ancient Greece, they have left intellectual monuments every bit as imposing as the pyramids of Egypt or the walls of Babylon.

Turbulent Centuries

The Near East in Tumult

When civilizations first emerged in Mesopotamia and Egypt in the fourth millennium B.C.E., they were solitary flowers blooming alone in a world of Paleolithic hunter-gatherers, Neolithic villages, and wandering pastoralists. By the second millennium B.C.E., however, when Hammurabi ruled in Babylon and the powerful twelfth dynasty in Egypt, a number of other islands of civilization had come into existence around the globe. The ships of the Minoans, precursors of the ancient Greeks, were sailing the blue Mediterranean. In northwestern India—Pakistan today—an impressive center of civilized living had emerged around the great cities of Harappa and Mohenjodaro. Still farther to the east, the states of North China were about to be drawn together into a loose-knit Bronze Age civilization dominated by the Shang dynasty. And beyond the wide Atlantic, metals were being worked in Peru.

Civilization had also emerged among other Near Eastern peoples on the frontiers of the Mesopotamian world. The turbulent centuries between 2000 and 1000 B.C.E. were particularly fecund producers of new centers of civilized living. During these centuries, nomadic peoples from the great Eurasian steppes or the deserts of Arabia and North Africa buffeted the city-based cultures of the Near East. In so doing, they helped bring about a fertile mixture of cultures and traditions. They brought skills with them from their earlier wandering lives, and they learned from the more settled peoples whom they frequently conquered.

The invaders thus contributed largely to the emergence of such satellite cultures at the periphery of the cultural zone around Mesopotamia and Egypt as the Hittites and the Phoenicians. And this tumultuous little world at the eastern end of the Mediterranean sea was the world of the ancient Hebrews.

Culturally, this was an immensely productive corner of the globe. From this time and place came such achievements as Hittite ironworking and the Phoenician alphabet. And it was here that the Hebrews developed their astonishing new religious ideas, leading the world definitively beyond polytheism to the worship of one God in the first successful monotheistic religion.

The Hittites and the Iron Age

The Hittites were Indo-Europeans, speakers of languages ancestral to those of modern India, Iran, and most of Europe. The Hittite subdivision of this great steppe-dwelling people wandered down into Asia Minor, subdued the natives of the hill and mountain country north of Mesopotamia, and evolved a powerful empire in the second millennium B.C.E. For roughly two hundred years, 1400 to 1200 B.C.E. the Hittites ruled the eastern end of the Mediterranean, collected tribute from the Egyptians, and raided Babylon. For several centuries, at least, they were a power to be reckoned with in the Near East.

Like most less developed cultures, the Hittites borrowed heavily from the more complex civilizations with which they came in contact. From the Land of the Two Rivers they carried home such cultural booty as cuneiform writing, Mesopotamian myths, and the concept of a codified system of laws. The charioteers from the steppes retained much of their own culture too, legends and styles of art that looked back to their days as nomads of the great northern grasslands. Hittite religion particularly reminds us that they were a people whose culture had developed on the edge of the civilized world: There is, for instance, evidence of human sacrifice among them.

From the Hittites, however, came one great contribution to the civilization of the ancient Near East: the working of iron.

Bronze, alloyed usually of copper and tin, had been the hard metal since civilization first appeared in Sumeria. Now, in the smithies of Hittite towns and villages and the double-walled mountain capital of Hattusas, brawny Hittite metalworkers discovered that iron ore, more plentiful than bronze, might also be used for hard-edged tools and weapons. The secret, which may have reached the Hittites from their old steppe homeland, involved much pounding of the heated but not melted ore to remove impurities, followed by a sudden quenching in cold water. The result was a sort of semisteel more readily available and cheaper than the alloy of copper and tin on which older, more aristocratic Bronze Age cultures had been built.

Understandably, the Hittites did not distribute the secret of the new metal widely. But when new waves of invaders swept down across Asia Minor and tumbled Hattusas into ruin, skilled ironworkers were widely scattered. The working of iron would have a significant impact on societies all across the Old World. It gave ordinary people weapons to match the bronze of the aristocrats. It also opened up land which could not readily be cultivated with stone, wood, or bronze-edged plows. The Hittites themselves vanished from the historical record until modern archaeologists unearthed their lost civilization. But their technological contribution was so important that some historians still date a new age of world history from the Hittites' twelfth-century prime—the Iron Age.

The Far-Trading Phoenicians

The Phoenicians were a Semitic-speaking people who settled the harbors and inshore islands along the coast of what is today Lebanon and Syria. They rose to prominence at the end of the second millennium, following the collapse of Hittite power, and flourished from 1100 to 800 B.C.E. They became the most famous traders on the sea before the Greeks and the chief bearers of developed Near Eastern culture to other peoples around the Mediterranean.

Politically, the Phoenicians were city-state dwellers, like the Mesopotamians. Failing to achieve political unity of their own, they were frequently absorbed into the larger polities of such powerful neighbors as the Egyptians, Hittites, and Assyrians. They borrowed Babylonian business methods and weights and measures and used Babylonian astronomy as a navigational aid. Their mythology was replete with Mesopotamian echoes, though their religion harked further back. Like the Hittites, the Phoenicians sometimes sacrificed human beings on the altars of their gods.

In one way, however, the Phoenicians made a major break with the practices of their Near Eastern neighbors. Unable to feed their numbers on the thin strip of mountain-girt coastline they inhabited, they turned gradually from agriculture to manufacturing and above all to trade.

The Phoenicians seem to have turned to profit everything their 120-mile stretch of coastline had to offer. The famous cedars of Lebanon provided them with a valuable early export item. After learning glassmaking from the Mesopotamians, they used a fine local sand to produce glass gewgaws that sold well to simpler folk around the Mediterranean. Even a tiny shellfish called the murex was used to make perhaps the most famous dye of all times, the Tyrean purple that would color the robes of emperors in centuries to come.

The location of the Phoenician cities—on the Mediterranean and astride the main trade route between Mesopotamia and Egypt—encouraged the Phoenicians to become traders as well as handicraft manufacturers. Byblos, Tyre, Sidon, and other cities were famous commercial centers in Old Testament times. The Phoenicians founded colonies on the islands of Cyprus and Sicily and on the coasts of Spain and North Africa. Among these Phoenician colonies was the North African metropolis of Carthage, Rome's great rival in later centuries. Other adventurous Phoenician sailors even passed out of the Mediterranean through the Strait of Gibraltar, the "Pillars of Hercules," beyond which few ancient seamen dared to venture. There is evidence that their little vessels braved the heavier swells and rougher winds of the Atlantic to trade for tin in western Britain.

The Phoenicians were *carriers of culture,* transplanters of ideas, styles, and folkways, rather than cultural originators. Their impact, however, was not small. Their city of Byblos, which became famous for the export of Egyptian papyrus, gave its name to the Greek word for *book*—and our word *Bible.* And whether the Phoenicians developed their own written language or borrowed it from their neighbors, they passed that too on to the Greeks. The twenty-two consonants of the Phoenician alphabet, together with the vowels added by the Greeks, would evolve down the centuries into all the written languages of the Western World.

THE ANCIENT HEBREWS

The Wandering Years

The Hebrew people of Palestine never produced an empire to rival that of the Hittites, nor did they wander as far as the Phoenicians, at least in ancient times. Yet they too left a great legacy to future ages, a heritage at least as valuable as either iron or the alphabet: monotheistic religion.

At the beginning of the second millennium before Christ, the Hebrews were part of the nomadic population of Semitic-speaking peoples that wandered and settled along the edges of the Arabian Desert, between the developed civilizations of Mesopotamia and Egypt. Abraham, the patriarch of the Hebrew tribes, trudges into history heading west from Ur with his wives and children, servants, shepherds, and flocks around him. The twelve Hebrew tribes apparently settled for a time in Palestine—or Canaan—between the Jordan River and the sea. Some of these, perhaps driven by drought, drifted on southward into Egypt, the great pillar of civilization at the other end of the fertile crescent from Mesopotamia. Oppressed—according to tradition actually enslaved in New Kingdom Egypt—they burst out once more in the thirteenth century B.C.E. to resume their wanderings.

Their liberator, and the leader of the folk migration known in the Bible as the Exodus, was a fiery preacher named Moses. Moses managed to hold his people together for forty years in the scorching deserts of Sinai. To accomplish this feat, he seems to have rallied the Hebrew tribes around a single divine being, Yahweh. By the 1200s B.C.E., then, the Hebrews had become monotheists—believers in one God, sworn to obey the commandments of the divine Lord whose laws Moses had brought down from the mountain to Yahweh's chosen people.

According to tradition, Moses was the author of the *Torah,* also called the *Pentateuch,* the first five books of the Bible. In a gesture known to every Western schoolchild, he is believed to have descended from Mount Sinai with the *Ten Commandments,* binding his people to a high standard of moral conduct, engraved on two stone tablets. Even his death was dramatic, coming within sight of the promised land he was never to enter. Leader, law-giver, and shaper of one of the world's great religions, this liberator of a small Near Eastern people became through the power of the word a world-historical figure.

The Kingdom of David

The wanderings of this pastoral nomadic people had taken them back to Palestine, which they now saw as the homeland promised to them by Yahweh. A hilly barren land along the Mediterranean Sea, Palestine nevertheless looked good after two generations in the wilderness. The region, however, was already settled by the Canaanites, a people who had built modest cities and established laws on the Mesopotamian model. Furthermore, in the second millennium B.C.E. this area was still subject to incursions by other nomadic peoples besides the Hebrews, including the powerful, iron-armed Philistines. To conquer and hold their promised land, then, the twelve tribes evolved once more, this time politically rather than religiously. In the fires of combat the Hebrew kingdom was forged.

Despite their monotheistic faith, the Hebrew tribes had frequently been disunited. A clan-based as well as an extremely religious society, they were guided by leaders called "judges" and sometimes by charismatic prophets who claimed divine inspiration for their warnings and injunctions. Shortly before 1000 B.C.E., however, all the tribes agreed to follow a single king, a war leader who might bring them final victory over their foes. Thus was the kingdom of Saul, David, and Solomon born.

The first of these rulers, Saul, was an impressive fighter, but he proved unable to win the definitive victories his people demanded. When he fell in battle, King David (ca. 1010–960 B.C.E.) took his place. And under David and his son Solomon (ca. 960–920 B.C.E.), the new state of Israel flourished as it would not do again until the twentieth century C.E.

A gifted military leader, David crushed the Philistines and completed the conquest of Canaan. He cemented the political unity of the twelve tribes, established a Hebrew state, and began to build a Hebrew capital at Jerusalem. Generally recognized as the mightiest

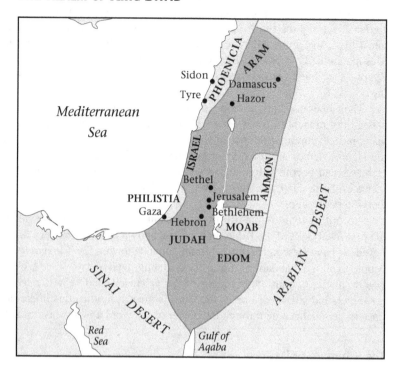

of Hebrew rulers, David became the center of an admiring body of biblical legend and literature chronicling his rise from shepherd lad to war hero and finally to founder of a centralized Near Eastern monarchy, the tenth-century B.C.E. kingdom of Israel.

The Splendor of Solomon

David was the founder, but Solomon brought a genuine splendor to the newly united Hebrew state. His reign would leave almost as deep a mark on the minds of future generations as the heroic achievements of the nation's first ruler.

Celebrated in the Bible for his wisdom, Solomon was apparently a shrewd diplomat and a great builder. His harem, his huge stables, the palace he built for himself, and the temple he raised to the glory of Yahweh were all in the most opulent Near Eastern style. He strengthened his army and equipped it with chariots and new iron-age weapons. He built, rebuilt, and fortified a number of cities. He constructed ships and traded with the Phoenicians and even down the Red Sea.

In the powerful imagery of the Old Testament, Solomon looms as the wisest and wealthiest of kings. Symbolically, he plays as important a role in the historical memory of Jews and Christians as Asoka does in the Indian past, the Duke of Zhou in early China, or Plato's philosopher kings in the classical tradition of the West—all to be discussed below. He embodies the governmental ideal of wisdom and power in the service of the people.

But tensions and divisions underlay the success of the Hebrew kingdom. The work of Saul, David, and Solomon would be undone within a single generation. And the Hebrew

The Kingdoms of Israel and Judah, c. 800 b.c.e.

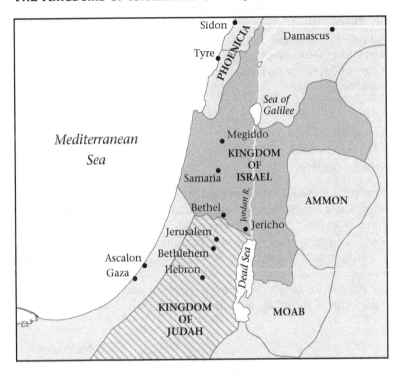

people, divided once more, would soon fall victim to larger and more aggressive neighboring peoples.

Division and Disaster

Solomon's efforts to make the Hebrew kingdom a powerful player on the Near Eastern chessboard of nations cost huge amounts of labor and money. Oppressive taxation, forced labor, and other expedients made Solomon increasingly unpopular among his own people. Differences between the more sophisticated, urban, and commercial northern reaches of the kingdom and the pastoral, agricultural, more pious south further weakened the monarchy. Simmering rebellion split the kingdom after Solomon's death.

The result was the creation of two smaller nations: Judah in the south, inhabited by two of the Hebrew clans and still ruled from Jerusalem; and the new nation of Israel in the north, including ten of the original dozen tribes. Neither half of the old kingdom proved viable in the shark-infested waters of ancient Near Eastern politics. In the eighth century B.C.E., Israel fell to the powerful Assyrian Empire; in the sixth century B.C.E., Judah was overwhelmed by the New Babylonian Empire of Nebuchadnezzar. At the time of the latter cataclysm, in 586 B.C.E., Jerusalem and Solomon's great temple were leveled and many Hebrews were carried off into captivity in Babylon. Others scattered to Egypt and beyond, beginning the *diaspora*, or dispersal, of the people who became the Jews across the Western world.

Some returned from Babylon to rebuild the temple to their Lord, as they increasingly called Yahweh, before the end of the sixth century B.C.E. But though there were short-lived Jewish states at later periods, this small, intensely creative people would remain vassals of other peoples—Persians, Macedonians, Romans, Arabs, Turks—for most of the next twenty-five centuries. Only in 1948, in the middle of the twentieth century, did a new nation of Israel, approximating in size the nation ruled over by David, rise once again in Palestine.

THE BIRTH OF MONOTHEISM

Hebrew Society

A people without a country for most of their history, the ancient Hebrews organized themselves along familiar social lines. Before the political state came social allegiance. Before government came law. Before kings came to rule, traditional authorities provided leadership. And throughout their history, the ancient Hebrews experienced their share of the sort of jarring societal changes that have marked the histories of most peoples down the centuries.

Among the earliest Hebrews, as we have seen, tribe, clan, and family were the primary forms of social organization. The twelve tribes were believed to be descended from

The Hebrews were the first "People of the Book," the first to center their faith on sacred writings detailing God's will toward his people. The Torah, illustrated here, provides the same sort of religious inspiration for modern Jews that it offered to their spiritual ancestors in ancient times. (S. Meltzer/Getty Images, Inc.)

the twelve sons of the patriarch Abraham. Within the basic family unit, patriarchy—domination by the father—prevailed, giving male heads of families great power over wives and children. Polygamy was allowed for men wealthy enough to support several wives. Only sons could inherit property, since daughters would become the responsibility of the families into which they married. A wife retained control of the dowry she brought with her to her marriage, but had few other property rights. Divorce was easy for men but very difficult for women to secure.

It is a familiar pattern among earth's earlier civilizations. Yet here as elsewhere, there are mitigating points to be made. The Book of Proverbs in the Old Testament praises the righteous and God-fearing woman who feeds, clothes, and supervises a sizable household in terms that suggest larger responsibilities:

> She considereth a field and buyeth it; with the fruit
> of her hand she planteth a vineyard.
> She girdeth her loins with strength, and
> strengtheneth her arms.
> She perceiveth that her merchandise is good . . .[1]

Some women, furthermore, clearly stepped outside the family-centered system entirely. Some exercised political power as judges or religious authority as prophetesses. Some, like Judith, who slew the commander of an invading host, were even hailed as national heroes for their deeds.

Religion played a central role in Hebrew life, and the many ancient Hebrew laws recorded in the Old Testament had a deep religious core. These traditional rules of life, however, were also rooted in the Hebrew sense of identity and, to some extent, in the influences of the older and larger peoples among whom they lived.

Thus it is easy to see such principles as letting the punishment fit the crime—"an eye for an eye"—in the collections of laws sanctioned by both Moses and Hammurabi. Both formulations probably reflected a popular sense of fairness and equivalence among these ancient peoples. Yet the Hebrew tribes also accepted distinctive laws that prescribed what one might eat, whom one might marry, and what punishments might be meted out for violations of these taboos. And both dietary regulations and practices like endogamy—marriage only within the Hebrew community—forged a strong Hebrew sense of identity long before the Hebrew state emerged.

On top of this structure of traditional society and law, a changing cast of recognized authority figures led the chosen people down the centuries. In early nomadic times, as noted above, charismatic personalities called "judges" took the lead. These influential individuals, often claiming divine inspiration, included women, like the wise Deborah or the heroic Judith. With the emergence of the kingdom, however, patriarchal male dominance was established at all levels. The Hebrew kings claimed a hereditary right to rule, appointed officials to impose their will, and governed by royal fiat like other Near Eastern monarchs.

The society of David and Solomon's day, finally, was as much divided by social tensions as any other complex society. Rural people soon came to resent the wealth and sophistication of their urban fellows living in Jerusalem and other Hebrew cities. The rough

---

[1]Proverbs 31: 16–18.

egalitarianism of earlier, less affluent times gave way to class conflicts between landowner and laborer, aristocrat and commoner, rich and poor. Socially speaking, at least, the Hebrews who were carried off to captivity in Babylon in the first millennium B.C.E. had little in common with those who had followed Abraham out of Mesopotamia well over a thousand years before.

The Worship of the One God

The Hebrew story was in many ways a paradigm case, a history and a society like many another in the long dawn age of human history. In one area, however, the ancient Hebrews stood out. The remarkable development of their religious beliefs would take them—and many generations yet unborn—to a new plateau of spiritual understanding.

The Hebrews seem to have been particularly concerned with religion, even by Near Eastern standards. Hebrew prophets in goatskins wandered among them like loin-clothed holy men in Hindu India, preaching an ever more rigorous faith. The Hebrews carried the words of their god Yahweh carved on two stone tablets in a chest, and they believed that they were divinely ordained to rule a promised land somewhere in Palestine. Over the millennium and a half between Abraham and the return to Jerusalem from Babylon, the Hebrews evolved a unique conception of divinity and of humanity's relationship to it.

The Hebrews of Abraham's day prayed and sacrificed to their own god much as Babylonians worshiped Marduk or as ancient Greeks might have venerated Athena—as their special patron among the many gods who ruled above. By the time of Moses, however, Hebrew spiritual leaders began to insist that Yahweh demanded exclusive worship in return for his special patronage—and then that he was the *only* real God in the universe.

During the course of the second millennium B.C.E., then, the ancient Hebrews came to believe that their God demanded an exclusive devotion from Hebrews that other Near Eastern gods did not. A Mesopotamian or an Egyptian could sacrifice to any number of divinities, but Yahweh was a jealous god and would tolerate no others. From this early Judaic view it was only a step further—albeit an immensely significant one—to the denial of the existence of other gods altogether.

Over the centuries the Hebrews added to this startling monotheism a powerful emphasis on the spiritual aspects of religion. Like Allah after him, Yahweh allowed no graven images of himself. He thus remained a purely spiritual presence, lacking the carven habitations where the gods of other peoples dwelt. Though the God of the Old Testament "spoke" to his human creations, from Adam to the prophets and beyond, he had few of the human feelings or relations of such widely worshiped gods and goddesses as the Egyptian Isis and Osiris, India's Shiva and Vishnu, or the familiar Greco-Roman pantheon—Jupiter, Mars, Venus, and the rest. He remained an incarnation of such suprahuman qualities as all knowledge, absolute power, and benevolent caring who had, miraculously, selected the ancient Hebrews as his chosen people.

In addition, Yahweh's prophets of the first millennium B.C.E. preached a strongly ethical monotheism, stressing the moral dimension of the worship of the one God. In passionate sermons to the Hebrews, preachers like Samuel, Jeremiah, and Isaiah insisted that Yahweh had imposed strict ethical requirements on his people. Sacrifice was not enough: Believers must rigorously obey the commandments that forbade murder, theft, lying, covetousness, and a whole array of sins. Beyond personal morality, furthermore, the prophets

PROBING THE PAST

This portion of the biblical book of Isaiah was probably composed by a Hebrew prophet living at the time of the captivity in Babylon (550 – 538 B.C.E.). During this period, when the Hebrew states of Judah and Israel had been absorbed by Assyrian and Babylonian conquerors and many Hebrews were living in exile in the New Babylonian Empire, the future of this small band of people must have seemed very dim indeed. At such a time, the powerful preaching of Isaiah revived their confidence that their God would save them in the end.

To what does Isaiah compare Yahweh when he wants to emphasize God's <u>care</u> for his chosen people? Why was this comparison likely to move his hearers? How is the <u>greatness</u> of the Lord expressed here? Who are the "nations" and "princes" whom the Lord "maketh as nothing?" Why would claims that worldly power is vain and that divine power will strengthen true believers appeal to the Hebrews in Babylon? To Christians in Rome centuries later?

> *"O Zion, that bringest good tidings, get thee up into the high mountain; O Jerusalem, that bringest good tidings, lift up thy voice with strength; lift it up, be not afraid; say unto the cities of Judah, Behold your God!*
>
> *Behold, the Lord God will come with strong hand, and his arm shall rule for him, and his work before him.*
>
> *He shall feed his flock like a shepherd: he shall gather the lambs with his arm, and carry them in his bosom, and shall gently lead those that are young.*
>
> *Who hath measured the waters in the hollow of his hand, and meted out heaven with the span, and comprehended the dust of the earth in a measure, and weighed the mountains in scales, and the hills in a balance? . . .*
>
> *Behold, the nations are as a drop of a bucket. . . . All nations before him are as nothing; and they are counted to him less than nothing, vanity. . . .*
>
> *It is he that sitteth upon the circle of the earth . . . that bringeth the princes to nothing; he maketh the judges of the earth as vanity. . . .*
>
> *But they that wait upon the Lord shall renew their strength; they shall mount up with wings as eagles; they shall run, and not weary; and they shall walk and not faint."*

Isaiah 40: 9–15, 17, 22–23, 31. *The Holy Bible* (Cambridge, England: Cambridge University Press).

insisted that the one God demanded social justice from his people. The rich should not oppress the poor, nor the powerful trample the humble underfoot.

God had made a special agreement, or *Covenant,* with the Hebrews, their prophets told them. When they fell into sin, God punished them with such historical calamities as the enslavement in Egypt or the captivity in Babylon. But if they remained loyal to him alone and kept his commandments, God's covenant promised them a land of their own and a place of respect among the nations.

Monotheistic, highly spiritual, and rigorously moralistic, the religion of the Hebrews would maintain the cultural distinctness of this vital people through a long and often tragic history. The Hebrews may have borrowed their flood story from Mesopotamia, proverbs from Egyptian wisdom literature, and psalms from both of these developed civilizations; but the faith of the children of Yahweh was distinctly their own, and a major contribution to the spiritual history of the world.

The Hebrew Heritage

Some Hebrews at least were called *Yehudim*—whence, via a Greek intermediary, the English *Jew* is derived—even before the sixth-century B.C.E. Babylonian captivity. The *Judaic* religion as it has evolved since that time was clearly built on these ancient foundations of ethical monotheism, emphasis on the spirituality of God, and belief in the historicity of his manifest will in the world. In the first century C.E., Jesus Christ, born and raised in the Jewish community of northern Palestine, became the founder of the Christian faith, a creed that would spread around the world. And in the seventh century C.E., the Prophet Muhammad, an Arabian merchant conversant with both Judaism and Christianity, founded the third major world religion to emerge in this region—Islam. Down through the centuries, Hebrew leaders like Moses and Solomon would be honored, not only in later Judaism but also in the Christian Old Testament and the Muslim Quran.

The walls that enclose the narrow, winding lanes and crowded *souks* (markets) of Old Jerusalem today are mostly Ottoman Turkish battlements, built in the sixteenth century by Suleiman the Magnificent. Pass in through the Damascus Gate, however, and you can visit in fifteen minutes three of the most sacred sites of the great religions that emerged in the western portion of Eurasia: the golden Dome of the Rock, built on the spot from which Muhammad is believed by Muslims to have ascended into heaven; the Church of the Holy Sepulcher, allegedly encompassing the site of the Crucifixion of Christ; and the Wailing Wall, all that is left of Solomon's long-vanished temple, the holy of holies for Jews the world over. Amid the tensions and explosive violence of this long-fought-over corner of the globe, it is chastening to remember that all three of these militant faiths derive in large part from the spiritual intimations that first took shape in the minds of a single people three thousand years ago.

EARLY GREECE

Mountains and the Sea

> The mountain looks on Marathon—
>   And Marathon looks on the sea;
> And musing there an hour alone,
>   I dream'd that Greece might still be free.[2]

Lord Byron's famous lines tell us as much about Greek geography as they do about the continuing Greek dream of freedom. Greece *is* mountains and the sea. Greece is a jagged peninsula protruding some 350 miles southward from the Balkans into the Mediterranean, the central sea of European ancient history. The land of the Hellenes, as the Greeks called themselves, was all mountains and narrow valleys, capes, blue bays, strings and clusters of rocky islands—a place very different from the vast continental expanses of China and India, or the inward-looking Near Eastern river valleys of Mesopotamia and Egypt.

Greek civilization—the first of European civilizations—thus developed in a naturally fragmented little world. Each mainland city-state was walled off by mountains from its

---

[2]George Gordon, Lord Byron, "The Isles of Greece," from *Don Juan*, ed. Leslie A. Marchand (Boston: Riverside Press, 1958), p. 127.

ANCIENT GREECE

Athenian Empire, 450 B.C.E.

■ Battle sites

Black Sea

THRACE

MACEDONIA

Byzantium

*Propontis
(Sea of Marmora)*

Aegospotami

CHALCIDICE

EPIRUS

Mt. Olympus ▲

Dodona

*Aegean
Sea*

Troy

THESSALY

LESBOS

LYDIA

PHRYGIA

ARGINUSAE IS.

Thermopylae

ITHACA

Delphi

EUBOEA

Thebes

Sardis

CHIOS

Gulf of Corinth

Athens

SAMOS

Mycenae Corinth

Olympia

Argos

Miletus

PELOPONNESUS

See Inset
Below

DELOS

Halicarnassus

COS

Sparta
LACONIA

*Ionian
Sea*

MELOS

CYTHERA

*THERA
(SANTORIN)*

RHODES

*Cretan
Sea*

PHOCIS

Chaeronea

EUBOEA

Delphi

BOEOTIA

Thebes

Delium

Leuctra

Plataea

Gulf of Corinth

Marathon

Eleusis

ATTICA

Megara

Athens

Corinth

Piraeus

Saronic Gulf

Mycenae

AEGINA

Mantinea

Tiryns

Argos

Epidaurus

Mediterranean Sea

CRETE

Knossos

Areas of Greek settlements

A L P S

ILLYRIA

CRIMEA

Panticapaeum

PYRENEES

Massilia
(Marseilles)

Adriatic

Black Sea

IBERIA

CORSICA

Rome

ITALY

Sea

Byzantium

Trebizond

SARDINIA

Neapolis
(Naples)

Paestum

Apollonia

ASIA

Cadiz

MAGNA

Croton

GREECE

MINOR

Strait of Gibraltar

Segesta

GRAECIA

Corinth

IONIA

Carthage

Selinus

SICILY

Athens

Syracuse

RHODES *CYPRUS*

MELITA

CRETE

SYRIA

PHOENICIA

AFRICA

Mediterranean Sea

Cyrene

LIBYA

EGYPT

neighbors. Many Greeks, furthermore, lived on islands in the Aegean or in colonies along the nearby coasts of Asia Minor (Turkey today).

The institutions of the Greek city-states, taking shape in isolated valleys, on islands, or in colonies along the coasts of other peoples' countries, were deeply influenced by this geographical fragmentation. The passionate sense of independence that was the glory and the downfall of the Greeks emerged quite naturally in this divided land. Fiercely independent toward other nationalities and even other Hellenes, the Greeks also developed a powerful sense of loyalty to their own isolated communities.

The Minoans

We know very little about the first people to drift into this sunny, sea-washed world of gray rock and gray-green islands. We believe that they filtered in from Asia Minor as early as 3000 B.C.E., while pyramids were rising in Egypt and ziggurats in Mesopotamia. By about 1800 B.C.E., however, a great palace had been built at the city of Knossos on Crete, the largest of the islands. Around this center, a pre-Greek seaborne civilization briefly flourished.

The civilization of Minoan Crete and its scattering of trading posts around the Aegean were clearly built on commercial exchange. Minoans traded in Egypt and the Levant, exporting pottery and bronze, olive oil and timber, and bringing back, among other things, the forms of writing we call Linear A and Linear B. Minoan culture, in turn, dominated the islands and much of the mainland of Greece.

The kings who ruled at Knossos lived in considerable splendor in the vast, labyrinthine palace excavated by archaeologists thirty-five centuries later. There were scribes and bureaucrats in attendance and an elegant court life. But there were few soldiers, if we are to judge from archaeological evidence. Theirs was a network of trade, not a military or political imperium.

Life at the center of this small island world, the frivolous, fragile, lovely court life of the Minoan sea kings, comes vividly to us across the centuries in the brightly colored wall paintings of the royal palace at Knossos. In these murals, bare-breasted, bejeweled court ladies stroll in gardens full of flowers, and bronzed youths lift goblets of Cretan wine to a future that must have seemed as unlimited to them as our own does to us—and as pleasant as the life of any civilization we know.

The end seems to have come swiftly. They lived, traded, and prospered for a few short centuries: the standard dating of Middle Minoan, the heyday of Cretan civilization, is from 2200 to 1500 B.C.E. Then they vanished, swept away in a series of catastrophes perhaps partially the work of nature—earthquakes and volcanic eruptions have been suggested—but almost surely in part the work of humans. The first Greeks had lived among them and learned to read and write and worship their gods. But other Greeks came later, perhaps around 1500 B.C.E., from the mainland city of Mycenae, bringing fire and sword.

The Mycenaeans

The Mycenaeans who next dominated this Aegean world were part of the great wave of migrating barbarian conquerors who intruded upon most of the main Eurasian enclaves of civilization during the second millennium B.C.E. These so-called Indo-Europeans— "tamers of horses" as Homer called them, chariot fighters, speakers of the lost Indo-

European tongue that would father all the major languages of Europe—constituted one of the most terrible of all barbarian onslaughts on civilization.

But the Mycenaeans were builders too. There was a structure of authority within the typical Mycenaean city-state—rule by an independent kinglet, rather than by council and assembly as in later centuries—and some records were kept in Minoan script. Their economic life is sometimes dismissed as little more than piracy and conquest, but they were traders too, exchanging goods around the Near East as the Minoans had done, pressing in where the declining Hittites and Egyptians gave way. Mycenae was a rich city, if we are to judge by the gold unearthed from the tombs of their nobles and kings.

Most noticeable from the distance of many centuries, they built walled cities and stone castles to garrison the lands they conquered. They raised the Lion Gate and the beehive-shaped *tholos* tombs of Mycenae. Sometimes they built on Minoan foundations; and Greek cities would rise in turn on the sites of Mycenaean ones.

But they were warriors above all, ruling the blue seas and rock promontories by the strength of their arms and the power of their bronze-tipped spears. Their most celebrated exploit was the great armada of ships and soldiers that descended on Troy, a wealthy Near Eastern city on the shores of the Hellespont. That famous conquest, probably undertaken by a loose confederation of warlords bent on plunder and headed by the king of Mycenae, would provide the half-legendary basis for the first great monument of Greek literature, the *Iliad* of Homer.

The Greek Dark Age

After the Mycenaeans, the mists close almost totally over the life of this southeastern corner of Europe where Western civilization began. Other tribes and clans of northern barbarians followed the Mycenaeans and crushed them in their turn. For at least three centuries—from around 1100 B.C.E., when the city of Mycenae itself fell to new invaders, to approximately 800—a genuine dark age settled over Greece.

Wave after wave of Indo-European peoples drifted down the valleys and on to the neighboring islands and the shores of Asia Minor beyond. There were rude Dorians, who settled in the Peloponnesus and became the ancestors of the militaristic Spartans of later centuries. There were Ionians, who moved on to the islands and the Asian coast of the Aegean, where, fertilized by contact with the older civilizations of the Near East, the Greek intellect would soon kindle into life with particular vigor.

But wherever these people came during the dark centuries, they blighted what remained of the wealth and culture of Minoan-Mycenaean times. The kings of the Mycenaeans disappeared, monumental architecture ceased, pottery grew cruder, the use of the Minoan script was forgotten.

It was not all dark, of course. Toward the end of this period, in the eighth century, two of the most famous of Greek poets, Homer and Hesiod, composed their works—or, more likely, sang or chanted them before gatherings of Greeks in rude halls or village squares. The more basic arts of agriculture were not forgotten; settlers old and new went on scraping a meager living out of the dry, light Mediterranean soil. The petty Mycenaean kingdoms were destroyed, but this may have been an advantage in the long run, since imperial, divine-right monarchies like those of the ancient East were thus prevented from gaining a firm foothold in Greece, leaving the way open for wider participation in government during the next age.

CLASSICAL GREECE

Wealth and Colonies

One thing that did continue to grow during the Greek dark ages was the population. And one consequence of population growth was the spread of Greek-speaking people still further around the Mediterranean world.

The dry soil of Greece simply could not support all the newcomers. Many Greeks were thus driven to emigrate by pure Malthusian pressure; their numbers were pressing too hard upon the food supply. Others, especially after the revival of the city-state around 800 B.C.E., emigrated as traders or as mercenary soldiers.

This surge of expansion, which was especially intense from about 750 to 600 B.C.E., carried Greek-speaking people much further than their Mycenaean or Minoan predecessors had gone. Greek colonies were established not only on nearby islands and along the Ionian coasts of Asia Minor, but farther to the east around the Black Sea, and much farther to the west—in southern Italy and Sicily, in Libya and France, and on the coast of Spain at the far end of the Mediterranean.

The Greeks maintained a loose cultural unity wherever they traveled and settled. No matter how great a colony became in its own right, it tended to retain ties with the city-state that had fathered it. All Greeks spoke dialects of the same language. They worshiped the same gods and goddesses, some brought down from the north, some found among the older peoples of the eastern Mediterranean. Early on they gathered for athletic competitions in honor of their gods. Among these contests were the first Olympic Games, traditionally believed to have been held as far back as 776 B.C.E.

At home the Greeks produced elegant pottery, olive oil, and wine for sale overseas. From more lavishly endowed lands they brought back staples such as grain, essentials such as copper and tin and iron, and—from the Near East, for the second time—a written language. The characters were Phoenician in origin, but the language was Greek. The earliest surviving written record of the language in which Homer had already sung and in which Plato was to write appears on a Greek pot dating from perhaps 750 B.C.E., the early days of the great Greek diaspora.

The Greek City-State

The Greek form of city-state, the *polis,* was one of the wonders of human social organization, a delicate balance that could not and did not long endure. But while it lasted, it gave some selected human beings more say in their own lives than some peoples know even today.

Physically speaking, the *polis* was two cities: a lower city, where the people lived, and an *acropolis* (high city) on a hill in the center of town, where the gods had their temples. In fact, however, the whole of the *polis* became in classical times the possession of the Greek citizenry. The all-too-human gods, glorified in white temples, were more objects of civic pride than sources of superstitious awe. The citizens owned the *polis,* and the city itself, with its unique political, social, economic, and military structure, governed and shaped the lives of its people.

The Greek-speaking invaders from the north brought with them the tribal and clan organization of the distant steppes. The typical *polis* thus took shape initially as an alliance of such tribes, governed by a council of leading families. This aristocracy, tribal in origin

The Acropolis of ancient Athens, with its white-columned temples, still rises above rocky, tree-fringed slopes. The Parthenon, dedicated to Athena, is right of center in this picture. Despite the carefully chosen angle from which this photograph was taken, the Acropolis actually sits in the center of the modern city of Athens, where the ancient stone is seriously threatened by pollution. (D. A. Harissiadis Photographic Agency, Athens)

and now commonly including the leading landowners, sometimes tolerated a chief or petty king for a time, "a first among equals" like the kings of the ancient Mycenaeans. But real power lay with the landowners and the tribal leaders, and the last generation of Greek kings seems to have faded away without much struggle, transformed into elected magistrates or simply expiring as an institution.

In the seventh and sixth centuries, however, the aristocracy soon followed the monarchy into decline, opening the way to an astonishing degree of freedom among the Greek cities. A number of factors contributed to the decline of the aristocrats. One was the continuing growth of trade, which raised the social status of merchants as well as of farmers and potters, who produced wine, oil, and jars for overseas sale. Another cause was a radical change in military tactics, the replacement of the chariot-fighting aristocracy by a heavily armed phalanx of citizen infantry. The phalanx, composed of all who could afford the sword, spear, shield, helmet, and basic body armor of a *hoplite* (infantryman), rapidly replaced the Homeric charioteer as the backbone of Greek armies.

Land, money, and military service simply could not be excluded forever from political power. A military assembly of hoplites—the farmers, merchants, and craftsmen who could afford the weapons—was one road to political involvement for these solid citizens. Frequently also, men called "tyrants" (without the negative connotation of later times) became their spokemen. These extra-legal rulers, often former military leaders, proceeded to modify political institutions in order to strengthen their citizen-supporters. Tyrannies tended to last only a generation or two. But the citizen assemblies they fostered survived, establishing the predominance of the middle ranks in the Greek *polis*.

By 500 B.C.E., in fact, the evolving Greek city-state was on the verge of producing the prosperous, comparatively democratic Athens of Pericles.

Not everyone strolled the streets discoursing about public policy, of course. Greek women were largely excluded from the public sphere of social and political life. Confined instead to the private sphere of the home, respectable women were honored for such traditional skills as feeding and clothing their families, raising children, and supervising sometimes quite large house-holds full of relatives, servants, and slaves.

The images of powerful or heroic Greek women which have come down to us were thus for the most part mythical. They were goddesses like Athena, Aphrodite, queen of love, or the warlike Amazons. Or they were heroines in plays or poems like the beautiful Helen of Troy, the witch woman Medea, or Antigone, who defies political authority for a higher cause.

There were exceptions. Spartan women exercised as their men did and owned most of the property. The exercise, however, was intended to help them bear strong sons, and they cared for the family property in order to free their husbands for a higher calling—war. Aspasia, consort of the Athenian statesman Pericles, was famed for her wit and wisdom. But she was also a foreigner and a courtesan—hardly a respectable woman at all by orthodox Athenian standards.

The famous "Greek democracy" was thus far from democratic by any modern definition of the term. The total population of Athens and its surrounding villages in the fifth century B.C.E. was perhaps two hundred thousand—of whom thirty thousand were free citizens. Only native-born free adult males of a certain economic standing—hoplite material—could be citizens. The rest—women and children, slaves, resident foreigners, and the lower orders generally—had no voice in the state or any place in the philosophical conversations of thinkers like Socrates.

Nevertheless, this is still a long way from the autocratic rule of pharaohs or Near Eastern kings. Greek citizens did meet in political assemblies to thrash out public policy. They did elect their own magistrates, war leaders, even a surviving electoral monarch here and there. They were citizens, not subjects. And it made a difference.

The Persian War

Against this small, bustling people, the biggest empire in the western half of Eurasia came awesomely in arms at the beginning of the fifth century B.C.E. The Persian Empire, built by Cyrus the Great less than half a century before, stretched from the eastern Mediterranean to the banks of the Indus, from the mountains of the Caucasus to the shores of the Arabian Sea. Cyrus and his son had overrun Mesopotamia and Egypt and pushed their frontiers eastward to the nearest of the rivers of India. Darius I, who had inherited this vast realm in the late sixth century, built roads and canals, divided his domain into twenty more or less efficiently governed satrapies, adopted the enlightened faith of Zoroaster, and reigned in civilized splendor from his great palaces at Persepolis and Susa.

Darius, of course, suppressed rebellion wherever it emerged among his many peoples. It was the suppression of one such insurrection, among the Greek city-states of Ionia, that triggered the Greek Persian War, a struggle that lasted decades but ended in a totally unexpected Greek victory.

The Ionian city-states of Asia Minor revolted in 499 B.C.E., under the leadership of the famous trading city of Miletus. Like others before them, the Milesians and their allies were crushed. But before they fell, the Ionians sent pleas for help to the Greeks of the mainland; and some small assistance was sent, most notably by the Athenians. For this act of defiance, Darius of Persia resolved to punish the mainland Greeks.

Of all the cities of the Hellenes, two were already prominent at the beginning of the fifth century: Athens, the largest and the most civilized, and Sparta, the most militaristic and most disciplined. These two were to dominate the history of that turbulent and splendid century. It was the Athenians, however, who bore the brunt of the Persian War and carried off the rewards of victory.

The first Persian punishment force drew their ships ashore at the edge of the small plain of Marathon, north-east of Athens, in 490 B.C.E. The mere sight of the iron-armed hosts of the Medes and the Persians, twenty thousand of them, with their royal guard of "Immortals" in the van, was enough to shake most enemies. The Athenian phalanx, outnumbered probably two to one, charged them at a dead run. The Athenian center broke, and the Persians poured through. But the Greek wings overwhelmed the Persian flanks, closed upon the Asian center, and drove the invaders in disarray back to their ships.

Retribution, however, was sure. Darius died before he could take further action, but his son Xerxes spent four years preparing a huge fleet and a massive army to avenge his father's humiliation and to add the lands of the Hellenes to his already swollen empire.

The new Persian host arrived in 480. They swarmed into northern Greece in unstoppable numbers, perhaps sixty thousand strong: Medes and Persians in leather breeches and fishtail iron jerkins, with their short, powerful bows; Assyrians with their bronze helmets and long lances; Arabs in long robes; Ethiopians in leopard and lion skins; and many more. The Spartans headed a coalition army that tried to halt them at a narrow northern pass called Thermopylae—the Hot Gates—and died almost to the last man when a Greek traitor showed the invaders a way to take the defenders in the rear. The Persians moved on southward, like locusts over the land, while a Persian fleet closed in on southern Attica by sea. Athens was taken and burned. All northern Greece lay open to Persian arms, and the defense of the south seemed no more than a forlorn hope.

But the Greeks bred brilliant leaders as well as soldiers who knew how to die for their homeland. Themistocles the Athenian had for years urged his countrymen to pin their faith on their fleet. Hundreds of new *triremes*—the long, oar-driven warships of the Mediterranean—had been built. These vessels, with their contingents of disciplined Greek hoplites, now turned the tide against the Persian host.

The turning point came at Salamis. Between this small island off the port of Athens and the shore, the Athenians tricked the larger Persian fleet into giving battle. Ramming and swarming aboard the demoralized Persian vessels, the Athenians once more routed their enemies. "No longer could we see the water," a Persian in a Greek play later lamented, "charged with ship's wrecks and men's blood."[3]

The Persian army was thus left without the support of its fleet. They wintered in Thessaly and marched south again the following year, 479. But this time a large Greek force led by a Spartan general met them at the village of Plataea, northwest of Athens, and shattered them on land as the Athenians had by sea. What was left of the Persian army stumbled home in defeat.

The war was not over. It dragged on nominally for some thirty years. But after Salamis in 480 and Plataea in 479, the struggle took the form of annual plundering raids by Greek fleets on the shores of the Persian Empire. The Persians never came again to Greece.

The Athens of Pericles

The history of Athens was in some ways similar to that of other Greek city-states. Its kings were replaced by a government of aristocratic councils early in the seventh century B.C.E. At the beginning of the sixth century the *archon* (magistrate) Solon—a member of the city's chief elected council—became Athens' most famous lawgiver. The laws of Solon freed poor farmers from debt slavery and opened up public office to citizens of less than aristocratic birth. Later in the sixth century the tyrant Pisistratus destroyed the residual power of the old clan-based aristocracy and transferred land from the aristocrats to the landless farmers who supported him. Pisistratus also encouraged handicraft manufacture and foreign trade and began the vast program of temple building that Pericles would carry to a triumphant climax.

Paradoxically, it was the aristocratic Cleisthenes who, during the last decade of the sixth century, brought participatory democracy to Athens. Winning popular support in 508, Cleisthenes instituted a Council of Five Hundred, chosen by lot, which was given sweeping authority to guide foreign and domestic affairs, to control government finances, and to prepare the crucial agenda for assembly meetings. The assembly of citizens still elected archons, passed all new laws, voted on questions of peace and war. A citizen-jury system began to edge out the aristocratic Areopagus court in judicial power. *Demokratia,* the rule of the citizens, was from this time on—a dozen years before the onset of the Persian War—the basic political reality of Athens.

Pericles, who dominated Athenian politics between 450 and 429 B.C.E., was another of those descendants of the old aristocracy who seemed to flourish under Athenian democracy. The sculptured head that has come down to us, bearded and helmeted, the eyes gazing out calm and blank like those of all Greek gods and heroes, gives us only an idealized notion of what he was like. The Athenian historian Thucydides says he was famous for financial integrity and enormously popular among the people. Beyond these bare facts, Pericles seems to have been a man with a vision of Athenian greatness, a policy of *grandeur* that carried Athens to the climax of the Greek golden age.

Pericles put the finishing touches on the democratic constitution of Athens. He also presided over the conversion of Athens' victory over the Persian Empire into an Athenian empire among the Greeks.

---

[3]Aeschylus, *The Persians,* trans. Seth G. Benardete, in *The Complete Greek Tragedies,* Vol. 1, eds. David Grene and Richmond Lattimore (Chicago: University of Chicago Press, 1959), pp. 234–235.

Pericles, the most celebrated statesman of ancient Greece, broods on the fate of nations in this idealized funerary sculpture. Is this a "realistic" representation? Look particularly at the hair, beard, and eyes. (New York Public Library Picture Collection)

The decades of naval warfare against Persia that followed Salamis added a new element to the turbulent mix of Athenian politics. The Athenian sailors, fundamentally oarsmen whose straining backs propelled Athenian triremes into battle, were typically landless city dwellers too poor to afford arms and armor. Thanks to their military contribution, this less affluent group now acquired a share of power in the assembly comparable to that of the hoplite class. Their growing participation in government represented a clear gain for *demokratia* in the Athens of Pericles.

Meanwhile, to keep up the pressure on the Persians and to bring home as much of the pillage of Asia as their arms could win, the Greeks organized the Delian League. This military alliance, originally voluntary, was gradually transformed into an Athenian empire. Under the leadership of Pericles, membership in the league became compulsory for some fifty Greek city-states. The headquarters—and the treasury—of the league were moved from the sacred island of Delos to Athens. Free contributions became required tribute. And the funds contributed by all the members began to be spent to build temples on the Athenian acropolis.

Under such leadership Athens flourished. Trade boomed, and the docks at the Athenian port of Piraeus were jammed with long ships and jars of wine and oil. There was plenty of work in the city—laboring on the public works on the acropolis or producing goods for export. And the city itself was a joy to live in. Philosophers such as Socrates disputed in the agora; the hands of Phidias sculptured stone among the columns of the Parthenon; Aeschylus and Sophocles produced moving tragedies for the annual festival of Dionysus.

Loyalty to the *polis* had never been greater. An aging Pericles appealed to it when he urged his hearers to "draw strength . . . from the busy spectacle of our great city's life as we have it before us day by day, falling in love with her as we see her."[4] These men of ancient Athens, with all their faults, had come as close to genuine self-government as any ancient people ever would. And they had found uses for their freedom that would seldom be matched, perhaps never exceeded.

The Peloponnesian War

The Greeks were always a rivalrous, contentious people. The war between Athens and Sparta that brought the fifth century B.C.E. to its disastrous close was more than a typical Greek feud, however. It was a clash of principle, a conflict between two irreconcilable ways of life.

Sparta had retained the virtues of virile Homeric warrior heroes, the stress on personal courage, and the conservative institutions of an earlier day. As late as the fifth century the Spartans still had not one but two kings, and their politics was dominated by an old-fashioned council of elders. Military service was normal for full citizens of any *polis,* but in Sparta all males lived in barracks till the age of thirty.

There was more to all this than conservative sentiment, of course. The fields of Sparta were worked not by Spartan citizens but by subject peoples called *helots.* Since the helots vastly outnumbered the Spartans, every Spartan had to be a soldier simply to keep the helots in their place. This need to dominate by force had also led the Spartans to impose their will on their neighbors in the Peloponnesus, the sprawling peninsula of southern Greece, through a compulsory alliance called the Peloponnesian League. In the last decades of the fifth century, the Peloponnesian League and the Delian League—the land-based Spartan coalition and the seaborne empire of the Athenians—came to an all but inevitable conflict.

The rise of Athenian power was bound to cause concern in Sparta. When the Athenians began to interfere in the affairs of Spartan allies, the leaders of the southern alliance responded violently. The Peloponnesian War, 431–404 B.C.E., dragged on for more than a quarter of a century. It was a civil war, pitting Greeks against Greeks, and it was the Hellenes as a whole who suffered.

From the beginning the Athenians had the worst of it. Sparta, located in the interior of the Peloponnesus, was safe from the Athenian navy, which had been Athens' most powerful military arm ever since Themistocles. Athens, by contrast, lay open to repeated incursions by the redoubtable Spartan army. Other misfortunes fell upon the Athenians. In the second year of the war, a plague ravaged the city, costing many lives, including that of Pericles.

There were battles without number, bloody massacres and shocking betrayals, tangled alliances involving even the Persians, the old enemies of all Greeks. In the end, the Spartans emerged victorious in 404 B.C.E. Athens was humiliated, stripped of its navy, deprived of its empire. The city was forced to raze the "long walls" connecting it with the Piraeus and the sea, which had been the source of its wealth and power. The Spartans im-

---

[4]George Willis Botsford and Charles Alexander Robinson, Jr., *Hellenic History,* 3rd ed. (New York: Macmillan, 1950), p. 202.

posed upon the city the notorious Thirty Tyrants—a council of Athenian collaborators—and returned home in triumph.

Athens was the loser, but no one gained permanently. The Athenians regained their freedom almost at once, but other wars and intrigues followed, dragging on into the fourth century. Peace was at last imposed from without—by a half-barbaric northern power called Macedon. Long before the Macedonian conquest, however, the Greeks had sacrificed their freedom on the altar of their own eternal contentiousness.

Alexander the Great: Long March to Glory

Philip and Alexander of Macedon, father and son, composed a strange, brief dynasty of power. Philip's triumph brought unity to Greece at least. Alexander's unrivaled string of victories spread at least an approximation of Greek ways and Greek culture from the Nile to the Indus.

Philip II seized the throne of the northern kingdom of Macedon from his own ward in the middle of the fourth century. He built up a powerful army of hard-bitten Macedonians, conquered his more barbarous neighbors, and soon became involved in the tangled wars and alliances of the Greeks. In 338 B.C.E., Philip's soldiers smashed the combined armies of Athens and Thebes on the brutal field of Chaeronea. Two years later Philip was dead, murdered by his own officers.

His son, Alexander, replaced him as king and warrior lord. He was apparently a youth of more subtlety than his father. Having been tutored by the Athenian philosopher Aristotle, he was perhaps capable of imagining a more sophisticated world order than conquest and pillage. But he was a warrior first and always. He began at once a twelve-year trek across western Eurasia seldom matched in the annals of warfare.

The tale of Alexander's victories reads like a gazeteer of the ancient Middle East. He crossed the Hellespont into Persia in 334, repeatedly defeated the Persians, swung south into ancient Egypt, and founded Alexandria in the delta of the Nile. Plunging back into Asia Minor, he finally crushed the Persian emperor Darius II at the Battle of Gaugamela in 331 B.C.E., and then marched farther and farther east across the far-flung Persian satrapies. He passed south of the Caspian Sea, crossed what is today Afghanistan, and went beyond the reach even of the Persians, into northern India. After tracing the Indus south to the Indian Ocean, Alexander turned back across the great desert to bring his odyssey to an end in Babylon. Here, his destiny accomplished, he died suddenly of a fever in 323 B.C.E. He was thirty-three years old.

For good or ill, Alexander's long march accomplished more than can ever have been imagined in his narrow Macedonian skull. He himself had "gone native" on the long road east, adopting Persian garb, marrying a Persian princess, declaring himself a king and a god after the Oriental manner. But he had also founded twenty-five Greek city-states along his march, and married off thousands of his Macedonian officers and soldiers to native women. Henceforth Greek administrators, Greek traders, Greek ways of living, thinking, and carving stone would become part of the life of this half of Asia.

A new and wider world was opened up by Philip of Macedon and Alexander the Great. But an old world died too—the untidy little world of craggy mountains, blue water, and white cities where a small, combative, immensely energetic people had brought to a climax one of the great human efforts at civilized living.

The Art of the Acropolis

Greek sculpture apparently began, as the Greek dark age ended and the city-state emerged, with models borrowed from immemorial Egypt. The stiff frontality of Greek archaic statuary—the gowns like a fluted column, the fixed "archaic smile"—seem to look back to Memphis and Karnak. However, these stiff sixth-century Apollos and skirted female figures probably also reflect the limitations of the log from which earlier figures were fashioned by Greek woodcarvers.

Yet from these crude beginnings developed the perfect physical proportions and idealized shapes of fifth-century sculpture. The classic simplicity of the head of Pericles or Phidias's *Athena Lemnia* became a model for later ages. The calm strength of the *Apollo* from the Temple of Zeus at Olympia and the incarnate majesty of the great bronze *Zeus* from the sea off Euboea have a power that challenges all efforts at emulation since.

But the restless mind of the ancient Greeks appears never to have been content, even with classic perfection. Greek sculptors of the fourth, third, and second centuries went on to more intricate, more violent, and perhaps more human things. Hellenistic sculpture included the tangled draperies of the *Winged Victory,* which stands in the Louvre today, and the writhing bodies of the muscular *Laocoön* and his sons in the serpent's coils. It also included the living flesh of perfect Hellenistic Aphrodite—the Greek goddess of beauty— and the wrinkled skin, taut tendons, and swollen veins of the *Old Market Woman.* Realism, melodrama, and sentiment thus replaced classic idealized forms as human concerns replaced ideal ones among the ever-changing Greeks.

Greek building, for all its subtlety of proportion, was very simple. Post-and-lintel structure—pillars and pediments and a gently sloping roof—made a Greek temple. The plain Doric order predominated, at least through the fifth century: a flat abacus at the head of the column and no base at all below. Yet the ruined beauty of the Parthenon, the Temple of Athena Parthenos (Athena the Virgin), on the Athenian acropolis testifies to what could be done with such economy of means.

A city crowned with such beauty—marble temples against the mountains and the sky—was a city that any people could, as Pericles said, fall in love with day by day.

Homer's Epics and Athenian Tragedy

"Sing, goddess, the wrath of Achilles," begins Homer's *Iliad,* the oldest and for many still the greatest of Greek poems. It dates from the Greek dark ages—perhaps 800 B.C.E.—and harks back for its warlike theme to the wars of Mycenaean times. But it was as close to a Bible as the worldly Greeks ever got, even in the vastly more sophisticated centuries after 500 B.C.E.

The strength of Homer's twin epics, the *Iliad* on the Trojan War and the *Odyssey* on the wanderings of the hero Odysseus, would not be easily equaled. The *Iliad* in particular stands alone in the classical canon as a powerful poem of men at war. The long hexameter lines boom with the rolling of the sea and the clash of battle on that distant Asian coast where Bronze Age Greeks and Trojans fought before Troy. The story of the wrath of Achilles—vain of honor, grieving terribly for the friend who dies in his place, and exploding at last, a blood-stained meteor across the battle-field—brings back with unparalleled power a savage age long gone.

Later Greek times produced lovely poetry as well. There are the fragile lyrics of Sappho, the Greek poet of the islands. Only fragments of her verse remain, yet they combine with unmatched beauty the poet's love of other women with a sensitive awareness of the legends of her people and the loveliness of the Greek isles. There are Pindar's famous odes, celebrating the transient glory of the heroes of his day and later imitated by many Western poets.

The ancient Greek theater apparently began with primitive hymn-singing and dancing in honor of Dionysus, god of the grape in particular and of fertility and generation in general. By the fifth century B.C.E., this simple celebration of divine beneficence had evolved into a complex dramatic form. In this classic Greek tragedy, characters in stylized masks acted out the story while a chorus danced, sang, and chanted a commentary between the "acts" of the play. The stories themselves normally derived from Greek mythology, but the old tales of gods and heroes often emerged with universal reference in the work of the fifth-century Athenian playwrights Aeschylus, Sophocles, and Euripides.

The dramatic heroes of Sophocles perhaps best embody what Aristotle considered the perfect tragic type: the noble character marred by a single tragic flaw. Thus *Oedipus the King* attempts to discover the crime against the gods that has brought divine retribution in the form of a plague upon the city he rules. The dramatic tension of the play grows out of the inability of this great king to see what would be obvious to the audience even if they did not know the story: that Oedipus himself is the criminal, the man who in defiance of all the laws of gods and humans has inadvertently murdered his father and married his own mother.

There was laughter in ancient Greece as well, evidently, and a comic theater to stimulate it. Most celebrated is the so-called Old Comedy of fifth-century Athens, embodied in the plays of Aristophanes. A comedy such as *The Clouds,* which lampoons the generation gap, the teachings of the philosopher Socrates, and much else, is typical. Aristophanes offers a rich mixture of social satire and personal innuendo, of bawdy farce and lyric flights of great beauty. We would expect nothing less complex and subtle of the Age of Pericles. Even Greek laughter was a many-splendored thing.

Philosophy: Socrates, Plato, Aristotle

From ancient Greece, as from Confucian China and ancient India, however, it is not shaped stone or patterns of words that have survived the longest, but the ideas of Greek teachers. These equivalents of the Hebrew prophets or the sages and gurus of the East are called the Greek philosophers, "lovers of wisdom."

In the cosmopolitan city-states of the Ionian coasts in particular, a handful of choice spirits among the Hellenes went beyond mythology to ask themselves, "What is the universe *really* made of?" The answers Thales, Anaximander, Pythagoras, and others came up with—water, the four elements, fire, number, and so on—are of largely antiquarian interest. But from them descended both the philosophy of the fifth and fourth centuries and the Hellenistic science of the fourth century and after.

The most famous of Greek philosophers were Socrates in the fifth century B.C.E. and Plato and Aristotle in the fourth.

Socrates called himself the "gadfly" of Athens, an intellectual horsefly stinging Athenians into questioning traditional values, examining their own lives, thinking seriously about the real meaning of life itself. More of a crackerbarrel philosophizer than a systematic thinker, Socrates buttonholed his fellow citizens in the agora, asking judges what justice was, querying poets about the function of art, discussing with the young people who gathered around him how society ought to be organized, how the good life ought to be lived. "The unexamined life" he told his disciples, "is not worth living." In the terrible years after the Peloponnesian War, Socrates was tried and executed by his fellow countrymen, less for his words than for his insistence on his right to speak them.

One of the admirers who mourned Socrates was a broad-shouldered, poetic young man called Plato. For the rest of his life, this most influential of all Western philosophers would immortalize his teacher in a series of *Dialogues* expounding first the views of Socrates and later Plato's own mature notions of the nature of reality, of the good society, of the ideal life, and much more.

This most famous of Greek philosophers insisted that there is more to reality than meets the eye. There are two levels to the universe, said Plato, a lower world of matter, or "particulars," and a higher, nonmaterial realm of Ideas, Forms, or Absolutes. A triangle drawn in the dust by a Greek geometer is a particular triangle, and it ceases to exist with a sweep of a sandaled foot. The Form of the Triangle—the definition of a triangle, we might say—is an Idea, invisible, immaterial, and eternal. The courage you show in a tight spot, your sense of justice, whatever wisdom you may have—all these are temporary, finite, bounded by one imperfect human heart and mind. The Idea of Courage, of Justice, of Wisdom would survive even if there were not one wise or just or brave person left alive to think such thoughts, or to embody them. Ultimate reality, then, is not material at all but rather is pure, transcendental Idea. The Idea of Man, the Form of the Good, Absolute Beauty—these Platonic formulations would be powerful shapers of Western minds for centuries to come.

Plato's ethical teachings stressed one of these capitalized abstractions especially: Reason. The goal of life, Plato said, was happiness. But happiness comes from the practice of virtue, and the highest of virtues is wisdom. Since wisdom is achieved through reason, the best possible life is a life dedicated wholly to rational inquiry and the pursuit of truth. Philosophy ("love of wisdom") is thus itself the highest of human activities, and the philosophical life is the best life.

The good society, in turn, would be one in which philosophers were kings, or kings philosophers, and in which the rest of us performed the functions to which we are best suited by nature, class, or profession. Plato was no democrat: His family was an ancient aristocratic one, and it was the popular demagogues who had executed Socrates. Let the best minds guide the state, said Plato, as the brain rules the body. It was a beguiling notion, one that can tantalize us even today.

Other Greek sages proposed other theories of the ultimate nature of things, and of the good life for human beings. For Plato's disciple Aristotle—himself "the master of those who know" to later ages—the Forms are real enough but exist only *within* the particulars that derive their structure from them—not in some transcendental realm of nonmaterial being. On ethical and political matters, Aristotle took an eminently practical view. After studying the constitutions of more than 150 Greek city-states, he classified them under three heads—monarchy, aristocracy, and democracy—and found strengths and weaknesses in all three. In the realm of personal morality, Aristotle agreed with Plato that the truth-seeking life of the philosopher was the best life possible. Recognizing, however, that most people were not capable of such a life, he urged that for the average person, virtuous conduct is a "golden mean" between two extremes. The good person, he believed, avoids excess and seeks moderation in all things.

Aristotle's wide-ranging mind left Western people ideas on every subject, from metaphysics, politics, and morality to science and the arts. He meticulously catalogued biological species and left theories that dominated physics until modern times. His writing on poetry and drama explained the "cathartic" effect, the sense of psychological purging and relief, that comes from great drama. Aristotle also laid out the means of constructing a "well-made play," methods still taught in drama and film schools today.

History and Science

The eager Greek intellect explored this world as well as the transcendental realm of the philosophers. Both Western science and Western history were founded by the ancient Greeks.

The two most honored of Greek historians were Herodotus and Thucydides, chroniclers of the two great fifth-century B.C.E. wars that bracketed the age of Pericles. Herodotus's *Persian War,* perhaps the first real history book ever written, recounted in colorful detail the epic struggle between the Greek city-states and the huge Persian Empire. Breaking with the ancient tradition of mythic and poetic accounts of the past in which gods and goddesses always played important parts, Herodotus sought to explain how human beings, Greeks and Persians, settled their differences by a resort to arms. Though he was not above inventing inspiring speeches for kings and generals and reading sententious morals into past events, Herodotus did travel widely, seeking evidence and talking to eyewitnesses, conducting a genuine historical investigation for the first time.

Thucydides' history of the grim and disillusioning *Peloponnesian War* offers subtler analysis and more thoughtful syntheses than his predecessor. Thucydides' account of the cruelty, corruption, follies, and defeats of Athens at war is all the more moving when we remember that he was himself an Athenian commander. Exiled by his fellow citizens for an early failure in the struggle, he gave the rest of his life, not to justifying himself, but to compiling an unbiased yet deeply moving history of the great conflict.

There seemed to be no end to the intellectual curiosity of the Hellenes. By Hellenistic times much of the Greek thirst for ultimate understanding had shifted from philosophy to science. Here the Greeks made more substantial contributions than did any Western people before the Scientific Revolution of Copernicus and Newton.

The names of some of the early Greek scientists are well known still. Pythagoras is most familiar as a mathematician. His famous theorem about the squares of the sides of a right-angle triangle is part of the bric-a-brac of every school-child's mind today. Aristotle's researches in biology and physics were so impressive that later ages would revere even his mistakes. Euclid's *Elements* of geometry remained standard for more than twenty centuries, and doctors to this day begin their careers with the Oath of Hippocrates, most renowned of ancient Greek physicians, to "do no harm" to any patient. Archimedes's promise to move the world itself if you could give him a lever long enough and a place to stand has the ring of Greek speculative daring at its best.

Perhaps as far back as Pythagoras, Greek astronomers recognized that the earth is a ball. They calculated its size by mathematics and used trigonometry to estimate its distance from the sun and the moon. They made one fundamental error; in the end they agreed with Ptolemy's earth-centered theory of the structure of the universe rather than with Aristarchus's sun-centered view. For Ptolemy's elaborate cosmological explication and mathematical calculation—it took some doing to present so erroneous a theory convincingly—carried the best scientific minds of Roman, Byzantine, Arab, and medieval Christian times along with him, till Copernicus in the sixteenth century set them right.

Reason was the heart of it, the core of Greek achievement in the linked fields of philosophy and science. When they set their minds to work, this ancient Mediterranean people produced a body of rational speculation and calculation that is a major human effort to explain the meaning of it all, the nature of things.

SUMMARY

The first age of human history saw the emergence of other peoples besides the Mesopotamian states and ancient Egypt. Around the eastern end of the Mediterranean and on across western Asia, new cities, kingdoms, and empires bubbled up, many of them during the turbulent second millennium B.C.E. Among these, the Hittites added iron to civilization's repertoire of workable metals, while the Phoenician city-states of what is today Lebanon traded the length of the Mediterranean and left the Western world its basic alphabet.

Much more influential in the long run were the ancient Hebrews and the ancient Greeks. The Hebrews were a small but immensely significant people who entered history as a group of pastoral nomads shortly after 2000 B.C.E. They established the short-lived kingdom of Israel under David and Solomon around 1000 B.C.E. The kingdom soon split into two halves, the northern half falling to Assyrian conquerors in the eighth century, the southern half to the Babylonians in the sixth century B.C.E.

Through these trials and tribulations, however, the Hebrews developed a unique religion. Focused on a divine Covenant between themselves and their God, the faith of the Hebrews was monotheistic, highly spiritual, and fostered both personal morality and a sense of social justice. This ancient faith survives today as modern Judaism. It also became the direct ancestor of both Christianity and Islam.

European history began in southern Europe, in the islands and mountainous mainland of Greece, where a series of cultures flourished between 2200 and 200 B.C.E. climaxing in the fifth century with the Age of Pericles.

The first two societies to develop in this area were those of the Minoans and the Mycenaeans. The Minoans (2200–1500 B.C.E.) migrated from the Near East to the large island of Crete, which they made the center of a city-based, seaborne, commercial hegemony over neighboring islands and coasts. The Mycenaeans (1500–1100 B.C.E.), Indo-European nomads from the north, overran this first European urban culture and became pirates, traders, and builders of rude cities.

As early as the eighth century B.C.E., Greek traders also took to the sea. The Greek city-state, or *polis,* ruled by a popular assembly with elected magistrates and other officials, became perhaps the most democratic of ancient urban institutions. The history of the celebrated fifth century B.C.E. began with Greece's victorious war against the huge Persian Empire. The century centered on the rich and culturally brilliant age of Pericles in Athens, and it ended with the self-destructive civil war between Athens and Sparta in which Sparta won but all Greece was the loser. In the fourth century the Greek peninsula fell under the military domination of Philip and Alexander of Macedon. Alexander brought the long feud with Persia to a climax by over-running the empire and scattering Greek cities across much of western Asia.

Greek culture, like that of the ancient Hebrews, provided a vital legacy to later peoples. Greek literature—from Homer's epics the *Iliad* and the *Odyssey* to the delicate lyrics of Sappho or the dramas of Sophocles—provided models for later writers. Greek sculpture idealized the human form in lifelike figures of gods and famous citizens.

Above all, the philosophy of Greek thinkers like Socrates, Plato, and Aristotle left the West a legacy of daring ideas. From Socrates's challenge to "know thyself," through Plato's belief in absolute Ideas like Truth and Beauty, to Aristotle's conviction that ethics is a golden mean between extremes, their views have shaped Western thinking ever since.

SUGGESTED READING

Ahlstrom, G. W. *The History of Ancient Palestine.* Minneapolis, Minn.: Fortress Press, 1993. Massive scholarly study.

Ben-Tor, A. *The Archaeology of Ancient Israel.* New Haven, Conn.: Yale University Press, 1992. Trans. R. Greenberg. From the Neolithic through the Bronze and Iron Ages.

Bernal, M. *Black Athena.* London: Free Association Press, 1987. Controversial study emphasizing Egyptian influence on Greece.

Bryce, T. *The Kingdom of the Hittites.* New York: Clarendon Press, 1998. Strong on political and military history.

Cantor, N. F., *The Sacred Chain: The History of the Jews.* New York: HarperCollins, 1994. Sweeping overview.

Chadwick, J. *The Mycenaean World.* Cambridge: Cambridge University Press, 1976. Overview by a scholar known for his exposition of the Minoan script, Linear B.

Dothan, T. K., and M. Dothan. *People of the Sea: The Search for the Philistines.* New York: Macmillan, 1992. Archaeological investigation of the Hebrews' great enemies.

Flanders, H. J., R. W. Crapps, and D. A. Smith. *People of the Covenant.* New York: Oxford University Press, 1988. Hebrew history through the Old Testament.

Freeman, C. *Egypt, Greece, and Rome: Civilizations of the Ancient Mediterranean.* Oxford: Oxford University Press, 1996. Greek and Roman history set against an Egyptian background.

Grene, D., and R. Lattimore, eds. *The Complete Greek Tragedies* (4 vols.). Chicago: University of Chicago Press, 1959–1960. All the surviving plays by the three greatest Greek tragic dramatists—Aeschylus, Sophocles, and Euripides—translated by various hands.

Hammond, C. L. *Alexander the Great: King, Commander, and Statesman.* London: Chatto and Windus, 1980. Combines deep classical learning with first-hand knowledge of the lands Alexander traversed.

Herodotus. *The History of Herodotus,* trans. G. Rawlinson. Chicago: Encyclopaedia Britannica, 1955. The first Western historian's account of the Persian War and of the Near East in his own time.

Homer. *The Iliad,* trans. R. Lattimore. Chicago: University of Chicago Press, 1951. Excellent rendering by an experienced translator and poet. See also *The Odyssey.*

Just, R. *Women in Athenian Law and Life.* London: Routledge, 1991. Illuminating anthropological approach.

Lefkowitz, M., and M. B. Fant. *Women's Life in Greece and Rome.* Baltimore, Md.: Johns Hopkins University Press, 1982. Perhaps the best description, but see also the highly praised S. Pomeroy, *Goddesses, Whores, Wives and Slaves: Women in Classical Antiquity* (New York: Schocken Books, 1975).

Podlecki, A. J. *Perikles and His Circle.* New York: Routledge, 1998. Useful new life based on re-reading of the very limited evidence available.

Seltzer, R. M., ed. *Judaism: A People and Its History.* New York: Macmillan, 1989. The Jews and the evolution of their faith.

Shanks, H. *Jerusalem: An Archaeological Biography.* New York: Random House, 1995. Illustrated history of the holy city.

Smith, M. S. *The Early History of God.* San Francisco: Harper & Row, 1990. Early Hebrew beliefs about God. See also K. Armstrong, *A History of God* (New York: Knopf, 1994), which takes the story into Christian and Islamic times.

Taylor, C. C. W., ed. *From the Beginning to Plato.* London: Routledge, 1997. Development of Greek philosophy.

Walbank, F. W. *The Hellenistic World.* Cambridge, Mass.: Harvard University Press, 1982. Scholarly introduction to the fascinating later Greek centuries.

Please refer to the document CD-ROM for primary sources related to this chapter.

CHAPTER 4

BRAHMAN, BUDDHA, AND THE AGE OF THE SAGES
The Emergence of India and China

(2500–200 B.C.E.)

A Glance Ahead: Two Giants Emerge in the East

While Egyptians and Mesopotamians were building cities, kingdoms, and even small empires, while Hebrews and Greeks were enriching the cultural life of the world around the Mediterranean, great civilizations were also taking shape much farther to the east. Much larger empires—and cultures as profound—emerged in the states that would become the India and China of later centuries.

Both are enormous. China is as wide as all Europe, and India is often called "the subcontinent" of Asia. Between them, China and India are home to one third of the population of the earth today.

Historic India generated not one but two of the major world religions—Hinduism and Buddhism. China was a unified superstate many centuries before the modern great powers were dreamed of. These two civilizations dominated their zones of civilized living down the centuries as no single people did in Europe, Africa, or the Americas. And while most of the ancient empires discussed in this book are honored names in history today, India and China are here still—and likely to make more history in years to come.

Lost Civilization of the Indus

The Indian Subcontinent

The raw physical reality of India is mud in the monsoon, dust in the dry season. It is the high thin cold of the Hindu Kush and the glittering snowfields of the Himalayas, the lush green valley of the Ganges, the dry hills of the south. It is a mixture of peoples, a babble of many languages, a meeting place of some of the world's greatest religions. To Westerners today it is a richly physical world of hot curries and importunate bazaars from which, mysteriously, has emerged the profound spiritual tradition of the yogi and the guru, enlightenment and Nirvana.

Indian civilization, like the civilizations of the Near East, was born in its river valleys, but it expanded inexorably thereafter, till it encompassed the entire subcontinent. On the map, this Indian subcontinent is one of the most readily recognizable of global features. It is a vast triangle, two thousand miles from north to south, about half the size of the United States. Like Arabia to the west and Indochina to the east, India is a gigantic peninsula jutting down from the underside of Asia.

Within this huge triangle, three main geographical subdivisions stand out. In the north the colossal ranges loom—the Hindu Kush and the snow-shrouded Himalayas. Just south of the mountains run India's most celebrated rivers: the arid basin of the Indus in the northwest, the five rivers of the Punjab and the long green valley of the Ganges in the northeast, flowing from the Himalayas to the Bay of Bengal. South of the rivers, finally, lies the wedge-shaped Deccan, a dry, hilly plateau fringed by narrow coastal plains as it runs down to Cape Comorin at the southern tip of the subcontinent.

Each of the major regions of India has its distinctive and historic features. But the first center of Indian civilization was along the low, intensively cultivated banks of the great northern rivers, especially the sacred Ganges. It is along the shores of these rivers, then, that any history of India must begin.

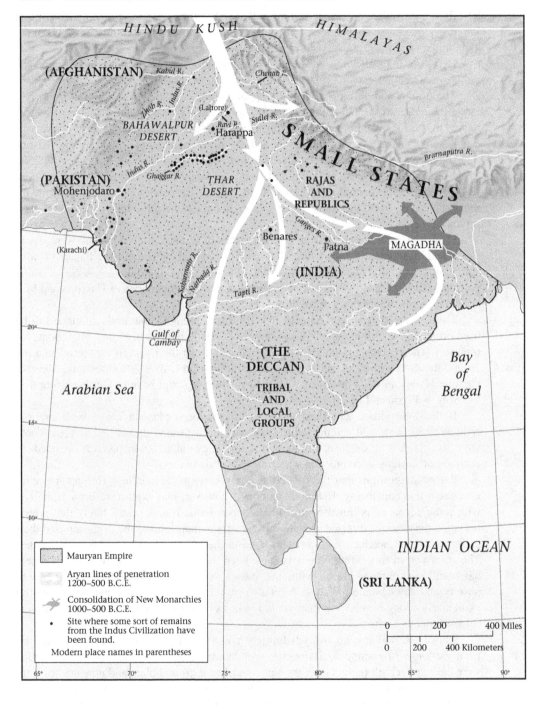

HINDU KUSH
HIMALAYAS

(AFGHANISTAN)
Kabul R.
Chenab R.

Zhob R.
Indus R.
(Lahore)
BAHAWALPUR
DESERT
Ravi R.
Sutlej R.
Harappa

SMALL STATES

Brarnaputra R.

(PAKISTAN)
Mohenjodaro
Indus R.
Ghaggar R.
THAR
DESERT

RAJAS
AND
REPUBLICS

(Karachi)

Benares
Ganges R.
Patna

MAGADHA

Sabarmutir R.
Narbada R.
(INDIA)

Tapti R.

20°

Gulf of
Cambay

(THE
DECCAN)

Bay
of
Bengal

Arabian Sea

TRIBAL
AND
LOCAL
GROUPS

15°

10°

INDIAN OCEAN

(SRI LANKA)

Mauryan Empire

Aryan lines of penetration
1200–500 B.C.E.

Consolidation of New Monarchies
1000–500 B.C.E.

• Site where some sort of remains
from the Indus Civilization have
been found.

Modern place names in parentheses

0   200   400 Miles

0   200   400 Kilometers

65°   70°   75°   80°   85°   90°

Harappan Culture

The first of the Indian civilizations may well have been the work of speakers of Dravidian languages like those spoken today in southern India. This ancient culture emerged, however, in the northwest, in what is now Pakistan.

Here, not long after the appearance of civilization in Mesopotamia and Egypt, the culture centered in the twin cities of Harappa and Mohenjodaro took shape.

The origins and development of Harappan culture, as the civilization that flourished along the banks of the Indus between 2500 and 1500 B.C.E. is called, remains to a large degree mysterious. We know that Harappan culture dominated an area larger than present-day Pakistan, leaving ruins scattered up and down the Indus basin and along the coast of the Arabian Sea. We know that it endured as long as a thousand years, from roughly 2500 to about 1500 B.C.E. We know nothing of Harappan kings and dynasties and wars, or even if they had kings or central government at all. But we can learn a good deal from the remains about the lives, the social organization, and even the attitudes of the people who produced them.

Harappan culture was built on agriculture, as most ancient civilizations were. As in Egypt and Mesopotamia, a system of dikes and drains enabled Harappan villagers to cultivate grain, especially wheat and barley, along the Indus and its tributaries. A considerable portion of this produce found its way down the rivers to the granaries of Harappa and Mohenjodaro, probably as taxes or tribute.

This ancient people worked copper and bronze, though stone tools continued to be used even after Neolithic times. They knew how to build bullock carts and small boats for transport. They exchanged goods, not only up and down the rivers of northern India but around the shores of the Arabian Sea and up the Persian Gulf to Mesopotamia. The rectangular Harappan seals inscribed with their distinctive script have in fact been found as far away as Persia and Egypt.

Both Mohenjodaro and Harappa seem to have been planned cities, with straight, right-angled streets and a remarkable system of underground drains and sewers. There were also citadels for defense, city granaries, and large public pools, perhaps intended for ceremonial washing in connection with religious observances.

Earlier suggestions that the two cities were the twin capitals of a Harappan empire now seem less convincing. Religious authority, however, may well have been combined with some degree of political control in Harappan India. It now seems likely that priests occupied the citadels, directed artisans and farmers at their labors, and even imposed their authority on the merchant families who lived in the large two-story houses in the cities. The chief god of this ruling elite may have been the horned male figure whose likeness has been found in many places, while the masses worshiped a female divinity heavy with jewelry and an elaborate hairstyle. Animals also seem to have been venerated, including particularly a long-horned bull that would retain its position as an object of religious worship in India thereafter.

Above all, perhaps, an overwhelmingly conservative cast of mind is indicated by what we know of Harappan civilization. For hundreds of years, the cities of the Indus were built and rebuilt on precisely the same rectilinear ground plan, and new houses were raised on the foundations of old. Foreign ideas seem to have been consciously rejected. Harappan merchants must have seen the elaborate irrigation works and the records on clay

The ruins of ancient Mohenjodaro shimmer beneath the blistering sun of the Punjab. Built of clay brick, the walls, streets, and stairs still follow the carefully laid-out plans of their vanished builders. (Anthony Esler)

tablets developed in the Tigris-Euphrates valley, for instance, yet these valuable innovations were apparently never introduced along the Indus.

The Aryan Invasions

The passing of Harappan culture is in some ways as obscure as its origins. Shifts in the course of the Indus or repeated flooding of the cities may have contributed to its decline. But the final fall of the Harappan world was almost certainly due to the intrusion of a new people into northwestern India: the Aryans.

The Aryan invaders who broke in upon the peaceful Indian world of 1500 B.C.E. were drifting tribes of Indo-European pastoralists and intermittent agriculturalists. They traveled like many nomadic peoples, seeking water and pasturage for their herds of cattle, horses, and sheep. Their gradual filtering through the passes of the Hindu Kush and down into northwest India was a folk migration lasting several centuries, not an organized military campaign like those of Mongols and other later nomads. But the impact of the Aryans was every bit as devastating.

We have no detailed contemporary accounts of the Aryan conquest. The Hindu Vedas, a collection of Aryan hymns to their northern gods, give us our best information, but they tend to be couched in highly figurative language. We do know that the newcomers charged into battle in chariots against Harappan foot soldiers, and there is good evidence that at least some of the Aryan tribes wielded iron weapons against the native bronze. We know that Indra, the Aryan war god, proudly styled himself *Purandara,* "Breaker of Cities," and that his followers left the corpses of their foes to rot in the streets of Mohenjodaro.

Cities, Family, and Caste

The period of the Aryan predominance in India, roughly 1500 to 500 B.C.E., thus began with the destruction of a civilization. Cities were abandoned for hundreds of years. Writing was forgotten. Much of Vedic India—the Aryan-dominated northern India described in the Vedas—returned to the village life that had characterized pre-Harappan, Neolithic India. Then, during the first half of the first millennium B.C.E., urban culture did reemerge—and its primary architects were the barbarian conquerors themselves.

The process began with an eastward migration by the restless Aryans from the Indus into the valley of the Ganges. The heavy rain forest there, which had resisted the bronze tools of Harappan times, yielded to the iron of the Aryans. The result was the opening up of rich soil for cultivation. The broad Ganges also contributed significantly to the economic development of the region, emerging as a busy avenue of trade.

Another aspect of the new India was the mingling of peoples and blending of cultures known as the Aryan-Dravidian synthesis. This subtle interpenetration of everything from religious beliefs to modes of production eventually turned the nomadic Aryans into settled farmers and their worship of anthropomorphic nature gods into the sophisticated concepts of Hinduism.

Accompanying the eastward migrations and the cultural synthesis of later Aryan centuries was the transformation of society. Some Aryans became sedentary landowners along the fertile Ganges valley, the more powerful of them using Dravidian farm laborers to work their land. Other Aryans became traders on the river itself. Crafts increased in complexity, providing heavy iron plows, trade goods, and the rough luxury items favored by the new, primarily Aryan aristocracy of landed and commercial wealth.

Here and there along the Ganges valley, finally, cities reappeared. Mere clearings in the jungle initially, these stockaded villages expanded into recognizable urban centers with substantial populations of artisans, traders, resident landowners, priests, warriors, and kings. Thus emerged such rude metropolises as Patna, the future capital of the Mauryan Empire, and Benares on the Ganges, still the holy city of the Hindus and perhaps the oldest continuously functioning city in the world.

Other institutions dominated Indian life in villages and cities—and from that day to this. The ancient Indian family seems to have been originally rather more open to power and prestige for women than would later be the case. Dravidian traditions, at least, were often matriarchal and matrilineal and allowed women to accumulate great wealth and enjoy high status in society. Among the invading Aryans, on the other hand, patriarchy prevailed. Wives were required to move to their husbands' families, bring substantial dowries, and accept their husbands' authority.

Even in the Aryan north, however, women could own property and run businesses. Some even became famous as philosophers or renowned for their religious piety in the Hindu or Buddhist traditions. Others found relative independence as temple dancers, prostitutes, or skilled courtesans, admired for their wit and gracious companionship as much as for their physical charms.

The caste system would play at least as important a role in Indian society. The word for caste was *varna,* meaning "color" and clearly referring to the old racial differences between conquerors and conquered. But the actual basis of caste divisions was social and economic rather than racial. These divisions represented a clear shift from color bar to social classes in Indian society.

The four original castes were *kshatriyas,* the warrior nobility; *brahmans,* the priests; *vaisyas,* landowners and merchants, and *sudras,* cultivators of the land and other manual laborers. As warfare became less perpetual and religion more complex and important, the ranking of the top two castes was reversed; priests came to be regarded as the highest caste, followed by warriors.

The caste system grew more complicated and more rigid, however, with the passing of the centuries. In time the system would subdivide into hundreds of occupational categories. The religious sanctions would grow more strict, forbidding all forms of social interaction between castes, from eating together to intermarriage. Even the touch of the "untouchables" at the bottom of Indian society would come to be thought of as polluting to a high-caste Indian.

But there was also an open-ended quality to the caste system that made it remarkably easy for later immigrants—and there were many of them—to be absorbed into Indian society. Newcomers in later centuries would be assigned a place in the structure of castes based on their traditional skill, craft, or occupation. Paradoxically, this undemocratic system of traditional classes thus made India a very tolerant society into which newcomers could be accepted with minimal social tension.

The Rise of the Rajas

Politically, the Aryan invaders had been loosely organized into tribes, clans, and families. Tribes were headed by chiefs or kings called *rajas,* most of them elected or chosen by rotation among the leading families. Councils of elders and assemblies of adult males normally shared political power with their kings. But the centuries of social evolution that carried India out of the dark ages following the Aryan conquest also transformed these simple tribal political institutions.

Most important, two new forms of state emerged in northern India: republics and kingdoms. The republican form retained many tribal institutions, including powerful councils and an oligarchy of leading families. In the developing kingdoms, however, the power of the *rajas* grew steadily at the expense of councils and assemblies. The new monarchies frequently became hereditary. They also developed administrative systems, headed by chief priests and military leaders, that exercised some degree of central control over the villages that composed the state.

As the caste system acquired religious support, so too did the institution of the monarchy. The brahmans conducted elaborate sacrifices, sometimes lasting as long as a year, to consecrate each new *raja.* The *rajas* in turn supported the evolving Hindu priesthood, establishing a close relationship between throne and altar. In India as elsewhere, the odor of sanctity thus hovered early over the kings of the Ganges, augmenting their growing authority over their people.

By the sixth century B.C.E. there were at least sixteen separate little states—many monarchies and some surviving republics—in the Ganges valley. These states retained some of their ties with the more traditional Aryan societies left behind in the Indus region to the west. They also continued the long-established Aryan tradition of incessant warfare among themselves and against the Dravidian peoples of the Deccan to the south.

Increasingly, however, one principality loomed larger than any of the others in the little world of the Ganges—the kingdom of Magadha. Its rulers, the Nanda clan, had by the fifth century B.C.E. expanded its power at the expense of its neighbors, pushing their way down the delta of the Ganges to the head of the Bay of Bengal. Domination of the Ganges valley thus came into the hands of a single state. From this power base the dynasty that followed the Nanda to the throne of Magadha would provide the foundation for the first genuine Indian empire—that of the Mauryas.

The Mauryas: Chandragupta

The Mauryan dynasty (321–185 B.C.E.) was the first to bring almost the entire subcontinent under a single government. And the earlier Mauryas—Kings Chandragupta and Asoka in particular—seem to have presided over one of those rare occurrences in human history: a genuine golden age.

Legend—which must here make do for history—has it that Chandragupta Maurya (321–297 B.C.E.) was the son of a concubine at the Nanda court. He is supposed to have seized the throne of Magadha from the last of the Nandas with the help of his mentor and evil genius, a shrewd but unscrupulous brahman named Kautilya. With their authority thus firmly established along the Ganges, Chandragupta and Kautilya turned their eyes to a field of operations much larger than any of the princelings of the Ganges had ever dreamed of—the whole of India.

Chandragupta first led the large and powerful army of Magadha back to the old Aryan heartland on the Indus for a confrontation with the Greek forces of Alexander's heir in that part of the world, the shrewd general Seleucus. The founder of the Seleucid dynasty, however, chose not to fight for his distant Indian satrapies. He ceded to Chandragupta not only the Indus and the five rivers of the Punjab, but also much of what is today Afghanistan.

Thus strengthened, the Mauryan leader turned back eastward and pushed the frontiers of his growing domain all the way to the mouth of the Ganges in Bengal. He thus came to rule an empire that stretched some two thousand miles across northern India, from the head of the Bay of Bengal in the east to the high passes of the Hindu Kush in the west.

We know little of Chandragupta Maurya personally. He is said to have been a severely autocratic ruler, and indeed he would almost surely have had to be to hold such an expanse of recently conquered territory together. A Greek ambassador records that the self-made emperor, who had seized the throne by force, employed a notoriously efficient secret police, and was heavily guarded in his palace at Patna.

Chandragupta's heir Bindusara expanded the Mauryan empire southward almost to the tip of the continent. Most of India thus acknowledged the overlordship of the Mauryas when the third of that redoubtable line came to the throne—Asoka, the most famous of them all.

The governing of such vast lands and peoples evidently required some doing in the third century before Christ. Some historians have suggested a rough system of more or less feudal allegiance on the part of local *rajas* to the Mauryan ruler at Patna. There is also some evidence of appointed Mauryan officials governing sizable chunks of the empire. However it was ruled, the Mauryan Empire was an amazing accomplishment, one of the most impressive feats of empire-building in all of ancient history.

Asoka, the Philosopher King

The reign of Asoka (ca. 268–231 B.C.E.) was an even more astonishing achievement than that of Chandragupta. Like the Greek Age of Pericles or the Augustan Age in Rome, the Age of Asoka seems to have been one of the high points of human governance.

Asoka's royal lion capital once crowned a seventy-foot-tall column at Sarnath, on the site of Buddha's first sermon. The style shows Persian influence, but the symbolism and the inspiration are distinctly Indian. Can you think of other cultures in which the lion was the royal beast? (Lauros-Giraudon/Art Resource)

Specific facts about the life of the celebrated Asoka are very hard to come by. He is reputed to have had to fight for his throne, a struggle that may have involved an older brother. He almost certainly completed the conquest of the eastern coastal region of Kalinga, on the Bay of Bengal. And he was beyond doubt a very pious king. On this thin scaffolding of fairly well-attested fact, an awesome edifice of tradition, elaboration, and symbolic truth has been raised.

It seems to have been the bloody Kalinga campaign that changed Asoka's life. Before he saw the heaped-up corpses and heard the wailing of women seeking their kindred among the dead, he was a Mauryan sovereign, wielding power and expanding the empire as his predecessors had. After the horrors of Kalinga, he was a man determined to live and rule in a different spirit.

That spirit was not that of Brahmanical Hinduism, but of Buddhism, a religion then two and a half centuries old in India. Asoka became a convert and apparently dedicated much of the rest of his life to the pursuit of *dharma*, the saving truth of the Buddha. He founded many shrines, sponsored a Buddhist council that dispatched missionaries to spread the faith as far as Tibet and Ceylon, and devoted the rest of his reign to Buddhist virtues, public service, and the spiritual unification of his vast empire.

Asoka declared his new principles in an extraordinary series of public inscriptions carved on the walls of caves and on stone pillars erected along high roads from the Northwest Frontier to Mysore in the south, from the Arabian Sea to the Bay of Bengal. Some of these sermons in stone clearly reflected Asoka's conversion, urging upon his people such Buddhist virtues as reverence for parents and teachers, compassion, religious piety, and *dharma*. Others declared the emperor's larger public policies, a firm intent to see that his government would follow righteousness and serve the people.

Asoka particularly advocated the distinctly Indian virtue of *ahimsa*—nonviolence— and promised to live by this principle as king. He would be mild toward his own subjects and would refrain from foreign conquests—as in fact he did. He renounced violence even toward animals, curtailed the mass animal sacrifices of Vedic days, and imposed a vegetarian regimen upon himself and his court.

A good deal of more practical public service accompanied Asoka's edicts. He dug public wells, built rest houses for weary travelers and clinics for the sick, and lined the roads of his empire with shade and fruit trees for the use of passersby. His masterpiece was the Grand Trunk Road, the commercial artery of North India, which ran many hundreds of miles from Patna to the Northwest Frontier and was still in use more than two thousand years later.

THE SOUL OF INDIA

The Lost Arts of Ancient India

Nature and history have not been kind to the earliest achievements of Indian art. The cities of Harappan India were built of clay, those of Mauryan times of wood, and only the faintest traces of either have survived. Yet enough fragments remain to give us some idea at least of the high levels of artistic accomplishment reached by the earliest dwellers along the Indus and the Ganges. This is especially so of the Harappan and Mauryan high points of India's ancient history.

The geometrical beauty of what we know of the "planned cities" of Harappa and Mohenjodaro, with their rectilinear street patterns and public bathing places, has already been mentioned. The meticulously laid-out blocks with water gurgling under the streets of residential structures rising two or more stories above them must have made an imposing spectacle in a world of Neolithic villages and tent-dwelling nomads.

The pieces of Harappan sculpture that remain—hundreds of carven seals and small figurines of terracotta, stone, or copper—reveal even more sophisticated traditions. The small rectangular seals usually depict animals, beautifully chiseled in low relief, as well as inscriptions in the unknown Harappan tongue. There are also examples of much more sophisticated sculpture, such as a lovely limestone torso only three and a half inches high, yet so exquisitely and naturalistically carved that it is often compared with the classic sculpture of Hellenic Greece. The lost civilization of the Indus would indeed have been a world worth seeing before the breakers of cities swept down from the north.

But the new civilization that eventually emerged in the Ganges valley to the east, the jungle-girt world of the first *rajas,* also nurtured builders of great skill. The palace of Chandragupta at Patna was described by Greek envoys as more splendid than the Persian cities of Susa and Ecbatana. Its pillared audience hall echoed the columns of Persian Persepolis. Patna itself stretched for miles along the river. Contemporary Buddhist bas-reliefs show high walls, many towers, and railed balconies over the streets. But all of it was made of wood cut from the great rain forests, and today only sections of the palisaded teak walls remain.

Among the Mauryan carvings that survive, most famous are the large animal figures—lions, bulls, and others—that top Asoka's famous inscribed pillars. In particular the conventionalized lion capitals of these smoothly polished forty- to fifty-foot freestanding columns show clear Persian influence. But they are nonetheless triumphs of Indian art.

There was a more completely Indian style in Mauryan sculpture, however, a style notably embodied in the massive statues of *yakshas,* or nature spirits. These big-bellied, larger-than-life figures are depicted naked to the waist, their powerful legs swathed in what looks like the *dhoti* that Indian men still wear in the villages. The *yakshis,* the female of this spiritual species, clearly reveal the supple, swaying stance, the narrow waist, and the swollen breasts that would be hallmarks of the female figure in Indian sculpture for centuries to come.

Epic Poetry: The Song of God

The literature that survives from these early Indian centuries is also sparse. There are, however, three literary peaks in that dawn age of Indian civilization. Two of these are epic poems: the *Mahabharata* and the *Ramayana.* The third is a hard-boiled treatise on statecraft called the *Arthasastra.*

The *Mahabharata* is, at 100,000 verses, the longest poem in the world. It is a Homeric saga of the struggle between two powerful Indian clans, the five Pandava brothers—particularly Prince Arjuna, the famous bowman—and their cousins the Kuravas. It clearly reflects the Aryan age of chariot fighters and kinship loyalties, of great archers, wild gamblers, and pious holy men wandering in the uncut Gangetic forest. Gods and other supernatural beings also play their part in a story that has a cosmic as well as a human dimension. The final victory of the Pandavas comes only after a colossal battle that, in the final version at least, seems to pit half the peoples of India against the other half.

The other great Indian epic, the *Ramayana,* is the more romantic story of how Prince Rama of one of the settled Ganges states rescues his lovely wife, Sita, from Ravana, the demon king of Ceylon. There is plenty of excitement in the adventures of Rama, Sita, and the friendly general of the apes, Hanuman, first exiled in the northern forests, then fighting epic battles in the south. But the original adventure story has been thoroughly reworked by brahman editors, so that Rama emerges as the ideal Hindu man, Sita as the perfect woman, and their relationship a model of the sort of conjugal loyalty and devotion expected in the settled agricultural states of the middle of the first millennium B.C.E.

The political commentary called the *Arthasastra,* attributed to Kautilya, Chandragupta's unscrupulous chief advisor, is a tract for a ruthless time of territorial state-building. For Kautilya, as apparently for his royal master, efficiency and success are the sole criteria of princely governance; morality is never taken into account. The people are to be kept in line by any means that work, including draconian laws vigorously enforced, hordes of bureaucrats, and battalions of what we would today call secret police.

A hard-nosed realist, Kautilya advises the shrewd *raja* to consider all his neighbors as enemies and all states beyond that inner ring as potential allies against the future victims between them. The *Arthasastra* thus projects a grimly convincing image of political and diplomatic affairs among the raw new states along the Ganges.

Before pious brahmans had done with the *Mahabharata* and the *Ramayana,* on the other hand, central figures in both these epic adventures had turned out to be incarnations of the god Vishnu or of Brahman, the spiritual foundation of the universe. This is illustrated most vividly in the section of the *Mahabharata* called the *Bhagavadgita,* the famous Indian *Song of God.* This best-loved of all Hindu texts is a dialogue between Arjuna the archer, youngest of the Pandava brothers, and his divine charioteer Krishna. Its climax comes when Krishna reveals that he is actually the incarnation of Brahman, the divine ground of all things, in a vision that dazzles Arjuna like "a thousand suns":

> O Lord of the universe [cries Arjuna] I see You without beginning, middle or end . . . endowed with numberless hands, having the moon and the sun for Your eyes and the blazing fire for Your mouth, and scorching the universe with Your radiance.[1]

The great victories of Prince Rama, the god-hero of the *Ramayana,* have become major festivals in the Hindu religious calendar. The feast of Diwali, a night of lights, candy, and toys for children rather like Christmas in the West, celebrates the victorious return of Rama and Sita to their kingdom in this ancient epic, which is still widely read. Even Hanuman the monkey prince has his share of temples and festivals over the length and breadth of India.

Hinduism: From the Sacred Cow to Brahman

We know little or nothing about the religion of Harappan India. Worship of a mother goddess, mentioned earlier, seems a likely explanation for the many small female cult figures found in Harappa and Mohenjodaro. Harappan seals point to some veneration of animals, and one in particular may indicate a Harappan origin for the cult that was to grow up around the great god Shiva as Lord of the Beasts.

The Aryans brought to India the gods of the northern steppes, gods of thunder and sun—Indra, the god of war; Agni, the spirit of the sacrificial fire; and Varuna, lord of the big sky over the endless Eurasian plains. Aryans sacrificed to these divinities, slaughtering dozens or even hundreds of animals, and sometimes human beings too. The hymns, prayers, and rituals committed to memory syllable by syllable by the brahman priests were passed down to become the core of the oldest Hindu scriptures, the Vedas (1000–500 B.C.E.).

Hinduism as it developed in Vedic times involved a merging of the pantheons of the Aryan invaders and the conquered Dravidians, and perhaps even a certain gentling of the brawling gods of the breakers of cities. Most important, there was a striking evolution from naïve anthropomorphic divinities to a profound philosophic search for the deepest spiritual principle of the universe, the Brahman of later Hindu thought.

For ancient Hindus, there were many nature spirits like the *yakshas* and *yakshis* mentioned above, while hordes of demons lurked in the shadows, ready to tear and rend the souls of the unwary. Living among the teeming life of the Ganges rain forest, early Hindus saw some of their gods in the shape of monkeys, snakes, or the sacred cow, which was the measure of wealth and source of life for their pastoral Aryan ancestors. To this day sacred cows browse more or less unopposed in the lanes and market squares of Indian villages. Grocers shoo them away from the vegetables and pedestrians step around the piles of dung they leave in their wake, but no one would deny them the streets.

The most important of all the gods were—and are—Brahma, the rather hazy creator god; Vishnu, the preserver of the universe; and Shiva, the four-armed dancing divinity who is often presented simplistically as the destroyer of all things. These three were in

---

[1]*The Bhagavadgita or The Song Divine* (Gorakhpur, India: Gita Press, 1975), pp. 233–235.

time subsumed theologically under the persona of Brahman, the universal spiritual principle underlying all that exists. Brahman is not a personal god at all, but the unimaginable spiritual essence permeating the entire cosmos, "the One . . . hidden in all things."

The fabric of Hindu belief generated such peculiarly Indian concepts as the brotherhood of all living beings, reincarnation, karma, and *ahimsa*. For Hindus, all life is one and all living things have souls. This view was amplified by a later belief, first expressed around 500 B.C.E. in the philosophical dialogues called the Upanishads, in reincarnation, the transmigration of the soul. The Hindu doctrine of transmigration holds that each human soul is reincarnated, or reborn, in the body of some other creature—human, animal, or even supernatural—over and over again. In precisely what form one is reincarnated depends on *karma*, the "actions" one takes during one's present life. If you lead a good and pious life, you may be reborn as a brahman or other high-caste Indian; if you wallow in self-indulgence and sin, you may live your next life in the body of a rooting hog or a worm to be crushed by any passing sandal. From belief in reincarnation and the brotherhood of all life, finally, sprang the doctrine of *ahimsa*, or nonviolence. Arising first among Buddhists and Jains (see below), it eventually permeated all of Indian society.

VOICES FROM THE PAST

This discussion from the Hindu *Upanishads*—religious speculations on the philosophical dimensions of the faith—depict a teacher and a pupil discussing a key point for a religion whose temples swarm with gods and demons: How many gods are there, really? How would an ancient Egyptian or Greek have answered such a question? An ancient Hebrew?

1. Then Vadagdha Sakalya asked him: "How many gods are there, O Yajnavalkya?" He replied with this very Nivid: "As many as are mentioned in the Nivid of the hymn of praise addressed to the Visvedevas, viz. three and three hundred, three and three thousand."
"Yes," he said, and asked again: "How many gods are there really, O Yajnavalkya?"
"Thirty-three," he said.
"Yes," he said, and asked again: "How many gods are there really, O Yajnavalkya?"
"Six," he said.
"Yes," he said, and asked again: "How many gods are there really, O Yajnavalkya?"
"Three," he said.
"Yes," he said, and asked again: "How many gods are there really, O Yajnavalkya?"
"Two," he said.
"Yes," he said, and asked again: "How many gods are there really, O Yajnavalkya?"
"One and a half (adhyardha)," he said.
"Yes," he said, and asked again: "How many gods are there really, O Yajnavalkya?"
"One," he said.
"Yes," he said, and asked: "Who are these three and three hundred, three and three thousand?"
2. Yajnavalkya replied: "They are only the various powers of them . . .
He asked: "Who is the one god?"
Yajnavalkya replied: "Breath (prana), and he is Brahman (the Sutratman), and they call him That (tyad)."

S. E. Frost, *The Sacred Writings of the World's Great Religions* (New York: McGraw-Hill, 1972, pp. 23–24.)

The heart of developing Hinduism, however, lay not in its ceremonies and scriptures but in the central role of the mystical element in Indian religion. As early as the first millennium B.C.E., Hindus decided that they might escape the endless round of lives filled with human suffering through the mystical concentration of their psychic forces known as meditation.

The goal of the yogi's meditation is not "life everlasting" for the individual soul but rather the submergence of the ego in the supreme unity of Brahman. This mystic merging of the self with the spiritual oneness of the universe is sometimes compared to the dissolving of a drop of water in the ocean. It is to be achieved through spiritual enlightenment—the simple realization that all differences are illusions, or *maya,* that all that really exists is the totality of Brahman.

The Naked Philosophers

Hinduism as it emerged in the first millennium B.C.E. had already established itself as a basic social cement for evolving Hindu society. The ancient faith sanctified the caste system and sanctioned the rule of the *rajas.* The brahmans were the highest caste in society and could demand rich rewards for putting their ritualistic expertise at the service of rulers and people.

But the middle of the first millennium B.C.E. was a time of many changes and strains in Indian society. Out of these tensions a restless new impulse toward spiritual exploration emerged in northern India. In particular, this spirit produced the gurus (spiritual teachers) of the sixth century whom Western envoys would later describe as *gymnosophists*—the "naked philosophers."

Some of these wandering holy men were in fact naked, going unclothed in monsoon rains and under the Indian sun to discipline the flesh. Others starved themselves for long periods or engaged in exhausting exercises that would soon develop into the sacred discipline of yoga. A few sought to rediscover ancient sorceries in backwoods tribes, or even attempted spiritual growth through alcohol and orgiastic sexual practices. Of all the gurus of this age of intellectual ferment, however, two left by far the most important imprints on the Indian mind—Mahavira and Gautama Buddha.

Mahavira (ca. 540–476 B.C.E.), the founder of the religion of the Jains ("Conquerors") actually accepted a broad range of conventional Hinduism, from the caste system to reincarnation. But he did have some extreme notions—such as complete celibacy, total honesty, and the rejection of all earthly possessions. Like the most extravagant seekers of his generation, he practiced rigorous asceticism, meditated intensively, and went naked in rain and sun.

His major contribution to Indian thought, however, was the doctrine of *ahimsa,* which he defined as the nonviolent refusal to take a life. In pursuit of *ahimsa,* the Jains carried brooms to sweep insects from under their feet, fed ants, and filtered the water they drank and the air they breathed in order to avoid accidentally extinguishing some minute form of life. Their piety took extreme forms. But it sometimes takes extremists to get a hearing for a new doctrine, and the notion of nonviolence was clearly thrust into the mainstream of Indian thought by the extravagant commitment of the followers of Mahavira.

Buddhism: The Teachings of Prince Siddartha

One approaches the historic Siddartha, or Gautama Buddha (563–483 B.C.E.), through a thick incrustation of image and legend. And the fairy-tale version of Siddartha's life has an undeniable charm. He grew up in splendor as a king's son, protected from any sight of human suffering. On one fatal day in his youth, however, he beheld a sick man, an old man, and finally a dead man—and learned that such evils came in time to all human beings. The stricken prince thereupon left his young wife and infant son and set out to find a way to escape the wheel of human misery. After many years of self-denial, he found enlightenment at last under the great bodhi (or bo) tree at Gaya, and devoted the rest of his life to spreading his new gospel.

He was not actually a *raja*'s son: His Sakya people were an undeveloped hill tribe among whom the headship rotated, his father being one of a number of sturdy *kshatriyas*—farmers who had a right to a turn as chief. But the rest of the legend—the years of rigorous asceticism, the meditation under the bo tree at Gaya, the famous first sermon in the deer park at Sarnath outside Benares, the monkish order he founded, and the long lifetime of wandering the roads of India with his disciples—all these are likely enough, given the spiritual ferment of the times.

Gautama Buddha found the fundamental cause of all suffering in one great human failing: desire, the almost universal human attachment to the good things of this world. Desire in turn fosters the central human illusion: that the things of this world are real. The Buddha agreed with orthodox Hinduism that worldly things are a grand illusion, a fantasy world of *maya*. Behind this illusory separateness of things, he further agreed, lies an ineffable spiritual unity—what the Hindus called Brahman. Buddha himself tended not to call it anything. His goal was to get there. Escape from desire, from the wheel of life and the *maya* world, was to be found along the eight-fold path that Buddha preached for half a century in the growing cities and along the jungle trails of Gangetic India.

The eight steps to Nirvana—union with the ultimate spiritual reality of things—begin with the recognition and rejection of selfish worldly desires as the blind follies they are. Next comes the cultivation of unselfishness, compassion, and honesty; then rejection of such injury to others as murder, theft, and adultery; and finally the choice of a source of livelihood that does not bring harm to other living things. The path leads through a turning away from evil thoughts and all physical concerns to deep meditation and final escape from the wheel of unending lives through Buddhahood—that is, enlightenment—and Nirvana, the extinction of the suffering ego in the great ocean of eternal peace.

Buddha and his followers wore only the simplest of robes, owned nothing but their begging bowls and staves, traveled always on foot, and never slept under a roof—a striking contrast with the patrician, sometimes greedy and worldly brahmans. The Buddha presented his faith to live by in simple language that the layperson could understand, without the elaborate theology of developed Hinduism. Perhaps most radically, he accepted people of all castes as equals on the eightfold path.

Men joined him to escape the chains of caste, women to break with the exhausting load of family obligations. Men and women both shaved their heads and donned the saffron robes of the mendicant in search of the higher truth he preached. His orders of monks and nuns would carry his doctrines far across the eastern half of Asia over the next thousand years.

The results are still visible today. You can still see Buddhist temples in the People's Republic of China or at Kamakura in businesslike modern Japan. And in Tibetan monasteries beyond the Himalayas, the gold-painted Buddhas of the Past, the Present, and the Future gaze down at you over flickering candles of yak butter.

Paradoxically, after becoming royal orthodoxy under sovereigns such as Asoka, Buddhism would all but die out in India in later centuries. But there are temples in all the architectual styles of the East in the Buddhist shrine at Bodh Gaya on the Ganges today. There pilgrims from many lands remove their shoes and pass reverently under the shadow of the giant bo tree where Prince Siddartha found enlightenment and into the hall where a huge gold statue of the Buddha still meditates on human folly and desire.

THE FIRST CHINESE DYNASTIES

The Middle Kingdom of East Asia

Sprawling across the far end of Eurasia, China is the world's third largest nation today. It has the largest population: Well over a billion strong, the Chinese constitute a fifth of the population of the earth. A great power and a powerful influence on all its neighbors, China is to East Asia what India is to South Asia—and then some.

Nor is China's preeminence a new thing in the world: It has probably been the most populous of nations since its first unification in the third century B.C.E. Cut off from other centers of civilization by formidable barriers such as the Gobi Desert, the jungles of Southeast Asia, and the Pacific, the giant of East Asia has inevitably emerged as the predominant force in its own very substantial corner of the globe, from Tibet to Korea and Japan.

Isolation and cultural supremacy have bred a strong belief in China's uniqueness, a sense of being "the Middle Kingdom," the center of civilization, indeed the only civilized people in a barbarous world. This conviction—which China shares with many other peoples—would help to hold together a huge nation marked by great geographical diversity over many centuries.

China today is slightly larger than the United States, stretching, like America, roughly three thousand miles from west to east and two thousand north to south. The land stairsteps down from the inhospitable Tibetan Plateau, the world's highest landmass, to the densely populated sea-level plains along the Pacific rim. North to south, China is divided into three main regions, two of them defined by great rivers. The Huanghe (Yellow River) of north China, with its light yellow loess soil blown south from the Gobi, has been the political core of Chinese development. Beijing, the political capital, is the metropolis of north China today. The Yangzi River of central China is the main artery of a spreading web of tributaries and lakes that water some of the nation's most fertile farm land. Central China, with its wheat fields and rice paddies, bamboo groves and mulberry trees, has a major outlet at Shanghai today. The more mountainous south is monsoon-drenched and semitropical, rich in rice and tea production, the nation's historic commercial center and not infrequently the center of revolt. Guangzhou (Canton) and Hong Kong are its gateways to the world.

In the northeastern corner of this huge and ancient land, then, another center of civilization emerged sometime in the second millennium B.C.E.

Neolithic Chinese still hunted and fished along the Yellow River, but they also farmed, cultivating millet and vegetables with the aid of hoes and other polished-stone tools. They domesticated dogs and pigs—both for meat—and oxen and horses for their labor. They made pottery much like that of other Neolithic people all across Eurasia.

These Stone Age farmers and hunters, squatting before their round mud houses along the Huanghe and its tributaries, did not of course see themselves as precursors of anyone. It is barely possible, however, that they did recognize the crucial change that they had pioneered: the invention of agriculture in the Far East. For it was on the backs of laboring Chinese farmers down the centuries, and with the leisure that labor made possible for a favored few, that one of the great world civilizations would be built.

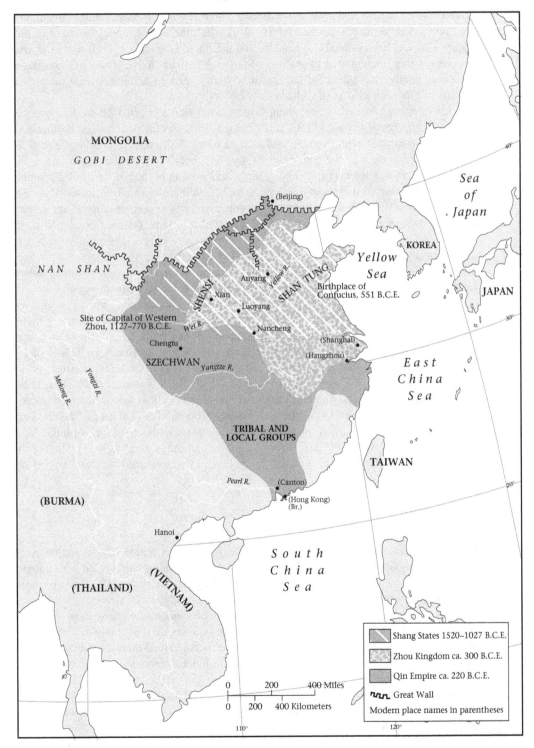

MONGOLIA

GOBI DESERT

NAN SHAN

(Beijing)

SHENSI

Xian

Anyang

Yellow R.

SHAN TUNG

Luoyang

Site of Capital of Western
Zhou, 1127–770 B.C.E.

Wei R.

Nancheng

Chengtu

SZECHWAN

Yangtze R.

Mekong R.

Yongzi R.

TRIBAL AND
LOCAL GROUPS

(BURMA)

Hanoi

(THAILAND)

(VIETNAM)

Pearl R.

(Canton)

(Hong Kong)
(Br.)

Sea
of
Japan

KOREA

Yellow
Sea

Birthplace of
Confucius, 551 B.C.E.

JAPAN

(Shanghai)

(Hangzhou)

East
China
Sea

TAIWAN

South
China
Sea

	Shang States 1520–1027 B.C.E.
	Zhou Kingdom ca. 300 B.C.E.
	Qin Empire ca. 220 B.C.E.
ᴧᴧᴧ	Great Wall

Modern place names in parentheses

0   200   400 Miles

0   200   400 Kilometers

110°

120°

40°

30°

20°

The Shang State

Traditionally, Chinese history begins with the Three Dynasties—the Xia, the Shang, and the Zhou. Of these, the Xia may have been mythical; the Shang, once dismissed as legendary also, has been proved real enough; and the Zhou, China's longest historic dynasty, is as thoroughly documented as any age so far back is likely to be. It was in the wake of the Zhou, finally, that China for the first time found genuine unity under the short-lived dynasty of Qin—the climax of China's early history.

As far as we presently know, then, Chinese civilization began with the hazily documented Shang dynasty, roughly 1500 to 1000 B.C.E. This was the period when northeastern China moved from Neolithic agricultural villages along the banks of the Huanghe to cities and kingdoms. It also saw the emergence of some of China's most ancient traditions.

Granted, most subjects of the Shang kings still lived in pit houses or similarly simple dwellings and worked their fields with stone tools. But there were other classes of society too. There were skilled artisans, workers in bronze and silk as well as in stone and ceramics. There was an embryonic merchant class that traded at some distance in salt and shells and the metals needed by the bronze workers, especially copper and tin. At the top of Shang society, finally, there was an aristocracy who hunted, fought, and enjoyed the finer things of Shang life—jade jewelry, bronze weapons and ritual vessels, silken robes, leather armor, and four-horse chariots from which to direct their frequent wars.

Presiding over this developing society were kings who, despite their titles, enjoyed only very limited powers. Shang kings were above all military leaders, defending northeastern China from border raids or embarking upon campaigns for loot or tribute. In peacetime, the monarch performed essential religious rituals and sacrifices on behalf of his people, entreating the gods for victory or good harvests. In performing these narrowly defined but important functions, rulers were aided by a still modest number of officials. These included expert scribes and diviners, the earliest specialists in the Chinese administration.

This Shang state was thus probably a loose confederation of clan states. The clans acknowledged the Shang king as leader in war and as a special intermediary with the gods. Beyond that, the power of the monarchy was almost certainly circumscribed by that of the more ambitious nobles. Royal authority probably seldom extended very far beyond the capital.

Families, Cities, Culture

The core of Chinese society has always been the traditional Chinese family, and the roots of this institution probably go back at least this far. The Shang father ruled with patriarchal authority, owning all property, arranging marriages, dictating to all other members. "Filial piety"—reverent obedience to the father—was the highest of virtues.

Women were expected to obey their fathers in childhood, their husbands after marriage, and their sons as they grew older. Men could take more than one wife, but women could not even remarry if their husbands died. Sons were valued more than daughters, because only males could perform the all-important religious ceremonies in honor of ancestors discussed below.

As we will see, an older woman might have considerable influence over a son who had inherited headship of the family. But in the ideal Chinese family, at least, woman's lot was not an enviable one.

Shang cities were substantial if in some ways rudimentary accomplishments. The city walls, sometimes as high as thirty feet, were made of pounded earth and must have involved the regimented labor of thousands of workers. Within the walls were the large houses of nobles and kings and the temples of the gods, all constructed of wattle and daub hung on a framework of heavy timber.

Yet this newly civilized folk also produced the beginnings at least of one of the most sophisticated cultures the world has seen. Shang artisans, for instance, learned very early to alloy bronze out of copper, tin, and sometimes other metals. Writing also developed early, as a means of recording prophecies. Religion was polytheistic, embracing a welter of nature gods, goddesses, and other spiritual beings. These included the ancestral sky god Shangdi, later referred to as Tian (Heaven), and the Dragon Woman, as well as countless local spirits of earth and air and water. Among Shang aristocrats, however, one other element of Chinese religious belief began to take shape: the worship of ancestors.

The elite seem to have believed that Shangdi in particular was too awesome and elevated to be approached directly. Therefore they prayed to their own most celebrated ancestors, now transported to that spirit world where Shangdi reigned, to intercede with the god on behalf of living generations here below. This procedure had the practical advantage of giving the aristocracy, who alone *had* celebrated ancestors, exclusive access to the greatest of the gods. Ancestor worship thus effectively excluded all other classes from any concern with public affairs.

The veneration of ancestors was therefore a powerful conservative force from the beginning. It was not the least important legacy from the Shang period of Chinese history.

The Kings of the Western Zhou

The Zhou dynasty, which seized power in the eleventh century B.C.E., would carry China from its first civilization to the age of Confucius, China's most revered philosopher.

According to the traditional dynastic histories, the house of Shang reigned, and sometimes ruled, for more than five hundred years during the second half of the second millennium B.C.E. The last Shang king, however, was a royal monster, a man steeped in crimes against gods and humanity. Then, out of the west, came two brothers, King Wu and the famous Duke of Zhou, at the head of a great army. These two princes of the western tributary state of Zhou are the heroes of this version of the change of dynasties.

The Zhou dynasty did in fact come to power in north China shortly before the year 1000 B.C.E. This house was to be recognized as at least the nominal overlord of China's political heartland until the year 221 B.C.E. Within this broad tract of time, two major periods are customarily distinguished: the comparatively successful Western Zhou comprising the first two and a half centuries of the period, and the long debacle of the Eastern Zhou, five hundred years of anarchy under a house that reigned in name only. And yet, paradoxically, the turbulent later-Zhou centuries may have seen more progress than the more renowned reigns that began the dynasty.

The Western Zhou is so called from the fact that the early Zhou kings continued to rule from their hereditary lands in the west. Here in the mountain-girt Wei River valley, on the edge of civilization, they were able to retain the martial spirit of border lords while profiting from the more advanced institutions of the principalities they had conquered to the east. Their nominal rule reached as far north as the future site of Beijing, as far south as the Yangzi valley of central China.

Zhou Feudalism

Zhou China was essentially a feudal state, as Shang China had been. The kings of the Western Zhou did, however, boast a more elaborate bureaucracy than those of Shang times. They also propounded a far more ingenious—and influential—set of justifications for the power they had seized with the sword.

At the top of the Zhou administration was a chief advisor who could sometimes be the actual formulator of royal policies. The prototype of this traditional chief minister was the Duke of Zhou, who labored by his brother King Wu's side through the long struggle that led to Zhou supremacy. The best of later-Zhou ministers strove to emulate this spirit of selfless dedication to the welfare of the monarchy. The worst of them exploited their power for their own benefit.

Beneath the king and his chief minister, six administrative departments, charged with such matters as agriculture, war, public works, and religious observances, developed under the Zhou. These administrators collected tribute and issued communiqués, though the tributary princes were often too involved with their own affairs to pay much attention to royal officials.

Zhou kings, or their shrewder advisors, did, however, evolve what became the standard Chinese rationalization for their rule: the Mandate of Heaven. As Sons of Heaven, Zhou rulers claimed to govern by a special mandate, a divine charge to govern the land. They further claimed that it was the heinous crimes of the last Shang king that had led Heaven to dispatch the princes of Zhou to replace the Shang. This ingenious doctrine had only a single drawback. Any failing of moral force in the Zhou themselves—or any striking series of public calamities, from earthquakes to invasions—could lead to the charge that the Zhou in their turn had lost the Mandate of Heaven. And without the clearly perceived divine right to rule, how long would the descendants of the Zhou continue to govern China?

The doctrine of the Mandate of Heaven thus introduced by apologists for the Zhou dynasty remained an essential feature of Chinese political theory. The chaotic rise and fall of later Chinese dynasties was explained by this cosmic pattern of interrupted harmony and reestablished order. It was a pattern that would be repeated over and over again throughout the long history of the Middle Kingdom.

The Eastern Zhou: Progress in a World at War

In the eighth century a military disaster signaled a fundamental turn in the fortunes of the dynasty—but this one a turn for the worse. Barbarians broke through into the Wei valley and sacked the Zhou capital. The monarchy thereupon prudently moved the capital eastward to Luoyang, in the civilized heart of northeast China. It was, apparently, a mistake.

From that time on, the authority of the Eastern Zhou—as the royal house is henceforth called—declined to the merest nominal allegiance. Feudal barons frequently failed in their tribute payments, sometimes refused even to respond when summoned to support the king in arms. During the latter part of the Eastern Zhou—the so-called Warring States period (fourth and third centuries B.C.E.)—this loose feudal empire dissolved entirely into a patchwork of separate states and clashing ambitions.

The Eastern Zhou has traditionally been considered a long decline after the more coherently ordered Western Zhou. More recently, however, historians have discovered some strikingly progressive elements in the politically anarchic later-Zhou centuries.

Veterans of the last wars of the Warring States, this soldier and his horse helped bring the Qin dynasty to power and unify China for the first time. These figures were among the hundreds of life-sized clay statues excavated from the underground tomb of China's First Emperor, Shi Huangdi. (Courtesy of the Cultural Relics Bureau, the People's Republic of China, and the Metropolitan Museum of Art, New York. Photograph by Seth Joel.)

Perhaps most obvious—but no less important—the population grew substantially. By the third century the civilized areas of northeastern and central China had the largest population of any center of civilization in the world. The dynasty that succeeded in unifying the warring states would thus emerge as master of the world's most populous nation, a rank China would continue to hold down to the present.

Economic development seems to have accompanied demographic growth. For one thing, China moved from the Bronze Age to the Iron Age during the later Zhou, producing iron axes, scythes, plows, and swords from approximately 500 B.C.E. on. New crops such as soybeans were introduced, and large-scale irrigation works sponsored by later-Zhou princes are mentioned for the first time. The merchant class particularly seems to have prospered during the Warring States period, making use of new military roads, and the first real Chinese coins, copper "cash" with holes in the center. Strung on cords, copper cash was from that time on China's most common medium of exchange.

Some historians have also detected a decline in the nobility and the rise of a new, self-made social type in the more fluid society of the Eastern Zhou. Men of humble background could rise at the courts of competing princes on the basis of energy, intelligence, and expertise in war or politics. This was especially so if the ambitious new man also possessed the winning social grace and air of spiritual force called *shi*. Shi was a debonair mastery of gentlemanly forms, religious ritual, and traditional wisdom that seems to have gained the pushiest social climber an entrée at the courts of the warring states.

Finally, the later Zhou was one of China's cultural golden ages. The book was invented during these centuries, and learning came to be respected for the first time in China. Princes and barons supported schools at their capital cities that would teach an aristocratic elite reading and music as well as archery and chariot fighting. From court to court, finally, there wandered not only unemployed officials and military commanders but sages as well. For the later Zhou was also, as we shall see, the Age of Confucius.

THE QIN DYNASTY UNIFIES CHINA

The Rise of the House of Qin

The state of Qin was located in modern Shaanxi in the mountain-walled valley of the Wei River, where the old Zhou capital had been. But the kings of Qin, rising to prominence eight hundred years later in China's social evolution, developed along very different lines from the loose feudalism of Zhou.

The Qin began with much of the border-lord military spirit that had distinguished their predecessors. They too evolved as a society on the dangerous edge, between the barbarian intruders from the north and west and the heart-land of Chinese civilization to the east. To this militant heritage they added a rigorous new approach to governance—a philosophy known as Legalism. The result was a potent mix of military toughness and authoritarian control that carried the Qin state to mastery of China in the third century B.C.E.

Defending the mountainous northwestern frontiers of Chinese civilization against raiders on horseback from the northern steppes, Qin warriors became expert cavalrymen themselves. During the fourth century B.C.E., the Qin kings used this cavalry arm to conquer a number of neighboring states in the northwest. In the third century, finally, they turned their powerful cavalry and the large armies recruited from their new subject states upon the civilized Zhou states to the east.

Discussion of the theory of Legalism may be deferred to a later section on the philosophical schools. In practice, however, Qin Legalism meant emphasis on law and punishment, rationalization and strengthening of the bureaucracy, and autocratic control from the center. Legalist administrators made appointments and promotions exclusively on the basis of merit and pushed policies that would keep the whole nation productively at work for the good of the state. They also put heavy stress on the military, planted secret police across the land to spy on the populace, and inflicted savage—if rigorously impartial—punishments for infractions of their draconian laws.

In the middle of the third century B.C.E., then, this militarily powerful, rigorously authoritarian state marched east against the collection of separate little kingdoms that still formally acknowledged the primacy of the decaying house of Zhou. The King of Qin was a young and aggressive prince surrounded by cadres of ambitious advisors, most prominent among them Li Si, a latter-day Legalist. The Qin army was ready, the rival Zhou monarchy moribund. Luoyang fell, and with it the house of Zhou.

One by one thereafter the other major states were overwhelmed, gobbled up, as a famous Chinese historian later put it, "like a silkworm devouring a mulberry leaf." In 221 B.C.E., the last of them fell. The King of Qin assumed a new throne, and Chinese chroniclers later gave him a new name and title to go with it—Qin Shi Huangdi, the First Emperor.

Shi Huangdi: The First Emperor

Shi Huangdi is one of those larger-than-life figures who sometimes erupt into history, wrenching events out of their time-worn course, dazzling and often horrifying their contemporaries. "Cracking his long whip," even a hostile Chinese historian admitted, "he drove the universe before him, swallowing up the eastern and the western Zhou and overthrowing the feudal lords. He ascended to the highest position and ruled the six directions, scourging the world with his rod, and his might shook the four seas."[2]

Certainly Shi Huangdi was a man of feverish energy. By 221 B.C.E. he ruled the largest part of modern China. But he did not stop there. His armies hurled back the nomadic barbarians of the northern steppes and pushed far south into what is today Vietnam. His archers and spearmen in their bronze and leather armor, his lumbering chariots and light cavalry clattered back and forth across the land, garrisoned the passes, held princes and people alike in awe. He was by far the greatest conqueror China had yet seen.

Yet it is the domestic achievements of Huangdi that most boggle the historical imagination. In the decade left him after unification, the First Emperor seems almost to have lifted the land out of one path and set it upon another.

Almost at a stroke he abolished both the warring states and the feudal system that had spawned them. The strongholds of the defeated princes were destroyed, and the nobles of the old order were decimated or compelled to live in the new Qin capital under the watchful eye of the emperor. The new China was divided into thirty-six districts, each with a military and a civil governor, and into many more country-sized subdistricts, each with its appointed administrator. A centralized bureaucracy thus for the first time genuinely governed a united nation in East Asia.

Within the nation Shi Huangdi labored to effect a degree of uniformity never attempted before. He standardized weights and measures for the whole of China, issued a uniform coinage, and commissioned scholars to produce a simplified standard set of Chinese characters for writing in all parts of the empire. Even the length of cart axles was made uniform by decree, so that cart wheels could all follow the same ruts in the soft loess soil of north China.

The Great Wall of China

Like kings and conquerors in other lands, the First Emperor also embarked upon an astonishing number of large-scale building projects. Roads crisscrossed the empire as never before, facilitating troop movements but also encouraging merchants to ply their trade once more. Canals were dug or refurbished, both for inland transport and to irrigate cropland. The emperor constructed elaborate palaces in his capital, including one allegedly large

---

[2]Theodore de Bary, Wing-tsit Chan, and Burton Watson, eds., *Sources of Chinese Tradition*, Vol. 1 (New York: Columbia University Press, 1960), p. 151.

enough to house ten thousand people. And he built himself a tomb at Chang'an—modern Xi'an—which traditional Chinese historians described as one of the miracles of the age. And in fact it awed a later age when parts of it were excavated in the 1970s.

All this, and still more. Somewhere between conquest and unification, among irrigation projects, royal palaces, and tombs, the First Emperor found time to build the Great Wall of China. In its final form, this amazing monument would stretch for fifteen hundred miles across China's northern frontier. It would average twenty-five feet in height over all those hundreds of miles, with watchtowers every two or three hundred yards. Huangdi did not build it all, of course. Sections had already been constructed by the lords of the northernmost Zhou states, and much of the emperor's work consisted of joining up these sections into a continuous barrier. Later rulers and dynasties revamped and added to the marvel, and most of the ramparts up which tourists toil and camera-toting Chinese teenagers mill today were actually raised in the sixteenth century C.E. rather than the third century B.C.E. Yet the Great Wall remains a monument to the will and vision of Shi Huangdi, and one of the undoubted wonders of the world.

To accomplish so much in so little time, the First Emperor had to drive his people mercilessly. Heavy taxes were laid on the peasant population. Forced labor was utilized for his enormous building projects. Whole populations were moved from one part of the country to another to carry out the emperor's orders. It was a triumph of the will unparalleled in China's ancient history—and one that many laboring Chinese probably could just as well have done without.

Legalists like Li Si particularly urged Huangdi to clamp down on intellectuals, the Confucian officials and other philosophers who objected to the rigors of the new regime. The books of philosophers who disagreed with the Legalists were collected and burned. Dissidents were imprisoned or executed, sometimes by the hundreds. They were harsh measures, but the men around the emperor justified them by the most powerful of Legalist arguments: success.

And then, when the first empire died suddenly in 210 B.C.E., the vaunted Legalist order collapsed like a house of cards.

Huangdi's chief ministers turned upon his heirs and then upon each other. Intrigue, executions, and royal suicide turned the dreamlike pleasure palaces of the First Emperor's capital into a nightmare world. Popular uprisings broke out among a people pushed to the breaking point and beyond. Within four years of Huangdi's death the dynasty of Qin followed its founder into extinction.

The unifier and his house perished; his capital was ravaged and looted, his tomb defiled. The Mandate of Heaven passed on to new hands. But the First Emperor's greatest achievement, the united China to which the Qin (Ch'in) dynasty had given its name, lived on.

ART AND THOUGHT OF ANCIENT CHINA

Art: Bronze Dragons and Clay Soldiers

There was much that was harsh and violent about the history of the first three Chinese dynasties. But even a sketchy survey of the architecture and sculpture, the poetry and philosophy of the first millennium and a half of Chinese history will strikingly brighten the perhaps too grim political picture thus far presented.

A serious problem arises at the outset for the student of Shang, Zhou, and Qin architecture. Since it was built primarily of wood, like Indian architecture of that period, there is simply none of it left to study. Yet it is possible, on the basis of surviving postholes and poetic descriptions, to reconstruct at least the shape and color of those vanished cities.

We read of luxurious noble residences set in large courtyards and raised on high platforms reached in many cases by a double ceremonial staircase. Spacious halls and chambers are mentioned, as well as pergolas, terraces, galleries, and balconies. Gardens and lotus pools and banks of blooming flowers glimmer through the pages of Zhou poetry. Descriptions of scarlet-painted pillars, carved and polished rafters, and similar princely indulgences are convincing evidence that these kings and barons of the Chinese Bronze and Iron ages built splendidly in their own way.

Where sculpture is concerned, we need no convincing. Considerable quantities of cast bronze in particular remain, collectors' items in China for hundreds of years. The archetypal Shang bronze is not a human figure but a vessel for holding meat, grain, or wine at a religious sacrifice. These ritual vessels stand on three or four legs and are typically covered with curvilinear or rectilinear designs in low or high relief, representing schematically the faces and bodies of animals. These animal-mask or monster-mask patterns became increasingly abstract and geometrical, until little remained but the eyes, polished bosses still peering out of the rhythmic interweaving of the sculptured bronze.

Fully figural sculpture still survives, some in marble or jade, but most elegantly cast in bronze. Animal motifs again are most common, including the water buffalo and rhinoceros as well as birds, horses, and dragons. The Chinese dragon shape in particular is fully developed by late Zhou times, with its undulating reptilian body, its wings and dorsal spines, and a scalelike patterning over its metal skin.

All this carved and cast sculpture from early China is small in size, and most of it is more decorative than realistic in style. But in 1974 the fabled tomb of the First Emperor of the Qin was discovered at Xi'an, and the emperor's fantastic army of life-size terracotta soldiers saw the light of day for the first time in twenty-two hundred years. There are reputed to be seven thousand of these clay statues—men, horses, even chariots—all life-size. Lined up in proper military formation, armed with real weapons, they were buried in underground tunnels to protect the emperor's subterranean tomb. Each figure is individualized and precisely detailed, from leather or bronze armor and intricate coiffure to the furrowed brow of an officer or the smooth-faced good looks of an infantry recruit.

These clay figures in their silent hundreds, idealized though they may be, give some indication of how convincingly these ancient Chinese could model the human figure when they wished to. They bring us as close as we will probably ever get to the living faces of the human beings who built the Great Wall of China.

Literature: Chinese Characters and the Book of Songs

Writing was invented in China during the Shang period as a means of communicating with spirits. During the Zhou dynasty, when writing began to be directed to human readers, books appeared—slips of bamboo or wood fastened along one edge. Under the First Emperor the characters were standardized. They have changed very little since—another instance of the remarkable continuity that is so central a feature of Chinese civilization.

The Chinese characters thus established are very different from any Western written language. Each character stands not for an alphabetical sound but for an entire word. The shapes themselves, executed with brush and ink, have a beauty of line that has made calligraphy a major art in China. Most striking, perhaps, there is a distinctly pictorial quality to many Chinese characters. Thus the symbol for *dragon* originally looked like a dragon; the character for *good* resembled a picture of a mother and child.

The sheer difficulty of learning these thousands of complex written signs—by contrast with the twenty-six letters required for written English, for example—severely limited the number of people who would become literate in China. The prestige of the scholar and the powerful place of the mandarin administrator in Chinese government are among the most important results of this elaborate Chinese system of writing.

There is no literature beyond oracle bones from the Shang, but the eight centuries of the Zhou dynasty were seen by subsequent generations of Chinese as a literary golden age. Perhaps the most immediately appealing products of this first great age of Chinese literature are poems, most notably the three-hundred-odd lyrics of the *Book of Songs,* first collected around 600 B.C.E.

The *Book of Songs* includes a variety of material, from elegant poems on the deeds of kings and courtiers to simple folk songs illustrating the lives of Chinese peasants. The latter, composed most commonly in short, rhymed lines comparable to those of European folk ballads, deal with many aspects of life in the fields and villages of ancient China. Farmers complain of the eternal tax collector. Soldiers lament the hardships of military service. Young people glow to the first tremor of love in an idyllic setting of pasturelands and country gardens:

> Mid the bind-grass on the plain
> that the dew makes wet as rain
> I met by chance my clear-eyed man,
> > then my
> > joy began.[3]

There are human misfortunes to complain of, and much talk of millet and rice, mulberry leaves, and the farmer's year. But after the hard work is over, there always seems to be a bountiful harvest, with country music and baskets full of food.

> > . . . guests to feasting
> strike lute and blow
> pipes to show how
> feasts were in Chou [Zhou]
> > drum up that basket-lid now.[4]

Like Huangdi's soldiers in clay, these lines present an idealized version of ancient Chinese reality—but a salutary reminder too of the good times that, though perhaps rarer than the songs allow, were nonetheless a part of life in old China.

The Sages: The Teachings of Confucius

Nothing undercuts the stereotyped Western image of the mysterious East more sharply than Chinese philosophy. To plunge into the writings of these Chinese sages after an immersion in the religious teaching of ancient India, for example, is to move from mysticism

---

[3]Cyril Birch and Donald Keene, *Anthology of Chinese Literature from Early Times to the Fourteenth Century* (New York: Grove Press, 1965), p. 8.

[4]Ibid., p. 12.

to humanism, from metaphysical to social thought, even—dismayingly—from a longing for the infinite to a pious emphasis on good manners. It can be a disturbing experience; for a Westerner hungering for mystical insights, it can even be a bit of a let-down.

It should not be. The sages of China, like the philosophers of Greece, were concerned above all with *human* relations, with life in the world of living, breathing men and women. Considering how human affairs have commonly been managed down the centuries, this was surely no ignoble concern.

The sages and schools of the period between the sixth and third centuries B.C.E. left a mark on the mind of China that no subsequent school of thought could match. And the first and greatest of them, at least in the admiring eyes of later generations, was Kongfuzi—"Master Kong"—known to the West by the Latinized name of Confucius (551–479 B.C.E.).

The Founder of Confucianism, China's national philosophy in later centuries, was born in what is now Shandong province in northeastern China, apparently in humble circumstances, though of aristocratic descent. He became one of the gentlemanly seekers after posts of authority at the courts of the kings of the later Zhou. Failing in this quest, he fell back upon teaching. Like Socrates and Jesus, he does not seem to have written anything himself, but his discussions with his students were preserved in the collection called the *Analects*. Respected in his own day, he was to be China's most honored sage in later centuries.

There is a deceptively conventional sound to many of Confucius's teachings. He earnestly urged such commonplaces of his day as respect for one's social superiors, reverence for one's elders and ancestors, pious observation of traditional religious rites, and formal courtesy. But Confucius had more startling things to say to his contemporaries. In a land where petty wars were more the rule than the exception, he was a pacifist. In a society still dominated by an arrogant hereditary aristocracy, he declared that the true gentleman was the man of wisdom and virtue, whatever his social origin. And in a Middle Kingdom ravaged by official exploitation, Confucius insisted that the care of the people should be the primary concern of their rulers.

His overall goal seems to have been social harmony. He dreamed of an ordered society in which each individual recognized his place and each group performed its proper function. In such a world, the loyal subject and the benevolent ruler would complement and support one another. The family would be the linchpin of society. And on the individual level, all would live by a maxim that has a certain resonance for Christians: "What you do not want done to yourself, do not do to others."

The Hundred Flowers

The later Zhou period, for all its social and political misfortunes, was hailed in later centuries as the age of the "hundred schools" of thought, the time when a "hundred flowers" of wisdom bloomed across the Middle Kingdom.

Mencius, a Confucianist who lived a couple of generations after Confucius, was a philosophic optimist. Mencius declared that human nature is fundamentally good, all appearances to the contrary. He urged self-perfection, the cultivation of virtue through study directed at bringing out our innate capacity for human decency. He was a political utopian as well, proposing the redivision of the land of China on a basis of eight parts for the people, one for the king. The voice of the people, he suggested, is the real voice of the gods, since it is they who will finally decide by their actions whether a ruler possesses the Mandate of Heaven or not. There were enough rebellions in China's history to give this last point more of a realistic edge than some of Mencius's other ideas.

Han Faizi (died 233 B.C.E.) and the Legalists declared by contrast that human nature is basically selfish and undisciplined. To govern such people required rigorous laws rigorously applied, as in the authoritarian state of Qin. "A 'tender mother,' " said Han Faizi, "has spoiled the children!" There is a grimly Machiavellian ring to maxims like "When a sage governs the state, he does not count on the people to do what is beneficial to him. Instead, he sees to it that [they] can do him no harm."[5] Ironically, this most celebrated of Legalist sages died in the dungeons of the Qin, according to tradition imprisoned and compelled to commit suicide by his most illustrious pupil—the First Emperor's Legalist chief minister, Li Si.

Perhaps the most influential of all the hundred flowers to bloom after Confucius's day, however, was Daoism, a school that was more a religion than a philosophy. It was a mystical view of the human condition whose founder may himself have been a myth.

The name Laozi, the legendary founder of Daoism (Taoism) means simply "Old Master." According to tradition, he was a sage of Confucius's own day, a keeper of the archives in the state of Zhou. Confucius once met him, so the story goes, and later told his pupils that he had seen that day a being that was neither fish nor fowl—but a dragon. At the end of his life Laozi, seeing Zhou China collapsing around him, left by the western gate and disappeared, leaving behind him only one short book, the *Daodejing (Tao Te Ching, The Classic of Virtue and the Way)* the most commented upon and most widely translated of all the Chinese classics.

Dao means *the Way*—but what the Way means is a mystery wrapped in an enigma. The Way is the way of virtue; it is the way of nature. And it is something more. It is the ultimate ground of all being, the way things work, the way things are.

Virtue for many Daoists was to do nothing at all but relax and get in tune with the universe, with nature and the ultimate. Confucianists and Legalists argued incessantly, labored interminably to change things. Daoists tended to feel that the best society was a simple preliterate life synchronized with the rhythms of nature, and they would rather go fishing than argue about it.

Chinese hermits, nature poets, and landscape painters of later centuries would all practice in their various ways this philosophy of simplicity, acceptance, and harmony with the larger natural forces of the universe. Pressed to define the Way, the philosophical Daoist could only join the muted chorus of mystics down the ages in asserting that

those who know do not talk
and talkers do not know.[6]

SUMMARY

City-based civilization emerged in both India and China between 2500 and 200 B.C.E., reaching a first climax under the Mauryan dynasty in India, the brief Qin dynasty in China.

India's first civilization, that of Harappa, was born in the Indus River valley around 2500 B.C.E. The Harappans built gridlike cities and had an integrated agricultural society.

---

[5]Han Fei Tzu [Faizi], *The Complete Works*, vol. 2, trans. W.K. Liao (London: A. Probsthain, 1959), pp. 306–307.

[6]Lao Tsu [Laozi], *The Way of Life*, trans. R. B. Blakney (New York: The New American Library, 1955), p. 109.

The Aryans, nomadic Indo-European cattle-herders from the northern steppes, destroyed the cities of the Indus and drove most of their Dravidian builders southward into the Deccan around 1500 B.C.E.

Civilization reemerged between 1000 and 500 B.C.E. in the Ganges River valley, east of the Indus. During this period the Aryans merged with the more settled Dravidians. Aryan iron tools succeeded in opening up the dense jungles of the Ganges valley and in rebuilding urban society once more. Although the institution of caste erected rigid barriers among races, classes, and occupations, it also made a place for future newcomers as new castes.

Magadha, one of the small kingdoms ruled by divinely sanctioned *rajas* along the Ganges, unified much of the Indian subcontinent under the Mauryan dynasty (322–185 B.C.E.). But the greatest of the Mauryas, the Buddhist Asoka, rejected the use of force and ruled as an Indian philosopher king.

Hinduism, the complex faith of most Indians, evolved during the Aryan-Dravidian synthesis shortly after 100 B.C.E. It developed a range of religious sects and practices ranging from veneration of sacred cows to the mystical meditations of Indian gurus. Buddhism emerged as part of a new religious ferment around 500 B.C.E. Prince Gautama the Buddha and his monks preached escape from earthly suffering and desire through spiritual enlightenment. Even India's most famous epic poems, the *Mahabharata* and the *Ramayana,* reflect not only the warlike ways of the Aryans but the spiritual insights of the brahmans who edited them as well.

Shang China (1500–1000 B.C.E.) was really a collection of separate states in northeastern China.

The Zhou dynasty (1000–221 B.C.E.), a clan of border lords from the rugged northwest, conquered Shang China in the eleventh century. Their claim that they had the Mandate of Heaven helped them to govern in a loose feudal fashion longer than any other royal house. But it was the short-lived Qin dynasty (221–206 B.C.E.) that first imposed a centralized imperial order on all the Chinese states under the hard-driving First Emperor Huangdi. Huangdi linked the nation's northern defenses against nomadic invasion in the Great Wall of China.

Shang bronzes, the sculptured metal dragons of Zhou times, and the astonishing life-size clay soldiers from Huangdi's tomb are marvelous artistic achievements. The poetry of the *Book of Songs* has been beloved in China for more than two thousand years.

Most important, however, the philosophers of the later-Zhou period, around 500 B.C.E., played a central part in Chinese cultural tradition. Confucius's call for good government and human decency would echo down the Chinese centuries. So would Mencius's faith in human virtue and self-improvement, the Legalists' demand for rigor and justice, and the gentle urgings of Laozi to follow "the Way" of nature, goodness, and the cosmos.

SUGGESTED READING

Allan, S. *The Shape of the Turtle: Myth, Art, and Cosmos in Early China.* Albany: State University of New York Press, 1991. Intriguing analysis of Shang beliefs and art.

Burton, T. R. *Hindu Art.* Cambridge, Mass.: Harvard University Press, 1993. Brilliantly illustrated survey.

Chakravarti. *The Social Dimensions of Early Buddhism.* New York: Oxford University Press, 1987. Useful focus on social teachings and consequences. See also C.-S. Yu, *Early Buddhism and Christianity* (Delhi: Motilal Banarsidass, 1981), comparing Christ and the Buddha in terms of authority, community, and the discipline they taught.

Confucius. *The Analects of Confucius,* trans. A. Waley. London: G. Allen and Unwin, 1938. Two valuable recent studies are R. L. Taylor, *The Religious Dimension of Confucianism* (Albany: State University of New York Press, 1990), and W.M. Tu, *War, Learning, and Politics: Essays on the Confucian Intellectual* (Albany: State University of New York Press, 1993).

Corless, R. *The Vision of Buddhism: The Space Under the Tree.* New York: Paragon, 1989. Good introduction to the life and teachings of the Buddha. Two readable lives of the Buddha are R. A. Mitchell, *The Buddha: His Life Retold* (New York: Paragon, 1989), and D. J. Kalupahana, *The Way of Siddartha: A Life of the Buddha* (Lanham, Md.: University Press of America, 1987).

Cotterell, A. *The First Emperor of China.* Harmondsworth, U.K.: Penguin, 1989. Readable life of Shi Huangdi.

Fu, Z. *China's Legalists: The Earliest Totalitarians and Their Art of Ruling.* Armonk, N.Y.: M. E. Sharpe, 1996. Strong Chinese condemnation of Legalist rigor by a Chinese who has lived under modern totalitarianism.

Kostermeier, K. K. *A Survey of Hinduism.* Albany: State University of New York Press, 1989. Expert overview of the world's oldest religion. See also D. M. Knipe, *Hinduism: Experiments in the Sacred* (San Francisco: Harper, 1991), and D. R. Kingsley's brief but penetrating *Hinduism, a Cultural Perspective* (Englewood Cliffs, N.J.: Prentice Hall, 1982).

Lewis, M. E. *Writing and Authority in Early China.* Albany: State University of New York Press, 1999. How the unifying power of the written word in the minds of a classically educated ruling class shaped a united China.

Li, H. C. *Eastern Zhou and Qin Civilization,* trans. K. C. Chang. New Haven, Conn.: Yale University Press, 1985. Emphasizes the emergence of centralized imperial government in a feudal world.

Li, Y.-N. *Chinese Women Through Chinese Eyes.* Armonk, N.Y.: W. E. Sharpe, 1992. Chinese essays, including studies of ancient China.

Loewe, M., and E. L. Shaughnessy, eds. *The Cambridge History of Ancient China: From the Origins of Civilization to 221 B.C.* New York: Cambridge University Press, 1999. Wide variety of views in a rapidly expanding field as Chinese scholarship piles up new evidence.

Pruthi, R., and B. R. Sharma, eds. *Buddhism, Jainism, and Women.* New Delhi: Anmol Publications, 1997. Considerations of women's role.

Quigley, D. *The Interpretation of Caste.* Oxford: Clarendon Press, 1993. Anthropological analysis of India's "peculiar institution." On the origins of caste, see B. K. Smith, *Classifying the Universe: The Ancient Indian Varna System and the Origins of Caste* (New York: Oxford University Press, 1994), and H. A. Gould, *The Hindu Caste System: The Sacralization of a Social Order* (Delhi: Chanakya, 1987).

Roy, K. *The Emergence of Monarchy in North India.* New York: Oxford University Press, 1994. Theoretical social analysis of a complicated subject.

Strong, J. S. *The Legend of King Asoka.* Princeton, N.J.: Princeton University Press, 1983. Translation and analysis of the *Asokavadana,* an early account of the Buddhist philosopher king.

Thapar, R. *Asoka and the Decline of the Mauryas,* rev. ed. New York: Oxford University Press, 1997. Critical look at the philosopher king.

Waldron, A. *The Great Wall of China: From History to Myth.* New York: Cambridge University Press, 1989. Carefully researched history of the wall, debunking many myths.

Willier, R. "Confucian Ideal of Womanhood," *Journal of the China Society,* 13 (1976). An apologia for the Confucian view of women.

Wiltshire, M. G. *Ascetic Figures Before and in Early Buddhism.* New York: Mouton de Gruyter, 1990. Scholarly study of the religious framework.

 Please refer to the document CD-ROM for primary sources related to this chapter.

CHAPTER 5

THE FURNACES OF MEROE AND THE OLMEC HEADS

Ancient Civilizations of Africa and the Americas

(1500–150 B.C.E.)

A Glance Ahead: Lost Civilizations across Three Continents

Early civilization happened elsewhere besides the places we have visited already. Ancient cities rose in other parts of Africa besides Egypt. Across the Atlantic in the Americas, long-vanished peoples laid the foundations of future civilizations too.

In North Africa, Kushite kings conquered ancient Egypt, and Carthage was Rome's most powerful rival for mastery of the Mediterranean. In Middle and South America, thousands of years before the more familiar Aztecs and Incas, the Mexican Olmecs carved huge stone heads and the ancient Chavín culture raised towering temples in Peru.

All that is left today are scattered artifacts, ruined structures, and the accounts of travelers many centuries ago. Archaeologists, anthropologists, and other scholars add to our knowledge of these long-vanished cultures. But until they can tell us more, historians can only poke admiringly through the ruins of these lost civilizations.

Nubia, Kush, and Inner Africa

The Second Largest Continent

There was once a predisposition—rooted perhaps in too many old Tarzan movies—to imagine Africa as one vast jungle inhabited by "natives" who lived in grass huts and were constantly being devoured by tigers and crocodiles. Even people with some knowledge tended to fall in with this "dark continent" image, claiming that Africa had been cut off from progress through lack of intercourse with other peoples throughout its history. The reality, as usual, is a good deal more complex and interesting than the myth.

The world's second largest continent—only Asia is larger—covers a little less than twelve million square miles. More than two fifths of that vast area is covered with grassy plains. Another two fifths is arid-to-desert land. Less than one fifth is forested, and only a small part of that is genuine tropical rain forest, most of it in the Congo River basin and along the Guinea coast of West Africa.

The geography of the continent falls into a series of clearly definable bands: fertile Mediterranean coastal lands in the north, the wider swath of the barren Sahara, the sudannic belt of grasslands, the equatorial rain forests, then grassy plains again, the Kalahari Desert, and finally the fertile uplands of South Africa. This simplified pattern of east-to-west bands is complicated by a curving north-to-south trench composed of the Nile and the Great Rift Valley with its attendant lakes, running almost the length of East Africa.

Historically speaking, the peoples and cultures of Africa have been as varied as those of any other continent. Black Africans have apparently always been important, constituting 70 percent of the population today. But there are also Arabs and Berbers in large numbers in the north and in recent centuries influential immigrations from Europe and Asia. Even the "black" majority is normally subdivided into a variety of culturally diverse peoples and language groups, from the Bantu-speaking agricultural people of the central and southern portions of the continent to the food-gathering Khoi-San and Mbuti peoples still to be found in the deserts and deep woods.

For Western explorers and imperialists as recently as a century ago, Africa was the dark continent, a symbol of the unknown and the primitive. In fact, Africa was making crucial contributions to the human story long before civilization was dreamed of.

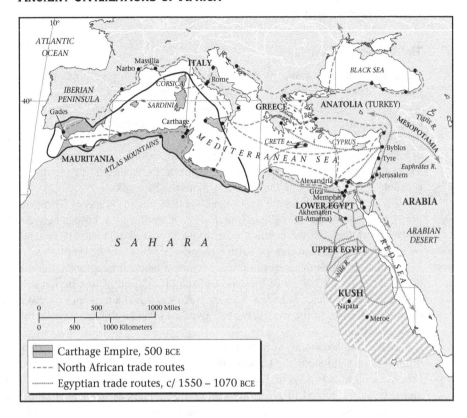

Early Contributions

As the evidence now runs, the earliest hominids first evolved into human beings in Africa. Africa probably maintained a long lead in the production of basic stone tools throughout the Old Stone Age. One of the oldest civilizations, that of ancient Egypt, took shape in northeastern Africa, though as we saw in the last chapter, the history of the lower Nile was also closely bound up with the early history of the Near East. Civilization, however, emerged, in parts of Africa besides Egypt, and it is with these historic beginnings that the following sections will be concerned.

The existence of these early African cultures argues strongly against the notion that Africa was cut off from progressive outside influences. Several of the early cultures to be considered here—Nubia and Kush on the upper Nile and Carthage on the western Mediterranean—developed in fruitful interchange with other areas. Their stories clearly illustrate the process of sociocultural development in the usual historical web of influences and interchange of goods and ideas.

Edgar Rice Burroughs, the creator of Tarzan and his fairy-tale Africa, once said that the best way to get ahead as a writer was to write about something you know absolutely nothing about. His vision of a dark continent thick with jungle, peopled by Hottentots, and stalked by man-eating tigers (who don't live in Africa at all) would seem to illustrate his theory to perfection. But that fictional vision does not tell us much about Africa. As a

Swahili-speaking East African might put it, shaking his head over this Wild West legend of his own land: "More *Wazungu* lies!"

The Nubian Corridor

Out of the south they came, by river and by caravan into Egypt: gold, ivory, ebony, ostrich feathers, slaves. And more: cattle, grain, leopards (and their skins), giraffes (whose tails were used as fly whisks), oils and perfumes, "amazon stone," carnelian, gum, and red ocher and ostrich eggs. Century after century the largesse of the mysterious lands beyond the cataracts of the Nile came north—in booty, in tribute, and in trade goods. Sometimes, especially during Egypt's long decline, African armies came down the Nile to smite Thebes and Memphis, and African kings from the south to sit on the throne of the pharaohs, to negotiate with the Greeks or fight the Romans.

For at least two thousand years there were rich lands south of Egypt, in that part of northeastern Africa once called Nubia, today straddling the border between Egypt and Sudan. From the eleventh century B.C.E. to the fourth century C.E., these lands were ruled by the powerful African state of Kush.

Nubia, or the Nubian corridor, has become a catchall geographical term for the area between the First Cataract of the Nile and the bifurcation of that immense river into the Blue and White Niles. On a map of modern Africa, it is the region of the cataracts and the enormous S-curve of the river between Egypt's Aswan High Dam and the Sudanese capital of Khartoum.

Before the beginning of history, the Nubians lived much as other Paleolithic or Neolithic peoples did along the banks of the Nile. From the Mediterranean in the north to the Ethiopian highlands and the Great Lakes of Central Africa, these early Africans hunted and fished and learned to grow crops and herd animals as other peoples did around the globe. Like other African peoples, they lived in small groups, in nomadic bands or agricultural villages. Some of the same tools and styles of pottery were produced in Nubia, south of the First Cataract, as in Egypt, north of it.

Then, around 3000 B.C.E. came the great change in Egypt. Led by the first pharaohs, centralized government mobilized the villages to bring the Nile under control. The resulting system of levees, catch basins, and irrigation ditches turned the Nile River north of the cataracts into one of the most productive agricultural zones in the world. Bureaucratic government, social classes, monumental building, and other elements of a developed civilization followed.

Life in Nubia, just south of the emerging Egyptian kingdom, could not help but be affected. In time, as we will see, many of the characteristics of Egyptian civilization would spread up the Nile into Nubia. Soon also, indigenous Nubian kingdoms—including Kush and Meroe—would emerge in the south and begin to play a key part in the history of the Nile valley as a whole.

Perhaps most important, however, Nubia continued to serve as the most important link between Egypt and the Mediterranean world in the north and inner Africa to the south. Though the cataracts required that boats be transported overland around them, the long river remained the easiest north-south route across the desert.

It is not surprising, then, that Egyptian rulers, eager for ivory, ebony, incense, and other products, sent trading expeditions up the Nile toward the heart of Africa. Up and down the Nubian corridor, goods, ideas, and power thus flowed for many centuries. As early as the Egyptian Old Kingdom, a pharaoh gratefully accepted a Pygmy dancer from Central Africa,

Women of ancient Kush, illustrated in a black stone relief sculpture from Meroe. The figure on the left is a Kushite queen. Note the elaborate headdresses, necklaces, bracelets, and decorated skirts, as well as the impressive throne on which the sovereign sits. (Werner Forman Archive/Art Resource)

sent to him as a gift from Nubia. As late as Roman times, Kushite raiders carried off a carved head of Augustus Caesar from an attack on an Egypt that had become a Roman province. Nubia was thus a vital link in the chain that bound the civilizations of the Old World together.

The Kingdom of Kush

From the beginning, Egyptian influences were of paramount importance in the development of these southern lands. The pharaohs of the Middle Kingdom went south of the first cataract and raided the region of the upper Nile. Around 1500 B.C.E., the aggressively expansionist pharaonic empire builders of the New Kingdom overran the area, and made the wealth—and the fearless bowmen—of the region prime resources in Egypt's most ambitious bid to master the Fertile Crescent.

During these centuries of northern domination, Egyptian governors and garrisons, priests, and artisans left an indelible mark on the lands and peoples of the upper Nile. The sons of Kushite kings were educated at the Egyptian royal court at Thebes. Egyptian temples and gods, Egyptian royal rituals, and Egyptian hieroglyphics were all transplanted to the Sudan. The Egyptian religious complex at Napata in particular became a center for the spread of Egyptian culture among the Africans beyond the cataracts.

When the long decline of Egypt began around 1100 B.C.E., the kingdom of Kush regained its independence and flourished as the master of the Upper Nile. But the black kings of Kush still followed Egyptian ways and worshiped Egyptian gods. They glorified their own deeds in hieroglyphic inscriptions and were buried under pyramids like those of the Old Kingdom. It was a new Egypt—upriver.

As old Egypt fell under foreign domination during the first millennium B.C.E., the Kushites may well have seen themselves as the true guardians of the old ways and ancient values they had shared with their neighbors down the river for so many centuries. Around

750 B.C.E., the Kushite kings Kashta and Piankhi marched north to liberate Egypt from its Libyan rulers, the mercenary North African princes who had seized the throne. For more than half a century thereafter, the Kushite pharaohs of the twenty-fifth Egyptian dynasty ruled a dual kingdom that stretched perhaps fourteen hundred miles from the Blue Nile to the shores of the Mediterranean.

But the future of Kush lay in the Sudan. Within sixty years the savage Assyrians had expelled the twenty-fifth dynasty and replaced the Kushite kings in Egypt. Assyrian predominance would be succeeded by that of other peoples, including the Greek Ptolemies and the Roman Caesars. Upriver, beyond the cataracts, Kush went its independent way.

The Furnaces of Meroe

The golden age of Kushite civilization was the period of the ascendancy of the city of Meroe, from the third to the first century B.C.E. Much of what follows will refer to these centuries.

The centers of Kushite civilization were populous cities, built from sun-dried brick, like those of Egypt and Mesopotamia, and garnished with palaces and temples. But there were differences too. The Kushite kings lived like Egyptian pharaohs, but the succession in Kush was decided by consensus among the royal princes, and the queen mother was uniquely powerful among the Kushites. There were powerful Kushite queens as well, though we know little about them. One, called Candace, attacked the Romans in Egypt, and another Kushite Candace earned a mention in the Bible.

Egyptian-style priesthoods, notably that of the sun god Amon, were extremely influential, but Amon's central place was later usurped by the Kushite lion god Apedemek, whose graven image is frequently found among the ruins of Kushite cities.

The wealth of Kush lay in its land, its location, and its energetic people. The Kushite capital of Meroe was watered not only by the Nile but by a significant annual rainfall. The result was a broad expanse of pasture and cropland, a green island in the desert where cattle grazed and grain stood tall. There were minerals of great value under the soil of Kush as well, including gold and iron. Kush was fortunate also in its locale, up the river from Egypt and on the trade routes that wound east through the Ethiopian up-lands to the Red Sea. From these advantages a vigorous people—farmers and herders, soldiers, traders, builders—made a very good life indeed for several hundred years.

Kushite artisans in particular exploited the iron ore of southern Kush so industriously that Meroe became the greatest center for the production of iron in Africa. Its surviving heaps of slag have led some Africanists to see Meroe as the Birmingham—or Pittsburgh—of the continent.

Culture seems to have flourished too in the inner African world of Kush. Carven images of Kushite victories in nameless wars are still to be seen in low relief across ruined walls. There are long lines of prisoners and royal processions parading in Egyptian silhouette, though their royal figures are more solidly built than the leaner, more sinuous people downriver, and the jewelry they wear is of Kushite make. There are animal gods and royal beasts, the lion and the elephant soon replacing the Egyptian vulture and cobra.

The wars the Kushites fought remain for the most part nameless because just about the time that the independent greatness of Kush began, the Kushites evolved their own form of writing—and we cannot read it. They developed a true alphabet, like that of the Phoenicians or the Greeks. But there is no Rosetta stone for Kushite; we can pronounce the words, but we cannot tell their meanings.

Gradually over the centuries, Kush lost touch with the Mediterranean world to the north. The passing of Kushite glory during the first centuries of what was elsewhere the Christian era has been explained in various ways. The limited land was probably over-grazed and perhaps dried out by the slow southward creep of the Sahara. Kush's best customers in Egypt were ruined by Rome's insatiable demands upon this breadbasket of empire, and business in Meroe suffered as poverty spread along the Nile. Trade to the east was taken over by new Red Sea powers. And around C.E. 350 one of these East African states, the Kingdom of Axum, put an end to what had been the greatest early civilization of inner Africa: "I made war on them [the Axumite king Ezana declared]. . . . I burnt their towns . . . and my army carried off their food and copper and iron . . . and destroyed the statues in their temples, their granaries and cotton trees and cast them into the [Nile]."[1]

The traveler approaching Meroe by train from Cairo today sees a scattering of ruined temples, huge broken pyramids, and heaps of slag from the famous ironworks. There is little left of the royal city at the center, the baths, the processional way running through row on row of rectangular roofs and courtyards up to the Kushite temple of the sun.

CARTHAGE: EMPIRE OF THE WESTERN SEAS

The Phoenician Diaspora

At the other end of North Africa from Egypt, and facing the Mediterranean Sea rather than inner Africa, stood the great city of Carthage and its seaborne empire. Founded by Near Eastern immigrants from Phoenicia—discussed in Chapter 3—Carthage became an independent African empire strong enough to challenge both the Greeks and the Romans for mastery of the western Mediterranean. Modern historians have tended to see the founding of Carthage as part of a larger, primarily economic Phoenician diaspora. In this view, the far-trading Phoenicians first came ashore at the site of the future Carthage to establish a way station—one of many—on the road to Spain. On Spain's Atlantic coast, beyond the Pillars of Hercules—now called the Straits of Gibraltar—they had established a major base at Gades, modern Cadiz. There they traded with the indigenous Spanish population for silver mined nearby and for tin imported from France and England.

It was a profitable trade. But the Atlantic coast of Spain was 2,000 miles from Lebanon, a long voyage even for the intrepid Phoenicians. The merchants of Tyre needed way stations along the North African coast where they could get food and water and repair their ships. It was probably for this purpose that Phoenician ships first anchored in the sheltered harbor where Carthage would later be built.

For the rest of the story of the rise of imperial Carthage, we must depend on legends that may well contain a kernel of fact. For legend has it that the city that became the capital of a vast commercial empire was built by a Near Eastern queen in the ninth century B.C.E. Elissa—known to the Greeks and Romans as Dido—was the royal sister of the king of Tyre, a wealthy Phoenician trading city on the coast of Lebanon. Caught up in a bloody feud in her Phoenician home, she fled the city at the head of many Tyrian nobles. Gathering support from other Phoenician cities as they moved westward, she and her followers settled at last on the coast of what is today Tunisia, where she built her city.

---

[1]Robert W. July, *A History of the African People* (New York: Scribner's, 1970), p. 38.

By all accounts, Elissa's "New City"—*Qart Hadash,* later Latinized to "Carthage"—was a splendid piece of work. In his epic poem, the *Aeneid,* the Roman poet Vergil described the exiled queen—here called Dido—raising her palaces and temples. Vergil's own hero, Aeneus, future founder of Rome, dawdles and watches, falling in love with the builder of the city that would become Rome's greatest rival. Legends also tell of Elissa's tragic end, dying by her own hand for love of Aeneus. These latter tales are probably poetic inventions. But the city she built was a concrete and powerful reality.

Peoples of the Maghreb

The Tyrian immigrants built their city on land bought or leased from the African people who already lived there. The peoples of this northern bulge of North Africa, later known as the Maghreb, would play an important part in the history of this African commercial empire.

The ancient peoples of North Africa west of Egypt have traditionally been called Libyans. We have no way of knowing what they called themselves, and they may have had little sense of being one people at all. We know, however, that they spoke one language and shared a precarious living space between the scorching Sahara and the Mediterranean Sea. Ethnically, they were probably the ancestors of the modern Berber population who share the land today with the later Arab conquerors of North Africa.

The Libyans were farmers and herders, growing grain and herding oxen, sheep, and goats. They rode horses and used them to pull carts and war chariots. They worked their land with stone tools, though some Libyans wore copper bracelets, anklets, and other metal items of personal adornment. Their religion, like that of ancient Egypt, seems to have focused on animal-headed gods and goddesses, especially on a ram-headed sun god called Ammon. Politically, they were originally organized into tribes and clans. In Carthaginian times, as we will see, some Libyan peoples developed hereditary kingdoms in the Maghreb.

These were the people, then, who agreed to sell a strip of coastal land to a handful of immigrants from the east in the eighth century B.C.E. In the centuries that followed, the lives of both the indigenous population and the intruders would be transformed by this fertile fusion of cultures.

The Carthaginian Empire

From the eighth to the second century B.C.E., the naval and commercial power of Carthage grew till it dominated the western Mediterranean and the seas beyond.

The Phoenician cities from which Carthage sprang foundered and fell in the welter of near Eastern peoples. On its own, the commercial empire or trading zone dominated by Carthage emerged by the sixth century as mistress of its own seaborne domain. Its power dominated all the other surviving Phoenician settlements of the west. The Carthaginian Empire included territories across the Mediterranean in southern Europe—parts of Spain and the islands of Sardinia, Corsica, and Sicily. In time it embraced trading centers on the Atlantic, from settlements in Britain and French Brittany through Cadiz in Spain down to the west coast of Africa.

Closer to home, the nearby peoples of the Maghreb, including the sizable Berber states of Numidia and Mauritania, were subject to or allied with Carthage. Even desert tribes such as the Garamantes fed the insatiable hunger of the Carthaginians for trade, bringing goods by the Saharan ways only they could follow from the oases of Fezzan.

A laughing mask from vanished Carthage reminds us that ancient peoples also saw the comic side of life. Power and wealth, conquest and defeat filled their history, but some may see more life in a face like this than in many pages of historical heroics. (Anthony Esler)

From this western, largely maritime empire the Carthaginians derived such valuable goods as pottery and glass, textiles and ivory, tin, silver, and gold. Much of this trade was by barter. The famous "silent trade" in African gold, described by the tireless Greek historian Herodotus, is perhaps not atypical of the trade that took place without money or a common language in these early times. The Greek explained how the Carthaginians, when trading with a certain African nation "beyond the pillars of Hercules," laid out their trade goods on the beach and then withdrew to their ships until the local people had brought forth sufficient gold to pay for what they wanted. No words were exchanged, only Mediterranean goods for West African gold. Herodotus added that "neither party deals unfairly with the other," as if it were rather an oddity in that world of shrewd horse traders.

There is evidence of voyages even farther down the coasts of Africa in ancient times. The most important of these was apparently undertaken by the respected Carthaginian Hanno, who set out with a large fleet on a voyage around West Africa in the fifth century B.C.E. According to descriptions copied from the walls of a Carthaginian temple, Hanno's ships slowly rounded the great bulge of West Africa, founding colonies, trading with the local people, and discovering strange lands. There were rivers filled with hippopotamuses and crocodiles and coasts lined with fires and drums in the night. There were people dressed in animal skins who pelted them with stones and hairy "savages" called Gorillas who resisted capture by clawing, biting, and climbing up trees. There were mysterious islands and erupting volcanoes with lava flowing down into the sea.

Hanno may have got as far as the modern country of Cameroon, at the inner angle of West Africa. If he did, it was a feat that would not be duplicated for almost two thousand years.

Rivals of the Greeks and Romans

Carthage was governed by an oligarchy of increasingly wealthy commercial families. These plutocrats sat on the Carthaginian ruling councils and held the main magistracies, called *sufets,* which apparently were similar to the Roman consuls. These civilian authorities kept close watch over the military in particular, so that Carthaginian generals seldom challenged the civil government, as happened so often in Rome.

As seen by their rivals across the Mediterranean, these empire builders of northern Africa were a dour and grasping lot, possessing a streak of cruelty that even the Romans professed to be shocked by. And there does seem to be some substance to the charge that the lords of Carthage sacrificed even their children to the gods who brought the city its wealth and power. For human sacrifice was practiced among them, as among other Phoenician colonists, and the burned bones of children have been found in special tombs in the Carthaginian holy place, the *tophet,* close by the harbor.

Carthage in its prime in many ways resembled a Tunisian town of today. The white-washed walls of the multistory tenements of the lower city must have been crammed with humanity, since estimates of the population run higher than half a million. Nicer homes and gardens lay in the northern suburbs. On the high city, or Byrsa, stood the temples of Baal the sun god, the even more popular goddess Tanit, and other divinities. A wall sixty feet high stretched across the neck of the peninsula on which the city stood, protecting Carthage from attack by land, while its fleet guarded it by sea.

To maintain its supremacy on the western seas, Carthage fought a long series of wars, particularly with the Greeks and the Romans on the other side of the Mediterranean. A brief glance at these conflicts may round out this overview of Africa's most celebrated early empire.

The Greeks were the great trade rivals first of the Phoenicians and later of the Carthaginians. Greek colonies in the western Mediterranean early ran afoul of Carthage's trade monopoly, and the two peoples fought intermittently through the fifth and fourth centuries B.C.E. Greeks even invaded the Maghreb and for a short time threatened the very survival of Carthage, only to be turned back in the end by Carthaginian forces.

During the third and second centuries, the rising power of Rome, almost due north of Carthage across the narrow waist of the Mediterranean, collided with this rich nation of traders. The results were the three Punic Wars, the most desperate struggles of Rome's own violent climb to mastery of the Mediterranean world.

The two empires first fell out with each other in the third century B.C.E. over rival claims in Sicily. Roman arms triumphed in the long run, but Carthage accepted only a temporary setback. The Second Punic War dealt the Romans a shock from which they did not recover for generations: the sudden descent of the Carthaginian general Hannibal's war elephants, come round by way of Spain, through the Alpine passes and into northern Italy. The armies of the great North African power ravaged the Roman heartland almost at will during the last years of the third century. But the Romans, fighting on their home ground, finally wore the invaders down once more. And fifty years later, in the middle of the second century, they launched the war of revenge that destroyed Carthaginian power forever.

It must have been a laborious as well as a bloody business to burn and topple into ruins a significant portion of a city that had once held half a million people. But the soldiers of Scipio the Younger managed it. Today the outer promontory of the double harbor is a dangerous underwater reef, and the line of the sixty-foot wall that once crossed the peninsula is detectable only from the air. The best that modern archaeology can muster has found very little of old Carthage in between.

THE FIRST NORTH AMERICANS

The Americas Before Columbus

The geography of the Americas is of course familiar in broad outline to all Americans; we have seen the globe turned our way all our lives. We have some notion of the mountainous spine that runs down the western side of the new World, the Rockies and the Andes. We know about the great plains and icy tundras of Canada, the plains and deserts of the western United States, and the dark forests that once covered eastern North America. We should know more than we do of the mountains and jungles of Central America and the Caribbean, of the world's largest rain forest in Brazil, of the southward-flowing pampas of Argentina, and of the howling seas and bitter winds around Cape Horn.

As recently as five centuries ago, this vast and varied sweep of continents and islands was inhabited by a single people, known through Columbus's fundamental error of geographical judgment as Indians. Among these Native Americans, a series of civilizations had arisen long before Columbus came.

Highly developed cultures emerged in two parts of the New World especially, in what are today Mexico and Peru. They are usually represented in the modern imagination by their final formulations, those that the European conquerors encountered—the Aztecs and

ANCIENT AMERICAN CIVILIZATIONS

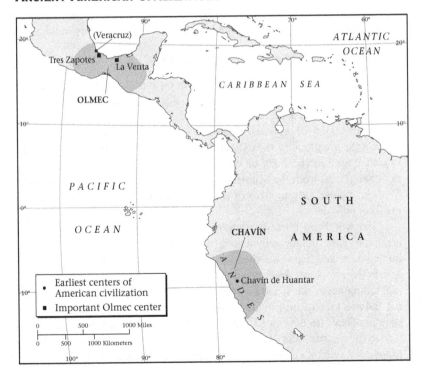

the Incas. But civilizations far older than these flourished and faded in the Americas hundreds and even thousands of years before the coming of the conquistadores. It is with these beginnings of civilization in the New World—with the long-vanished Olmec people of Mexico and the Chavín culture of Peru—that this chapter must finally concern itself.

We will begin, however, with a look at the earlier Amerindian cultures from which these first American civilizations emerged—the food-gatherers and farmers of Stone Age America.

Hunters and Farmers

In 3500 B.C.E. the great hunts on the western plains of North America were already thousands of years in the past. When the first Paleolithic hunters had passed through the gap in the Canadian ice sheet into what is today the western United States, they had found a hunter's paradise of big game. Endless herds of mammoths and mastodons, camels, prehistoric horses, giant bison, lion-sized cats, and many other creatures roamed the grasslands. The hunting bands from Asia had grown fat in this Eden of raw meat on the hoof. They had also spread rapidly southward, as we have seen, occupying both continents of the New World in no more than a millennium or two.

Then things began to change.

The last ice age drew to a close. The retreat of the glacier and the resulting changes in temperature and vegetation transformed the New World environment. The warmer, drier climate substantially diminished the variety and numbers of the great herd animals of earlier times. In addition, the growing numbers and increasing skill of human hunting bands may have led to vast overkill and the extinction of whole species. Most of the big game, the so-called megafauna of the Americas, was thus wiped out thousands of years ago.

A changing environment inevitably led to changes in the ways of life of the people who lived on the land. By the time civilization began to take shape on the far-off plains of Sumer, cultural change was also under way among the peoples of the Americas.

Regional Economies and Family Structures

The native population of North America was once dismissed as a uniformly primitive collection of tribes. Archaeological and anthropological studies, however, have emphasized the range, diversity, and achievements of even the earliest peoples of North America. This is evident in the variety of regional economies which emerged in this part of the New World.

On the great plains, the extinction of most of the American megafauna led the Indians to concentrate increasingly on one surviving species: the enormous herds of bison or buffalo that grazed from the Mississippi to the Rockies. Using spears tipped with deadly new "Folsom points," the hunters of the plains brought down these large meat animals with growing efficiency.

The woodland hunters of eastern North America prowled vast forests of hardwoods and pine. Like hunter-gatherers in many lands, they foraged for fruit, nuts, and roots, hunted deer, and fished the rivers and streams of eastern America.

In the Far North, Inuit peoples, lacking plant foods, lived entirely by hunting and fishing, killing bears, seals, and other mammals for food and clothing. In the Pacific Northwest, the Indians killed forest animals and depended heavily on the rich harvest of the salmon streams. They also developed boats, including kayaks, birch-bark canoes, and log dugouts.

In the deserts west of the Rockies and north of the Rio Grande, finally, a surprisingly productive foraging economy took shape, killing lizards, birds, and other small game and collecting prickly pear in the lowlands, berries and nuts on the flat-topped mesas. These desert gatherers lived in caves and rock shelters, made early baskets, nets, and traps, and, like most of their fellow Native Americans, chipped tools out of stone. It was to these foraging peoples of the American southwest that agriculture would first spread up from Mexico around 2000 B.C.E.

Among those many peoples, a remarkable variety of gender and family relations developed. Some evolved small nuclear families composed only of parents and children. Others developed extended families, uniting several generations and the nuclear families of grown siblings. In some cultures, men ruled with a heavy patriarchal hand. In others, matrilineal and matrilocal patterns made succession through the woman's side the rule. In these cultures, the husband was required to move into the wife's family, giving women the whip hand.

A similar variety prevailed in the assigning of traditional roles and tasks. Among northern Indians, where clothing was mostly made of animal hides and leather, men were primarily responsible for making it. In the south, where cotton and other vegetable fibers were used, women were the weavers. In some areas, including the far north, gender roles were sometimes scarcely defined at all, leaving men and women free to divide up the work as they pleased!

Harmony with Nature

The religious views of these first Americans are almost entirely inferred from beliefs that survived into modern times and from parallels with preurban peoples elsewhere in the world. In North America, as in South America, Africa, and indeed, almost everywhere in early times, people had a strong sense of the oneness of the natural world and of the need to live in harmony with nature. Like animists elsewhere, early Native Americans attributed life to all things and sought only to take their fair share of nature's plenty.

Modern examples must suffice. Thus, for instance, a twentieth-century Papago woman, digging in the Arizona earth for clay to make a pot, expresses her gratitude to the clay. "I take only what I need," she declares. "It is to cook for my children."[2] Far to the east, in the forests along the Mississippi, a Fox Indian explains his people's attitude toward the timber they use for many things:

> We do not like to harm the trees. Whenever we can, we always make an offering of tobacco to the trees before we cut them down. We never waste the wood, but use all that we cut down. If we did not think of their feelings . . . all the other trees in the forest would weep, and that would make our hearts sad too.[3]

MEXICO: THE OLMECS

Origins of the Olmecs

The geography of Mesoamerica ("Middle America"—Mexico plus Central America) is confusing at first glance. It appears to be a twisting line of mountains and lowland plains choked with tropical rain forest that winds between the continents. A cross-sectional view,

---

[2]Ruth M. Underhill, *Red Man's Religion: Beliefs and Practices of the Indians North of Mexico* (Chicago: University of Chicago Press, 1965), p. 116.
[3]Ibid.

however, reveals an underlying symmetry. There are frequently coastal plains on both Pacific and Caribbean shores, inland mountain walls, and, especially in Mexico, high plateaus among the mountains. Civilization developed toward the center of this three-thousand-mile isthmus, in the region that today comprises southern Mexico, Guatemala, and Honduras, in areas that included both highlands and the coastal plains.

Mexico's jungle-shrouded Yucatán Peninsula, home of the Maya, and the fertile Mexican plateau called the Mesa Central, the center of the Aztec Empire, are the sites of the most famous Mesoamerican civilizations. But they were not the oldest.

America's first civilization emerged in southern Mexico between 1500 and 400 B.C.E. It did not develop in the highlands, as the more celebrated cultures of the Aztecs and the Peruvian Incas did, but on the coastal lowlands around present-day Veracruz. This oldest American civilization is called Olmec culture, after the Aztec name for the tribes who lived there at the time of the Spanish conquest. We have no idea what the people who created that ancient civilization called themselves.

We know that much of the Old World pattern of cultural evolution was duplicated in Mesoamerica. We have stone tools left by hunter-gatherers who drifted south twenty thousand years ago. We have archaeological remains of the villages of their Neolithic descendants in Mexico, settled village-dwellers who were making the delicate transition from foraging to agriculture. We know that the population grew, here as elsewhere, until it reached numbers sufficient to produce more complex forms of social organization. And we have the beginnings of Mexican art and religion in the thousands of small figurines—almost always female, as in the Old World—found among the hearths and burial sites of these vanished village peoples.

Olmec Culture

And then, out of the mists of the first millennium before Christ, looms the high culture of the Olmecs, ancient Mexico's first civilization.

The head is nine feet high, carved from solid stone, and weighs perhaps fifteen tons. It stands on the grass, bodiless, neckless, wearing a round, close-fitting helmet, staring back at you. This is not some Easter Island primitive, but a startlingly realistic face. It is one of a number of similar monumental heads unearthed so far, carved by the Olmec Indians while Greece still languished in its dark age and before Rome existed.

The famous Olmec heads are only part of a growing archaeological treasure of sculpture and architecture, all clearly linked by the Olmec style, the best of it dated between 800 and 400 B.C.E. Most of the finds are clustered in such tropical lowland sites on the Caribbean shore of Mexico as La Venta, in the Veracruz region. These sites include ruins that clearly point ahead to Mayan and Aztec culture. And they have yielded up artifacts that would not be bettered by these later civilizations—that would not in fact be matched by them, for their realistic mode was developed by the Olmecs alone in Middle America.

La Venta and similar sites are usually described not as true cities but as ceremonial centers for the surrounding villages. Typical architectural finds include large pyramidal earthern mounds, precursors of the stone pyramids of the Mayans and Aztecs. There are also engraved stone altars, stelae, and sarcophagi. Such complexes are quite large and must have required the labor of all the surrounding peoples to build.

Besides the great carved heads there are smaller heads and figurines in clay, jade, serpentine, and other stone. Some of these are masks, as lifelike as the great heads, or perhaps even idealized portraits. Some are either infants or dwarfs, the latter freighted with

An Olmec head. The realistic modeling was rare in pre-Columbian American art. The flattened nose and ears may have been carved this way to avoid breakage when the sculptured heads were drawn overland from the deposits of basaltic rock where they were carved to the Olmec ceremonial center where they were displayed. (Museo Nacional de Antropología)

supernatural significance for Mesoamerican Indians. There are lifesize clay "tomb watchers," some of them sinister enough to suit their grim task admirably.

The most common motif of all, however, is that of the jaguar, which was probably a rain god, and the strangest of these are the half-human, half-cat were-jaguars. So pervasive is this feline presence that one authority has called his study of the Olmecs simply *The Jaguar's Children.* Were-jaguars in the form of children are a particularly common—and startling—form of this sculptural type. We do not know what a smoothly sculptured, soft-fleshed infant with jaguar claws on its little hands and jaguar teeth just showing between softly parted baby lips may have meant to the ancient people of Mesoamerica. But we can be properly terrified ourselves.

Olmec Society

What then can we say with any confidence about the builders of Olmec culture?

Much more can be deduced with some certainty about socioeconomic and even intellectual achievements than about the precise political organization or history of the Olmec people. Olmec culture seems to emerge full-blown on the Mesoamerican scene; there is little evidence of the slow development we would expect. It ends as suddenly, around 400 B.C.E., when the great complex at La Venta apparently expired in violence. Whether it was a rebellion against priestly overlords or an invasion by less developed peoples we do not know.

What political structure the Olmecs had, or whether any large political unit existed at all, also remains controversial. Some archaeologists have suggested that an Olmec empire, headed perhaps by priests or warlike traders, linked the Veracruz centers with more distant Olmec-influenced areas as far away as central Mexico and even Guatemala. Others have postulated the spread of a new religion centering in the worship of the jaguar god, or the simple exchange of Olmec goods in distant parts of Middle America.

More can be said about the economic aspects of Olmec life. Most Olmecs, to begin with, seem to have lived in pole-and-thatch houses in the tropical lowlands along the Caribbean, or in adobe-and-stone huts on the highland fringes. They grew corn and beans and other vegetables and wore clothing made of cotton and maguey. They made clay pots and small figurines by hand.

Social classes higher than peasant agriculturists are also indicated. Priests ran great ritual centers like La Venta. Richly furnished tombs indicate an aristocratic elite, as does the depiction at one site of a man kneeling before another, a much more gorgeously clad person. Farmers, artisans, priests, and perhaps nobility, then, existed in the Olmec world.

Something more, finally can be said about the highest expressions of the culture. The religion of the Olmecs was evidently of primary importance to them; no palace ruins have been found, only the remains of temples. Their cults very probably included sky gods and earth gods, a female fertility goddess, the jaguar divinity, and the strange jaguar people who were perhaps that rain god's human representatives. Gods are also shown in bas relief hovering over clubwielding soldiers locked in combat, indicating that war too had its divine patrons in this oldest of Middle American civilizations.

PERU: CHAVÍN CULTURE

Origins of the Chavín Culture

The condor is the largest of all flying birds. Balancing on ten-foot wings, it cruises above the longest mountain range in the world, from Patagonia in the far south to the peaks that loom above the Amazon. It is an ugly bird close up, vulture-headed and ungainly on the ground. But riding on the icy winds that whistle among the crags, it is the sovereign of the Andes skies.

A condor's-eye view of the Peruvian Andes, where civilization first appeared in South America, would reveal a rather simpler topography than the tangled mountains and jungles of Mesoamerica. To the east of the north–south mountain chain, the jungles of the Amazon basin flow eastward beneath mist and rolling clouds two thousand miles to the Atlantic. To the west the Andean foothills descend to a narrow strip of desert between the mountains and the Pacific shore. Rain is rare, but river valleys carve their way through the arid land to the ocean. The mountainous highlands are much less fertile than the high plateaus of Mexico. Corn will not grow there naturally, though flocks may be grazed on the slopes.

Tropical jungles, forbidding heights, and a strip of rock and sand along the sea—it seems an unlikely area for civilization to emerge in. But that is precisely what happened on the western slopes of the Peruvian Andes and the arid Pacific coastlands early in the first millennium B.C.E.

In the end, civilized societies were to evolve over a large part of the central Andean region of South America, including portions of what are today Peru, Bolivia, Ecuador, and northern Chile and Argentina. But it began with the Chavín culture of Peru, named for the highlands site of Chavín de Huantar and usually dated between 800 and 400 B.C.E. Like Olmec culture in Mexico, Chavín culture was to spread widely and to be hailed by later archaeologists as a mother culture for the entire region.

The cruising condor probably paid no particular attention to the first people to appear in Peru, filtering southward through the Andean gorges perhaps twenty thousand years ago. These Paleolithic people hunted deer and llamas in the mountains and hauled in huge catches of fish along the shore. Within ten or twelve thousand years, they had settled into the universal Neolithic village. Soon they were raising potatoes and herding woolly llamas and alpacas in the highlands, growing cotton and making fishnets on the coast. They learned, probably as late as the second millennium B.C.E., to make ceramic pottery and to grow corn.

Corn cultivation required elaborate irrigation and terracing procedures, and these soon appeared in both the dry coastal valleys and the highlands. Regional exchange also developed, with potatoes, meat, and wood flowing down the mountains, and corn and cotton coming up from the lowlands.

Then, early in the first millennium B.C.E., came the oldest of Peruvian civilizations, Chavín culture.

Ruins in the Andes

Chavín de Huantar is not the center of the culture that is named for it. Indeed, Chavín culture seems to have had no single center. But the Chavín site, almost 9,000 feet up in the Cordillera Blanca of northern Peru, is a splendid example of the style that would impose itself on much of the central Andes over succeeding centuries.

This extremely old temple complex of truncated pyramids, plazas, and raised platforms impressed the conquistadores in the sixteenth century and continues to impress archaeologists in the twentieth. Perhaps the best brief description is still that of a Spanish chronicler who was closer to the living reality than we are. The temple at Chavín de Huantar, wrote Vasquez de Espinosa, was "a large building of huge stone blocks, very well wrought . . . one of the most famous heathen sanctuaries, like Rome or Jerusalem with us." The Indians, he said, "used to come and make their offerings and sacrifices, for the Devil pronounced many oracles from here, and so they repaired here from all over the kingdom."[4] That was written in the days of the Inca Empire; two millennia before, there was very probably no "kingdom." But the ceremonial center was there, and flourishing.

From the battered walls and chambers of dry stone-masonry that remain, here and elsewhere, a lost way of life may still be reconstructed today.

Agricultural terracing had become extremely elaborate by the first millennium B.C.E., and the multilevel stone terraces followed many winding rivers through the mountains and down to the sea. Large numbers of disciplined workers labored on the temple complexes. Common textiles and ceramics still flourished on the coast, where the temples tended to be built of sundried adobe brick instead of stone. In the uplands, the llama and the alpaca

---

[4]George Bankes, *Peru before Pizarro* (New York: Phaidon Press/E. P. Dutton, 1977), pp. 132–133.

provided meat, wool, and the beast of burden that was so notably lacking elsewhere in the Americas. Trade was well established between regions in Peru, and pilgrims may have threaded the mountain trails to cult centers like Chavín de Huantar, where organized priesthoods served as intermediaries between native American people and their gods.

Chavín Religion and Art

Beyond such concrete details, however, early Peruvian society, even more than that of Mexico, is generally the object of speculation or dispute. Was there a Chavín polity, an empire coextensive with the reach of the culture? It seems extremely unlikely, given the broken country and the size and resources of the population. How then, was that culture disseminated over so wide an area of the central Andes? Opinion inclines to a spreading religious cult that perhaps included a feline god like the Olmec jaguar. It has recently been suggested that the new religion spread together with a new form of corn, which provided the caloric intake to support larger populations and a more diversified society of specialists.

As with Olmec culture, finally, art and religion are the heart of what we know or guess about Chavín.

Chavín religion, like that of the Olmecs, probably involved nature and animal divinities, gods of earth and air and water, and deities who manifested themselves primarily as great cats with snaky hair and monstrous fangs. Sacrifice was also important: one gallery at Chavín de Huantar is heaped with the bones of sacrificial beasts and with fragments of exquisite ceramic ritual vessels. Goods found buried with the dead indicate some hope for an afterlife. Beyond such basic guesses we can know little about the rites, myths, and theologies of the people in the long fringed shirts and simple loincloths who came down the mountain paths to the temple, or of the priests who met them at the gates.

The stone itself remains, as does the ceramic ware and, on the dry coast of Peru, some remarkably preserved textiles and rudely worked gold. All tell us something of the artistic sensibilities of the people who created the Chavín culture.

Unlike the La Venta and other Olmec temples, those of Chavín de Huantar are not solid but are honeycombed with rooms and passages. The largest of them, nicknamed the Castillo (Castle), was originally a three-story structure 250 feet square. Inside, it was a maze of chambers, narrow corridors and galleries, ramps, stairways, and an intricate system of air shafts that brought the bracing air down to the lowest level. It was decorated inside and out with carved heads of eagles, cats, and other creatures—many of them, puzzlingly, native to the Amazon jungles rather than to the mountains or the coast.

These examples of Chavín sculpture look much more like the highly stylized, symbolic carving we associate with pre-Columbian America than does the precocious realism of the Olmec. It is mostly flat bas-relief on stone, though there are some decorative heads, human and animal, protruding from the exteriors of the more elaborate temples. It is as hard to see the falcons in the symmetrical lines and curves and scrolls of a low relief at Chavín de Huantar as it is to pick out the animal masks in a Shang bronze. But the space is as full of restless movement, and the sense of design is as strong in America as it is in the first Chinese culture five hundred or a thousand years before.

Distinctive "stirrup-spout" pottery, woven cloth with painted designs and representations of the cat god, gold beaten into sheets and worked by the technique of *repoussage* into the familiar snarling feline face—all reveal the presence of the common culture we call Chavín.

Then as now, the mountains changed color in the sunset, the wind cried among the peaks, and the big bird floated on the wind. From the height of the drifting condor, the changes in the world below could not have looked like much. Stone terraces along the rivers, temples in isolated valleys or on far coastlines, perhaps larger clusters of dry-stone or wattle-and-daub huts here and there. But in the large cult centers, in the restless patterning of stone and clay and cloth, in the cat god and the unknown prayers of Chavín people, there was something new in the Andean world. There was a shared spirit, a common culture, the beginning of a pan-Andean civilization before any documentable political union had yet emerged on the wrinkled land below.

SUMMARY

Civilization emerged beyond Eurasia in these early centuries as well. Parts of both Africa and the Americas still have their share of shards and ruins dating from this period more than twenty centuries ago.

Egypt, discussed in an earlier chapter, was the oldest of these early African civilizations. Others were Kush, located in Nubia south of Egypt, and the commercial empire of Carthage.

Both the Kingdom of Kush and the Carthaginian Empire were at their height during the later first millennium B.C.E. Kush evolved under Egyptian influence farther up the Nile, in what is today Sudan. Kushite kings even ruled Egypt for a time in the eighth century B.C.E. During the golden age of Kush (third to the first centuries B.C.E.), the furnaces of Kushite Meroe may have spread iron and ironworking across much of Africa, enabling that continent to skip the Bronze Age entirely.

Carthage established a commercial empire including most of the western Mediterranean, with trading posts beyond Gibraltar on the Atlantic coasts of Europe and Africa. At its height in the middle of the first millennium, Carthage repelled the Greeks, but it fell at last to the Romans in the middle of the second century B.C.E.

The first Native American peoples to make their way from the Old World to the New settled in America north of the Rio Grande. After thousands of years as hunters and gatherers, they moved toward the settled life of predominantly agricultural villages.

The larger Amerindian populations south of the Rio Grande moved still further from their food-gathering beginnings. The mother cultures of Middle and South America were those of the Olmecs and the Chavín, both of which flourished during the first millennium B.C.E.

Olmec culture, which produced the famous giant stone Olmec heads, developed on the Caribbean coast of Mexico around modern Veracruz. Sites like La Venta were probably religious ceremonial centers rather than cities. But the structured society and uniquely naturalistic art of the Olmecs indicate a highly sophisticated culture.

The Peruvian culture named for the elaborate stone temples at Chavín de Huantar was also socially complex. Elaborately terraced fields and large stone structures reveal an impressive material culture. As with the Olmecs, however, there is no evidence of centralized political institutions.

SUGGESTED READING

Adams, R. E. W. *Ancient Civilizations of the New World.* Boulder, Colo.: Westview Press, 1997. Brief survey of both Mesoamerican and South American civilizations.

Ben Khader, A. B.A., and D. Soren, eds. *Carthage: A Mosaic of Ancient Tunisia.* New York: American Museum of Natural History and W. W. Norton, 1987. Western and North African perspectives, beautifully illustrated by many color photographs.

Burger, R. L. *Chavín and the Origins of Andean Civilization.* New York: Thames and Hudson, 1992. Brief illustrated overview of the oldest South American civilization.

Burstein, S., ed. *Ancient African Civilizations: Kush and Axum.* Princeton: Markus Wiener, 1998. Useful introduction to these two successive East African states.

Clark, J. E., and M. E. Pye. *Olmec Art and Archaeology in Mesoamerica.* Washington, D.C.: National Gallery of Art, 2000. Authoritative discussions of the Olmec achievement.

Coe, M. D. *Mexico: From the Olmecs to the Aztecs,* 4th ed. New York: Thames and Hudson, 1994. Short, readable overview.

Hansberry, W. L. *Africa and Africans as Seen by Classical Writers,* ed. J. E. Harris. Washington, D.C.: Howard University Press, 1981. Discussion of references to Africa by Greek and Roman scholars, poets, and others.

Hassig, R. *War and Society in Ancient Mesoamerica.* Berkeley and Los Angeles: University of California Press, 1992. Sophisticated examination of empire-building and war-making capacities.

Hurt, R. D. *Indian Agriculture in America: Prehistory to the Present.* Lawrence: University of Kansas Press, 1987. Includes some emphasis on pre-Columbian agriculture.

Krech, S. *The Ecological Indian: Myth and History.* New York: W. W. Norton, 1999. Challenges the view that Native Americans consciously acted to preserve their environment.

Lazenby, J. F. *Hannibal's War: A Military History of the Second Punic War.* Warminster, England: Aris and Phillips, 1978. Detailed narrative account of the great African general's long struggle against Rome. See also his account titled *The First Punic War: A Military History* (Stanford: Stanford University Press, 1996).

Shinnie, M. *Ancient Nubia.* New York: Kegan Paul, 1996. A leading archaeologist's summary account. See also her *Ancient African Kingdoms* (New York: New American Library, 1970), a quick overview.

Soren, D. *Carthage: Uncovering the Mysteries and Splendors of Ancient Tunisia.* New York: Simon & Schuster, 1990. Recent illustrated view.

Taylor, J. H. *Egypt and Nubia.* Cambridge, Mass.: Harvard University Press, 1991. The British Museum's excellent holdings illustrate many aspects of Nubian life.

Welsby, D. A. *The Kingdom of Kush: The Napatan and Meroitic Empires.* Princeton, N.J.: Markus Wiener, 1998. Brief but scholarly treatment.

Yamauchi, E. M., ed. *Africa and Africans in Antiquity.* East Lansing: Michigan State University Press, 2001. Up-to-date papers on ancient Kush and Meroe, Nubia, Carthage, and the Maghreb.

Please refer to the document CD-ROM for primary sources related to this chapter.

OVERVIEW II

THE CLASSIC AGE

(500 B.C.E.–C.E. 500)

....

Classic is a word with a ring to it. It conjures up the polished enamel and gleaming chrome of ancient automobiles, or orchestras tuning up. A classic age should be something splendid.

What makes the half-dozen centuries centering upon the time of Christ so distinctive as to earn them such a label?

In the first place, there is a certain scale and grandeur to them. Both the Roman Empire and Han China were about the size of the United States today. The Guptas ruled the subcontinent of India, and successive Persian empires filled most of the Middle East most of the time. Important political units of this second age of human history were thus considerably larger than those of earlier times.

A special feature of the so-called classic age of world history is an increased level of contact between neighboring societies, particularly between the formerly islanded civilizations of Eurasia. Goods could travel from China to Rome in the time of Christ.

Still, there is more to the claim that these centuries constitute a classic age than the size

of empires and the reach of trade. There is a breadth and depth of accomplishment here too that is hard to match in even the most brilliant of the earlier cultures.

The civilizations of the classic age had, after all, the advantage of being able to draw upon the cultural, political, economic, and technological heritage of their predecessors—and go on from there. The Classical Maya, for instance, had hundreds of years of Mesoamerican experience in monumental architecture, stone carving, even mathematics and astronomy, to build upon. The people of Axum brought with them into East Africa the skills at building and trading developed over centuries in their Yemeni homeland.

To some degree, it is perhaps a matter of tone—a tone of confident supremacy that few before or since can match. Like the rich, full tones of a symphony orchestra, the civilizations of the classic age radiated a powerful confidence that they knew what they were doing.

Roman poets or Han historians spoke with confidence of their place in the world as one of absolute supremacy—of Rome as "the City and the World" or of China as the "Middle Kingdom" ringed by hopelessly inferior barbarians.

A grand scale of political organization, sustained trade and communication between peoples, breadth and depth of cultural achievement, and a tone of confident certainty about it all are perhaps as close as we can come to defining the classic age. Yet there is an undeniable feel of cultural climax to these centuries immediately before and after Christ—we can scarcely be more precise—that other ages of civilization can only envy.

CLASSICAL CIVILIZATIONS

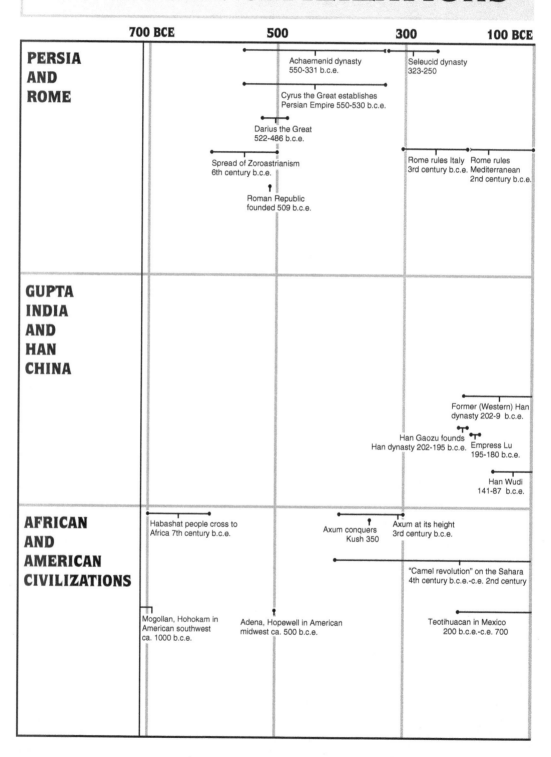

	700 BCE	500	300	100 BCE

PERSIA AND ROME

Achaemenid dynasty 550-331 b.c.e.

Seleucid dynasty 323-250

Cyrus the Great establishes Persian Empire 550-530 b.c.e.

Darius the Great 522-486 b.c.e.

Spread of Zoroastrianism 6th century b.c.e.

Rome rules Italy 3rd century b.c.e.

Rome rules Mediterranean 2nd century b.c.e.

Roman Republic founded 509 b.c.e.

GUPTA INDIA AND HAN CHINA

Former (Western) Han dynasty 202-9 b.c.e.

Han Gaozu founds Han dynasty 202-195 b.c.e.

Empress Lu 195-180 b.c.e.

Han Wudi 141-87 b.c.e.

AFRICAN AND AMERICAN CIVILIZATIONS

Habashat people cross to Africa 7th century b.c.e.

Axum conquers Kush 350

Axum at its height 3rd century b.c.e.

"Camel revolution" on the Sahara 4th century b.c.e.-c.e. 2nd century

Mogollan, Hohokam in American southwest ca. 1000 b.c.e.

Adena, Hopewell in American midwest ca. 500 b.c.e.

Teotihuacan in Mexico 200 b.c.e.-c.e. 700

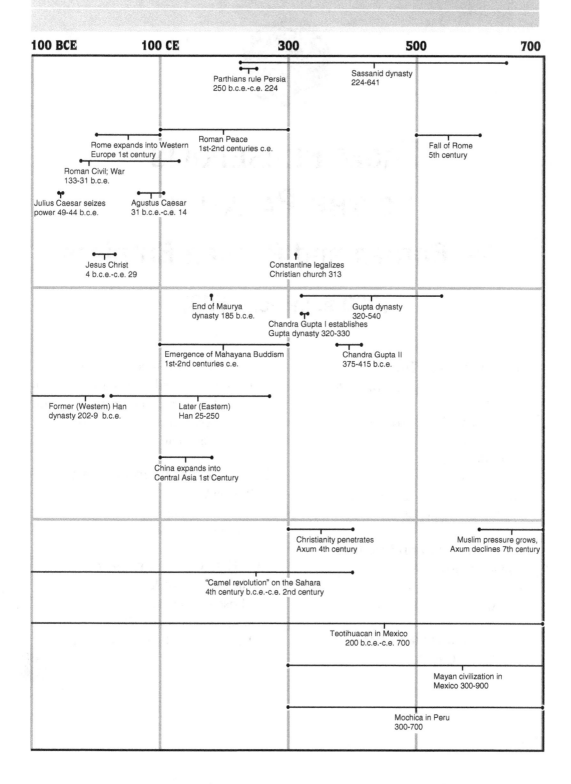

100 BCE	100 CE	300	500	700

Parthians rule Persia
250 b.c.e.-c.e. 224

Sassanid dynasty
224-641

Rome expands into Western
Europe 1st century

Roman Peace
1st-2nd centuries c.e.

Fall of Rome
5th century

Roman Civil; War
133-31 b.c.e.

Julius Caesar seizes
power 49-44 b.c.e.

Agustus Caesar
31 b.c.e.-c.e. 14

Jesus Christ
4 b.c.e.-c.e. 29

Constantine legalizes
Christian church 313

End of Maurya
dynasty 185 b.c.e.

Gupta dynasty
320-540

Chandra Gupta I establishes
Gupta dynasty 320-330

Emergence of Mahayana Buddism
1st-2nd centuries c.e.

Chandra Gupta II
375-415 b.c.e.

Former (Western) Han
dynasty 202-9 b.c.e.

Later (Eastern)
Han 25-250

China expands into
Central Asia 1st Century

Christianity penetrates
Axum 4th century

Muslim pressure grows,
Axum declines 7th century

"Camel revolution" on the Sahara
4th century b.c.e.-c.e. 2nd century

Teotihuacan in Mexico
200 b.c.e.-c.e. 700

Mayan civilization in
Mexico 300-900

Mochica in Peru
300-700

CHAPTER 6

FROM PERSEPOLIS
TO THE PALATINE
The Roman and Persian Empires

(500 B.C.E.–C.E. 650)

A Glance Ahead: The Wide Empires of Western Eurasia

Rome and Persia were wide empires indeed. The Roman Empire encompassed Western Europe, plus slices of North Africa and the Near East. At its height, the empire of the Persians reached from the Middle East to Central Asia.

The Roman Empire, whose ruins dot the landscape of Western Europe, is as well known as any slice of ancient history is to modern Western people. The Persian Empire is less familiar—yet it was unified earlier and lasted longer than Rome did. Between them, these two sprawling dominions brought order to roughly half of civilized Eurasia.

The thousand years of Roman history break down into two five-hundred-year chunks, the Republic and the Empire. Persia's twelve hundred years are subdividable into a series of ruling dynasties. Yet both preserved a remarkable unity and continuity across their broad swathes of the globe. It was a unity that would never be matched again in either Europe or the Middle East, two regions that have been notable for divisiveness and violence for most of their history since.

Dynasties of Persian Power

The Middle East

To many Westerners, the Middle East means mostly oil—or oil and bloody little wars that never seem to settle anything. It is a tangle of states, middling or small in size but almost uniformly underpopulated, barren, and of interest only because of the oceans of petroleum beneath their sun-baked soil. Historically, the region is much more interesting than that. Geographically, it is certainly more complicated.

Even by a conservative definition, the Middle East is a huge slice of land.[1] It stretches from Arabia in the west to modern Afghanistan in the east, from the Black and Caspian seas in the north to the Red Sea, the Persian Gulf, and the Arabian Sea in the south. It is as far from one end of this region to the other as it is from New York to California.

The region is also much more heterogeneous topographically than the popular impression of a desert floating on oil might indicate. The northern tier of large Middle Eastern nations—Turkey, Iran, and Afghanistan—consists of high plateaus ringed by protecting mountains. The southerly tangle of states including Israel, Jordan, Lebanon, Syria, Arabia, the states of the Persian Gulf, and Iraq have their share of rolling sands; but they also have such important rivers as the Tigris, the Euphrates, and the Jordan.

North or south, however, most of the Middle East is low on both rainfall and population. The region has produced more than its share of nomads moving their flocks from one oasis or stubbly pasturage to the next. From the deserts of Arabia to the rugged Anatolian Plateau of Turkey and on to the mountains of Afghanistan, the area has bred hard people leading hard lives. Perhaps for this reason they have taken special pleasure in each historic Middle Eastern metropolis, from ancient Thebes and Babylon to Persian Persepolis and Islamic Damascus and Baghdad.

---

[1]The terms *Middle East* and *Near East* are frequently used almost interchangeably. In this book, *Near East* means primarily the states and regions of the eastern end of the Mediterranean, from Mesopotamia up through Palestine and the Levant to Constantinople and the Straits connecting the Mediterranean and the Black Sea. The term *Middle East* will usually be used to denote the considerably larger area described in this section.

During the millennium centering roughly on the time of Christ, this diversified region enjoyed a period of intermittent unity presided over by a series of powerful Persian dynasties. Of these, the first unifiers of the Middle East were the Achaemenids (550–331 B.C.E.), the royal house founded by Cyrus the Great.

Cyrus the Great

Cyrus the Persian (550–530 B.C.E.)—Cyrus the Shepherd, as they called him in his own time—was a self-made emperor if there ever was one. He seems to have been shrewdly merciful with defeated foes, judiciously tolerant of all religions, and automatically and totally courageous. He lived, fought, and died with the modest simplicity we would expect of a man who might have had trouble making his own mark on a Babylonian clay tablet. The fact that he devoted nearly all of his life, as far as we know it, to fighting with his fellow men is all the staunchest modern moralist could hold against him. And that, as they say, was a vice of the times rather than of the man.

The Persians and their overlords the Medes were Indo-Europeans, descendants of steppe nomads who had drifted south onto the Iranian Plateau hundreds of years before. In the sixth century B.C.E., they were still a warlike, semipastoral people living in the mountains of what is today western Iran. There they were within easy striking distance of the rich valley of the Tigris and Euphrates. The Medes had in fact participated prominently in the destruction of the penultimate Mesopotamian empire, that of the Assyrians.

By the middle of the sixth century B.C.E., however, the Medes had grown soft. This apparently put ideas into the head of Cyrus, hereditary chief of the tributary Persian tribes, in his mountain city of Pasagardae. In 550 B.C.E. Cyrus marched on the last Medean king, overthrew him, and made himself king of the Medes and the Persians. The twenty years of victories that followed constitute one of the most astonishing careers of blood and glory in the history of western Eurasia.

Cyrus's horse soldiers wore leather breeches and heavy felt boots, sat upon their rugged mountain ponies like centaurs, and were armed with the short, powerful compound bows of their steppe ancestors. They had a leader of genius in Cyrus. In his reign and that of his two successors, the Persians made themselves masters of the largest empire the sixth-century world had seen.

Three years after seizing control of the Median confederacy, Cyrus crossed the Taurus Mountains into what is today Turkey and there overthrew King Croesus of Lydia. The Lydians may have been the inventors of coinage, and Croesus was widely believed to be the richest king in the world. With the fabled wealth of Croesus at his command, Cyrus swung eastward, accepting submission from most of the tribes and peoples of modern-day Iran and Afghanistan. Only then, with a huge army and many victories behind him, did Cyrus turn south for the richest prize of all: Babylon.

The New Babylonian Empire was in decay and disarray. The unworthy heirs of Nebuchadnezzar, feuding with the powerful priesthoods of the city, had lost their authority over the people. With the help of a shrewd propaganda campaign, a Babylonian collaborator, and a well-placed victory or two, Cyrus was able to take possession of Babylon in 539 B.C.E. without even a token siege. It was the end of Mesopotamian independence and the beginning of Persian greatness in the Middle East.

Cyrus died in the saddle nine years later, struck down in a war with the queen of a nomadic tribe in eastern Iran. His son Cambyses conquered the other earliest center of civilization, Egypt. Cambyses' successor, Darius I, extended the power of the Persians still further. His armies crossed both the Indus River into northwestern India and the straits of Bosporus and Dardanelles into southeastern Europe, where he accepted the submission of Macedonia, on the northern frontiers of Greece.

By 500 B.C.E. the Persian Empire was thus the master of the Middle East, the great power between Europe and farther Asia. For a thousand years, the Persians and their successors would maintain that position. Persia would be a powerful threat to its neighbors east and west and a crucial link in the chain of commerce and cultural influences that would connect the Roman and the Han Chinese empires in the days of the Caesars.

Cyrus the Shepherd was buried in a simple, house-shaped tomb on the grounds of his palace in mountain-girt Pasagardae. The Persian Empire itself was a far more splendid monument to the barbarian king.

Darius the Great

But Cyrus was first and last a soldier. It was his successors Cambyses and particularly Darius I who transformed a patchwork of conquered tributary states into the most impressive political structure—and the most physically impressive empire—in the western Eurasia of that time.

Some of the pillars of the Persian emperor's royal audience hall in Persepolis, in modern Iran, still tower against an evening sky. If you had only the destruction of this palace by Alexander the Great to go by, whom would you judge more "civilized"—the Greeks or the Persians? (The Oriental Institute, the University of Chicago)

Darius I (522–486 B.C.E.), also sometimes called the Great, ruled a huge realm. He had to govern a considerable variety of peoples, from sophisticated Egyptians and Babylonians and businesslike Lydians and Greeks to his own vigorous Persians and Medes and the wilder steppe peoples, such as the Scythians and Parthians, with a handful of Indians from beyond the Hindu Kush thrown in. And he and those who followed him on the throne of Cyrus had to hold this vast empire together without the benefit of modern technology, modern bureaucracy, or the faintest shadow of modern national feeling. That they were able to do it at all is a tribute to the ingenuity and organizing ability of these barbarians turned empire builders.

Achaemenid Persia—so called after a revered ancestor of Cyrus—was divided into a couple of dozen provinces called satrapies. Each of these was headed by an appointed satrap, or governor, often a member of the imperial family or a prestigious local nobleman. The satraps were normally granted wide-ranging political, military, and financial autonomy. Indeed, as long as a satrapy paid its tribute on time and provided its share of recruits for the army, the province could pretty much go its own way in matters of local concern.

This loose-reined autonomy was balanced, however, by an ingenious array of imperial controls. There were garrisons of royal troops at strategic points across the empire. There were also royal agents, known as "the king's eyes and ears," who kept tabs on both the satraps and their people, alert for signs of official conspiracy or popular rebellion.

Beyond these coercive measures, a more subtle web of common institutions brought a deeper unity to the empire. Darius formulated a single imperial code of laws, based on Mesopotamian models going back to Hammurabi, for all his peoples. He borrowed the idea of a minted coinage from the Lydia of Croesus, and soon royal gold and silver coins were in use all across Persia. A common set of weights and measures was also established, a system of royal couriers and mail, a common calendar (borrowed from Egypt), and a lingua franca, the Aramaic tongue already widely used for business purposes in the Near East.

Darius built extensively too. A network of hundreds of miles of roads linked the far places of the Persian Empire. The Royal Road from the capital at Susa in central Persia to the western city of Sardis, not far from the Aegean, was more than fifteen hundred miles long. Darius and his heirs took their ease in gardens they called "paradises" and in great palaces at Susa, Babylon, and, most splendid of all with its hundred-columned hall, Persepolis.

Gone were the rough leather breeches of Cyrus's rude cavalry; the marching soldiers sculptured on the walls of the palace at Persepolis wear the long robes called *kaftans*, heavy bracelets, and their hair and beards carefully curled in the Mesopotamian fashion. King Darius or Xerxes, his heir, robed in Tyrean purple, heavy with gold embroidery, gold jewelry, and a high tiara of gold, awed his prostrate nobles into the conviction that they were "in very truth . . . looking upon the lord of all the earth."[2]

The Seleucids and the Parthians

The Achaemenid Persian Empire marks the climax of the strain of urban-imperial civilization that had first emerged in Mesopotamia and Egypt three thousand years before. But Persia also marks a transition from the relatively small polities of these earlier millennia to the much larger empires of later ages. And the Persian Empire itself remained at least an intermittent player on the great-power stage for more than a thousand years.

---

[2]A.T. Olmstead, *History of the Persian Empire* (Chicago: University of Chicago Press, 1948), pp. 282–283.

At the beginning of the fifth century B.C.E. a handful of Ionian Greek city-states on the Aegean coast revolted against Darius and found support from the newly emergent Greek city of Athens. Darius suppressed the Ionian Greeks, but the punitive expeditions he and his successor Xerxes sent against Athens and the other Greek cities of the West were decisively defeated. As the fifth century advanced, palace intrigues and harem plots undermined the power of the kings of kings. Persian women took the lead in such conspiracies, proving as ruthlessly ambitious as the men who had founded the dynasty. And in the fourth century B.C.E., as we have seen, the young Macedonian king Alexander the Great led the forces of the Greek West in a counterattack that shattered the Achaemenid empire.

Later dynasties labored with varying success to rebuild the greatness of Persia. Two of these were dynasties of foreign kings, the Greek Seleucids and the Parthians, another wave of intruders from the northern steppes. The third was a new Persian dynasty, the Sassanids. Among them they carried the history of this ancient empire throughout the classic age.

The Seleucids (323–250 B.C.E.) were the Greek dynasty who ruled Persia for the better part of a century after Alexander the Great conquered it. Seleucus was one of Alexander's chief lieutenants. Within a decade or so after the Macedonian conqueror's death in Babylon in 323 B.C.E., his generals had parceled out his vast empire among themselves. Seleucus got the best of it—most of the Persian domain, minus Egypt. He and his successors were great builders of cities and great Hellenizers, spreading the Greek way of life at least to urban enclaves across the Middle East.

The Parthians replaced the Seleucids around 250 B.C.E. and ruled till C.E. 224, five long and tumultuous centuries. A warrior people from east of the Caspian Sea, the Parthians challenged the Romans for dominance of the ancient Near East. Their cavalry attacks and volleys of arrows combined with the blistering sun of the region to swallow up whole Roman legions.

These rugged fighters also played a more constructive role in the establishment of trade across the Eurasian continent. As we will see in a later chapter, this series of trade routes linked China in the east with the Roman Empire in the west. In so doing, the Great Silk Road curved down from the mountains of Central Asia into Persia. In Persia, Parthian and later Sassanid rulers guaranteed merchants safe passage—and took their share of the profits of this legendary road.

But the Parthians seem to have lacked the organizing ability of the Persians. They let much power go by default into the hands of local nobility, the Iranian barons who would play such an important part in Persian history from this time on.

The Sassanid Revival

The Sassanids, finally, expelled the Parthians in C.E. 224 and ruled the empire until 641, several centuries after the fall of Rome. The Sassanids—the word originally meant simply "Commanders"—were of Iranian stock, like the first Persians, and they claimed an Achaemenid connection. The four-hundred-year reign of the Sassanids is thus often seen as a restoration of the realm's legitimate rulers. Of the three dynasties, it certainly came the closest to equaling the splendor of the days of Cyrus and Darius.

During their four centuries on the Persian throne, the Sassanids constructed an elaborate system of power. It was a system based on a carefully structured bureaucracy and on two influential groups—the Iranian barons and the magi, or priests of Zoroaster.

A cluster of state officials directed the affairs of this most developed of Persian governments. In most periods, the chief of these was the grand vizier, the king's right hand

and the operational head of the state. Other powerful officials were the chief priest, head scribe, and general of the armies. Below this exalted level, appointed officials spread out to the four main provinces, the lesser satrapies and other districts.

The Iranian barons, or Persian nobility, granted estates along the frontiers of the empire, and provided a flexible border defense. In defending their own lands, these Iranian barons protected the Sassanid Empire as well. The ancient Zoroastrian priesthood, whose religious ideas will be discussed below, also served the state well. The magi collected the crucial peasant land tax on which government finances depended and provided religious sanction for Sassanid imperial power.

Under the Sassanids, that power was great enough to challenge the West once more, as Persia had done in the days of Darius and Xerxes. Under these rulers, Persia expanded until it briefly matched the vast extent of the original Persian Empire of the Achaemenids. At its greatest extent, Sassanid power reached from today's Pakistan in the east to Egypt in the west and northward into Central Asia, and up to the suburbs of Constantinople.

The building of this vast empire, however, brought Persia once more into conflict with Western powers, first with ancient Rome, then with the medieval Byzantine Empire, whose capital was Constantinople. In later Sassanid times, when Rome and Byzantium were Christian states, the struggle acquired overtones of a religious clash between Zoroastrian and Christian. Exhausted by these wars, the Sassanid regime fell in its turn to the first wave of Muslim conquerors to come galloping out of Arabia.

The Persian achievement was a monumental one indeed, with a geographical and historical dimension that reaches through classic and even into the medieval period of Western history. It is a powerful illustration of the scope of human political achievement across the western end of Asia.

PERSIAN SOCIETY AND CULTURE

Peoples, Classes, Genders

The Persian Empire, like most large ancient empires, made no effort to homogenize its diverse populations into a single people. Instead, Persia remained a land of many peoples, a hierarchy of classes, and a variety of patterns of gender relations.

At its height, the empire included such ancient peoples as Mesopotamians and Egyptians, as well as citizens of newly emerging Greek city-states. It encompassed both sophisticated Mediterranean peoples and Central Asian tribes. As a result, the satraps who governed these very different provinces enjoyed a large degree of autonomy to deal with local problems appropriately.

In terms of class, there is a certain similarity. At least within the wealthy urban societies of the empire, aristocrats, officials, priests, merchants, artisans, peasants, laborers, and slaves were to be found. The imperial government could relate to such groups much as their former governments had—again, probably a source of stability.

Gender relations could, however, differ significantly from one part of the empire to another. In Mesopotamia, for instance, a rise in the slave population undercut the traditional claim of women workers to jobs in handicraft industries. In Egypt, by contrast, we have documents testifying to the persistence of many legal rights for women. A marriage contract, for instance, guaranteed the bride not only the return of her dowry in the event of the marriage's dissolution, but also a third of her husband's earnings.

ACHAEMENID PERSIAN EMPIRE

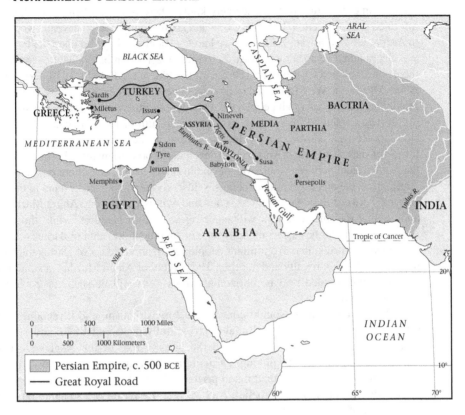

Like the Roman Empire, then, the Persian Empire of the classic age was a complex assemblage of communities and groups. That these groups were able to function in tandem at all is a testimony to the success of the succession of dynasties who ruled Persia for more than a thousand years.

The Faith of Zoroaster

The earliest religion of the Persians was probably the sort of polytheistic worship of natural forces that was common among ancient peoples. Indo-European Persians prayed to the powerful Anahita, goddess of the life-giving waters, and to Mithra, god of the sun. They sensed the presence of the numinous, the wholly other, the divine in the forces of light and darkness, earth and wind. Sacrificial fire played a central part in the religion of the early Persians, as it did among their Aryan relatives in India. There was a caste or tribe of priests among them—the magi—who like Indian brahmans performed all religious ceremonies.

Then, in the same sixth century that saw the emergence of the Persian Empire under Cyrus and Darius, a new and startlingly different religion appeared in Persia. Its founder was a prophet called Zoroaster, a mysterious figure about whom almost nothing is known with certainty. There are legends in plenty, of course, as there are surrounding most religious leaders. There are stories of his miraculous birth, his visions, his ten years' labor to find his first convert; of the Persian satrap who became his first patron, of his temporary happiness and later misfortunes, even of his murder by barbarous nomads while he prayed before the sacred flame. In actual fact, we scarcely know where or even when he lived, though best-informed guesses seem to be eastern Iran and sixth century. We do have his words, however, in *Avesta,* the Zoroastrian Bible, and we know what effect they had upon the Persians.

Six hundred years before Christ, Zoroaster preached a religion that had many of the elements of developed Christianity. There was, he said, not a multiplicity of gods but one god: Ahura Mazda, the Wise Lord, god of light, goodness, and truth. Ahura Mazda was the creator of all things, the judge of all people, the rewarder of virtue with an infinity of spiritual bliss.

It was a splendid vision. But, as in the later faith of the Christians, there was a dark side too. Zoroastrianism saw a principle of evil in the world also—the cosmic Liar, the prince of darkness, called Ahriman in developed Zoroastrianism. The universe itself was the battleground between Ahura Mazda and his chief lieutenant Mithra on the one side, and Ahriman on the other. All human beings, said Zoroaster, must take a stand in this eons-long struggle between light and darkness, good and evil. For in the end Ahura Mazda must win, and on that day his followers will enter rejoicing into paradise, while those who have served the Liar will be cast from the Bridge of Judgment into a pit of darkness and torment.

It was a creed suited to a militant people, and from the days of Darius the Great it was the faith of Persian royalty and nobility. The symbol of Ahura Mazda—a small human figure in profile, framed by vast horizontal wings—can still be seen carved in the ruined stone of Persepolis.

The Persians seldom sought converts to Zoroastrianism, and it remained largely the religion of an aristocratic elite. But even so carefully preserved a faith underwent change, as all faiths do. The fire sacrifice and the priestly role of the magi were annexed to Zoroastrianism from the beginning. Particularly under the Sassanids, every village had its sacred fire and two magi to tend it and perform all sacrifices. Other gods clustered around Ahura Mazda in popular folk belief. And Mithra, the Wise Lord's champion, became the protagonist of a growing cult of his own.

The Persians' Zoroastrian vision had its influence on neighboring peoples too. The faith spread eastward into India, where the Parsi sect comprises the largest body of Zoroastrians in the world today. The cult of Mithra the sun god, champion of light against darkness, spread westward to become a popular mystery religion in Rome and the favorite cult of Roman soldiers all over the empire. Even the Zoroastrian Liar found a place in foreign pantheons as the Satan of the Christians—the Father of Lies whose pit of fiery punishment carries more than an echo of the pit of Ahriman.

The Art of Imperial Persia

The pillars of Persepolis are the best-known relics of Persia's early glories. On a huge stone-faced platform projecting from a wall of cliffs, Darius the Great and his son Xerxes raised an intricate complex of palaces, monumental portals, harems, and audience halls in the fifth century B.C.E. Here was the celebrated hall of a hundred columns where Darius sat in state—the hall that Alexander and his drunken generals gave over to the flames a century and a half later.

One may climb the broad double stairway today, with its flanking bas-reliefs of marching soldiers and subjects bearing tribute, and pass through surviving doorways and porticos carved with the royal figures of massive human-headed bulls. There is a huge fallen capital crowned with back-to-back bulls' heads that would be echoed centuries later on the pillars of Asoka in far-off India. And there are the soaring columns, sixty-five feet high, that once supported the lofty roofbeams of Achaemenid palaces.

Achaemenid glazed brick from Susa shows Persian soldiers in long embroidered kaftans, bows and quivers on their backs, long spears held vertically before them. Such figures give an idea at least of the blaze of color that once dazzled the eye of a Herodotus—or an Alexander—approaching a Persian royal residence for the first time. Persian treasure troves include gold and silver jewelry, cups of bronze and ivory, chased daggers, and plates of silver. From such exquisite work we may get an idea of life at the top among the most ancient Persians.

There is a monumental, formal, ceremonial quality to much of this art of ancient Persia that clearly derives from the Mesopotamian provinces of the empire. It is an art of audience halls and throne rooms, of silhouetted soldiers in embroidered robes. But there is a flowing freedom of movement to the bronze and gold and silver animals, the lions and griffins, a winged ibex leaping into space. There is a freshness and vitality here that breathes the cooler air of the Iranian Plateau—or the winds of the distant steppes.

And from time to time a living face looks out. From Susa the marble head of a Parthian queen, smooth-cheeked and calm, carved in polished stone in the Greco-Roman manner, gazes thoughtfully upon the world. From the distant Asiatic province of Tajikistan, a clay-sculpted head of a man, short-bearded and warmly capped, eyebrows raised, mustache tilted in a smile, radiates a sense of life. Such faces remind us that life did in fact once beat between the ribs of men and women who moved through the streets of even such exotic places as Persepolis and Susa.

ROME—REPUBLIC INTO EMPIRE

The Roman City-State

The Romans have an image in history very different from that of the creative, liberty-loving, self-destructive Greeks who preceded them as the dominant European people in the Mediterranean world. In fact, however, these two strikingly dissimilar peoples were descended from common Indo-European origins somewhere on the Caucasian steppes. Speakers of various Italic dialects, including Latin, probably drifted into the Mediterranean basin at roughly the same time—early in the first millennium B.C.E.—as the Greek speakers to the east. Their histories were to be closely linked from then on.

Other peoples lived and flourished in the Italian peninsula before Rome rose, of course, most prominent among them the Etruscans. But, like the Minoans and Mycenaeans, whose civilizations preceded that of the Greeks in the Aegean, the ancient Etruscans are a people all but lost in the mists of history.

The Etruscans probably came, like the Minoans, from somewhere in Asia Minor. They imposed their rule upon the Iron Age natives living north of the Tiber River in central Italy sometime early in the first millennium B.C.E. They built a loose league of fortified cities, made lovely pottery, and furnished their tombs with grave goods of bronze. They learned to read and write from Greek colonies established in southern Italy and Sicily, and they passed this skill on to the Romans. By 500 B.C.E., however, Etruscan sovereignty over central Italy was drawing to a close. In the fourth century a decadent Etruria was absorbed by Rome; in the third the Greek colonies of the south followed the Etruscans into the Roman maw. It was a fate that awaited many other peoples then tilling their tiny fields and fighting their petty wars around the Mediterranean in blissful ignorance of the powerhouse that was building on the Tiber.

The core of Roman power lay for centuries in the hard-fisted Roman peasantry and their grim patrician overlords. Between them they provided the backbone of the Roman army. They were a hardy people, practical, disciplined, and traditionally brave. They were, above all, an intensely conservative lot. Not for these Romans the restless political experiments of the Athenians, or the Greek delight in the free play of the intellect. As their Roman forefathers had done, so would they do. "This thing, Rome," the Roman historian Ennius said "is simply men who know what their past means."

They were, in their own judgment, a people made to rule. "Others, I know," wrote Vergil, the most famous of all Roman poets, "will mould the breathing brass with a finer touch; in marble trace the features to the life." But "these shall be your arts, [Romans:] to rule the subject nations with imperial sway . . . to impose the arts of peace, to spare the humbled, and to crush the proud."[3] In time, much of the Western world would come to accept that judgment—and that imperial sway.

There were many myths of Roman origins, among them Aeneas's flight from burning Troy, and Romulus and Remus suckled by a wolf. In fact the city of Rome seems to have been founded by descendants of a number of tribes—Latins, Sabines, Etruscans—living among the seven hills, meeting in the little valley that would become the Forum. Among these Latin tribes there were two important classes: *patricians,* who were the better-off farmers, and *plebeians,* the poorer. The real centers of authority among them remained for a long time the old tribes and clans, whose heads were the chief men in the emerging Roman state.

Under the Etruscans Rome became a sizable city, important for trade and a power in that part of Italy. Probably sometime around 509 B.C.E., the traditional date of the founding of the Roman Republic, the Latin tribes overthrew their Etruscan kings. The constitution they established to replace the old Etruscan monarchy was dominated by the Senate, a patrician council composed of elder statesmen, former magistrates, and other leaders of the old clans. The magistrates, especially two executive officials called *consuls,* were chosen for short terms by assemblies of the free male fighting men.

Roman women did have more freedom than Greek women did. Upperclass women joined their husbands at the theater, the circus, and the banquet table. Working-class women labored as servants, artisans, shopkeepers, garment workers, nurses, midwives, doctors, entertainers, actresses, dancers, prostitutes, and servers in restaurants and taverns.

The Romans settled their domestic disputes, between patrician and plebeian in particular, with comparatively little violence. The "struggle of the orders" in Rome was settled by a striking conservative compromise. The championship of the interests of the lower social orders was vested in elected officials called *tribunes of the people*—who more often than not supported the will of the patrician Senate. The Roman Republic was to have its share of destructive domestic conflict, but that lay centuries in the future.

The city on the Tiber River extended its sway over the entire Italian peninsula quite rapidly. Fear impelled some of the neighboring states to accept the protection and sovereignty of Rome—fear of a resurgence of Etruscan power, or of the barbarian Goths who had once stormed down from the north. The primitive ethnic organization of the other Italian tribes favored the Romans too: The loosely structured tribal societies that surrounded

---

[3]*The Aeneid,* in *The Works of Vergil,* trans. A. Hamilton Bryce (London: Bohn's Classical Library, 1907), pp. 320–321.

GROWTH OF ROMAN DOMINIONS UNDER THE EMPIRE

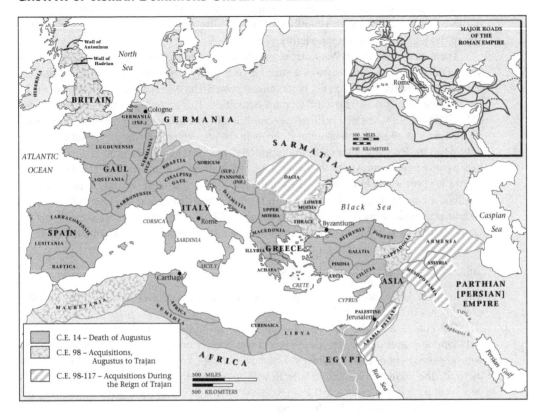

Rome offered little resistance to the imposition of Roman authority. By the end of the third century, Rome was the undisputed master of the Italian peninsula. And the centuries of the Roman conquest were just beginning.

Rome Rules the Mediterranean

During the last three centuries before Christ, then, Rome became the political center of the Mediterranean world.

The empire that grew up around the Mediterranean Sea in the later centuries of the Republic was an oddly improvised, ramshackle, even reluctant affair. The Romans fought a good deal during those centuries, but most commonly in defense of their own interests or those of their allies and their expanding provinces. The rule was unenthusiastic involvement—followed by famous victories—and an expanding empire that led the Romans into more foreign involvements, more wars, more provinces to rule.

Reluctant imperialists though they might be, the Romans were extremely good at empire-building. Italy was Roman by 285 B.C.E. Carthage, Rome's powerful North African rival, which had come to dominate the western Mediterranean, had been decisively defeated by 200 B.C.E. and was destroyed shortly after 150 B.C.E. Macedon and Greece also fell to Roman arms in the middle of the second century, western Persia and Ptolemaic Egypt in the first.

The Romans earned their place in history. Roman discipline and the Roman short sword, the eagle standards, and the tramping legions had a fierce implacability, tenacity of purpose. The epic wars with Hannibal's Carthage illustrate this determination as well as any in the long litany of Roman victories.

There were three Punic Wars, stretching from the middle of the third to the middle of the second century B.C.E. The first was a struggle over Sicily (264–241), where the Carthaginians had replaced the Greeks as the predominant power. The Africans were driven from the island only at the cost of fearsome Roman casualties. The second was the Hannibalic war (212–202), begun when that brilliant general brought an African army down from the Alps on the backs of elephants to take the Romans in the rear. Hannibal was dislodged from Italy only when the Romans, after suffering repeated defeats on their home ground, turned the tables by invading North Africa to shatter the Carthaginians at Zama in 202. The Third Punic War (149–146) was a bitter piece of Roman chauvinism. Carthage was taken, pillaged, and much of it burned. The stubborn Roman refusal to admit defeat despite Hannibal's victories and the pragmatic shrewdness of the Roman general Fabius "the Delayer" in wearing out the Carthaginians by refusing to give battle were typical of the builders of the Roman Empire.

Julius Caesar and the Roman Civil War

The greatest danger to the Roman polity during the last centuries of the Republic, however, lay not in foreign wars but in the threat of civil war.

The conquest of the eastern Mediterranean in particular made some Romans very rich. Opportunities multiplied for pillage in war and for corruption among the *proconsuls,* who governed conquered provinces. Land was cheap, tens of thousands of slaves were there for the taking, taxes and tribute flowed into the hands of the few. They spent their new wealth on broad estates and large houses, on Greek culture and Asiatic luxuries, and forgot the spartan virtues of earlier centuries.

The poor, by contrast, rapidly grew poorer as Roman power spread. Hannibal's campaigns in Italy ravaged the countryside, and long service in the East left farms untenanted. Rich men bought out small holdings, combined them into great estates called *latifundia*, and worked them with slave labor. Roman farmers, landless and unemployed, swarmed to Rome, where the Senate and the consuls now governed in splendor from the white-columned buildings that rose around the ancient Forum. Generals and proconsuls built themselves palaces on the Palatine Hill in Rome; the poor sweltered in multistoried tenements and lived on the grain dole taken in tribute from Sicily and Egypt.

The resulting bitterness of the masses was exacerbated by the increasingly violent political ambitions of the mighty. The very generals whose victories turned the Roman Republic into an empire brought their armies home with them and became a menace to domestic tranquility, indeed to the very existence of the state.

The result of this unhappy mix of social pressures and political ambition was a turbulent century of tension and recurrent violence called the Roman Civil War (roughly 133–31 B.C.E.).

The history of those troubled decades is studded with the names of famous politicians. But it is well to remember that beneath the surface of high politics and military challenge there rumbled the bewilderment, bitterness, and sudden furies of a whole people caught in the grip of trends and currents that were as far beyond their understanding as the political and economic pressures of our own times often beyond our comprehension.

The reforming brothers Tiberius and Gaius Gracchus, tribunes of the people in 133 and 123, respectively, stirred up the popular assemblies, passed laws to provide land for the landless at the expense of the *latifundia,* and were hounded to violent deaths by the Senate. A series of victorious generals next took the center of the stage, mobilizing conservative sentiment and factional political support in the capital to slaughter their enemies. This penultimate round of the Roman Civil War nearly tore the empire apart. It was a savage time, dominated by the powerful personalities of the generals Pompey the Great and Julius Caesar, the latter the only one of them all whose name is a watchword to this day.

As a general, Pompey won many victories for Rome. As a politician, he organized the so-called First Triumvirate, a loose political alliance including a rich nonentity and a much younger but equally ambitious man named Julius Caesar. Caesar spent most of a decade conquering Gaul—most of modern France. Then, feeling threatened by both allies and enemies at home, he turned back toward Rome to face more deadly enemies there than he had found among the Gallic barbarians.

In 49 B.C.E. Caesar crossed the Rubicon River into Italy with the famous remark that "the die is cast"—and all his future hung on that cast. In Rome he smashed an alliance of convenience between Pompey and the Senate. He thereafter drove Pompey from the Italian peninsula and crushed him for good in Greece. He pursued his foes around the Mediterranean, enjoyed a brief liaison with Cleopatra in Egypt, and returned triumphantly to Rome in 46 B.C.E.

He was the undisputed master of the Roman world. He had a little more than two years to live.

Julius Caesar seems to have been a somewhat more complex person than such pithy communiqués as the celebrated *Veni, vidi, vici*—"I came, I saw, I conquered"—might lead us to expect. A famous portrait head of him shows what appears to be a rather thoughtful man, half smiling, shadowed at the temples. He was as ambitious as other victorious Roman generals had been. He may also have had a touch of the reforming Gracchus brothers in his makeup. He claimed at least to be the people's champion, and the aristocratic Senate was terrified of him. The Republic, he said, was a hollow sham.

What exactly he might have done about it if he had lived we cannot know. What he did do was make himself dictator for life, packing the Senate with his officers, and give land to his soldiers. He also inaugurated a program of public works, reorganized the administration of Italy, reformed taxation in the provinces, extended Roman citizenship to at least some conquered peoples, lowered the debt burden, and reformed the calendar. His enemies said he planned to make himself king of Rome.

On the Ides of March, 44 B.C.E., he was stabbed to death in the Senate house by a group of senatorial conspirators led by two of his own lieutenants. Caesar thus died as he had lived—dramatically.

The battered shell of the Republic survived him by a dozen years. The wars and intrigues that followed were complicated and brutal, the last bloody gasp of the Roman Civil War. Caesar's assassins and his old commanders fought while champions of the old order such as the eloquent orator Cicero labored to save the Republic. In the end, they were all out-smarted by a young man who was only nineteen when Julius Caesar died: his grandnephew and adopted son Octavian, known to history as Augustus Caesar.

The year after his uncle's assassination, Octavian and his allies of the Caesarian faction formed the Second Triumvirate and forced the Senate to grant them—and their legions—the power to restore order to the state. In the year 42 B.C.E. at Philippi in northern Greece, they defeated the men who had murdered Caesar. Octavian then fell out with his own allies, most importantly with Caesar's old friend (and Cleopatra's new lover) Antony. In 31 B.C.E. Octavian's forces destroyed Antony's in a naval battle off Actium, and the Roman Civil War was over.

From the reign of Augustus Caesar, we date the most successful and prosperous period of Roman rule: the Principate at home and the Roman Peace over the length and breadth of their wide empire.

Augustus Caesar and the Roman Peace

Gaius Julius Caesar Octavianus, holder of the *imperium* (military command) and of the tribunician power (and hence spokesman for the people), *pontifex maximus* (chief priest), *princeps* (which then meant not "prince" but simply "first citizen"), voted the title of *Augustus* (the Fortunate and Blessed) during his lifetime and "the Divine" after his death, was never officially emperor of Rome at all. Nor were his successors during the most successful centuries of what we call the Empire, as contrasted with the Republic. The purple robe and the diadem, the bowing and scraping as before a Near Eastern potentate, were adopted at Rome only in the fourth century C.E. by rulers desperate to hold the empire together. Augustus had no need for such trappings.

Augustus, Rome's "second founder." The armor, the pose, the upraised arm all embody the force of character and confident authority that made Augustus not merely another successful general and shrewd politician, but the first ruler of Rome's golden age. This idealized portrait, however, probably bears little physical resemblance to the real Octavian. (Library of Congress)

Historians call the order he established the Principate—rule by the princeps. It was a typical conservative Roman compromise, yet it amounted to little less than a second founding of Rome after a century of civil strife.

During the forty-five years of Augustus's rule (31 B.C.E.–C.E. 14), the Senate and the popular assemblies still met. But the former was filled with friends of the first citizen's, and the assemblies seem to have lost all political function. Consuls, proconsuls, tribunes, and other officials were still elected, but only after securing Augustus's political blessing. He ruled the vast empire, whose frontiers now reached to the Rhine and the Danube, as commander of the Roman armies. He dominated Rome on the strength of his great-uncle Julius Caesar's name, his own military triumphs, and the simple fact that he had brought peace and order after decades of civil war. He earned a reputation for piety as the rebuilder of the temples and refurbisher of the cults of the Olympian gods, but he also built temples to the "divine" Julius Caesar and to "Rome and Augustus," thus surrounding the name of the emperor with the faint aura of divine right. He did not go beyond that. But then he did not need to.

The peace and prosperity fashioned by Augustus Caesar lasted for the better part of two hundred years. These were the centuries of the *Pax Romana*, the Roman Peace, an achievement Europe would not see again.

The "good emperors"—Claudius and Trajan, Hadrian, Marcus Aurelius, and others—who reigned during the first and second centuries C.E. perpetuated and expanded the Augustan heritage. They completed the building of the splendid city on the seven hills that future generations would revere as the Rome of the Caesars. They brought the protection of Roman power to more and more of their subjects. And they expanded the empire beyond anything the West had seen before.

Among the material benefits of the empire, three deserve special attention: Roman administration, Roman citizenship, and Roman law.

Roman administration under the Republic had been relatively simple, a matter of the short-term proconsuls, who not infrequently milked their provinces mercilessly. Under the

VOICES FROM THE PAST

Roman emperors like Claudius, as the author of this book points out, used spectacles in the Colosseum to "become 'one with the people.'" Do modern politicians ever give the impression that they share the popular tastes of the masses of the voting public?

[The Emperor] Titus noisily supported the Thracians and apostrophised their adversaries with gibes worthy of a bargee. Claudius proved himself, through simplicity it is true and not by calculation, a model in this respect:

'There was no respectable [situation] . . . in which he appeared more affable and more gay [than at gladiatorial combats]; he could be seen, in the manner of the vulgar, counting on his fingers at the top of his voice the gold pieces offered to the victor. He would urge all the spectators to enjoy themselves, calling them his 'masters' from time to time, and larding his remarks with jokes in fairly bad taste. . . . But what was liked above all was that he wrote notices addressed to the crowd on tablets and had these circulated among the spectators, instead of having them transmitted by means of heralds as was customary.'

Roland Auguet, *Cruelty and Civilization: The Roman Games* (London: Allen and Unwin, 1972), p. 186.

emperors of the first two centuries C.E., however, a much more elaborate system of imperial administration was carried out by paid permanent officials closely supervised by their superiors. It was a system that provided lower taxes and more effective government than most parts of the Roman world had ever known before.

Roman citizenship was also extended far more widely by Augustus and his successors; by approximately C.E. 200, all free provinces had been granted citizenship, making them equal in every way to their conquerors. The army, the bureaucracy, and even the higher reaches of the government were thoroughly opened up to Gauls and Spaniards, Near Easterners and North Africans.

Roman law, finally, embodied the benefits of Roman government more concretely and longlastingly than almost any other aspect of the Roman predominance. The first laws of the Romans had been inscribed on the famous Twelve Tablets as early as the fifth century B.C.E. Over the following centuries, Roman civil and criminal law grew through legislation by the assemblies and decrees promulgated by the emperors, but above all through precedents established by Roman magistrates down the years. The resulting system of justice was among the most impressive bodies of law ever produced.

"Let justice be done," the Roman maxim ran, "though the heavens fall." Mercy was not a Roman strongpoint; stern justice seems to have been.

The sheer size of the empire, as well as the complexity of its government, grew significantly under the *imperators* who followed Augustus. Roman legions pushed farther east into former Persian lands, north across the Danube into central and eastern Europe, north across the Channel to overrun most of Britain. There were setbacks and withdrawals, especially in what was to become Germany, but the legions were generally victorious. At its height, the Roman Empire covered more than three million square miles, only slightly less than the size of the United States today. Recent estimates of the population of the empire run to eighty million, about a third that of modern America.

The Crisis of the Third Century

There were breakdowns, of course, as there are in any human institution, even during the early centuries of the empire. There was the increasing interference of the Praetorian Guard—the elite troops who served as the emperor's bodyguard and policed the city of Rome—in selection of each new emperor. There were tyrants even among the good emperors, men such as the insane Caligula and Nero, who crucified the Christians and drove all Gaul to revolt. And there was plain brutality: the severed hands of those who took up arms against Rome, the enslavement of whole armies of her foes, the popular savagery of gladiatorial contests and public executions.

Neither anarchy nor tyranny, however, was new to either Europe or the Mediterranean. What was unprecedented was the level of general prosperity, the long years of peace. It was when these began to fail seriously that the decline and fall of the Roman Empire began.

It came in two stages. There was a first major breakdown in the third century C.E. This was followed by recovery under an increasingly autocratic regime in the fourth century. But the recovery was only temporary. In the fifth century came the collapse.

The good times seem to have ended with the reign of Marcus Aurelius (161–180), the celebrated Stoic emperor, last of the benevolent successors of Augustus. The next hundred years, the disastrous third century C.E., saw a bewildering series of short-term rulers, many of them provincial generals who were elevated by their troops and then killed by their own or rival legions. Standards of living declined sharply. The countryside was depopulated, the cities swollen with poor people living on the government grain dole, the solid middle classes of society shrinking under the pressures of government exactions. There were rebellious rumblings in the provinces—Gaul, Spain, North Africa—and new pressure on the frontiers from Germanic peoples in Europe and a revived Persian Empire in the East.

This century of disasters was ended by the reforms of the emperors Diocletian and Constantine, who between them at least temporarily restored the Roman order on a more autocratic basis than ever before.

Diocletian (284–305), a strong-willed Balkan peasant from Illyria who had risen through the army, attempted to quell anarchy by the installation of the so-called Tetrarchy. Imperial power was shared among four rulers, two senior *Augusti* and two junior men called *Caesars*. Diocletian strengthened the bureaucracy, reformed taxation in the direction of greater equality—and rigor—and even attempted to fix prices. In his last years he embarked upon the last major persecution of the Christian church, in whose growing power he apparently detected a threat to the restored authority of the state.

The Tetrarchy collapsed after Diocletian, and Constantine (306–337), son of one of the tetrarchs, fought his way to sole mastery of Rome. Constantine carried Diocletian's bureaucratic reforms to even greater lengths. He established two capitals, one at Rome and one at Byzantium (renamed Constantinople in his honor) in the east, where a Byzantine (or East Roman) Empire would survive for another thousand years. He set up an elaborate centralized system of administration involved four huge imperial prefectures, a dozen dioceses, and 120 separate provinces from Britain to Egypt. He also shrewdly separated civil government from the military and encouraged a series of army reforms in order to strengthen the frontiers.

At home the autocratic Constantine prescribed fixed hereditary membership in the crafts and professions. He levied taxes for defense that were so oppressive that free farmers had to be reduced to near slavery if they were to be kept on the land. Only the Christians had obvious cause to love him, for he finally legalized the Christian church in Rome in 313.

Decline and Fall

The fall of Rome in the fifth century C.E., the destruction of one of history's most impressive political achievements, still challenges historians. It clearly involved both internal weakening and external assault.

Of all Rome's preurban neighbors to the north—Germans, Celts, Slavs, and others—the Germanic tribes along the Rhine-Danube frontiers had generally been the most important. Half-Romanized Germans had infiltrated the empire for centuries, as settlers on deserted lands and as mercenary soldiers. Late in the fourth century, however, these Germanic peoples were thrust more violently against Roman frontiers by the onslaught of warlike East Asian nomads following the steppe gradient westward. Thus pressured from the rear, armies of Visigoths, Ostrogoths, Vandals, Franks, and others crashed through the Roman boundaries in force in the fifth century. Barbarian cavalry broke the Roman phalanxes, ravaged whole provinces, and twice sacked Rome itself, the Visigoths in 410, the Vandals in 455. The invaders ended by establishing kingdoms of their own all across the western half of the Roman Empire.

There is little argument about the unhappy sequence of events that Edward Gibbon, in perhaps the most famous of Western histories, christened *The Decline and Fall of the*

Roman Empire. What fills the pages of more recent historical studies are attempts to explain the underlying causes of this mighty fall.

Before the barbarians came, so most modern historians believe, the empire had been fatally weakened from within. It is these internal weaknesses that have preoccupied students of Roman history since Gibbon.

There were obviously political factors at work. The lack of orderly procedures for the transfer of power, thanks to Augustus's shying away from hereditary monarchy, clearly opened the door to political turmoil. After Diocletian and Constantine, there was also the increasing remoteness of government—of emperors in purple and gold glittering with jewels, of elaborate court ceremonies, of corrupt and arrogant bureaucrats.

A wide range of social and economic problems also existed. There was the widening gap between rich and poor, the heavy cost of bread and circuses to keep the poor properly docile, the squeezing of the middle classes of society by government regulation and economic pressure. And there were more technical problems: the diminishing quantities of silver available for coinage, the exhaustion of soil, the abandonment of farmlands. They all added up to a substantial decline in the prosperity that had been one of the empire's chief claims on the loyalty of its subjects.

Demographic factors have been stressed in some analyses. The "barbarization" of the army and much of the bureaucracy that took place when Romans refused to serve seems a major weakness to some. Population decline, especially among the millions of slaves who did much of the work of the empire, may also have weakened the empire seriously.

Cultural and ideological causes may also have played a part. A general malaise, or failure of nerve, as the center failed to hold and things fell apart may have further undermined Rome's will to fight. Gibbon himself put some of the blame on the subversive influence of early Christianity, which siphoned off the best minds for the church and encouraged pacifist and antistate attitudes among its other-worldly followers.

There are historians who throw up their hands at this complex array of causes and simply blame the colossal difficulty of governing so vast an assemblage of lands and peoples with the limited personnel and resources available in Roman times. The wonder was not that Rome fell, this school declares, but that it lasted as long as it did.

Other historians urge that what took place was less the "decline and fall" of a great civilization than the transformation of one society into another one. They emphasize the fact that the Germanic invaders of the Roman Empire had been living on its borders and infiltrating the empire itself for centuries. German chiefs had become landowners, married Roman ladies, taken Roman names, and tried to take part in Roman public life. Even the Germanic invaders of the fifth century sought less to destroy the sophisticated society they had long admired than to take it over and live as the Romans did. Their alien ideas and customs led to the failure of this effort; but the result was less a savage destruction than a slow change from ancient to medieval civilization in the West.

Nevertheless, by the end of the fifth century, there were barbarian kingdoms where once Roman eagles stood, from North Africa to Britain. And in centuries to come, though Rome later became the city of the popes and the center of western Christianity, the teeming metropolis of half a million souls shrank to tens of thousand. The villas of a ruder nobility were built within the gigantic shells of public baths, and goats grazed on the Palatine Hill where palaces had once stood. Difficult as it is to define or explain the end of an era, one surely ended here.

Roman Society and Culture

Roman Women

Ancient Rome, aggressively militaristic and imperialistic as it was, might seem a thoroughly male-dominated society. Yet women played a crucial part in Roman history—and often got some credit for it too.

During the period of the Republic—the first five centuries of Rome's history—women were nominally under the complete control of their fathers. Among the upper classes, at least, the *paterfamilias* or "father of the family" exercised life-and-death power over every member of it, from younger siblings, women, and children to slaves. Even after his daughter married, his power over her was officially greater than that of her husband.

This legal authority, however, seems not to have been much exercised in practice. More important was the belief that a "Roman matron" should be a worthy partner to her stern-faced husband. Virtue, character, and sheer competence were key qualities of the Roman matron. She was expected to be capable, not only of running a large household, but also of exercising political authority while her husband was away at the wars.

Roman women could also legally inherit and manage property, a right that gave them real leverage in society. During the late Republic and the centuries of imperial rule that began with Augustus, ruling-class women significantly expanded their range of independent activity. Moralists professed to be shocked when aristocratic women showed up at banquets, theaters, and horse races, attended gladiatorial combats in the Colosseum, and even took lovers. Poets, on the other hand, sang the praises of these emancipated women and sometimes even fell in love with them themselves.

In some periods, women also exercised significant political power in Rome. Emperor Augustus's wife Livia carved out a place for herself as empress, complete with a substantial staff. Imperial women of the second and third centuries C.E. sometimes actually ruled the empire through weak male emperors. The third-century empress Julia Domna was a powerful ally for her imperial husband Septimius Severus and became known as Julia the Philosopher in the intellectual circle she founded.

The arches of a Roman aqueduct still tower over the city of Segovia in Spain, once a province of the Roman Empire. Like Roman roads and Roman law, Roman cities—with their aqueducts, theaters, and other amenities—were major benefits of the only period of political unity in European history. Can you think of any structures in modern America that will probably still be standing two thousand years from now? (Barbara Rios/Photo Researchers, Inc.)

In Rome as elsewhere, then, the position of women as conventionally defined was considerably different from the positions some women at least were able to carve out for themselves.

Art and Engineering

Roman official religion, literature, art, and philosophy were all based to a considerable degree on Greek mythology, writing, carving, and thought. Over centuries of emulation, the Romans did succeed in absorbing much of Greek culture, in making its conventions theirs, even in going beyond their brilliant neighbors in some areas. But the overall consequence was as clearly derivative as, say, much of modern American culture is derived from that of Europe. Roman culture, therefore, cannot be discussed without repeated backward glances at the cultural achievements of the first of Western civilizations, that of the ancient Greeks.

The Greeks had produced highly idealized representations of gods and great leaders in the Hellenic fifth century B.C.E. and extremely realistic statues in the later, Hellenistic period. Both the ideal and the realistic legacy in sculpture were taken over wholesale by the Romans.

Many Greek statues, for instance, exist today only as stone copies preserved in Rome. But the Romans used Greek styles for their own purposes too. Portrait heads of Roman citizens from the late Republic were as hyperrealistic as any Hellenistic achievement. Yet Roman statuary projects a special force of its own. The strength of a Roman *paterfamilias*—the strength of character that befits the head of an old Republican clan— shows through the craggy features. The whole figure of *Augustus* in armor, one arm upraised, radiates idealized authority as effectively as any fifth-century Greek god—as the image of the refounder of the Roman Empire should.

Nowhere was that spirit expressed more powerfully than in Roman building. The Romans had vast spaces to cover, public baths and basilicas (law courts), palaces and temples built on an imperial scale. To roof such buildings they introduced the arch, the vault, and the dome. They embellished these great buildings with scrolled Ionic and complicated Corinthian columns, with carving and tile and gold leaf. Most of that ornate splendor is gone today. But even the ruins of the Baths of Caracalla and the Basilica of Constantine have a spaciousness and a grandeur not to be found in the Greek world.

In engineering, finally, the pragmatic Roman spirit found one of its truest expressions. The Romans criss-crossed Europe with more than fifty thousand miles of stone-paved roadway, a system not equaled until modern times. The soaring arches of Roman aqueducts awed and baffled the peoples who came after them; the one built to supply Segovia with water was known as the Devil's Bridge to medieval Spaniards. Into the city of Rome itself a total of fourteen aqueducts brought 100 million gallons of water every day.

Roman Poetry: Vergil

The Roman cultural debt to Greece is nowhere clearer than in Roman literature. Again, though, there are distinctive Roman accomplishments to admire.

Most of the common elements in the literature of the two peoples—style, themes, mythological foundations, literary conventions—were the result of conscious modeling of Roman work upon Greek. Thus, if Homer opens his epic *Iliad* by calling upon the gods for divine inspiration, Roman Vergil will not go many lines before he calls upon his Muse for inspiration too. If there is a catalogue of the ships that brought the Greeks to Troy with all their colorful crews in Homer's epic, there will be a catalogue of the peoples that followed Aeneas to Italy in the later poem. And so on, through much of Latin literature. The literary genres are the same for the two peoples: epic and lyric poems, tragedy and comedy, pastoral and satirical modes flourish among them both. There is similarly bawdy humor on both their stages, a common nostalgia for a simpler, pastoral past in much of their verse.

Roman poetry, however, needs no excuses: It clearly matched the best of its Greek precursors and left an influential legacy. There is a barbaric strength to Homer not to be found in later epics, but Vergil's *Aenid*, the Augustan epic of the founding of Rome, has a perhaps subtler power of its own. Vergil's Aeneas is a man with a mission, driven by a Roman sense of duty, yet he is tempted by very human feelings along the way. The mythic core of the story was simple enough: the ancient tale that Rome had been founded by the last Trojan, the hero Aeneas, escaped from flaming Troy and charged by the gods to found a new city in a new land. But it took the genius of Vergil to ask: How would the future founder of Rome feel when his wanderings took him to North Africa and he was welcomed by Queen Dido, busy raising the walls of her own city—Carthage? How would he react, and how would she, when the founders of the two great imperial rivals of Roman times fell passionately in love?

There is much more to the *Aeneid*. But the love of Aeneas and Dido has enthralled readers over the almost two thousand years since Vergil wrote it, in the days of Caesar Augustus.

THE RISE OF CHRISTIANITY

The Message of Jesus

"And it came to pass in those days," the second chapter of the third Gospel informs us, "that there went out a decree from Caesar Augustus, that all the world should be taxed." So Jesus of Nazareth was born in Bethlehem, where his parents had gone to render unto Caesar, around the year 4 B.C.E.

He was thus born at a time when the Roman Republic was turning into the Empire, and a time when Greek ideas had been thoroughly assimilated by the Romans. His story sits oddly in the middle of Roman history, so largely secular and practical in spirit. Yet the religion that grew up around the name and teachings of Jesus Christ constitutes a crucial part of the legacy of those times. Modified by Greek ideas, adopted as the Roman state religion, Christianity would survive the Greco-Roman world to become the dominant religion of the West.

We do not know what Jesus looked like—there are no dependable contemporary likenesses—but the traditional medieval image of a gaunt man with long hair and a beard is likely enough, given the styles of his time and province. The Bible does offer a vivid picture of his wandering ministry, of his style of preaching in vigorous parables, of his ability to move the hearts of his hearers. He was clearly a charismatic figure, whatever he looked like.

According to the Testament of his followers in the first and second centuries C.E., his birth was heralded by angels, his life replete with miracles, his passing accompanied by storms and earthquakes and climaxed by the greatest miracle of all, his rising from the dead and ascending to heaven. Jesus began his active ministry—which apparently was limited to the last three years of his life—at the age of thirty, when he became a wandering holy man in the far Roman province where he was born and put to death. Here his messianic claims—that he was the Messiah prophesied of old, come to save the world—led to his arrest at the instigation of the Hebrew priestly hierarchy in Jerusalem and his execution by the Roman authorities. And here in the eastern provinces of the empire, the Christian church began to grow.

The moral passion of Jesus had gone straight to the heart, and it would reach many others in the Roman Empire whose needs were like those of his first hearers: "Blessed are the poor in spirit, for theirs is the kingdom of heaven" (*Matthew* 5:3). His commandments had a scope that would stir even the skeptics of a later age:

> Thou shalt love the Lord thy God with all thy heart, and with all thy soul, and with all thy mind. This is the first and great commandment. And the second is like unto it. Thou shalt love thy neighbor as thyself. On these two commandments hang all the laws and the prophets. (*Matthew* 23: 37–40)

The new religion thus began with the law and the prophets of the ancient Hebrews and looked at first like a schismatic form of Judaism. From his Hebrew heritage Jesus derived the monotheism that had long distinguished the Jews and the ethical emphasis brought to their faith by the prophets of earlier centuries. But Jesus added his own unique beliefs to the faith of his fathers, and it was these additions that were to carry Christianity from obscurity and persecution to the top of the Roman world.

The two distinguishing features of the Christian message, as early Christians understood it, were, first, the assertion that he was not a mere prophet, like his predecessors, but the Son of God himself, and, second, that he came to bring to his followers the supreme gift of eternal life. "Dost thou believe in the Son of God?" he asked the man that was born blind. "Thou hast seen him, and it is he that talketh with thee" (*John* 9:35, 37). And to Martha: "I am the resurrection and the life: he that believeth in me, though he were dead, yet he shall live: and whosoever liveth and believeth in me shall never die" (*John* 11:25–36).

Christianity Under the Empire

This message was spread by the twelve disciples who had followed Jesus during his lifetime. But the new faith was carried outside the Hebrew community most effectively by a man who had never seen Jesus of Nazareth in life—Saint Paul. This Greek-trained Hebrew was able to preach the message of Christ to the Greek-speaking Eastern Roman Empire particularly. More than anyone else, he saw Christianity not merely as a Hebrew sect but as a religion open to all believers. Through his endless travels, his letters to Christian communities around the eastern end of the Mediterranean, and his total conviction of the truth of the Christian message, Paul became almost a second founder of the new religion.

There is no doubt that Jesus believed in his own divinity and in his mission to bring salvation to suffering humankind. Nor is there any doubt of the spark these messianic claims of divinity and salvation kindled in the souls of the faithful. The sign of the fish, under which Christians met in secret in the early years, was used because the letters that spelled *fish* in Greek—the lingua franca of the Roman East—were also the initials of the key words in the Christian message: "Jesus Christ—Son of God—Savior."

Various eastern "mystery cults" had made a similar offer of eternal life, and indeed had practiced some of the same rites and rituals that emerged in the early church. The cults of Dionysus, Demeter, the Egyptian Isis and Osiris, and others had promised life after death.

Osiris and Dionysus had returned from the dead themselves. Magna Mater—the Great Mother—and Mithras, the Zoroastrian god of light, required baptism of initiates. Dionysus, the Great Mother, and Isis and Osiris all offered a communion feast. But the Christian forms of these practices and promises, rooted in a claim of recent historicity rather than ancient myth, had a special appeal. Christianity gradually outdistanced all the rest.

The spread of the new cult was also fostered by men of learning who took up the new ideas, interpreted them in the familiar light of Greek philosophy, and thus made them acceptable to respectable Romans. In this way, the Greek doctrine of the *Logos* (the Word, or the spiritual manifestation of the World Soul) was used to explain Christ's coming into this world: "And the Word [*Logos* in the original Greek of the New Testament] was made flesh, and dwelt among us . . ." (*John* 1:14). Thus also Saint Augustine, writing in the last days of the Roman Empire, explained the problem of evil in a world made by a beneficent and all-powerful God by referring to well-known Neoplatonic doctrines of the distance between spirit and matter. From Paul in the first century to Augustine around 500, the simple story and dramatic claims of Jesus were supported and elaborated by men imbued with the rational spirit of Greco-Roman culture, till Christ's message emerged as the core of a formidable system of theology.

Women in the Early Church

Women also played a significant part in the rise and spread of Christianity. They seem in fact to have been rather more prominent in early Christian times than they would be in many later Christian centuries.

Jesus himself had included a number of women among his early followers, and the Apostles who took up his work also found many women converts. Wealthy women welcomed traveling preachers, accepted conversion for themselves and their households, and then turned their homes into "house churches" where fellow Christians might worship in safety. If persecution followed, women as well as men went heroically to their martyrdom, glorifying the new faith.

As church institutions took shape, women often served as deaconesses, converting and baptizing women and administering church charities. Some, feeling seized by the Holy Spirit, preached and prophesied themselves. Once the Christian church was legalized by Constantine, rich and powerful women like his mother Helena went on pilgrimages, brought home holy relics, and built churches to house them.

Without these dedicated women, it is difficult to imagine Christianity surviving through those early centuries, or taking the shape it did in generations to come.

The Triumph of the Early Church

The rise of Christianity was not as rapid as that of Islam seven hundred years later. The early Christians were accused of atheism as the Jews had been—they did reject all but *one* of the gods, after all—and were rumored to practice abominable rites in secret. There were brutal persecutions in the first three centuries, mob violence in provincial cities and mass executions in Rome. Saint Paul and other spreaders of the new faith were martyred for their beliefs.

Slowly but surely, however, the church found social and political recognition. Its own institutions were strengthened and systematized as its doctrine was. The isolated, persecuted Christian communities of the early centuries grew into a structure of episcopal sees, each headed by a big-city bishop. Even this early, furthermore, there was a tendency to defer on doctrinal matters to the bishop of Rome, the head of the Christian community at the imperial capital.

After one final round of savage persecutions under Diocletian at the beginning of the fourth century, then, the Christian church was finally recognized by the emperor Constantine in the Edict of Milan (313 B.C.E.). At the end of the fourth century, under Theodosius, the pagan temples were closed at last and Christianity became the state church of the Roman Empire.

The Greco-Roman world was a shell of its former self by then, deeply split and ready to crumble. But when the superstructures of the state fell away under the hammerblows of the barbarians, the Christian church would stand. It would go on alone into the darkness that lay ahead.

SUMMARY

Two vast empires divided much of Western Eurasia between them in the classic age. Rome dominated the Mediterranean and Western Europe, while Persia ruled Western Asia.

The Persian Empire, the largest in history up to that time, emerged with dramatic suddenness in the sixth century B.C.E., temporarily unifying the entire Middle East—western Asia—by 500 B.C.E. The founders and the most celebrated of Persia's four successive ruling houses were the Achaemenids (539–331 B.C.E.). Cyrus the Great and his rough, leather-clad Persian cavalry conquered most of the empire in the later sixth century B.C.E. Cyrus's heirs added to their inheritance, till by 500 the Persia of Darius the Great stretched from Egypt and Mesopotamia to the northwest frontier of India. Persian imperial administration of this sprawling system of satrapies, Persian roads, and palaces all set a new standard for western Eurasia.

The inheritors of the Persian imperial tradition were a diverse line of dynasties—the Seleucids, the Parthians, and the Sassanids.

Persian high culture was significantly influenced by neighboring peoples, east and west, but produced lasting monuments that were distinctly Persian. The militant religion of Zoroaster—preaching life as a struggle between light and darkness, good and evil—influenced Persia's neighbors in their turn. And Persian palaces like those at Persepolis were magnificent embodiments of Persian imperial achievement.

Farther to the west, the ancient Romans were also among the world's most successful empire builders—and the only ones ever to bring Europe under a single government.

Beginning around 500 B.C.E., the city of Rome in central Italy grew into another vast Eurasian empire. But Rome's endless wars and vast imperial holdings corrupted its aristocracy and tempted its generals to use their armies to advance their own political ambitions. Around the time of Christ, two remarkable men, Julius and Augustus Caesar, ended this civil strife, imposed order, and left Rome united, powerful, and prosperous.

The period of the Roman peace—the first two centuries C.E.—saw Roman power established all around the Mediterranean Sea and over most of Western Europe. The third century, however, saw political chaos in the capital once more. Diocletian and Constantine reestablished order during the fourth century. But Rome was decaying economically, socially, culturally, and in other ways; and in the fifth century, the Western Roman Empire collapsed under waves of invasion by less developed peoples who lived on its frontiers.

During their centuries of power, the Romans developed practical arts like engineering and architecture themselves, building roads, aqueducts, theaters, and temples across Europe. Roman administration was efficient, Roman law a major cultural accomplishment. Rome's great writers left an unexcelled literary heritage to the West.

Jesus Christ was born during the reign of Augustus Caesar and preached in Palestine at the beginning of Rome's golden age. Though persecuted in its early centuries, Christianity spread across the empire, won official recognition in the fourth century, and survived the fall of Rome to shape the civilization of medieval Europe.

SUGGESTED READING

Balsdon, J. P. V. D. *Roman Women.* Westport, Conn.: Greenwood Press, 1975. The best place to start. Equally scholarly are M. Lefkowitz and M. B. Fant, *Women's Life in Greece and Rome* (Baltimore, Md.: Johns Hopkins University Press, 1982). See also J. P. Hallett, *Fathers and Daughters in Roman Society: Women and the Elite Family* (Princeton, N.J.: Princeton University Press, 1984), impressionistic discussion of women's influence on society, exercised through family connections.

Cambridge History of Iran (7 vols.). Cambridge: Cambridge University Press, 1983. Volumes 2 and 3 deal with the first four dynasties of Persia in scholarly detail.

Cherry, D. *Frontier and Society in Roman North Africa.* New York: Clarendon Press, 1998. Challenges claims that native North Africans were effectively "Romanized" during the Roman period.

Cook, J. M. *The Persian Empire.* New York: Schocken Books, 1983. Achaemenid Persia in the light of recent archeological discoveries.

Curtis, J. *Ancient Persia.* Cambridge Mass.: Harvard University Press, 1990. Brief but authoritative introduction to the subject.

Deschesne-Guillemin, J. *Hymns of Zarathustra.* Boston: Beacon Press, 1963. Valuable introduction and commentaries accompany these translations of the Zoroastrain hymns, or *gathas.*

Evans, K. K. *War, Women and Children in Ancient Rome.* London: Routledge, 1991. Studies of the legal, familial, and workday problems of Roman women.

Ferrier, R. W., ed. *The Arts of Persia.* New Haven, Conn.: Yale University Press, 1989. Solid overview of the arts in ancient Persia.

Garnset, P., and R. Saller. *The Roman Empire: Economy, Society, and Culture.* Berkeley and Los Angeles: University of California Press, 1987. Particularly useful on government administration and social relations.

Giardina. A. *The Romans,* trans. L. G. Cochrane. Chicago: University of Chicago Press, 1993. Intriguing collection of essays on Roman social types, from citizens and priests to bandits and slaves.

Grainger, J. D. *The cities of Seleukid Syria.* New York: Oxford University Press, 1990. Scholarly account of the cities of this part of the Persian Empire under Alexander's successors.

Gruen, E. S. *Cultural and National Identity in Republican Rome.* Ithaca, N.Y.: Cornell University Press, 1992. Analysis of the republican ideology before the rise of the Caesars.

Harris, W. V. *War and Imperialism in Republican Rome 327–70 B.C.* New York: Oxford University Press, 1985. Scholarly account of Roman expansion around the Mediterranean Sea.

Jenkyns, R., ed. *The Legacy of Rome: A New Appraisal.* New York: Oxford University Press, 1992. New collection based on a classic anthology of scholarly essays on Rome's cultural legacy to later ages.

Lintott, A. *The Constitution of the Roman Republic.* New York: Clarendon Press, 1999. Analytical overview of the evolving Roman political system in the centuries before Augustus.

Meeks, W. A. *The First Urban Christians: The Social World of the Apostle Paul.* New Haven, Conn.: Yale University Press, 1983. Sees leading converts to Christianity as socially isolated people—wealthy women, Jews, freedmen—in need of a sense of spiritual community.

Stambaugh, J. E. *The Ancient Roman City.* Baltimore, Md.: Johns Hopkins University Press, 1988. Physical and social parameters of Roman urban life, based on literary sources as well as historical and archaeological materials.

Sherwin-White, S., and A. Kuhrt. *From Samarkand to Sardis.* Berkeley: University of California Press, 1992. Survey of Hellenistic Persia. See also their edited collection, *Hellenism in the East* (Berkeley: University of California Press, 1987).

Wells, P. *The Barbarians Speak: How the Conquered Peoples Shaped Roman Europe.* Princeton, N.J.: Princeton University Press, 1999. Focus on resistance to Roman imperalism, especially on the social and cultural side. See also G. Woolf, *Becoming Roman: The Origins of Provincial Civilization in Gaul* (New York: Cambridge University Press, 1998), for an archaeologist's view of Roman influence on conquered peoples.

Wiesehöfer, J. *Ancient Persia: From 550 b.c. to 650 a.d.* trans. A. Azodi. London: I. B. Tauris, 1998. Broad synthesis of Persian history from Cyrus to the Arab conquest.

 Please refer to the document CD-ROM for primary sources related to this chapter.

CHAPTER 7

FROM THE GANGES TO THE GOBI
Gupta India and Han China
(200 B.C.E.–C.E. 500)

A Glance Ahead: Evolving Empires of Eastern Eurasia

Due east of Rome and Persia in the classic age lay two more remarkable empires: those of Gupta India and Han China. The striking qualities of historic India often seem to lie in its capacity for generating spiritual insights, religions that have spread far across Asia. China's genius, on the other hand, has seemed to be more political, a capacity for building—and repeatedly rebuilding—political unity over a vast tract of eastern Asia.

The weaknesses of the two giants also complement each other. India was politically divided for most of its history, a collection of peoples united by commerce and culture. Han China, by contrast, established a political unity that would be replicated by succeeding dynasties. When it came to religion, the global faith that made the profoundest impact on China was Buddhism—which had to be imported from India.

Different in many ways, but alike in vast reach and historical longevity, India and China stand second to none among the giants of the classic age.

The Many Peoples of India

Invaders of the Punjab: The Kushans

From the fall of the Maurya dynasty in 185 B.C.E. to the rise of the Guptas in C.E. 320, India was without even a shadow of a central government. During this period of five centuries, foreign invaders shouldered their way down through the Northwest Frontier once more. Separate kingdoms rose and fell in the Deccan. But a tough nucleus of cultural elements, from religion to caste, was already binding India together. And even the foreign invaders of this period would enrich rather than undermine the traditional culture that was the heart of India.

During these centuries foreign invaders thrust far beyond the Punjab, the region of the five rivers that branch out of the Indus. Over several hundred years, these foreign intruders set up kingdoms of their own over various parts of northwestern India. The mongoloid Kushan Empire, in particular, stretched for a time all the way from the frontiers of Parthian Persia into the heart of the Ganges valley. But all the newcomers followed one of two patterns. Some adopted Indian names, religions, and culture, and were absorbed into a population that was already becoming adept at absorbing foreigners. Some were eventually dislodged and went their way. In either case, India survived the onslaught of each new intruder in turn.

Most of the invaders of these five centuries, however, left something of their own to add its tang to the rich mix of Indian tradition. The Greeks brought coinage to India, and helped develop trade between India and the Mediterranean. The Kushans patronized Buddhism and presided over the emergence of a new form, the Mahayana Buddhism that would spread far across Asia.

Kingdoms of the Deccan: The Tamils

Indian history thus far had centered in the north, in the valleys of the Indus and the Ganges, in the shadow of the Himalayas.

But there were also cities and kingdoms in the south during these centuries around the time of Christ—highly developed Dravidian cultures in the great southward-reaching triangle of peninsular India called the Deccan.

The Deccan was cut off from the north by the Narmada River and by ranges of thickly forested hills. But the hills of the Deccan stairstep down to fertile coastal plains on

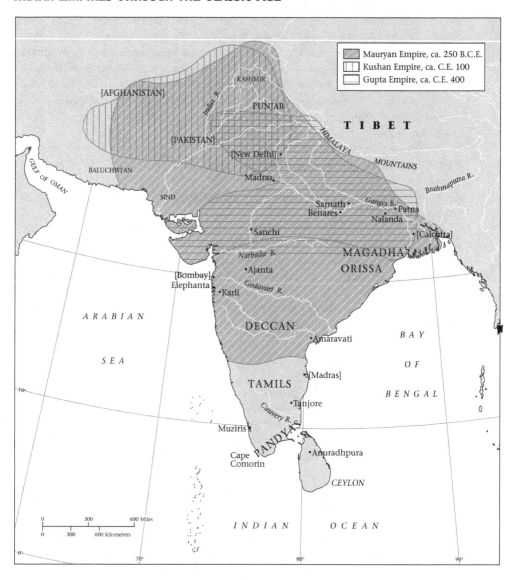

both sides of the peninsula, and these plains became increasingly prosperous centers of both agriculture and trade in the first centuries C.E.

The peoples of the south were still almost purely Dravidian stock, as yet little affected by the long-established Aryan predominance in the north. The southerners spoke their own languages and had their own culture and social patterns. Trade, both overseas and with north India, appeared and grew during this period. Commercial contacts with the cities of the Indus and Ganges began to bring such northern cultural characteristics as Hinduism and the caste system into the south. In the first centuries after Christ, there were southern kingdoms that could challenge the most powerful northern principalities.

The most important peoples of the further south were the Tamils. Their language was the most widely spoken southern tongue, and they dominated the whole region from what is today Madras down to Cape Comorin, at the tip of the subcontinent.

During the first centuries C.E. the Tamil peoples were just moving from village culture into larger political units—chiefdoms and monarchies. Village councils were still central decision-making bodies, even after hereditary monarchy was introduced. The people still prayed to commemorative "hero stones" or made sacrifices of blood and rice to ancient gods of fertility, regarding the elaborate Vedic rituals—so ancient in the north—as modern novelties.

But change came rapidly to the shrewd Tamils. The source was growing prosperity as they developed the agricultural potential of their converging coastal plains and above all the mushrooming trade that flourished on both coasts. Southern India thus became a booming center of commerce and handicraft industries, and the land along the southern rivers bloomed.

Political and cultural evolution came with economic growth. Matrilineal succession prevailed in many parts of the south. The queen of the Pandyas, a powerful Tamil people, could field an army of thirteen thousand infantrymen, four thousand cavalry, and five hundred elephants. Tamils for a time conquered and occupied northern Ceylon (Sri Lanka) where they are still a revolutionary force today—and they fought epic battles among themselves. Poetry also flowered among them very early, and the songs of the Tamil bards are among the treasures of India's literary heritage.

Nations of Shopkeepers

The lack of a strong central government during the five hundred years between the Maurya and Gupta empires seems in no way to have handicapped the rapid growth of hand manufacturing, trade, and cities in both northern and southern India. Indeed, the half-envious label applied to industrial Britain many centuries later—"a nation of shopkeepers!"—would seem almost equally appropriate to India in the last centuries before Christ and the first centuries C.E.

Over a region approximately half the size of the continental United States, Indians found raw materials in considerable quantity. Iron and copper, gold and silver and precious stones were mined. The subcontinent's still abundant forests provided woods of all sorts, from teak to aromatic sandalwood. Cotton was widely grown and silk introduced. Even the sea contributed, providing pearls for Indian jewelry and for export.

These materials were processed by a complicated array of guilds, most of them organized by castes or subcastes who traditionally practiced particular hereditary crafts. Guilds of carpenters, metalworkers, and ceramicists were especially powerful in many urban areas. Like guilds in medieval Europe centuries later, Indian guilds regulated quality, prices, and competition, contributed substantially to religious foundations—especially Buddhist and Jain—and made the streets of Indian cities colorful with banners and processions on their feast days.

Trade also boomed during these centuries. North and south were linked by sea trade along the coasts and by a more modest system of roads begun in Asoka's day. Flotillas of coastal trading vessels, caravans of mules, oxen, and camels bound all the regions from the Himalayas to Cape Comorin. Foreign trade also prospered as Greek and Kushan states in the northwest encouraged Indian trade with the Mediterranean and China. And

Indian merchants searching for the spices that brought such good prices in the West increasingly traded and even settled in Southeast Asia, where Indian religious influence was also growing.

It was, in sum, a bustling, prosperous time in the cities of India. Coinage replaced barter in the urban centers; gold, silver, and copper coins of many kinds were minted, and even Roman *sesterces* circulated freely. The literature of the age describes a colorful urban population of guild craftsmen, wealthy caravan masters, and shipowners mingling with Hindu brahmans and Buddhist monks, prostitutes and poets, in narrow city streets. The courts of the *rajas* and of kings with even more exalted titles borrowed from Persia or China were centers of luxurious living and cultivated taste.

THE GUPTA GOLDEN AGE

Chandra Gupta I: The Raja Of the Rajas

India was a highly literate society by this time, one with several written languages. But the destruction in later centuries of what records might have survived leaves us with almost as little detailed knowledge of the reigns of the Guptas (C.E. 320–540) as we have of their Maurya predecessors half a millennium earlier. Enough is known, however, to piece together some striking parallels between these two Indian empires.

To begin with, both centered in northern India, specifically in the Ganges valley, which had been the center of Indian development since the Aryan conquest. Both the Maurya and Gupta dynasties, in fact, rose to power first in the same Ganges state of Magadha. Both expanded westward from there to incorporate the old pre-Aryan heartland on the Indus and the five rivers of the Punjab. Both pushed much more tentatively southward. The greatest of the Guptas actually controlled less of the Deccan than Asoka had. The Mauryas ruled for only about a century and a half (321–185 B.C.E.), the Guptas nominally for two centuries (C.E. 320–540). But in both cases the first three reigns were the glory days, and then the empire began to fragment and decline.

The first of the Guptas, Chandra Gupta I, even had the same name as the founder of the earlier dynasty, Chandragupta Maurya, though they were not related. The second of the Gupta clan, Samudra Gupta, was the great conqueror. The third, Chandra Gupta II, presided, like Asoka, over the dynasty's golden age.

Chandra Gupta I (320–330) seems to have been either a minor princeling or a wealthy landowner in the Ganges valley who married well. His bride, Princess Kumara Devi of the powerful Lichchhavi tribe, brought him an alliance powerful enough to make him ruler of the state of Magadha. From its now ancient capital of Patna, Chandra Gupta expanded his suzerainty over enough of the surrounding territories to kindle dreams of empire. In C.E. 320 he took the grandiloquent title of *maharajadhiraja*, "great king of kings." Ten years later he left this title, with all its implied aspirations, to his son Samudra Gupta, who made good on them with a vengeance.

Samudra and Chandra Gupta II

Samudra Gupta (330–375) is shown on some of the gold coins he minted with the profits of his wars reflectively strumming a lute, and he is supposed to have loved poetry. The most important single record of his reign, however, is a record of his conquests. According to this eulogy, Samudra broke many kings in the field, forcing some to accept his overlordship and pay tribute and others to do homage. He brought most of northern India under Gupta rule and raided hundreds of miles into the southern jungles, returning laden with glory and plunder. He imposed direct Gupta government, collected tribute, or exercised a paramount influence from the mountains to a point well south of the Narmada. He became what his father had dreamed of being: *raja* of the *rajas,* great king of kings.

Chandra Gupta II (375–415), a grandson of the founder, fought his share of campaigns too. He completed the conquest of the northwest, so that Gupta power stretched all across northern India, from the Indus valley to the head of the Bay of Bengal. He also negotiated a shrewd series of marriage alliances with the preeminent princes of the south that cemented Gupta influence in the Deccan. An additional advantage of his wars and marriage diplomacy was that it gave the Guptas control of valuable west-coast seaports and their trade with the West.

Chandra Gupta II is most famous, however, for the cultural life of his reign and for his own patronage of the arts. Kalidasa the poet lived at his court, and literature and art flourished while he ruled. When we reflect that his forty years on the throne generally constituted a time of peace and prosperity, despite his celebrated conquest of the northwest, the "golden age" label so often affixed to the reign is easy to understand.

The first century of Gupta rule (the fourth century c.e.) was thus a time of expanding power, growing prosperity, and cultural splendor. The second Gupta century, however, was increasingly darkened by new invaders moving down from central Asia across the Northwest Frontier: the White Huns.

The White Huns were probably kin to those Huns who, under the notorious Attila, had reached the walls of Rome a hundred years before. Now, in the fifth century, while Rome foundered and fell to half-civilized Germanic invaders, the White Huns battered at the gates of Gupta India.

Gupta leaders succeeded in turning them back until late in the century. By 500, however, the Huns ruled the northwest and the Guptas were drawing back once more upon their Ganges base. They were a local power thereafter, and one that would disappear from the skimpy records in a few decades more.

Life in Gupta India

Government was probably less centralized and less intrusive in Gupta India than in Maurya times. Most of the day-to-day authority was in the hands of the provincial viceroys, district officers, and even the headmen and elders of the individual villages. The councils of major cities were chosen by local people—especially merchants and craft guildsmen—rather than appointed from the center, as was apparently done in Maurya times. Nor was there anything in the India of Chandra Gupta II to correspond to the secret police of Chandragupta Maurya's day.

Economically, the trends of more recent centuries continued. Indian farmers labored in fields of wheat and sugar cane in the west, rice in the east, and in orchards and vegetable gardens everywhere. Craftspeople in bustling Indian cities continued to produce large quantities of pottery, metal goods, and textiles for home and foreign consumption. Trade with the west, by caravan and ship, dwindled in Gupta times as Rome declined. But Indian merchants were still frequently seen in East African ports, and they increased their activities in Southeast Asia. Spices, gems, perfumes, and sandalwood were exported; silk from China, ivory from Africa, and horses from Arabia and Persia flowed in.

Women's lives in general were varied. Upper-class girls were given some education, and girls of all classes were married young. Outside of marriage and motherhood, the only ways of life commonly open to women were withdrawal to a Buddhist nunnery, acting in a theatrical company, or prostitution. There were women who were teachers and even philosophers. On the other hand, the sixth century saw the first recorded case of widow burning: pious self-immolation by a high-case Hindu widow who believed she would thereby become a *sati,* or woman of great virtue. This supreme act of loyalty was considered to prove the widow's faithfulness to her husband and to guarantee their reunion after death. Widows also occupied a very low social status, which may have encouraged some to commit suicide in this way.

A Chinese Buddhist pilgrim who visited northern India in the reign of Chandra Gupta II described the Indians as on the whole a fortunate people. The land was prosperous, yet the people, he said, religiously refrained from both meat and wine. Charity hospitals were provided for the poor by pious citizens. Even the untouchables, the caste at the bottom of society, knew their place. These pariahs never entered a city without beating on a piece of wood so that their betters might avoid being polluted by contact with them.

Even allowing for the exaggerations of an enthusiastic visitor, it was a model society by the standards of its time.

The sanctuary at Karli. The dimness, the heavy polygonal columns, and capitals thronged with spiritual presences generate the profoundly religious atmosphere for which India has been known for three thousand years. Note the balance of horizontals and verticals, circles and rectangles, in each column. (New York Public Library Picture Collection)

The Hindu Renaissance

Hinduism, meanwhile, underwent even more impressive transformations, both before and during the Gupta era. Some of these changes paralleled those in Buddhism. Hinduism too saw a turning away from older texts toward more popular religion, and a widespread belief in a divine incarnation as savior. But the Hindu Renaissance, as it is often called, was a unique series of developments within India's oldest and always majority religion. These developments involved the priesthood, the scriptures, and the basic beliefs of Hinduism.

The brahmans, the hereditary priestly caste, remained widely respected and essential for ceremonial occasions. But the public turned more and more to a new collection of religious literature. These were the Puranas, popular myths and chronicles of Indian dynasties infused with religious significance and a prophetic framework by brahman authors.

The many gods, or *devas,* of the Vedic tradition remained, but there was a trend toward monotheism, the ancient sun god Vishnu or the fertility god Shiva emerging as the one true God in the thinking of his followers. Thus Shiva *nataraj,* "lord of the dance," embodied the cosmic rhythms of the universe. Depicted as a four-armed deity dancing in a ring of fire, crushing the demon of ignorance underfoot, he was seen as the cyclic force that both created and destroyed worlds.

There was also a tendency to group three of the most prominent old divinities as a sort of Trinity, embodying the three main forces in the universe. In this Hindu tradition, Brahma was the Creator of the universe; Vishnu was the Preserver, frequently appearing in human incarnation to save the virtuous; and Shiva was the Destroyer who brings a deserved end to all things when evil has corrupted the cosmos beyond hope of salvation. The process is cyclical, however, and Brahma soon creates heaven and earth anew.

The richness of this evolved Hinduism made a wide variety of religious experience available to Indians. An individual might worship the *lingam* (phallus) in the temples of Shiva or practice one of the many forms of *bakhti* (personal piety) encouraged by the cult of Vishnu.

The Gupta rulers were Hindus: Chandra Gupta II was even a theologian of sorts. Yet religious toleration prevailed, as it had under the Buddhist Asoka. Comparative tolerance of other people's beliefs would continue to characterize Indian religion until the coming of more militant faiths from the western end of Eurasia in later centuries.

Mahayana Buddhism

The Buddhist visitor from China, cited above, noticed particularly the intense religious feeling of Gupta India. From the first century C.E., in fact, both Buddhism and Hinduism had been undergoing vital changes in the land of their birth.

The crucial changes in Buddhism took place in the centuries between the empires, particularly during the first two centuries C.E. It was in this period that Buddhist belief divided into the two great traditions that have characterized it ever since. This division, comparable to the Catholic-Protestant split in Christianity or the division between Shiite and Sunni Islam, produced two separate communities in international Buddhism. The older form, *Hinayana* ("Little Vehicle") Buddhism remained perhaps closer to the precise words and ideas of the founder. But the newer form, *Mahayana* ("Big Vehicle") Buddhism, was to reach much further, spreading in the end over most of East Asia.

Hinayana Buddhists saw Prince Siddartha the Buddha as the greatest teacher who had ever lived. He was the man who showed how an individual might, through right living, right thought, and assiduous meditation, escape from the endless wretched wheel of life into that blissful extinction of the self called Nirvana. It was a practical if profound message, from one enlightened human to those others, most commonly monks and nuns, who were capable of following him on the rigorous path of spiritual enlightenment.

Mahayana Buddhism expanded this conception drastically, and by so doing reached much larger numbers of people. Mahayana Buddhists saw the Buddha not merely as a wise teacher but as an incarnation of God. His goal, they asserted, was also larger: not only individual escape from the wheel, but the salvation of all humanity through the self-sacrificing labor of the spiritually enlightened few.

In the Mahayana theology there was in fact not one Buddha but a whole series of such incarnations of divinity, "blessed Buddhas . . . equal in number to the sands of the river" come to save humankind.[1] Before and after the historic Buddha there had lived, or would live, many other *bodhisattvas,* people who attained enlightenment but deliberately rejected escape into Nirvana in order to continue their pious work in this world, showing others the way to salvation. In addition, hosts of lesser gods clustered around the central figure of the Buddha in the art and thought of Mahayana Buddhism. Even Nirvana looked different to followers of the newer path, who envisioned a hierarchy of heavens and hells awaiting the faithful or the unbeliever after death.

Like Confucius, the historic Buddha had apparently refused even to speculate about gods; unlike Christ, he had never claimed to be divine himself. Seven centuries after Siddartha's death, many of his followers went further than the founder ever had, transforming Buddha into the central god of an immensely popular religion. His worship became a spectacle of impressive proportions, replete with huge temples and elaborate rituals. The Chinese visitor quoted earlier described a Buddhist festival in which towering floats were dragged through the streets, decorated with devas and spirits, Buddhas and bodhisattvas, canopies and streamers, and accompanied by singers, musicians, monks, and throngs of worshipers expressing their devotion with "flowers and incense."[2]

The larger conception of salvation for the multitude was splendid, but one wonders what the simply dressed man who had walked the dusty roads of the Gangetic states in the sixth century B.C.E. would have thought of the temples and the ritual, the incense and the bells.

The Art of Caves and Stupas

The classic art of the half-dozen centuries climaxing in the Gupta age is the architecture and, above all, the sculpture of Buddhism. It is the art of the cave temple and the stupa, and it shows what beauty Buddhism could inspire even in this dawning of the Hindu Renaissance.

The *stupa,* a center of worship that goes back before the time of Christ, was a large domed mound with a relic of the Buddha buried at the center of it. Around this masonry-covered mound ran a circular paved path where monks walked, murmuring their devotions. Enclosing the entire precinct was a circular railing with four ornamental gateways set at the four cardinal points of the compass.

---

[1] *The Smaller Sukhavati-Vyuha in Buddhist Mahayana Texts,* trans. E. B. Cowell (New York: Dover, 1969), p. 99.

[2] Fa Hsien, *A Record of Buddhist Kingdoms Being an Account by the Chinese Monk Fa-Hsien of His Travels in India and Ceylon,* A.D. 399–414, trans. James Legge (Oxford: Clarendon Press, 1886), p. 79.

It is on these high, elaborately carved stone gateways that we see for the first time the interwoven tangle of figures that will be so typical of later Indian temples of many faiths. Thus, the three transverse panels that top the gateways of the Great Stupa at Sanchi, in the northern Deccan, are already bursting with sculptured life—elephants and lions, peacocks and lotuses, kings and surging crowds. The gods are there too; benevolent bodhisattvas and fullbreasted, narrow-waisted *yakshis* (nature spirits) swaying under mango trees. Buddha himself is never shown, but the stone is thick with Buddhist symbols, from the glowing footprints left by Prince Gautama's departure from his father's palace to the bo tree—the throne of his enlightenment—and the great spoked wheel of life.

Perhaps even more striking to Western eyes are the "cave temples," rock-cut sanctuaries where the western hills stairstep down to the coastal plains above Bombay. These temples, complete with facade, long interior nave, flanking pillars, side aisles, and a mounded stupa at the far end, are carved entirely out of the living rock of the cliffs. They were sculpted, even to the obviously nonfunctional ribbed vaults overhead, in perfect imitation of the wooden, thatch-roofed temples then in use in the world outside.

In the dim light of the most imposing of these sanctuaries, the one at Karli, the rows of close-set polygonal pillars with their lotus and elephant capitals give one a dizzy sense of moving in a world where nothing is what it ought to be. All that would be needed to catapult the viewer back a score of centuries would be the murmur of shaved, saffron-robed monks moving down the shadowy aisle beyond the sixteen-sided pillars.

Nowhere does Buddha himself appear in these earlier monuments to Hinayana purity. Soon, however, the traditional figure of the more popular religion of later centuries begins to show. The Indo-Greek sculptors of the Gandhara school in the northwest offer an almost Hellenic Buddha, replete with acanthus leaves and even cupids. Farther south, however, the Mathura school presents a more convincingly Indian figure—the round face, the shaved crown, the bump of enlightenment, the right hand raised in a gesture not of blessing but of fearlessness. Here if anywhere the classic simplicity and calm strength of Gupta art look out at us.

To see the best of what remains of Gupta painting, finally, one would have to go to the famous Ajanta caves in the mountains of the Deccan. Here, on the walls of some thirty cave temples and monks' cells hollowed out over several hundred years, the lives of the aristocracy of that long-vanished age live on in faintly glowing colors. Here lovers lounge eternally on the veranda of an elegantly pillared palace. A prince and princess stroll among the palms and flowers. And a bodhisattva, his handsome head bowing under the weight of a high jeweled crown, gazes beneath half-lowered lids into his divine destiny. The smoky modeling of cheeks and lips, the glimmering colors on the cave walls, illuminate that forgotten world of sensuality and mystic faith with a somber beauty.

Beast Fables and Courtly Love

The age of the Guptas was the great age of Indian literature as well. It was the age of Kalidasa, frequently described as the Indian Shakespeare, of the final versions of the great Indian epics, and of the triumph of literary Sanskrit in plays, poetry, and prose.

The great technical breakthrough was the adoption of a version of Sanskrit, the language of the ancient Vedas and other Hindu religious texts, as the language of a brilliant living literature. Kalidasa and other playwrights and poets of this Indian "nest of singing birds" used this two-thousand-year-old tongue with refined and courtly elegance. They also used the vernacular Prakrit language in plays for the speeches of the lower-class characters.

If Buddhism shaped the painting and sculpture of the Gupta age, the Hindu Renaissance inspired much of its literature. It was at this time that the ancient epics—the *Ramayana* and the *Mahabharata*—were put into the versions we have today under the judicious guidance of brahmanical scholars. Thus interpreted, these old poems of war and adventure acquired heavy religious overtones: the *Song of God* episode, with its revelations of princely duty and the nature of the godhead, was added to the *Mahabharata* at this time. The *Panchatantra,* the widely popular collection of Indian beast fables and fairy tales, was also assembled during this period. The wisdom here is more worldly, but this world of talking animals, of beast and human life commingled, seems distinctly Hindu in spirit.

There is even a substantial mythological framework to the romantic plays and poems of Kalidasa, the most celebrated secular writer of the Gupta age. Shiva and Vishnu, the two ancient epics, and the even older Indian myths of gods and nature spirits hover over his works as Greek mythology informs Greek tragic drama. Kalidasa's most famous play, *Shakuntala,* is based on an incident from the *Mahabharata,* and gods move freely in and out of the story.

As writers have learned in many lands, however, much can be done with sacred material. *Shakuntala,* the story of a king's love for the lovely daughter of a pious hermit, is as romantic a piece as a Gupta court audience could have wished. The lyric passages, which were apparently sung, give the performance something of the air of a modern musical comedy. But the depth and endless variety of emotional tones, the joy in nature, the humanity of the middle-aged king, and the shy eagerness of Shakuntala herself have earned Kalidasa's masterwork a high place in Indian literature ever since.

Mathematics, Medicine, and Science

Religion seems to infuse so much of the Indian consciousness that it is perhaps surprising that some of the most impressive achievements of the Gupta age came not in mystic insight or theology but in science. As it happens, no great conflict was felt between science and religion in Gupta India. Buddhist monasteries and Hindu schools taught mathematics and medicine as well as philosophy and their respective sacred texts. The Buddhist college at Nalanda, the largest institution of higher learning in India, taught medicine and physics along with languages, literature, and metaphysics.

Gupta medicine was based too little on empirical observation to make much progress. Gupta astrology was very popular, but it is hard to establish progress in a pseudoscience. In astronomy and mathematics, however, Indian scientists clearly rivaled the Greeks and the Chinese.

The great leap forward made by Indian mathematicians was the development of what Westerners came to call Arabic numerals—a vast improvement over the Roman numerals that remained standard in the West for another thousand years. With nine numerical symbols and that wonderful little invention, the zero, India immensely simplified the process of mathematical calculation. With the decimal system and the concept of place value, new spheres of mathematical operation were opened up. The value of pi and the beginnings of algebra were also developed here.

Greek astronomy was in circulation among Indian scientists, and Greek scientific terminology was absorbed into Indian texts. But the astronomers of the subcontinent discovered for themselves that the earth was a rotating sphere and learned the causes of lunar eclipses. They also calculated the length of the solar year to the seventh decimal place.

The life of the scientific mind, at any rate, has never been limited to any one corner of this spinning globe.

THE HAN DYNASTY OF CHINA

The Exalted Founder: Han Gaozu

On the great eastward bulge of Asia, the first attempt at a unified China had collapsed in ruins in 207 B.C.E. The awesome First Emperor, Shi Huangdi, had scarcely been placed in his fantastic tomb when court intrigue, peasant rebellion, and rival warlord armies tore his empire apart. From the Great Wall in the north to the warm, typhoon-swept south, the river valleys and tile-roofed cities were tumbled into chaos once more. With the collapse of the Qin dynasty after a single reign, China seemed to be sliding back into Zhou feudalism and the anarchy of the Warring States.

But this was not what happened. When the Mauryas succumbed in India, no new unifying power emerged for five centuries. In China the violence burned itself out, and a new dynasty took up the task of unification in less than twenty years. The Han dynasty (202 B.C.E.–C.E. 220) would in fact be one of China's greatest—and most admired—ruling houses, a model to those that followed.

Two strikingly different rivals for supreme power emerged in the chaos of feuding warlords that followed the death of Huangdi. One was a dashing southern aristocrat named Xiang Yu. Xiang Yu was willing to leave other princes and warlords in possession of their own lands in return for the sort of semifeudal suzerainty that had been wielded by the Zhou kings. The other contender was a rare type in Chinese imperial annals: a one-time village official and former bandit turned rebel general named Liu Bang. Liu Bang was not an aristocrat or even a gentleman, and his ambitions went considerably beyond feudal suzerainty.

Liu Bang seems to have had a good deal of peasant cunning and more than his share of dogged determination. He was no great military leader; at one point he was even captured and held for ransom by the Xiongnu barbarians from beyond the Great Wall. In his protracted struggle with Xiang Yu, he won only one battle—the last one.

Surrounded, outmaneuvered, and outlasted, the aristocratic Xiang Yu committed suicide—and has lived on ever since as a tragic figure in Chinese opera. Liu Bang got on with the business of organizing power in China.

The Han dynasty he founded was to rule, with a single brief interregnum, for more than four hundred years, from 202 B.C.E. to C.E. 220. The Liu family took their dynastic name from the river Han, which flowed through the territory that had been Liu Bang's home base. The peasant emperor himself was posthumously awarded a new name by the historians of his reign. He is officially known to history as Han Gaozu, "Exalted Founder" of the Han dynasty. It was a dynasty that would be so honored in Chinese history that to this day the Chinese call themselves "people of Han."

In the few years left to him after his long struggle for power (he died in 195 B.C.E.), Gaozu set the dynasty on the basic political course it would follow thereafter. He chose to reject Zhou feudalism and to continue instead the centralizing policies of the Qin. But he also had the common sense to proceed with less rigor and more moderation than the hard-driving First Emperor had used. Taxes were easier to bear under Gaozu, punishments less savage than they had been under Huangdi's Legalist advisers. Some elements of the feudal order were preserved temporarily by the pragmatic Exalted Founder—notably, feudal domains for some of his own supporters and relatives.

The Chinese people, exhausted by Huangdi's grand schemes and by the years of civil war thereafter, responded to this more temperate course by conferring their support on the

VOICES FROM THE PAST

Sima Qian (Ssu-ma Ch'ien) (145–90 B.C.E.), the "Grand Historian" of Han China, was famous for his dramatic style and for his ability to bring historical figures to life. Here Gaozu, the founder of the Han dynasty, faces the difficult problem of rewarding his chief supporters after their victory and accession to power. Which does the new emperor seem to value more, military or administrative skills? From what you know about Gaozu, does this homely parable sound like something he might actually have said? Do you get a sense of his character from this anecdote?

"The king of Han, now emperor, considered that Hsiao Ho had achieved the highest merit, and hence enfeoffed him as marquis of Tsuan with the revenue from a large number of towns. But the other distinguished officials objected, saying, "We have all buckled on armor and taken up our weapons, some of us fighting as many as a hundred or more engagements, the least of us fighting twenty or thirty. Each, to a greater or lesser degree, has engaged in attacks upon cities or seizures of territory. And yet Hsiao Ho, who has never campaigned on the sweaty steeds of battle, but only sat here with brush and ink deliberating on questions of state instead of fighting, is awarded a position above us. How can this be?"

"Gentlemen," the emperor asked, "do you know anything about hunting?"

"We do," they replied.

"And do you know anything about hunting dogs?"

"We do."

"Now in a hunt," the emperor said, "it is the dog who is sent to pursue and kill the beast. But the one who unleashes the dog and points out the place where the beast is hiding is the huntsman. You, gentlemen, have only succeeded in capturing the beast, and so your achievement is that of hunting dogs. But it is Hsiao Ho who unleashed you and pointed out the place, and his achievement is that of the huntsman. Also in your case only you yourselves, or at most two or three of your family, joined in following me. But Hsiao Ho dispatched his whole family numbering twenty or thirty members to accompany me. This is a service I can hardly forget."

Ssu-ma Ch'ien, *Records of the Grand Historian of China: The Shih Chi*, trans. Burton Watson (New York: Columbia University Press, 1961), pp. 127–128.

---

new dynasty. The Han rulers, in turn, brought the Chinese a period of relative peace and prosperity comparable to that enjoyed by Romans after Augustus or Indians in the Gupta age. It established traditions that would shape the lives of generations far into China's future.

The Sustainer: Empress Lü

Life was easier along the Yellow River, the Yangzi, and their webs of tributaries wandering among the misty mountains of China. Labor in the millet fields of the north and the rice paddies of the south brought the peasant farmer a large share at least of his just reward, thanks to the dynasty established by the peasant emperor. But at the imperial capital at Chang'an (modern Xi'an), politics was still full of intrigue and violence.

After Gaozu's death, someone was desperately needed to carry on the work, to sustain the drive for unification and conciliation he had begun. Fortunately for China—if not for her court rivals—there was such a person: the empress dowager Lü.

Empress Lü was not Gaozu's only wife, nor was her son the late emperor's oldest or even his favorite. But Lü was well known to Gaozu's old comrades in the long struggle for power, now the chief ministers of the Han Empire. Two of her brothers had been generals in the wars, and she herself had contributed substantially to the successful struggle and suffered in the cause. When her undeniable intelligence, firmness of purpose, and driving ambition are added to this record, the rise of the empress to power has almost a ring of inevitability about it.

In fact, she rose through a court struggle as devious and cruel as anything the Hans had faced in the field. Lü ruled first through her son, a well-meaning but unaggressive sixteen-year-old. When the boy emperor suffered a nervous collapse, allegedly out of horror at his mother's brutal treatment of her defeated rivals, the dowager empress governed directly. There was no doubt of her vindictiveness toward rivals. There was no doubt either that hordes of ambitious members of the Lü clan descended on Chang'an during the years of her supremacy, challenging even the old fighters for the empress's favor.

Precisely because of her need for supporters, however, Dowager Empress Lü endeavored to earn the support of the people through moderate and humane policies. Like Gaozu, she eased the tax burden. She allowed the substitution of fines for physical punishments, and she rescinded the Qin book-burning laws. Her rule was strong and beneficent enough to earn the grudging admiration even of those of the old guard who objected to the growing power of the Lü clan.

Despite all the feuding of the factions, then, the great Han historian Ban Gu wrote approvingly of her reign:

> During the times of [Empress Lü] the world had succeeded in putting behind it the sufferings [during the period of] Contending States. . . . the world was quiet, [mutilating] punishments and other penalties were seldom used, the people were busy in sowing and harvesting, and clothing and food multiplied and were abundant.[3]

But the years rapidly grew heavy on the empress, who was not young when she acceded to power, and her strength waned as her years advanced. She appointed favorite nephews to supreme civil and military authority, advanced her family in the crucial tables of precedence—and then quite suddenly died. The cause of death was the bite of a black dog, which Lü swore on her deathbed was the spirit of a long-defeated rival come back to take its revenge.

Like the First Emperor of the Qin, the great sustainer of the Han could do nothing to impose her will from beyond the grave. Within weeks of her death, old fighters and members of Gaozu's clan had joined with leading officials and military men to massacre the entire Lü family and to put another of the Exalted Founder's line on the dragon throne of China.

The Martial Emperor: Han Wudi

The greatest of the Han emperors came to the throne half a century after the founder's death. Han Wudi, "the Martial Emperor" (141–187 B.C.E.), believed totally in the Mandate of Heaven and the mystique of the emperor. To fortify his claim to absolute sovereignty, he revived or instituted what became traditional imperial prayers and sacrifices to Heaven, to Earth, and to many other supernatural powers. To strengthen the developing system of

---

[3]Ban Gu, *The History of the Former Han Dynasty,* trans. Homer H. Dubs (Baltimore, Md.: Waverly Press, 1938), p. 210.

imperial administration, he recruited, trained, and appointed a pyramidal bureaucracy of tens of thousands of officials.

Wudi's economic policies built consciously on the prosperity of the earlier Han. To encourage continued economic growth, he expanded the transportation system through an extensive program of canal building. He established a system of imperial granaries to store grain for resale in time of bad harvest—a system that both stabilized agricultural prices and provided a tidy profit for the imperial treasury. To pay for his large-scale foreign and domestic projects, however, Wudi tapped the growing wealth of the empire through expanded taxation on trade, handicraft industry, and agriculture and through state monopolies on the sale of such essentials as iron, salt, and liquor.

The Martial Emperor's most obsessive concern, however, was with foreign wars, both defensive and expansionist. Perhaps his greatest military efforts were lavished on a series of campaigns against the nomadic Xiongnu north of the Great Wall. Wudi sent huge armies north to push the intrusive nomads back across the Gobi. He extended the Great Wall itself and set up military colonies to keep watch over the northern frontiers. He also developed what became a traditional Chinese policy of "using barbarians to control barbarians." This involved an intricate combination of marriage alliances, tributary relationships, and hostage taking in the guise of providing court education for the children of Xiongnu chieftains.

Besides these defensive measures, Wudi also embarked on a grandiose program of Chinese imperial expansion. Following in the footsteps of the First Emperor, the Martial Emperor pushed into both Korea and north Vietnam. His reaffirmation of Chinese authority made Vietnam a Chinese colony for most of the next millennium. His aggressiveness

CHINESE EMPIRES THROUGH THE CLASSIC AGE

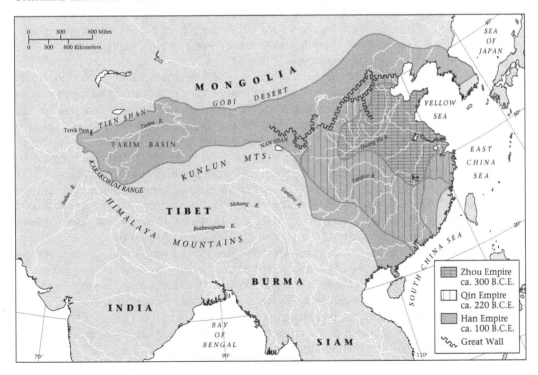

also helped transform Korea into the cultural base from which the offshore islands of Japan would later be reshaped in China's image.

But the ambitions of Wudi did not stop with domination of East Asia. He sent expeditions far across the northwestern frontiers as well, into the heart of Eurasia. His expeditions had several goals: alliances with western barbarians against the Xiongnu, acquisition of the famed war-horses of Ferghana in Central Asia, and quite possibly control of the east-west trade routes across Eurasia as well. These military campaigns established Chinese power from Mongolia to the borders of Tibet, pushed over the Pamirs into central Asia, and established Chinese control over crucial oases on the caravan roads around the Tarim Basin.

China's interest in westward expansion was to continue, and Chinese armies were to push westward still farther. But the Martial Emperor had done his share for Chinese territorial expansion north, south, and west. By the time of his death in 87 B.C.E., the borders of the Middle Kingdom were beginning to look a good deal like those of modern China.

Wang Mang and the Interregnum

In traditional Chinese historiography, the four centuries of Han rule are divided into two halves: the Former or Western Han, from 202 B.C.E. to C.E. 9, and the Later or Eastern Han, from C.E. 25 to 220. The thirty-five years in between constitute the brief, colorful period of the usurping emperor Wang Mang.

The emperors of the Former Han fell victim to what was to become a familiar combination of peasant unrest and weakness at the center. Peasant revolts broke out during the last two decades of the first century B.C.E., partly because of excess taxation, partly because of population growth that outstripped the land available to feed the people. At the same time, the government faced dwindling tax revenues as once-taxable peasant farmers became farm laborers on the traditionally untaxed estates of large noble landowners.

Amid this crisis, Wang Mang, nephew of a reigning empress, assumed power, proposing radical surgery to cure the ailing state. In the process he temporarily replaced the Han dynasty with his own imperial house.

The usurper claimed that he was reviving traditional policies of pre-Han rulers. In fact, some of his reforms look rather like revivals of some of the most extravagant policies of his great Han predecessor Wudi. Thus Wang also expanded government monopolies, strengthened the system of imperial granaries, and even indulged in inflationary coinage to put more money into circulation. His most drastic innovation, however, was a scheme to boost government revenues—and benefit the peasantry—by nationalizing the great estates of the aristocracy and parceling them out among taxable peasant proprietors.

Needless to say, this plan quickly alienated the great landowners from the new government. Bad harvests and terrible flooding by the Yellow River then triggered a new wave of peasant rebellions—the bloody revolt of the Red Eyebrows. Crusading for vaguely Daoist ideals, this group adopted red as its symbolic color because this was the color of the Hans, whose restoration they championed. They rose first in Shandong, China's great northeastern peninsula and the site of its most sacred mountain, and were soon ravaging the central plains. When nomads from beyond the Wall broke through the depleted border garrisons, it was clear to all that the Mandate of Heaven had not passed to Wang Mang after all.

Wang was slaughtered by rampaging rebels in his own capital in C.E. 23. Two years later the head of a branch of the ruling house of the Han Empire seized power, and the Han began two more centuries of rule over China.

New Frontiers

The first century of the Later Han dynasty—the first century C.E.—was a period of internal recovery and renewed external expansion. The restored Han moved the capital from Chang'an eastward, down to the city of Luoyang and reestablished the strong centralized administration of earlier Han times. Prosperity was revived across the country and relative peace reigned.

The Later Han, however, also saw a revival of Han imperial expansion. Armies from Luoyang reestablished Han authority over South China and north Vietnam, and Chinese influence grew in Korea. The first respectful embassy from one of the "hundred tribes" of Japan was received during Later Han times. The Xiongnu were dealt so crushing a defeat toward the end of the first century C.E. that they began the long westward drift across the steppes that would eventually bring them up against the walls of Rome—under the name of Huns.

Most striking, however, was the renewed westward drive under the Later Han emperors. The leading spirit in this expansion was Ban Chao, one of China's most celebrated proconsuls of empire. In two major expeditions he reestablished Chinese authority over the Tarim Basin and pushed on over the Pamirs and across central Asia as far as the region of the Caspian Sea. At the moment of Han China's farthest westward penetration, only the Parthian Empire of Persia lay between the great Empire of the East and the Roman Empire of the West. And the Later Han emperors actively encouraged trade with the West over the Silk Road—a connection that would continue for some time even after the fall of the dynasty.

The Mandate Passes

The second century of Later Han rule—the fourth of the dynasty's total tenure of power—was far less successful. As usual, the troubles were both political and economic, focusing in the court and in the country as a whole.

A special political difficulty was one that had surfaced as early as the reign of Empress Lü in Former Han times: the ambitious families of empresses. In the feudal times of the Shang and the Zhou, before unification was achieved, the kings of the various affiliated Chinese states could marry each other's daughters—their equals in rank. But under the unified empire of the Han, there were no other monarchs in China, and the neighboring peoples were dismissed as barbarians, unsuitable sources of Han empresses. Han emperors therefore had to marry the daughters of aristocratic subjects. The multitudinous kin of the empress invariably flocked to court to take advantage of the family's good fortune by establishing themselves in as many positions of power as possible. When an empress outlived her imperial husband and governed as regent for a minor emperor, the power drive of her clan could tear the Luoyang court apart. This in fact happened more than once under the Later Han.

Other centers of factional rivalry existed at the imperial court as well. These included the large numbers of eunuchs, whose power extended far beyond the imperial harem; the most successful generals; and the chief ministers of state. All these groups contributed to the downfall of this and more than one later dynasty.

Finally, economic factors and peasant upheavals once more played crucial parts in the coming catastrophe. Rich landowners, recovered from the disasters of Wang Mang's regime, once more acquired tax exemptions for their large estates. Buckling under the increased tax burden thus shifted to their shoulders, peasants sought to escape the tax collectors by fleeing into South China or by rebelling against the state.

Like the Red Eyebrows, the Yellow Turbans of the later second century C.E. had Daoist sympathies and social grievances. They also had the usual share of peasant superstitions; the yellow cloth they wore wrapped around their heads symbolized the color of Chinese earth, which would quench the red fire of Han. Like the Eyebrows, the Turbans rose first in the great northern peninsula of Shandong and were soon terrorizing much of North China.

The collapse of the Later Han thus came in a typical turmoil of court conspiracy, peasant revolt—and finally warlord generals carving up the crumbling empire into their own separate fiefdoms. By C.E. 220 China was once more divided, this time into the Three Kingdoms. The generals who headed these successor states began four centuries of political fragmentation and disarray in China. The first and one of the greatest of Chinese experiments in empire, that of the Qin and the Han, was over.

In a sense, the Han Empire was the victim of its own success. The centralized administration that was one of its greatest achievements could not work without close ties with the landed aristocracy. But the landed magnates milked this special relationship so successfully that they became too rich and powerful to control and created autonomous power centers all over the empire. Again, the very peace and prosperity of Han times seem to have led to an unprecedented growth in the peasant population—until there were simply more people than the government could support or control. Nevertheless, the Han dynasty had fathered a sense of political unity that would reassert itself time and again in centuries to come.

THE STRUCTURE OF HAN CHINA

The Imperial Mystique

China under the Han was the great empire of the east, as Rome—at almost exactly the same time—was the empire of the western end of Eurasia. The two had much in common: vast size and population; increasing power in the hands of the emperors; increasingly centralized bureaucratic administration; a sense of being the only truly civilized people, surrounded by barbarians; even an important breakdown of authority midway in their history, in both cases about the time of Christ. The two were aware of each other's existence and traded through intermediaries from one end of the world island to the other.

The Han emperors built a significant bastion of imperial authority on the Zhou doctrine of the Mandate of Heaven. It was under the Han that this doctrine of divine right to rule became associated not with a weak feudal regime like the Zhou but with a powerful centralized monarchy. From Han times the Chinese tended to believe that legitimate government meant strong rule by a single benevolent despot—a fatherly, authoritarian emperor whose governance was both virtuous and divinely sanctioned.

That the facts of political life at the Chinese court seldom corresponded to this pious theory was much less important for China's subsequent history than was the impact of the theory itself. This imperial mystique, the belief in paternal, virtuous, and divinely mandated governmental authority, was a powerful unifying and centralizing force in Chinese life. Reinforced by a common written language, shared traditions, and—as will be emphasized presently—Confucian beliefs and a classically educated centralized bureaucracy, this image of the emperor helped to weld China's tens of millions of people into something that Rome and India could never be: not a polyglot empire but a gigantic unified nation.

There were major breakdowns of Chinese unity still to come. But the centralizing rule of the Han set China on the road to national unity and strong central government infused with a sense of its own righteousness and right to rule. China has followed this road ever since, despite all that its huge size, vast population, and strong regional loyalties did to pull it apart.

The Scholar Bureaucrats

The Han period also saw a crucial institutional development that made the authority of the imperial government much more than a theory. For in Han times, China's famous system of scholar bureaucrats began to evolve.

The great shift from government by an autonomous feudal aristocracy to government by appointed officials of the central government had had a brief, violent trial run under the Qin. But the Legalist rigor of Qin administrators had made the system too brutal for widespread acceptance. Infused with the more moderate spirit of Confucianism—and with due concessions to the existing social elite of the countryside—China's administration under the Han dynasty became the most impressive in the world.

At the center of the Han administrative system were a small number of powerful court officials. These included a chancellor who chaired meetings and wielded substantial authority under the emperor; a director of the secretariat, whose power came from his control over what documents actually reached the emperor for signature; and a commandant of the Chinese armed forces. There were also nine ministers of state charged with the daily business of government, with running the huge imperial palace, and with the crucial religious rituals required of the Son of Heaven.

Outside the capital at Chang'an or Luoyang, the nation was divided and subdivided into administrative districts. There were a dozen main regions, 20 princedoms (holdovers from the feudal system), more than 100 commanderies, 240 marquisates, and 1,300 counties in Han China—all governed by officials appointed by the emperor. In the Han period, as noted above, most of these officials were still members of wealthy landowning families.

Also under the Han, however, the system of civil-service examinations that would eventually undermine the remaining power of the landed magnates slowly took shape. Exams on Confucian principles and classics were given annually at Chang'an to young gentlemen nominated for office. To prepare them, an imperial university was established at the capital. Again, the children of the wealthy, who had money for books and tutors, were evidently the ones most likely to succeed. Nevertheless, the result was to produce a ruling elite of government administrators who had a common family background and whose heads were filled with common Confucian theories, shared historical understanding, and the same basic values—a powerful force for stability in the ancient Middle Kingdom.

Around 100 B.C.E. China's governmental bureaucracy, divided into eighteen civil-service ranks, included upwards of 130,000 people—not many to govern tens of millions of Chinese, but an astonishing number of educated, centrally appointed officials for those days, when most of the world was still ruled by village elders, hereditary clan chieftains, and local princes.

Sixty Million Chinese—and Counting

The land they administered was large, populous, and generally prosperous in spite of some startling social and economic changes over the four centuries of Han rule. The size of the Han Empire, with the cementing of Chinese authority over northern Vietnam and the addition of Xinjiang—China's far west—was close to the size of twentieth-century China. The population, according to tax censuses taken around the middle of the dynasty, ran higher than sixty million people. We are thus dealing with a nation approaching the geographical size of the United States today, though with a population approximately one quarter that of the present United States.

Han society, however, underwent significant changes. Han China was particularly affected by the destruction of the ancient pattern of provincial feudalism by Gaozu and his successors. Gaozu abolished most of the autonomous states upon his seizure of power, leaving only a few such feudal enclaves to reward his own followers. Later Han emperors undermined even those few by edicts requiring feudal landholders to divide their estates equally among their male offspring. Within a few generations, this procedure had so thoroughly fragmented the great feudal holdings that they easily came under imperial control.

From this change emerged the basic social structure of China from Han times to the twentieth century. When feudal landholding was replaced by freehold property, three main classes quickly developed across the vast expanse of China's countryside. There was a class of locally powerful, often very wealthy large landowners. There was a larger class of peasant freeholders who often had to struggle to keep enough land to feed themselves. And there was an even larger class of tenant farmers and farm laborers. The interaction among these social classes, who composed the bulk of China's population, would determine much of its subsequent history.

The relative peace and prosperity of the Former Han transformed the nation economically as well. A true money economy, for example, was established for the first time. The widespread use of coins instead of barter brought with it such exotic problems as inflation and the need for a firm governmental monetary policy. But the growing wealth of China also filled the government's treasury with strings of copper cash, revenues that accumulated through so many reigns that the strings actually rotted away—an enviable situation for any government.

Under the expansionist Han emperors, furthermore, foreign trade expanded significantly. China traded, in the first instance, with the less developed tributary peoples around it. More important, Chinese goods moved westwards across Eurasia along the great Silk Road to India or to Rome, where Chinese silk became a major luxury import. Chinese merchants themselves did not travel that far. But the trade overland through central Asia or by sea through the archipelagoes of Southeast Asia became one of the basic ties that bound the world island into a single, if loosely linked, unit during the classical period.

The Women of Han China

The Han dynasty is commonly characterized as one of China's most splendid periods. In the lives of the female half of the huge Chinese population, it was also a time of considerable variety and significant achievement.

During this age in which much of the traditional Chinese way was first established, the position of women was also apparently set. Widely accepted maxims and popular anecdotes illustrating admired feminine qualities came into circulation: Like so much else, these precepts were sanctified in Han times by attribution to Confucian sages. They added up to a prescription for ideal womanhood that would prevail in China through most of its history.

According to this Confucian view—as in Christian, Muslim, and other groups in later centuries—women's virtues were family virtues. Chinese women were expected to be devoted to their parents in childhood and youth, to their husbands thereafter. Care of their

Chinese court ladies, hair elaborately dressed, hands concealed in long sleeves. The well-fed self-assurance of the Middle Kingdom in one of its greatest ages is eloquently captured in these clay figurines, which have survived remarkably undamaged over twenty centuries. (New York Public Library Picture Collection)

family and children was to be their central preoccupation as adults. Fidelity, chastity, and modesty were the ideal female qualities.

In actuality, however, Han China produced a number of women who transcended this image. Women of several important classes became highly educated and much respected for their learning during the Han dynasty. At the top of the social pyramid, Han empresses and imperial concubines were sometimes celebrated for their culture, as were the wives and daughters of some of the landowning aristocracy. Daoist and later Buddhist nuns might be both educated and relatively independent in traditional China. A few at least of the courtesan class were also highly cultured, as *geishas* would be in Japan at a later date.

We shall meet all these groups of learned ladies in later periods of Chinese history. But the Han period—the very time when the constricting Confucian ideal of womanhood was taking shape—was also a time of relative success, for the elite at least, of China's female population.

THE MIND AND ART OF THE HAN

The Triumph of Confucianism

If Shang bronzes were the glory of that dynasty, and if the supreme cultural achievement of the Zhou lay in philosophy and poetry, then Han China's major cultural monuments are to be found in the somewhat less exalted fields of scholarship and history. But Confucian scholarship and the study of the great dynastic cycle of Chinese history also had their contributions to make to the many-splendored culture and the amazing longevity of Chinese civilization.

The triumph of Confucianism in Chinese thought during the Han period was a complicated and in some ways rather unedifying spectacle. But that triumph would make a great difference to China's future.

All the schools of philosophy that had survived the "burning of the books" under the Qin had their place under the Han. The Qin Legalist tradition itself, with its justification of ruthless efficiency and rigorous punishment, was often the actual policy of Han emperors, even those who paid reverent lip service to Confucius. The romantic mysticism of Daoism became in Han times the basis of a widely popular farrago of nature worship, dietary regimen, research into methods of preserving life indefinitely and transmuting base metals into gold, and plain magic.

Nevertheless, the Confucian tradition did become the predominant philosophy of China during the Han period. Han emperors, from the classically uneducated Exalted Founder to the ruthlessly Legalistic Martial Emperor, filled their edicts with Confucian invocations of government for the good of the people, respect for the sages, and other pieties. The official examinations were based on the Confucian classics, so that all government administrators had at least studied the master's writings. Official sacrifices were made to his immortal spirit, and the classics themselves were engraved in stone and set up for all to see. From Han times on, Confucian philosophy was the national philosophy of the Chinese people.

In some ways the Confucianism thus established bore little resemblance to the social and ethical doctrine preached by Master Kong five hundred years before. Confucian scholars of the Han period attributed to their founder many views he never held. He was presented as a supporter of harsh punishments, as the author of a book on fortune-telling, and as an ardent champion of the doctrine that the emperor was the Son of Heaven. Like Buddha in India, Confucius was thus transformed at the moment of his triumph. Yet Confucius's canonization as the nation's official philosopher did bring a strong emphasis on learning and virtue as inextricably linked in human society.

A surprising product of this emphasis was the work of ancient China's most admired woman writer, Pan Chao. A member of an aristocratic family and educated in the Chinese classics, Pan Chao composed her widely admired verses, essays, and treatises—sixteen volumes in all—during the Han period. Pan Chao's classic *Precepts for Women* became the basis of Chinese women's education for most of the next two thousand years. Her *Precepts* included an idealistic view of marriage as "the fusion of Yin and Yang"—the male and female principles of the universe.[4]

Her main emphasis, however, was on the value of serious education for women. Only through equal access to knowledge, Pan Chao declared, could women and men ever find true equality in this world. It was a view that defenders of women's rights would take up with vigor in later centuries.

A broader consequence of this linking of learning and virtue was that many Confucian sages did not take official jobs or become pedantic scholars but remained poor men—and social critics—all their lives. Such men could still speak for the people whose ragged robes and torn sandals they shared. Official doctrines attributed to Confucius still included much of the master's spirit, including his insistence that virtue should rule, and even his radical notion that government should serve the people rather than exploit them. The endless repetition of these views over many centuries, by everyone from the emperor to the raggediest Confucian student, gave these principles of duty and decency, harmony and order, some weight at least in shaping the policies that ruled China.

---

[4]Pan Chao, *Nu Chieh: Precepts for Women,* in Florence Ayscough, *Chinese Women Today and Yesterday* (New York: Da Capo, 1975), pp. 240–241.

The Grand Historian

The study of history was another area in which the Han dynasty made significant contributions to Chinese culture and political understanding. Han China actually nurtured not one but two of the greatest historians Chinese civilization has ever produced. In addition, Han historical scholarship developed a central concept of Chinese social thought: the idea of the dynastic cycle.

Sima Qian lived during the Former, Ban Gu during the Later Han. Both men were close to great events and the great men of the age—Sima Qian as court historian to Wudi the Martial Emperor, and Ban Gu as the twin brother of Ban Chao, the most famous of Han empire builders. Their books followed what became a Chinese historiographical tradition by incorporating large amounts of source material, from government documents to snatches of poetry, into their texts. Otherwise, however, the two historians and their histories were very different.

Sima Qian's *Records of the Grand Historian* was a monumental attempt at a universal history of China, from the age of the mythical sages through the Shang, Zhou, and Qin to his own time. He passed judgments, told colorful stories, invented speeches for his historical figures, and generally filled his ten thousand or so pages with fascinating and thoroughly humanized history.

Ban Gu's *History of the Former Han* was more restrained in tone and more restricted in scope. But it became a model for a standard form of Chinese history thereafter: the history of a single dynasty, from vigorous beginnings to final collapse.

The interpretation of China's past as a series of such more or less uniform dynastic cycles became the core of traditional Chinese historiography—and the Former Han the great exemplar of this pattern. Each of the great dynasties thereafter was seen as beginning vigorously, rising to great achievement, then settling into a long decline and fall as the Mandate of Heaven passed on to strong new hands.

A more modern approach sees the dynastic cycle as a pattern of institutional, social, and economic development and decline. Thus, the success of a new dynasty is seen in its centralizing policies as much as in its personalities, and factional feuds built into the structure of the court contribute to its downfall. All dynasties build grandly, send out great armies, and in so doing overspend, leading to pressure on the tax-paying peasantry that will finally drive them to rebel. As revenues dry up, inadequately maintained dikes and border garrisons are likely to give way, leading to natural disasters and barbarian invasions. These catastrophes indicate that the Mandate of Heaven has been withdrawn—and yet another dynasty is swept away.

There seems to be truth in the concept of the dynastic cycle itself—one form of the eternal recurrence of rise and fall that plays over the history of all civilization. In China's case, however, we can chart the cycle in remarkable detail, thanks to the scrupulous efforts of Chinese historians to record the histories of their dynasties over the two thousand years since the Former Han.

Art in the Palace of Han

Surprisingly little remains of the art and architecture of Han China. The Han Chinese left us no crumbling Forum like that of ancient Rome, no Ajanta caves full of wonders. Their magnificent palaces were built of wood, and the paintings that literary sources describe have vanished with the plastered walls that held them. From such literary ac-

The vigor and dynamism of the Han Empire are powerfully conveyed by this beautiful bronze horse, dating from the second century C.E. Note the "flying gallop" pose. What conveys the sense of rapid motion in this statue? (New York Public Library Picture Collection)

counts, however, and from surviving fragments of metalwork and lacquerware, pottery, pressed tile, and the walls of tombs, we may get some idea at least of the subjects and styles of Han art.

The subjects are human, social, and historical: laborers in the fields, banqueters at the table, dignitaries parading in their parasol-shaded chariots, ancient sages, famous kings. There are few gods and no heavens, hells, or judgment halls of the dead, even in Chinese tombs. The style is simple, vigorous, and full of energy. Human figures are clearly outlined, rather flat, almost cartoonlike at first glance. But they move, gesture, reach out—their horses prance or charge at a flying gallop—with the dash and vigor that made the Han age great.

For the architecture of Han, we have some small pottery models, a few sketchy pictures, and the usual extravagant literary descriptions. From the models we get a sense of multistory tile- or thatch-roofed houses, walled courtyards, pig-pens and kitchens, balconies, people sitting in open doorways. From the written descriptions of Han palaces, we get a picture of something much more splendid.

The scale of Han public building clearly matched and even exceeded that of Huangdi. Gaozu's palace complex at Chang'an was more than a mile square and filled one ninth of the capital city. One of Wudi's even larger palaces, located outside the city walls, was connected to a royal residence inside the ramparts by an overpass that soared across the city moat as well as the walls. Inside a royal compound were many sumptuous buildings with ornamental gates and towers, mazes of courtyards, and vast audience halls, the whole surrounded by extensive parklands dotted with artificial lakes and stocked with exotic plants, beasts, and birds. Interiors of palaces or mansions were bright with plaster, paint, and gilt, bronze, and lacquer.

Gaozu, a peasant's son long used to field and camp, may have felt faintly ill at ease moving through such newly painted splendor in his elaborate silk robes. But the great Wudi surely strode with perfect confidence across an audience hall apparently larger than the one that graced the royal palace in twentieth-century Beijing. For the Han emperors built to their own measure, and that scale was often significantly larger than life.

SUMMARY

As in Persia and Rome, powerful centralizing dynasties ruled both India and China in the classic age.

India's second golden age, the reign of the Guptas, came as the climax of a long period of turbulence and growth in the subcontinent. After the disintegration of the unified Maurya Empire in the second century B.C.E., India did not know unity again for more than five tumultuous but prosperous centuries. During this period repeated waves of invaders swept down through the passes of the Northwest Frontier.

But prosperous cities and kingdoms also grew in southern India, which now rivaled the north in wealth and power for the first time. Increased urbanization, sophisticated crafts, and the expansion of trade both within and beyond the subcontinent made this prosperous period for the many peoples of India.

A true golden age came with unification under the Gupta dynasty (C.E. 320–540). The two earliest of these maharajas, Chandra Gupta I and Samudra Gupta, repeated the Maurya feat of conquering much of the land between the Himalayas and the southern cape. Chandra Gupta II gave India a Hindu Renaissance when order and prosperity pervaded the land, and the arts flourished. Then new invaders swept down across the Northwest Frontier, and the Gupta supremacy too passed into history.

Religious piety continued to be central to the high culture of India. Buddhism divided into two historic traditions, the Hinayana and Mahayana schools, and completed its evolution into an elaborate popular religion. Hinduism grew even more dramatically, tending toward monotheism and popular diversity and undergoing a genuine spiritual revival all across India.

Architectural remains reveal Indian piety, and sculpture projects a sense of the many forms of life. The plays of Kalidasa flourished in sophisticated princely courts and Indian scholars invented the zero and compiled a calendar very similar to our own.

China under the Han dynasty (206 B.C.E.–C.E. 220) laid the foundations for an imperial unity that would be reestablished again and again over the next two thousand years.

Gaozu, "Exalted Founder" of the dynasty, was a tough, hard-driving peasant who imposed order by force on the anarchy that had followed the death of Huangdi, the first unifier of China. His successor, the Empress Lü, established the new order firmly all across the Middle Kingdom. The empress's grandson and the most famous of all the Hans, Wudi, the "Martial Emperor," expanded China's frontiers by conquest, pushed back the Xiongnu nomads, built immense public works, and encouraged the establishment of a Confucian administrative system that would long outlast his dynasty.

Lesser Han rulers were briefly displaced around the time of Christ by the short-lived reforming regime of the usurper Wang Mang; but the Hans of the first century C.E. were again vigorous and successful. China's wealth and empire grew once more, until Chinese armies almost confronted Roman armies on the distant steppes of central Asia. Internal decay, rebellious generals, and invasions by northern peoples finally brought the Han dynasty down in the third century C.E.

Under this vigorous ruling house, the imperial mystique was honored, and the astonishing system of highly trained Confucian scholar bureaucrats, which would make China perhaps the best governed of all nations for many centuries, took shape. The population of China passed sixty million, and the wealth of the land supported such growth.

Confucius became the empire's official philosopher and the core of China's educational system under the Hans, and history writing emerged as one of China's major cultural achievements. Han emperors patronized art and literature on a scale suited to the wealth and splendor of the Middle Kingdom during one of its greatest ages.

SUGGESTED READING

Altekar, A. S. *The Position of Women in Hindu Civilization.* Banares: Motilal Banarsidass, 1956. Recommended survey of the subject; especially useful for earlier periods.

Champakalakshmi, R. *Trade, Ideology, and Urbanization: South India 300 B.C. to A.D. 1300.* New York: Oxford University Press, 1996. Scholarly study of city life in the south of the subcontinent.

Chattopadhyaya, B. *The Making of Early Medieval India.* New York: Oxford University Press, 1994. Useful summary.

De Bary, W. T., ed. *Sources of Indian Tradition.* New York: Columbia University Press, 1958. Valuable collection of source materials.

Dutt, N. *Mahayana Buddhism.* Calcutta: Firma K. L. Mukhopadhyay, 1973. Older but solid, exploring contrasts with the Hinayana tradition.

Flood, G. *An Introduction to Hinduism.* New York: Cambridge University Press, 1996. Balanced treatment.

Ganguly, D. K. *The Imperial Guptas and Their Times.* New Delhi: Abhinav Publications, 1987. Concise study of the dynasty and its achievements.

Juneja, M., ed. *Architecture in Medieval India: Forms, Contexts, Histories.* Delhi: Permanent Black, 2001. Substantial collection of studies of the age of the temple builders.

Kalidasa. *Shakuntala and Other Writings,* trans. W. Ryder. New York: Dutton, 1959. Highly praised translation of the Gupta dramatist.

Loewe, M. *Crisis and Conflict in Han China.* London: Allen and Unwin, 1974. Breakdown of the Former Han.

———. *Divination, Mythology, and Monarchy in Han China.* New York: Cambridge University Press, 1994. How supernatural beliefs supported imperial authority.

Needham, J. *Science and Civilization in China,* 6 vols. New York: Cambridge University Press, 1986. Massive ongoing study directed by a scholar who has given his life to examining China's scientific and technological achievements.

Nilakanta Sastri, K. A. *Development of Religion in South India.* New Delhi: Munshiram Manoharlal Publications, 1992. Brief survey of spread of Hinduism into the south.

Paul, D. Y. *Women in Buddhism: Images of the Feminine in Mahayana Tradition.* Berkeley: Asian Humanities Press, 1979. Cultural analysis.

Sima Qian. *Historical Records,* trans. R. Dawson. New York: Oxford University Press, 1994. Brief selections from China's Grand Historian.

Thani Nayagam, X. S., ed. *Tamil Culture and Civilization: Readings.* New York: Asia Publishing House, 1971. Anthology of classical Tamil writing.

Yang, L. "Female Rulers in Imperial China," *Harvard Journal of Asiatic Studies,* 23 (1960–1961), 47–61. Includes empresses during the Han, when women rulers were particularly prominent. For a contemporary life of Empress Lü, see Ban Gu's *History of the Former Han Dynasty,* Vol. 1, trans. H. H. Dubs (Baltimore, Md.: Waverly Press, 1938), chaps. 2 and 3.

 Please refer to the document CD-ROM for primary sources related to this chapter.

CHAPTER 8

FROM THE SAHARA TO PERU
The Classic Age in Africa
and the Americas

(600 B.C.E.–C.E. 900)

A GLANCE AHEAD: KINGDOMS AND CULTURES OF AFRICA AND THE AMERICAS

No other region could match the sheer size and scope of Rome, Persia, India, and China in the classic age. But old civilizations developed further and notable new ones emerged across Africa and the Americas as well.

North Africa made major contributions to Mediterranean culture with its fertile fields and famous cities like Alexandria. Down the east coast of Africa, ancient Kush was swallowed up by Axum—which also played an important part in the trade of the Indian Ocean. Across the Atlantic, great cities like Teotihuacán bloomed in what would become Mexico and Peru.

You can see classic grandeur in the towering obelisks of African Axum—in the immense stone pyramids of the classical Mayans in Middle America—or in the huge brick pyramids built by the Peruvian Mochica. There is impressive scale in the far-spread Amerindian trade routes or in the Camel Revolution that swept across the Sahara. Sit on top of the Huaca del Sol on the coast of Peru, or cruise the Saharan dunes on camelback, and you will feel some of the sense of mastery that is the hallmark of the classic age.

AFRICA NORTH AND EAST

Greek and Roman Africa

The centers of most of the world's more developed cultures during the classic age remained on the linked continents of Asia and Europe. On this huge landmass complex cultures interacted in ways that fostered comparatively rapid growth and development. But civilization had already begun outside the world island, and there were further developments on other continents during this period too.

Africa, closest to Eurasia and the home of one of the earliest civilizations, that of Egypt, continued to be integrated into the large patterns of Old World civilization. But sophisticated societies emerged outside the older cultural areas as well.

North Africa's ties to the Near East and the Mediterranean world remained strong in the classic age. Thus, Egypt was ruled first by the Ptolemies, heirs of one of Alexander the Great's generals, then by the Romans. The Romans especially squeezed the Egyptian peasantry unmercifully to ring all the grain possible out of the fertile Nile valley to feed the populous cities across the Mediterranean. Egypt's monuments and reputation for deep wisdom survived, however. Alexandria, in the Nile delta, became, as we will see, one of the great Mediterranean centers of learning.

By the time of Christ, all the rest of North Africa had also been incorporated into the Roman Empire. From the mouths of the Nile to the site of ancient Carthage and on west to the Strait of Gibraltar, Roman soldiers maintained domestic order and turned desert raiders back into the Sahara. The Romans also sowed the fertile strip along the Mediterranean coast with ordered farms and public wells, aqueducts and cities. The ruins are still there today, villas and temples, colosseums and aqueducts as impressive as any to be found in Italy or Greece, here on the northern edge of Africa.

Alexandria

The Egyptian city of Alexandria was famed for its harbor in Greek and Roman times. Its towering Pharos, a 400-foot lighthouse, was hailed as one of the wonders of the ancient world. Visitors from Africa, Asia, and Europe gazed in awe at the great Delta city's commercial wealth, palaces, and temples. Even more important, however, was the central part played by Alexandrian culture in the history of the classic age.

Alexandria's cultural institutions in particular were unrivaled. Its zoological and botanical gardens drew throngs of citizens. Its museum was true to its name, a temple of learning dedicated to the Muses. Most celebrated of all was the great library of Alexandria, which may have contained as many as 400,000 books. Here Egypt's Ptolemaic dynasty supported scholars, scientists, and other learned people, freeing them for study and writing in an atmosphere like that of a modern research institution.

Many writers and thinkers flocked to this new Athens on the southern shores of the Mediterranean. The geographer and astronomer Ptolemy worked here, assembling the theory of the structure of the universe that would dominate Western thought down to the time of Copernicus. The philosopher Plotinus, founder of the Neo- or New Platonism, probed the metaphysical limits of human understanding in the shadow of these brightly painted, multistoried buildings. The Greek-speaking Ptolemaic dynasty gave way to Roman emperors, but Egypt's reputation for wisdom continued to draw the best minds from Hellenistic into early Christian times.

The intellectual brilliance of Alexandria owed much to the city's Egyptian setting. Egypt's ancient skill at surgery and medicine, for instance, helped make Alexandria a leading medical center. There, thanks to the prevailing intellectual freedom, doctors conducted valuable anatomical studies by dissecting corpses. Greek and Egyptian styles of art and architecture began to blend and mingle here.

Greek and Egyptian taste for artistic representations of black Africans has left us a particularly valuable legacy of statuettes in marble, bronze, and terra cotta clay. Here these people of the Upper Nile are shown riding elephants, battling crocodiles, wrestling, dancing, juggling, making speeches, or playing musical instruments. These small figures are a vivid reminder that Hellenistic and Roman Alexandria was still an African city.

VOICES FROM THE PAST

This North African proudly described his own successful climb from rags to riches and community respect in the second century C.E. Does this inscription from ancient Africa remind you of any more recent attitude of "self-made men" toward their own success?

I was born of humble parentage. My father possessed neither money nor house of his own. Almost from the day of my birth I have lived by working on the land. I gave my plot of land no rest; nor did I spare my own labour. Came harvest time, when gangs of itinerant labourers set out on their rounds going as far afield as Cirta in Numidia and the Plains of Jupiter, I was always in the lead. For twelve years I toiled on these rounds under a broiling sun. From labourer I rose to the position of a contractor of labour, and for eleven years I led my troop of harvesters all over the Numidian plains. Hard work and thrift made me the owner of a house and a well equipped farm. My house lacks nothing in the way of material comforts. My life has earned its reward of distinction. I was co-opted to a seat on our local municipal Council by the Council's own decree, and from poor peasant I have risen to the position of municipal censor.

L. Thompson and J. Ferguson, *Africa in Classical Antiquity* (Ibadan: Ibadan University Press, 1969), p. 148.

Meanwhile, an impressive African civilization flourished far from the intersecting cultures of the Mediterranean during this period. This was the East African empire of Axum, south and east of Egypt on the shores of the Red Sea.

Axum and the Red Sea

Axum rose to supremacy in northeastern Africa on the ruins of ancient Kush and its capital, Meroe. The Axumite troops of King Ezana ravaged this ancient African kingdom on the upper Nile around C.E. 350. But Kush may already have been tributary to the kings of Axum when Ezana's armies desecrated its temples, for Axum was nearing the apogee of its power in the fourth century C.E. Axumite civilization, in fact, had its complex origins the better part of a thousand years before.

Axum was located southeast of the Sudan, in an area that straddles both the high Ethiopian plateau and the sun-bleached coast of the Red Sea. Perhaps as early as the seventh century B.C.E., Semitic-speaking Arab people had crossed the southern end of the Red Sea from Yemen to Africa. The newcomers, known as the Habashat people, settled both on the African shore and in the high country back from the coast. Here they met, dominated, and merged with a farming, herding Kushite-speaking people to produce the Axumites of the first millennium C.E.

The intruders came with experience in agriculture, trade, and other skills. The Habashat had already made southern Arabia bloom through the judicious deployment of dams and aqueducts. They had for generations been trading along the Red Sea and around the Indian Ocean. They were literate in their own Ge'ez tongue, and they knew how to build with stone.

Axumite Society

The new land the Habashat came to combined one of the hottest strips of territory on earth—the African Red Sea shore—with the mile-high mountains, deep gorges, and rushing rivers of the Ethiopian highlands inland. The Kushite people they found there lived in farming villages or followed their herds through the hills down to Lake Tana or the wide bend of the blue Nile. The Habashat blended with this older people on the land, as Aryans had with Dravidians in India, to produce a new African people—the people of Axum.

Such inland African products as ivory, hides, rhinoceros horn, and gold passed to the outside world through their highland capital, the city of Axum itself. Adulis, their port city in the lowlands, became a collecting point for goods from further down the coast of East Africa, or from as far away as India and Ceylon, across the Indian Ocean. From Axum and Adulis these African and Asian goods would flow north up the Red Sea to the eastern Mediterranean, to the Near East, Greece, Rome, and beyond.

During its most prosperous time, from the third century B.C.E. to the fourth century C.E.—the heart of the classical age—these Axumite cities were thriving centers of trade. Greek, Arab, and Jewish merchants mingled in its port cities, and caravans from the Sudan and beyond jostled each other in the streets of its capital. This bustling nation of traders became a key juncture in the flow of goods and ideas between the three continents of the Old World.

With wealth from overseas, furthermore, there came power in Africa. The Habashat invaders did not originally have a centralized political structure. Priests were important among them in the early days, and there were governors who collected tribute from local areas. Like so many others around the world, they were one people culturally but not yet a

A carved megalith from Axum, in today's Ethiopia, dwarfs the tiny human figure standing at its base. Notice the false door inscribed in the solid stone at the base of the structure. Where else have we seen inscribed vertical shafts set up as commemorative and decorative structures? (The Smithsonian Collections)

political nation. More centralized political institutions, however, evolved with time. By the first century C.E. the written guide to the Red Sea used by Greek traders reported that there was a king at Axum—and that he had some Greek education. A traveler of a later century described the Axumite ruler progressing in splendor, clad in gold-embroidered linen and standing in a four-wheeled chariot drawn by four elephants. Both the king and his counselors were armed with gilded spears and shields, and flutes made music for them as they passed.

The Culture of Axum

The soldiers of the kings of Axum carried the power of the coastal kingdom inland. Axumite armies pushed north through the Ethiopian mountains as far as the frontiers of Egypt. They thrust west across the grasslands of the Sudan to ravage Kush and Meroe. For a time they controlled all the land from the Ethiopian uplands to the Horn of Africa, dominated a long stretch of the Red Sea coast, policed the interior caravan trails, and kept all the neighboring pastoral peoples in awe.

The city of Axum itself, settled in the well-watered highlands some days' journey back from the coast, developed a unique material culture under the Axumite kings. The ruins that remain remind the traveler of no place else on earth. There are crenelated castles and thrones of carven stone. There are "stepped walls" and the giant obelisks of Axum, sixty-five feet high and carefully sculptured to look like towers with false doors and windows and strange round arches at the top.[1]

---

[1]G. W. B. Huntingford, "The Kingdom of Axum," in *The Dawn of African History,* Roland Oliver, ed. (London: Oxford University Press, 1961), p. 23.

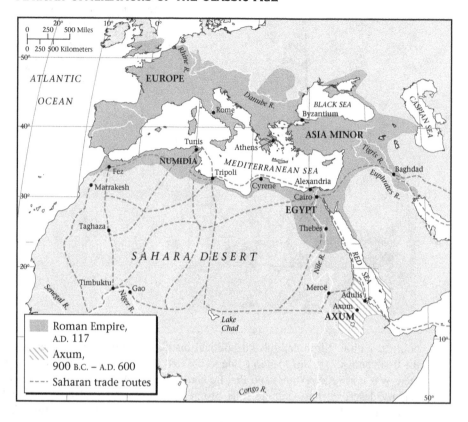

In pagan Axum there were temples to the old gods of Arabia—gods of earth and war and the blazing sun—and blood sacrifices to these deities, even of humans. But in the fourth century C.E. the celebrated King Ezana accepted conversion to Christianity at the hands of his old tutor, an Eastern Orthodox priest. Thereafter churches began to rise in Axum. Thereafter also the fortunes of the Axumites began to change.

In Christian Axum, many things changed. The blood sacrifices ended, if they had not ended before, and commercial ties with the Christian Near East grew still stronger. But conversion also had a powerful isolating effect on Axum, which became the only Christian country in this part of the world. This effect was intensified in the seventh century C.E., when Islam swept like a prairie fire across North Africa and down through Arabia. The Christian Axumites then found themselves alone indeed, between the pagan peoples south and west of them and the Muslims to the north and east.

These enemies encroached slowly upon the greatness of Axum. Adulis was taken by the Arabs, and other Axumite harbors by neighboring African peoples. The herdsmen that king Ezana had held in check now raided at will across the croplands of the Axumites. There were kings in the city of Axum for another century or two; then they too disappeared from history.

The survivors of once proud and prosperous Axum clung to the faith of Ezana, if they could not keep his wealth and power. Christianity persisted and strengthened them in their long isolation. They survived to become the ancestors of Africa's oldest continuously independent people, the Ethiopians of today.

Africa South of the Sahara

Saharan and Sub-Saharan Societies

During the thousand years before and after Christ, Africa south of the Sahara desert developed at its own pace. There were as yet no Alexandrias or Axums in these regions, any more than there were in Europe north of the Alps or Asia north of the Great Wall of China. Nevertheless, archaeological research reveals technological and economic progress and suggests the emergence of more complex political forms in the western and southern parts of Africa during the classic age.

Social structures for most of Africa remained solidly traditional during this period. The family, as in so many other places, was the foundation of all group life. Extended families grouped several generations and the families of several siblings in a single sizable compound. These family units in turn evolved into villages. Within the village, gender and age further organized society. Specific social roles were assigned to men and women, and special prominence and power went to village elders, whose long experience was deemed valuable to the community as a whole.

There was variety within these common patterns, particularly within the area of gender relations. Some African societies were patriarchal and patrilineal, recognizing power and inheritance in the male line, others matriarchal and matrilineal. Everywhere, however, family ties were the ties that bound African societies together.

Technology: Metals and Salt

Many African peoples of this period continued to shape stone into hard-edged tools for everyday use. Some of them also learned to work copper, iron, and gold and to mine salt during these centuries.

Of the chief metals, copper was mined in Mauretania in northwestern Africa in pre-Christian times. Copper ornaments and use objects have been found in tombs in this area. The West Africans of Senegal and the central and southern Africans of today's Zaire, Zimbabwe, and Zambia also worked copper, though we know less about these regions.

Ironworking, as we have seen, may have radiated from ancient Meroe or may have emerged spontaneously in several parts of Africa. Some authorities believe Africans outside of the Nile valley both mined and worked iron during the first millennium after Christ. Khoi-San peoples may have mined iron in southern Africa as Bantu-speaking Africans did in West Africa. Certainly, the great Bantu migrations, to be discussed in a later chapter, spread iron far across central and southern Africa.

Gold, which would emerge as a key African export in the next stage of African history, also came into use south of the Sahara this early. Far up the Senegal and Niger rivers of West Africa, people probably panned and mined for gold as early as the first millennium C.E.

The lowly mineral called salt became increasingly valuable as more and more Africans settled down in agricultural villages. Hunting peoples got plenty of salt from the animals they killed, but people dependent on crops had little salt in their diets. Living as they did in an increasingly hot climate, Saharan and equatorial Africans also lost much salt each day through perspiration. While archaeologists still have much digging to do, salt works from the first millennium C.E. have been found in the Sahara itself as well as in East Africa.

You can pick up the white, crusty stuff today in the salt pans of the northern Sahara, or buy lumps of it wrapped in plastic along the Niger south of Timbuktu. It is still as essential as ever to human survival in these dessicated lands.

The camel, which reached Africa from Asia in the early centuries of the Common Era, could carry heavy loads of trade goods through arid lands where horses or mules could not survive. Here camels are being loaded with salt in the modern West Africa state of Niger for the journey across the Sahara to the populations of the tropical African lands to the South. (James L. Stanfield/National Geographic)

Trade: The Camel Revolution

Commercial exchange, as we have seen, goes back a long way in Africa. Both food-gathering and agricultural peoples traded stone and metal for tools, decorative beads, meat, grain, dried fish, and many other things. Most of this exchange, however, was local and small in scale. Only with the spreading use of metals and the introduction of the camel into Africa did long-distance trade emerge.

Metal deposits were found only in widely scattered sites. As peoples began to work them, however, metals became the most widely valued of trade goods. Evidence of exchange includes the discovery of copper ingots in South Africa and of ornaments made of metals not locally available in West African graves. Other things were widely traded too, including salt from the Sahara and glass beads, which may have been made as far away as India.

A key development that made wider trade possible was the Camel Revolution. This major improvement in transportation spread westward from Asia during the centuries around the time of Christ. Capable of carrying as much as 500 pounds for many days with little water and only the scantiest grass, camels were ideally suited for desert travel across northern Africa. The hardy beasts were probably introduced from the Near East into Egypt by the Greek Ptolemies and to the rest of North Africa under the Romans. The African Berbers quickly adopted camels, using them for travel across the Sahara to the Western Sudan and the forests of the Guinea coast.

Camels are not friendly animals, and there seems to be little love lost between them and their keepers. Riding a camel up and down real Saharan dunes is rather like hanging onto a small boat bucking through heavy seas. But their introduction into North Africa by C.E. 200 revolutionized travel and transport across the northern half of the continent.

North American Cultures

The Desert Southwest: Mogollon and Hohokam

Agriculture replaced hunting and gathering in Mexico thousands of years before Christ. Slowly, this pattern of life, with its settled villages and increasingly structured society, spread north of the Rio Grande.

An early such shift north of Mexico occurred in what became the American southwest before C.E. 1000. In Arizona and New Mexico, a hotter, drier climate menaced the stable foraging society that had taken root there. Threatened with extinction, the Mogollon and Hohokam peoples moved toward settled farming.

The Mogollon people used digging sticks to cultivate the basic trio of crops that had first developed in Mexico: corn or maize, beans, and squash. They built permanent pit houses that were cool in summer and warm in winter. They also constructed underground storage rooms for harvested food.

The Hohokam were themselves immigrants from Mexico. One thoroughly excavated Hohokam site reveals a hundred pit houses. The site also includes perhaps the first irrigation system constructed in America, here used to bring river water to arid fields several miles away. The Hohokam grew not only the basic food crops mentioned above but cotton and tobacco as well.

The Eastern Woodlands: Adena and Hopewell

Farming began to spread to eastern North America about this time also, though it complemented rather than replaced hunting and gathering. This was particularly so in the eastern woodlands of what would later become the United States.

On the Ohio River, the Adena culture emerged earlier than the Mogollon tradition—before C.E. 500. The existence of settled villages shows that the Adena people spent a large part of the year in one place, probably tending crops. They combined pumpkins and other food plants with nuts, fish, and game gathered or hunted in the forest.

Around the first century C.E., the much more widespread Hopewell culture emerged in the Mississippi and the Ohio River valleys. Like their Adena predecessors, the Hopewell people combined foraging with limited farming. But maize was not yet effectively adapted to the colder northern environment. Further development would await both new strains of corn and some crucial technological advances.

Society and Culture

During the thousand years around the birth of Christ, however, these Native American peoples of the classic age did make some remarkable social and cultural breakthroughs. The people of the southwest, for instance, learned to weave cotton into cloth and to make pottery. Besides their impressive irrigation works, the Hohokam people mined for turquoise. This they traded with the city-dwellers of Mexico for copper bells and earrings, rubber balls, and other handcrafted products. They also imported from Mexico such cultural practices as mounds for religious ceremonies and large outdoor ball courts.

The eastern forest people traded even further and built even more impressively. The Hopewell culture constructed large and elaborate burial mounds for their most honored dead. These graves have yielded trade goods accumulated by Hopewell people, sometimes from halfway across the continent. Among these were shells from the Gulf Coast, copper from the Great Lakes, and obsidian from the Rocky Mountains. Their Adena predecessors were even greater builders. The Great Serpent Mound in southern Ohio, winding for some 1,300 feet, is the largest representational earthwork in the world.

The artistic achievements of these peoples could be striking. Human figures dance around an elaborately decorated Hohokam pot dating from the first millennium C.E. Hopewell artisans shaped a flat sheet of mica into a startlingly lifelike silhouette of a

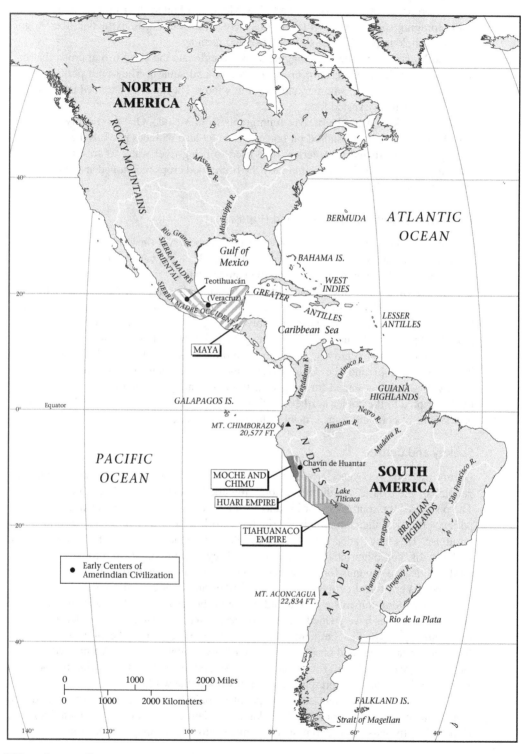

NORTH AMERICA

ROCKY MOUNTAINS

Missouri R.

Mississippi R.

BERMUDA

ATLANTIC OCEAN

Rio Grande

SIERRA MADRE ORIENTAL

Gulf of Mexico

BAHAMA IS.

Teotihuacán

WEST INDIES

(Veracruz)

GREATER

SIERRA MADRE OCCIDENTAL

ANTILLES

LESSER ANTILLES

Caribbean Sea

MAYA

Magdalena R.

Orinoco R.

GUIANA HIGHLANDS

GALAPAGOS IS.

Equator

Negro R.

MT. CHIMBORAZO 20,577 FT.

Amazon R.

Madeira R.

PACIFIC OCEAN

Chavín de Huantar

SOUTH AMERICA

São Francisco R.

MOCHE AND CHIMU

HUARI EMPIRE

Lake Titicaca

TIAHUANACO EMPIRE

Paraguay R.

BRAZILIAN HIGHLANDS

• Early Centers of Amerindian Civilization

MT. ACONCAGUA 22,834 FT.

Paraná R.

Uruguay R.

Rio de la Plata

0   1000   2000 Miles

0   1000   2000 Kilometers

FALKLAND IS.

Strait of Magellan

human hand around C.E. 500. The great traditions of Native American art thus began to take shape even before many of these people had settled into fully agricultural societies.

SOUTH AMERICAN SOCIETIES

Growing Populations

The rise of the United States to prominence over the past two centuries has fostered a completely unhistorical sense of "natural" North American predominance in the western hemisphere. For most of the history of civilization in the New World, Middle and South America have in fact been the leaders, and North America the less developed continent of our hemisphere.

Population densities in the pre-Columbian Americas are an intensely debated subject, but there does seem to be some agreement that the south was much more heavily populated than the north. In both Middle America and northwestern South America, intensive advanced agriculture centering in corn, beans, squash, and, in South America, potatoes had produced a population base adequate to support societies more elaborate than any to be found north of the Rio Grande.

The Olmec culture of Mexico and the Chavín culture of Peru had begun the social evolution of Mesoamerica and South America during the first millennium before Christ. During the first thousand years C.E., that process of cultural evolution continued in Mexico and Central America on the one hand, and in northwestern South America on the other.

In both these areas the process of state formation was a key element in this development. From agricultural villages linked by religion and culture, there evolved states with populations of tens and hundreds of thousands, specialization of labor, structured systems of social classes, and sometimes true cities and central governments as well. Unification into larger empires like those of the Aztecs and Incas of later centuries was rare. Nevertheless, during the classical period areas of advanced culture were scattered all over the highlands and lowlands of Mexico, Honduras, Guatemala, and through the central Andes and neighboring coastal lowlands of Peru.

While North America remained the preserve of hunting-and-gathering tribes and agricultural villages dominated by hereditary chiefs, impressive civilizations had thus emerged in Middle and South America. Three of the better known of these societies will be dealt with here, including perhaps the most sophisticated of all Amerindian cultures, that of the Classical Maya.

The Mochica Pottery Makers

We will begin with South America and the continuing evolution of civilization in the shadow of the Andes.

The first highly developed culture in Peru, the Chavín culture of the first millennium B.C.E., had faded several centuries before Christ. But its influence lingered on, giving rise to several successor cultures during the first millennium C.E. One among these has particularly impressed the archaeologists, who are once more our primary sources of understanding: the Mochica culture of the Moche River region of northern Peru.

The cult centers of the old Chavín culture had been in the Andes. Mochica culture, like most of the successor cultures to Chavín, developed on the coastal strip along the Pacific and in the river valleys that spread through the foothills of the Andes down to the sea. Like most of the classical American cultures, they flourished rather later than the classic civilizations of the Old World: Mochica culture was probably at its height between C.E. 300 and 700.

Although they were preliterate, the Mochica people have left us a great deal of concrete information about themselves in their unique pottery. In the naturalistically sculptured forms of many of their ceramic works and in the pictures with which they decorated them, a whole vanished culture comes to life. These, coupled with huge clay-brick ruins, reveal one of the most sophisticated South American societies before the Inca.

The Mochica civilization was almost surely that of an organized state, and one that dominated the coastal valleys of much of Peru. The ruling elite must have included a priestly class that supervised the large temple complexes. It must also have involved a warrior class, since the Mochica were a warlike people who built their empire, as empires have generally been built, by force.

The bulk of the population were farmers, though they supplemented their diet with game and fish. The Mochica were, in fact, very advanced agriculturists, cultivating maize, beans, potatoes, and other crops on the narrow green patches along the rivers. These they irrigated by elaborate systems of ditches and fertilized with bird dung fetched on large seagoing rafts from offshore guano islands.

The Mochica were also large-scale builders, mostly in adobe brick. They constructed genuine cities and raised massive step-pyramids in their religious ceremonial centers. One of these pyramids, the Huaca del Sol in the Moche Valley, towers 150 feet high and required as many as fifty million clay bricks for its construction.

Beyond all this, the Mochica became some of the most skilled artists and artisans in the Americas. Their metalworkers made masks of copper, headdresses of gold, and jewelry of various metals. Mochica women specialized in textiles, doing both the spinning and the weaving of cloth. They produced richly embroidered, elaborately decorated tunics, shirts, and mantels—most of them worn by men. Mochica potters manufactured the sculptured ceramic ware that has provided information about their culture and the gems of many ceramics collections since.

Many Mochica pots and jars are fully sculptured and as realistically representational as the Olmec heads of Mexico. There are actual portrait heads on these Peruvian jars.

Other ceramic works and the painted images on them show Moche warriors swinging their clubs in battle or leading home long lines of prisoners with ropes around their necks, probably for sacrifice. They depict reed boats on voyages to guano islands or peasant farmers laboring in shorts or even naked in the fields. And they provide detailed documentation of the rich sexual lives of Moche men and women in a ceramic record as vivid as India's *Kama Sutra* or any Japanese "pillow book."

This Mochica people of the north coast of Peru are only one of several Peruvian societies that developed on the Pacific coast and in the Andes between the ancient Chavín and the awesome achievement of the Incas. But thanks to their artistic and architectural accomplishments, they illustrate Peruvian civilization during the classical age more vividly and more impressively than most of the other societies of northwestern South America.

Peruvian Culture

Other cultures flourished in Peru, both on the coast and in the mountains, during this period. Archaeologists have a plentiful supply of ruins to explore, tombs to excavate, and surviving artifacts to evaluate. Partly because of the lack of a written script, however, firm

Teotihuacán's immense Temple of the Sun, larger than the largest pyramid at Egyptian Giza, dominates this revered Mesoamerican"city of the gods." A four-chambered cave recently discovered under the huge pyramid may have been dedicated to a primordial Mother Goddess believed to dwell underground. (Jim Fox/Photo Researchers)

conclusions are hard to come by. A brief survey of some of the remarkable remains of these vanished peoples will perhaps be more useful than a summary of debatable conclusions.

In the Peruvian highlands, multistoried stone buildings gaze out over the mountains, their purpose unknown. Statues of warriors or women and pottery decorated with hunting scenes give haunting glimpses of vanished civilizations. More striking are the gorgeous textiles discovered wrapped around mummies found on the arid south coast of Peru. Thanks to the dry climate, fabric thousands of years old has been perfectly preserved. Woven of a variety of threads—wool, cotton, even human hair—and dyed with more than a hundred different colors, the textiles of Paraca Necropolis have been described as among the most beautiful in the world. Yet we know almost nothing of the society that produced them.

Perhaps most tantalizing of all are the famous Nazca lines. These marks inscribed in the dry earth of southern Peru were discovered by accident when a plane flew over them in the first half of the twentieth century. Seen from that height, it was clear that many of the lines sketched out animals and birds, while others defined geometrical shapes or ran straight across the desert pointing at the horizon.

Those who have studied the enigmatic lines have seen astronomical significance in some, which point toward solstice or equinox points. The pictures, undetectable on the ground, must have been intended for the gods to contemplate.[2]

---

[2]Alternative explanations relating the Nazca lines to flying saucers have not found favor with archaeologists.

The Pyramids of Teotihuacán

There are more huge stone pyramids in Mesoamerica than there are in Egypt—striking testimony to the centuries of organized society and the sophisticated cultural heritage of Mexico and Central American before the conquistadores came. Some of the most impressive of these monuments are to be found not in the coastal Caribbean lowlands where Olmec and later Mayan culture flourished, but in the upland valleys of central Mexico. Of these peoples of the high plateau, the earliest and one of the most revered were the builders of the great city of Teotihuacán, the "sacred center . . . of the Mesoamerican world" around the time of Christ.[3]

The civilization of Teotihuacán emerged perhaps as early as 200 B.C.E. and expired in violence around C.E. 700. As usual, lacking significant documentary evidence, we know virtually nothing of the political history of this early Mesoamerican people and can do no more than speculate on their political institutions. But there is plenty of information—including, once more, pictorial evidence—concerning the economic life, social structure, and artistic capabilities of the people of Teotihuacán.

There is an aggressive tone to surviving Teotihuacán mural paintings—warriors with human hearts skewered on their blades—suggesting a predatory foreign policy similar to that of the Aztecs of later centuries. Evidence of Teotihuacán's cultural predominance is found as far afield as Guatemala. Whether this evidence proves trade and cultural contacts or actual conquest and rule must remain uncertain. We know only that we are dealing with a powerful people whose influence was widespread.

The best evidence of their greatness is, of course, the city of Teotihuacán itself. Several square miles in area with a population of well over one hundred thousand, this was one of the true cities—as opposed to ceremonial religious centers—in pre-Columbian America. It was a planned city, designed probably by priestly administrators. Its grid of streets and avenues provided space for the temples, palaces, and market plazas, the courtyards and arcades of the rich, and the single-story, flat-roofed "apartment houses" of the less affluent.

The arts of Teotihuacán included elegant ceramics, beautiful stone masks, and the carefully carved stone faces of the gods. There are also paintings, here in the form of thousands of murals found in houses and palaces throughout the city. The chief divinities of Teotihuacán were Tlaloc the rain god and Quetzalcoatl, the feathered serpent of later Aztec times. But the great monuments in the city are the gigantic pyramids of the Moon and the Sun. The Pyramid of the Sun, seven hundred feet long and more than two hundred feet high, built of stone over an earthen core, is one of the largest structures to be found anywhere in Amerindian Mexico.

Teotihuacán was a thriving place for nine hundred years before it perished by fire, perhaps in war or revolution, between C.E. 650 and 750. Eight centuries later the vast ruins of this dead city drew the Aztec emperor Moctezuma to pray and consult with the gods among its empty avenues and tumbled stones. But the gods of Teotihuacán, who could not save their own people from the common fate of empires, could not save the Aztecs either.

---

[3]Jill Leslie Furst and Peter T. Furst, *Pre-Columbian Art of Mexico* (New York: Ableville Press, 1980), p. 43.

The Mayan City-States

The Classic Maya of Mesoamerica, who flourished between C.E. 300 and 900, produced what many scholars consider the most brilliant of all pre-Columbian Amerindian civilizations. Every enthusiast for "lost civilizations" knows their huge step-pyramids, bursting vertically out of the jungle, vines and bushes sprouting picturesquely from the ancient stone. Fewer know their faces, the convincingly modeled middle-aged cheeks, hooked noses, heavy lids of men in ceremonial headdresses reproduced in ceramic figurines, or the painted figures of priests, nobles, and warriors in fantastic regalia marching across the walls of temples. But it is only when we begin to penetrate the minds of the Maya that we glimpse the true dimensions of their accomplishment.

There are many mysteries about Mayan civilization. We know that the Mayans lived in the lowlands of the Mexican Gulf Coast and in parts of Guatemala, Honduras, and El Salvador in the first millennium after Christ. We know that in some ways their culture derived from that of the ancient Olmecs—but even Olmec antecedents cannot explain mathematical insights that had not yet occurred to Europeans at that time. We know that after centuries of dynamic cultural development Mayan civilization withered and died. But we have only informed guesses as to why.

Even basic facts about the Mayan economy are debated. They were certainly a fully agricultural people, cultivating maize, beans, squash, and other foods and feeding a population of upwards of two million people. One of the long-standing puzzles of Mayan history has been how the Mayans managed to feed so many people using old-fashioned slash-and-burn agricultural methods. Recent research employing aerial photographs, however, seems to have detected intricate patterns of irrigation canals beneath the brush and forest that blanket the region today. So one Mayan mystery at least may be on its way to a solution.

The political and social organization of the Mayans is clearer than that of any Amerindian culture we have glanced at so far. The Maya region was divided into a number of small states, all speaking related but not always mutually intelligible languages. Warfare was common among these states, and prisoners were brought home and ritually sacrificed to the gods of the victors.

Like Mesopotamian or Greek city-states, the lands of the Mayans shared a similar hierarchic social and political structure. They were normally ruled by a hereditary elite of priests and nobles. There was an intermediate social class of artisans and artists, traders and civil servants. And there was a majority population of peasant farmers and a smaller number of serfs and slaves.

Among the peasant masses, men and women worked hard with stone tools clearing the jungle for planting. Their standard of living, however, seems to have been relatively high, perhaps higher than that of the Indians of Yucatan or Chiapas today. Their pole-and-thatch houses were built on platforms. Their cotton clothing included skirts and shirts for women, knee-length trousers for men. More aristocratic families flaunted jade and feather ornaments and pierced ears, noses, and lips for further decoration. Marriages were monogamous among the peasantry, polygamous among the upper classes, and if things didn't work out, divorce was easy.

Mayan Religion and Art

Like other lowland Mesoamerican peoples, the Mayans were not yet a truly urban culture. But they did build huge ceremonial centers with the famous stone step-pyramids, multistory palaces, wide plazas, ceremonial ball courts, intricately carved stone stelae, and other impressive structures and carvings. Thousands of people could live at centers like those of Tikal in northern Guatemala, with its 230-foot pyramid, or at Palenque in eastern Mexico, with its great palace towering over the surrounding jungle. Tens of thousands of others would live in wattle-and-daub thatched huts around the periphery of such a place. And countless more would come for the great celebrations before the temples of the gods.

Even experienced archaeologists can get dizzy climbing the steep, narrow steps of a Mayan pyramid—let alone descending! Sitting outside the temple you will find perched on top, gazing down at the hazy green of bush or jungle below, you are likely to develop a deep respect for what these Native Americans could do. This is especially true when you remember that under the green canopy, or in those hills and valleys on the horizon, countless other ruins remain, choked in roots or vines or rubble, still waiting for the excavator's pick.

In stone and plaster sculpture as well as in multicolored wall paintings, the Mayans have left even more detailed information about their daily lives than did the Mochica or the people of Teotihuacán. In these images from the past, a colorful aristocracy of warriors in jaguar skins and plumed headdresses and ladies in long white robes watch costumed dancers spin to the music of drums, rattles, and trumpets. Crowds cheer the young players of ceremonial ball games or watch the bloody sacrifices of prisoners from the last war. The excitement of these vanished spectacles lives still in moving limbs, an upraised hand.

But there were minds at work here whose concerns went far beyond such common pastimes as sports, music, and war. There was, for instance, as bewildering a pantheon of gods as we have encountered anywhere in the world. The chief of these was Itzamná, creator of humankind, inventor of the arts and sciences—a toothless old man often represented as a lizard, a crocodile, or a serpent. There was Ah Kinchil, god of the sun, and Ah Puch, lord of death, with his spotted body and protruding spine. There were gods who protected the interests of all sorts and conditions of people in this complex Mayan world. There were patrons of traders, travelers, farmers, hunters, fishermen, and beekeepers; gods of poetry and music, of war, sacrifice, and suicide; gods of the rain and the life-giving corn.

All of these divinities mingled traits of humans and animals, reptiles, or birds in monstrous, sometimes changing shapes. In the complicated Mayan theology, they presided over thirteen heavens above the earth and nine hells below it. Like gods in many other lands, they made the corn grow, the women fertile, and the warriors victorious.

Mayan Mathematics, Science, and Writing

Once again, however, we make them seem too simple. For the Classic Mayans are most famous not for theology but for science, mathematics, and their unique system of writing.

Mayan mathematical thinking was in some ways at least as advanced as that of the Old World. Their system was based on the number twenty—rather than ten, as in the later metric system. Like Gupta Indian mathematicians, the Mayans also understood the concept of zero. They were thus able to undertake calculations reaching into the millions.

Mayan astronomers were also remarkably accurate, both as observers and as calculators. Astronomer-priests recorded detailed observations of the movements of the moon and the planet Venus over generations. They were able to predict both solar and lunar eclipses. Temples were aligned with the heavenly bodies, and some temples may have been intended primarily as astronomical observatories. On the foundation of this astronomical knowledge, Mayan priests designed a 365-day calendar that came considerably closer to measuring the earth's actual annual revolution around the sun than the contemporary Julian calendar in use in Europe.

The Mayans, finally, developed the most advanced system of hieroglyphic writing in the Americas. Though all but a handful of their bark-paper codices (books) were destroyed by their Spanish conquerors in the sixteenth century, subjects of special literary concern seem to have included religion, science, and the political achievements of their rulers. Religious texts included sacred songs and spells, horoscopes and prophecies. Among subjects of political interest were the victories of their rulers in the many wars between the separate Mayan city-states.

A related document is the famous Mayan *Popol Vuh,* written after the conquest in a Mayan language but using European letters rather than Mayan glyphs. This book preserves a Mayan informant's view of history, from the creation of the world to the last Mayan kings, mingling the deeds of gods and men in a narrative that still fascinates modern students of this ancient people.

SUMMARY

Advanced societies continued to develop in Africa and the Americas during the classic age. North Africa continued to flourish as part of the Mediterranean culture that surrounded the world's largest inland sea. Alexandria, in Egypt, became a great intellectual center of the Mediterranean world during Hellenistic and Roman times. The fertile North African shores played an important role in the larger Roman imperium of these centuries.

Eastward in Africa, on the blistering Red Sea shore and in the cool Ethiopian highlands, the Kingdom of Axum (third century B.C.E. to fourth century C.E.) built its independent place in the commercial life of the Old World. Serving as a meeting place for goods from inner Africa, the Mediterranean, the Indian Ocean, and the lands beyond, Axum enjoyed many prosperous centuries before succumbing to isolation and conquest early in the Christian era. The Sahara itself, finally, was criss-crossed with trade routes as camel caravans transported goods between the Mediterranean and the southern half of West Africa.

Agriculture spread widely across North, Middle, and South America during the classic age. In the North American southwest, the Hohokam and Mogollon cultures drew from neighboring Mexico to build their own village societies. In the eastern woodlands, the Mississippi Valley produced the Adena and Hopewell cultures with trade links to distant parts of the continent.

Among a number of local cultures that rose in the Peruvian Andes on the foundations laid by the ancient Chavín "mother culture," the society of the Mochica people has perhaps most intrigued historians, archaeologists, and art collectors. These makers of some of the New World's most famous pottery also built a powerful state with a structured society and a brutally successful military class.

The metropolis of Teotihuacán in upland Mexico represented an urban achievement of the first order. Perhaps the most impressive of American cultures during the classic age, however, was that of the Mayans (C.E. 300–900) of Middle America. Mayan society, like that of ancient Greece, never evolved politically beyond the city-state. But Mayan art, religion, and intellectual achievement, from early writing to mathematics and astronomy, were dazzling. Mayan culture provided a cultural reservoir for later civilizations in Middle America.

Suggested Reading

Adams R. E. W. *Ancient Civilizations of the New World.* Boulder, Colo.: Westview Press, 1997. Brief overview of Mexican and Peruvian civilizations.

Alva, W., and C. B. Donnan. *Royal Tombs of Sipan.* Los Angeles: University of California Press, 1993. Golden burial of Peru's Lord of Sipan.

Anfray, F. "The Civilization of Aksum from the First to the Seventh Century," in *Ancient Civilizations of Africa,* Vol. 2 of the *UNESCO General History of Africa,* G. Mokhtar, ed. London: Heinemann, 1981. By a leading excavator of Ethiopian ruins.

Bawden, G. *The Moche.* Cambridge, Mass.: Blackwell, 1996. Solid study of Mochica society and history.

Bulliet, R. W. *The Camel and the Wheel.* Cambridge, Mass.: Harvard University Press, 1975. Spread of the camel revolution from the Middle East to North Africa. See also H. Gauthier-Pilters and A. I. Dagg, *The Camel: Its Evolution, Ecology, Behavior, and Relationship to Man* (Chicago: University of Chicago Press, 1981).

Canfora, L. *The Vanished Library.* Berkeley: University of California Press, 1989. Alexandria's vanished treasure trove of ancient learning.

Carrasco, D., L. Jones, and S. Sessions, eds. *Mesoamerica's Classical Heritage: From Teotihuacán to the Aztecs.* Boulder, Colo.: University Press of Colorado, 2000. New studies of the meaning of the classical tradition in Middle America.

Clancy, F. S. *Sculpture in the Ancient Maya Plaza: The Early Classic Period.* Albuquerque: University of New Mexico Press, 1999. Formative period in Maya carving.

Coe, M. D. *The Maya,* 5th ed. New York: Thames and Hudson, 1995. One of the best surveys of this much discussed ancient Mesoamerican people.

Ehret, C. *An African Classical Age: Eastern and Southern Africa in World History 1000 B.C. to 400 A.D.* Charlottesville: University Press of Virginia, 1998. Impressive attempt to use linguistic evidence to construct an overview of East African history over this long period.

Haas, C. *Alexandria in Late Antiquity.* Baltimore, Md.: Johns Hopkins University Press, 1997. Social conflict in the context of urban topography.

Joyce, R. A. *Gender and Power in Prehistoric America.* Austin: University of Texas Press, 2000. Thoughtful analysis, with some emphasis on the Maya. See also T. Ardren, ed., *Ancient Maya Women* (Walnut Creek, Calif.: AltaMira Press, 2002), for more studies of gender in Maya society and culture.

Lovejoy, P. E. *Salt of the Desert: A History of Salt Production and Trade in the Central Sudan.* New York: Cambridge University Press, 1986. Solid study of this key item in Saharan trade.

Munro-Hay, S. C. *Aksum: African Civilization of Late Antiquity.* Edinburgh: Edinburgh University Press, 1991. Scholarly and up-to-date.

Pillsbury, J., ed. *Moche Art and Archaeology in Ancient Peru.* Washington, D.C.: National Gallery of Art, 2001. Studies of the intriguing Mochica material culture that survives.

Schele, L., and M. E. Miller. *The Blood of Kings: Dynasty and Ritual in Maya Art.* Fort Worth, Tex.: Kimbell Art Museum, 1986. Mayan art in its social context.

Snowden, F. M. *Before Color Prejudice: The Ancient View of Blacks.* Cambridge, Mass.: Harvard University Press, 1983. Classic study of Greco-Roman views of Africa. See also W. L. Hansberry, *Africa and Africans as Seen by Classical Writers,* J. E. Harris, ed. (Washington, D.C., 1981).

Tedlock, D. *Popol Vuh: The Mayan Book of the Dawn of Life and the Glories of Gods and Kings.* New York: Random House, 1985. Translation of a Mayan religious classic.

Wolf, E. R. *Sons of the Shaking Earth.* Chicago: University of Chicago Press, 1959. Ecologically based poetic evocation of Mesoamerican cultures.

 Please refer to the document CD-ROM for primary sources related to this chapter.

Overview III

Expanding Cultural Zones

(500–1500)

Civilization survived, despite the widespread destruction that brought the classic age to an end. Out of the ruins, as so often before, areas of order, prosperity, and high culture emerged once more.

If anything, the new cultures—or the reconstituted older ones—were larger and more impressive than those that had collapsed during the middle centuries of the first millennium C.E. For civilization had grown until it transcended the reach of political authority. The result was a series of *zones* of culture, harder to define historically than any nations and empires, but real nonetheless.

Several types of cultural zone are detectable during the thousand years between C.E. 500 and 1500. The most obvious, perhaps, are the satellite civilizations that appeared around the fringes of great empires. In China's East Asian sphere, for example, related civilizations developed during these years in Korea, Vietnam, and, most important, Japan. Indian culture reached almost all of Southeast Asia, scattering trade and temples from Java to Vietnam.

A second sort of cultural zone was that created by the rise and spread of a new international religion. Medieval Christianity, in both its Roman Catholic and Greek Orthodox forms, completed the process of civilizing Europe that the Roman Empire had begun. Islam, born in the seventh century, spread so rapidly that by the fifteenth century a series of Islamic states stretched from West Africa to Southeast Asia. In each case, the particular forms of urban, literate culture that developed clearly reflected the shaping power of the religious faiths that dominated these two wide swathes of the Old World.

A third type of cultural zone was that created by the far-reaching conquests of a single people—the Mongols. And even when the Mongol Empire crumbled, a zone of Mongol culture still reached from the steppes of western Russia to the Pacific.

Larger cultural zones had by this time also emerged in the New World and in Africa south of the Sahara. The kingdoms and empires of the West African savanna constituted a zone of related cultures even before the shaping influence of Islam began to be felt there. The peoples of Mesoamerica and Peru manifested common cultural traits well before the unifying power of the Aztecs and the Incas welded them into empires in the fifteenth century. In these cases, similar geographical environment—the West African grasslands or the Andes, for instance—might help to explain the phenomenon.

Of course, cultural zones were not new in the world. A common civilization had infused the separate states of ancient Greece, of Shang China, even of ancient Mesopotamia. But the new zones of culture that flourished between 500 and 1500 had a size and a dynamism that pointed toward something still more impressive: the beginning of a truly global culture in centuries to come.

The major cultural zones remained separate for the most part during the period under consideration here. Except for the brief Mongol interlude, even Eurasia was without the unifying exchange of goods and ideas that had tentatively linked east and west during the classic age. But the new zones of culture were growing. And the time would come when one among them, around 1500, would launch a drive for dominion that would threaten to turn the whole world into a single cultural zone—the emerging global culture of our own time.

EXPANDING CULTURAL ZONES

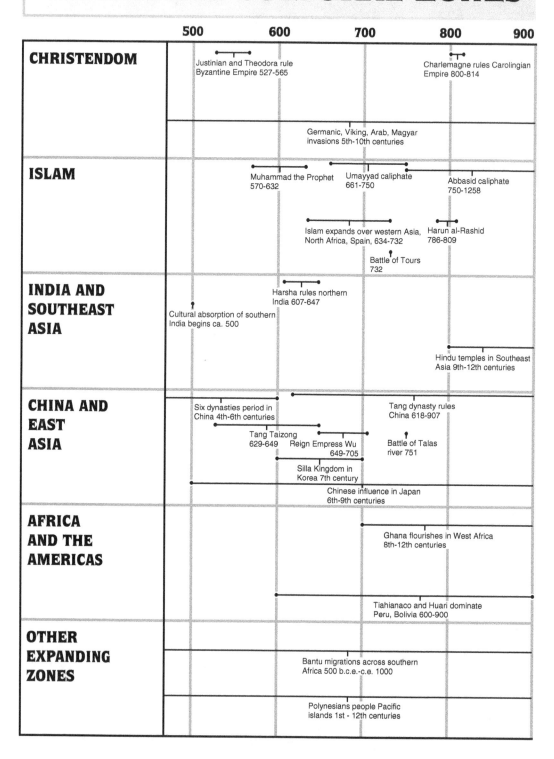

	500	600	700	800	900
CHRISTENDOM	Justinian and Theodora rule Byzantine Empire 527-565			Charlemagne rules Carolingian Empire 800-814	
		Germanic, Viking, Arab, Magyar invasions 5th-10th centuries			
ISLAM		Muhammad the Prophet 570-632	Umayyad caliphate 661-750	Abbasid caliphate 750-1258	
			Islam expands over western Asia, North Africa, Spain, 634-732	Harun al-Rashid 786-809	
			Battle of Tours 732		
INDIA AND SOUTHEAST ASIA	Cultural absorption of southern India begins ca. 500	Harsha rules northern India 607-647			
				Hindu temples in Southeast Asia 9th-12th centuries	
CHINA AND EAST ASIA	Six dynasties period in China 4th-6th centuries	Tang Taizong 629-649	Reign Empress Wu 649-705	Tang dynasty rules China 618-907	
			Battle of Talas river 751		
		Silla Kingdom in Korea 7th century			
		Chinese influence in Japan 6th-9th centuries			
AFRICA AND THE AMERICAS			Ghana flourishes in West Africa 8th-12th centuries		
			Tiahianaco and Huari dominate Peru, Bolivia 600-900		
OTHER EXPANDING ZONES		Bantu migrations across southern Africa 500 b.c.e.-c.e. 1000			
		Polynesians people Pacific islands 1st - 12th centuries			

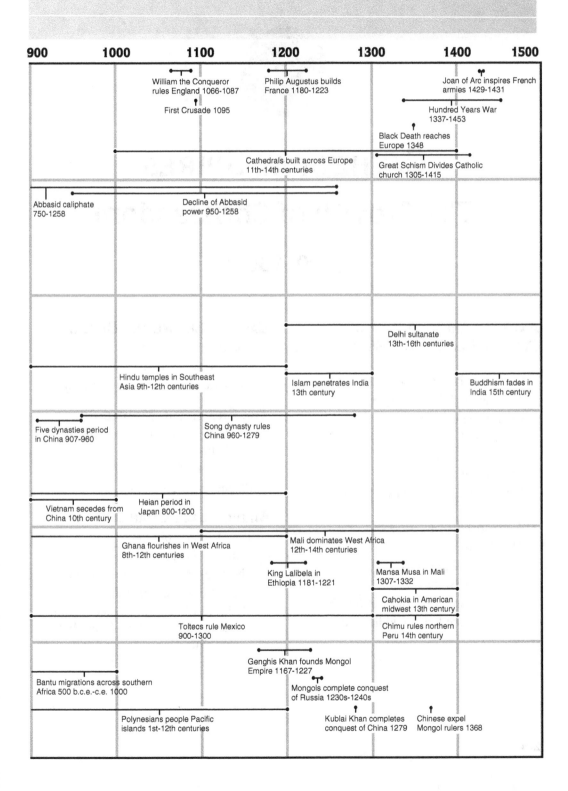

| 900 | 1000 | 1100 | 1200 | 1300 | 1400 | 1500 |

William the Conqueror
rules England 1066-1087

First Crusade 1095

Philip Augustus builds
France 1180-1223

Joan of Arc inspires French
armies 1429-1431

Hundred Years War
1337-1453

Black Death reaches
Europe 1348

Cathedrals built across Europe
11th-14th centuries

Great Schism Divides Catholic
church 1305-1415

Abbasid caliphate
750-1258

Decline of Abbasid
power 950-1258

Delhi sultanate
13th-16th centuries

Hindu temples in Southeast
Asia 9th-12th centuries

Islam penetrates India
13th century

Buddhism fades in
India 15th century

Five dynasties period
in China 907-960

Song dynasty rules
China 960-1279

Vietnam secedes from
China 10th century

Heian period in
Japan 800-1200

Ghana flourishes in West Africa
8th-12th centuries

Mali dominates West Africa
12th-14th centuries

King Lalibela in
Ethiopia 1181-1221

Mansa Musa in Mali
1307-1332

Cahokia in American
midwest 13th century

Toltecs rule Mexico
900-1300

Chimu rules northern
Peru 14th century

Genghis Khan founds Mongol
Empire 1167-1227

Mongols complete conquest
of Russia 1230s-1240s

Bantu migrations across southern
Africa 500 b.c.e.-c.e. 1000

Polynesians people Pacific
islands 1st-12th centuries

Kublai Khan completes
conquest of China 1279

Chinese expel
Mongol rulers 1368

CHAPTER 9

Cathedral Spires
The Growth of Christendom
(500–1500)

A GLANCE AHEAD: A WORLD RELIGION RISES IN THE WEST

Jesus Christ had lived in Roman times, but most of the citizens of Roman Europe were still pagans when Rome fell. The Christianization of most of Europe was the work of the thousand years of European history we call the Middle Ages.

Medieval Europe was a patchwork quilt of kingdoms and fiefdoms, city-states, and even smaller political entities. But similar political structures, common economic institutions, and above all the Christian Church united them all in a single vast zone of Christian culture.

This chapter will trace the rise of Christian civilization out of the ruins of Rome. It will outline the emergence of new European nations and their long feud with nearby Muslim powers. We will analyze the Gothic climax of the High Middle Ages and the series of cataclysms, from the Black Death to the Hundred Years War, which brought this cycle of European history to an end.

Medieval Europe was history by 1500, and western Christendom was on the verge of the greatest schism in its history. But the European nations shaped over the preceding millennium were poised to play an unprecedented role in the coming age.

THE EARLY MIDDLE AGES

The Reign of the Barbarian

Bordered by the glittering cultures of Byzantium and Islam, sharing the Eurasian land mass with the great civilization of India and China, Europe in the Middle Ages looks like a very backward cultural zone indeed. But medieval Europe did flower, briefly and brilliantly, in the High Middle Ages—the eleventh, twelfth, and thirteenth centuries. And its future greatness may be traced back this far at least, to the crusading religion, the increasingly productive agriculture, the enterprising merchants, the militaristic aristocracy, and the increasingly powerful kingdoms of the medieval centuries.

We must begin, however, where the story does, with a very different Europe from that of the High Middle Ages—with a Europe lying broken and helpless in the ruins of its greatest historic catastrophe.

From the fifth century to the tenth, barbarian kingdoms divided Europe among themselves, fought one another and each new wave of barbarian invaders, and gradually transformed life on the western end of Eurasia.

They came in two great surges. The first, composed mostly of semicivilized Germanic peoples, shouldered their way into the empire they had long admired and established themselves as early as the fifth century. They set up an Ostrogothic kingdom in Italy, a Visigothic one in Spain, Franks in what would become France, Angles and Saxons in Britain, and Alemanni in Germany. A second, more varied wave of invasions began in the eighth century. Vikings pressed down from the north by sea, Magyars from the eastern steppes, and Muslim Arabs up from the south across Spain and the Mediterranean.

Some of the intruders took what they could carry and headed home. Others settled among the peoples of the broken empire or the unstable barbarian kingdoms that replaced it. Some of those who stayed became Europe's new masters, a military aristocracy distinguished by cavalry skills and increasingly heavy arms and armor—the mounted knights of the new age.

The process of transition from the civilization of the ancient Romans to the culture of the early Middle Ages was more gradual than was once imagined, more evolutionary than revolutionary in nature.

The new peoples brought some new ways of life with them, of course. The German royal entourage, a war band called the *comitatus,* would provide the germ of the new feudal political order, based on personal allegiance to an overlord. The proclivity of the Germans for country rather than urban living would contribute to the disintegration of the network of cities that had dominated ancient Greco-Roman civilization. Yet when towns reappeared in the later Middle Ages, German social brotherhoods called *guilds* would evolve into the merchant and craft guilds that played a central role in the medieval urban economy.

But there were Roman roots for medieval civilization too. Roman estates called *villas* worked by slave labor probably evolved in some places into medieval manors with their labor force of serfs. The cities the Romans had built were abandoned slowly, over generations, but the Roman Catholic Church, with its structure of episcopal administration and its communities of monks and nuns who preserved some vestiges of Latin culture, would reach new heights in the Middle Ages.

A mingling of folkways accompanied by a slow merging of peoples thus lay at the root of the new society of medieval Europe. Germanic chiefs intermarried with Roman aristocrats, while German freemen settled beside Celtic or other indigenous peasant cultivators. The Vikings who descended from Scandinavia established themselves in parts of northern Europe, including Normandy (in modern France) and northern England. Muslims from the other side of the Mediterranean colonized Spain, Sicily, and other places along the southern fringes of the continent, producing enclaves of civilized living along the southern margins of Europe. From the glory of Augustus in his far-off city of marble, it was a long comedown to the "do-nothing" kings of the Merovingian Franks, who, according to a contemporary chronicler, were sometimes trundled along the rutty lanes of the kingdom in a farm wagon while a servant trotted ahead blowing a ram's horn.

Charlemagne's Empire

Here and there, however, strength and capacity existed even in Dark Age Europe. The most impressive attempt to restore order and unity to the Continent was led by perhaps the most famous of medieval monarchs, the Frankish king Charles the Great, known to history as Charlemagne.

Charlemagne (768–814) was a half-literate giant, six feet and several inches in height, a tremendous toper, trencherman, and womanizer, and a mighty warrior in a war-battered age. The greatest of the ambitious Carolingian kings of the Franks who succeeded the do-nothing Merovingians in the eighth century, Charlemagne spent most of his long reign fighting. He hammered together a rude but sizable empire, with modern France at its core and chunks of Spain, northern Italy, western Germany, and neighboring regions as outlying provinces. On Christmas day, 800, a pope, grateful for his help against barbarian intruders and the pope's political enemies in Rome, placed a crown on Charlemagne's head, hailing him "Pious Augustus, crowned by God," and heir of all the Caesars.[1]

He was scarcely that, this huge, thick-bearded man who spoke vulgar Latin as well as the Frankish tongue and kept a slate beside his bed so that he could practice tracing the letters of the alphabet in rare quiet moments. His endless campaigns spread Roman Christianity and Frankish rule far across western Europe. He organized his empire into a loose

---

[1]Robert S. Hoyt and Stanley Chodorow, *Europe in the Middle Ages* (New York: Harcourt Brace Jovanovich, 1976), p. 160.

provincial structure of *counties*—each headed by a count—and tried to keep tabs on them, both in person and through royal inspectors sent out from his court at Aachen near the Rhine. He even presided over a temporary revival of learning, the Carolingian Renaissance, which at least made a virtue of Latin literacy and theological scholarship at Aachen. Charlemagne's scholars both preserved much of Rome's literary heritage for the future and developed a new form of writing—*Carolingian minuscule,* the small or lower-case letters we still use, along with Roman capitals, today.

But Charlemagne's heir had none of his strength of will, and his three grandsons divided the Carolingian Empire among them less than thirty years after his death. The Carolingian Renaissance too proved to be a false dawn in the Dark Ages. But it did at least halt the long decline and point out one way in which peace and prosperity might be restored to Europe. To the extent that they accepted this obligation, the strong kings of centuries to come were all Charlemagne's heirs.

The Feudal Lords

The forces that pulled Charlemagne's empire apart were rooted more deeply in medieval society than in the rivalries of feuding heirs. For the real rulers of Europe in the Dark Ages were not the kings of the barbarian states but the powerful dukes, counts, knights, and other warrior lords of medieval Europe linked in a loose structure of power called *feudalism.*

Feudalism was a system of military service and land tenure that bound Europe's ruling classes into an elaborate pyramid of political and military power. Under this system

Charlemagne, looking almost larger than his horse in this bronze representation, wears the crown and holds the orb of imperial authority. Note the heavy sword under his cloak, a symbol of his many victories and conquests. Notice also the monumental feel of this representation, which is in fact only a small figurine. (Courtesy of the Library of Congress)

the less powerful knights—called *vassals*—sought political protection and economic support, commonly in the form of a grant of land, from the more powerful, who became their feudal lords, or *seigneurs*. In return, feudal overlords required military service, money payments, and general support from their vassals.

The ceremony of feudal vassalage was solemn and symbolic. The vassal knelt, placed his hands between those of his lord, and took an oath of *fealty*, or allegiance. He pledged perhaps forty days of military service each year, plus money payments when the lord's son was knighted, his daughter married, or the lord himself captured and in need of ransom. In return the seigneur handed the vassal a clod of earth or a sprig from a tree, and with it conferred on him a *fief*, a parcel of land replete with villages of serfs to cultivate it.

This structure of interlocking obligations was quite suitable to a violent age in which only local authority was strong enough to offer any real protection. In time, however, the system became immensely complex and sometimes self-defeating. Loyal vassals might find themselves with a number of overlords, some of whom might feud with each other, creating embarrassing conflicts of interest. The strong kings of later centuries sometimes came into conflict with the most powerful of feudal overlords, "overmighty subjects" who could rival even kings for power. The royal rulers of the High Middle Ages would thus often prefer to depend on hired mercenary companies, whose services could be depended on as long as the monarch's money lasted.

Throughout the Middle Ages in Europe, the feudal lords would hold much of the Continent's political power. In the early Middle Ages—the first half of the thousand years of medieval history—the military leaders were the real rulers of the land.

Serfs of the Manor

If feudalism constituted the political power structure of Europe in the early Middle Ages, the manor system was the heart of the earlier medieval economy. In a world reduced to isolated, county-sized political units, subsistence agriculture was essential. The manor system fed the farm laborers themselves, the feudal aristocracy, the priests, the kings. And it provided at least a modicum of protection for masses of people who could no longer look to garrisoned legions or civil authorities for defense against violence or help in hard times.

The typical medieval manor consisted of a village surrounded by arable land, usually with the manor house or castle overlooking it. A dozen, perhaps several dozen, stone or mud huts clustered along a single unpaved village street. A small, rude church might occupy one end of the street, and perhaps a mill, bakehouse, smithy, and other adjuncts were mixed in among the houses of the peasants. The surrounding land would include, besides the arable for spring and autumn planting, a third field left fallow in rotation each year so that it could recover its strength. These three fields were typically divided into strips so that all might have a share of the best as well as the worst land. Beyond the three-field system of strips were blocks of common pastureland for farm animals and portions of uncut forest for firewood and foraging pigs.

Medieval peasants were totally subservient to the lord of the manor. They paid portions of their produce to support the lord. They also worked the lord's land for him and did other manual labor around the estate—the *corvée* work on roads, bridges, and so on. The blacksmith's shop, the bakehouse, and similar amenities were the lord's, and the peasants paid to use them. Peasants were tried for all but the most serious crimes in the baron's court, and married outside the manor only with his consent. They were not chattel slaves, as in the ancient world. But they were serfs, bound to the land and the village for life—and thus to the lord, for as long as he held that land.

Life in the village under the hill during the early Middle Ages was a hard and narrow round. The typical peasant family—that is, the large majority of Europeans—lived in a meagerly furnished, earth-floored, one-room hut. They moved by day in a clutter of chickens and animals who shared the hut with them, slept whole families curled together for warmth on a straw-covered sleeping floor at night. They plowed with horses or oxen and a heavy wheeled plow, harvested and threshed their grain with rough homemade tools.

There had been such breakdowns of the great enterprise many times in many parts of the world. But this was probably the worst that Europe ever had to endure.

The Life of the Church

In this harsh, subsistence-level world, one institution worked still for higher ends and provided islands of culture in a backward Europe. The Christian Church survived the Fall of Rome and actually expanded and grew more powerful through the medieval centuries.

As we shall see, Christianity spread north from two radiant centers in the Mediterranean world during the Middle Ages. The popes of Rome sponsored the vast expansion of Roman Catholicism over Western Europe, while the patriarchs of Constantinople, capital of the Byzantine or Eastern Roman Empire, spread Greek Orthodox Christianity across much of Eastern Europe. Even in the early Middle Ages, daring missionaries converted pagan kings and queens, and through them their peoples. Churchmen like Charlemagne's advisor Alcuin preserved some Latin learning, produced beautifully decorated hand-written books, and presided over such heroic attempts at cultural revival as the Carolingian Renaissance.

Humbler monks and nuns sought refuge from worldly temptation behind the walls of monasteries and convents. There they lived according to the strict religious rules of St. Benedict, which prescribed poverty, chastity, and obedience to their superiors in the order. Alternating hard work in the fields or cloisters with religious meditation and prayer, they created islands of order, charity, and often relatively efficient agriculture in the medieval world.

Monastic establishments planted among non-Christian populations also provided centers from which these pagans might be converted to Christianity. Monks and nuns were also among the few literate Europeans during this period. By copying Latin works—partly to learn their letters, partly as discipline—these pious Christians preserved the classics of pagan Rome for later generations.

How many medieval villages had their own priests and little churches, or even a cross on a hill around which to pray, we do not know. Many probably did not, especially during the earlier medieval centuries. In many parts of Europe, old religions worshiping the forces of nature, pre-Christian cults, folk beliefs, and superstitions undoubtedly survived. But the Christian Church remained the most determined and dynamic of Western institutions even during this grim time.

Women in Early Medieval Society

The role of women at all levels of medieval life, finally, was extremely important. In a time when Western civilization struggled simply to maintain itself, women may in fact have played a particularly important part in society.

In a world reduced to fundamentals, the family was a central institution. The peasant household, which included the large majority of medieval people, was the basic unit of production, one in which women carried at least their half of the common burden. Caring for farm animals and children, tending vegetables near the house, preparing food, making all clothing by hand, and often doing a share of sowing or harvesting crops in distant fields as well, medieval peasant women needed nimble fingers and strong backs.

Higher up the social ladder, women of noble families often shared in the ruling functions and responsibilities of the upper classes. The structure of power and prestige, like the system of economic production, was based on the family, on inheritance and marriage. Women born of great families could inherit vast estates. As wives of fighting barons, they were often called on to administer and sometimes defend their lands and manor houses while their husbands were away at the frequent wars.

Women, finally, could also make an independent place for themselves, and even exercise considerable authority, within the Church. Women who found the burdens of family life oppressive could dedicate their lives to God by "taking the veil" and entering a convent. Women with large estates could even establish and run their own convents. Within these holy institutions, they could wield the absolute authority of a mother superior or an abbess. Women as well as men, finally, might lead lives so pious that they achieved the ultimate medieval accolade of saint-hood. Hildegarde of Bingen, whose convents carried Christianity to the Germanic peoples, was famed for her learning and visionary insights. The pope himself wrote to her that "We are filled with admiration, my daughter . . . for the new miracles that God has shown you in our time, filling you with his spirit so that you see, understand, and communicate many secret things."[2]

THE HIGH MIDDLE AGES

The Rebirth of Cities

In the year C.E. 1000, Europe was a cramped and drafty fortress on a hill, a dozen families huddled in huts along a muddy street below, and all around, a world of fen and forest stretching to an empty horizon. It was as though the Greek city-states and the metropolis on the seven hills of Rome had never existed.

A century later, two centuries, and it was a world transformed.

Once again the gates of cities swung wide, and to the braying of donkeys and the baaing of sheep, country folk could pass through an arched gateway into crowded cobble-stoned streets. Steep-roofed multistory houses pressed close above. There were market squares and gingerbready guildhalls, street after street of artisans and merchants, and rising against a misty gray sky, the half-finished towers of a cathedral. This was the twelfth century, or the thirteenth—the greatest of centuries, medieval enthusiasts have insisted since. Paris was the cultural capital of one of Europe's great ages—the Athens of the age of faith.

But where did it come from, this new urban sprawl, this urban splendor reborn? Among the causes most commonly credited, three stand out: agricultural improvements, population growth, and perhaps most important, the revival of trade.

The medieval European manor, primitive as it was in many ways, produced several crucial agricultural innovations. These included the three-field system, the heavy wheeled plow

---

[2]*Patrologia Latina,* Vol. 197, Col. 145, quoted in F. and J. Gies, *Women in the Middle Ages* (New York: Crowell, 1978), p. 81.

(both mentioned above), the horseshoe and the horse collar, and the windmill for grinding grain where no river was available for a water mill. After the year 1000 there was also a significant expansion in the amount of land under cultivation, due to the clearing of woodlands, the draining of swamps, and the movement of productive western European lords and peasants into less developed eastern Europe. Because of this increase in food production, the population began to grow, after centuries of stagnation, And some of these additional people concentrated in islands of dense population in which cities rapidly took shape.

The heart of the medieval cities, however, was commercial exchange and skilled handicraft manufacturing. The revival of trade in Europe in the eleventh, twelfth, and thirteenth centuries is thus a central cause of the rebirth of cities.

Trade grew up in Europe once more, partly because of the increased demand for goods created by the expanding population. Another cause was the taste for Eastern luxury goods encouraged by the Crusades, which began at the end of the eleventh century. And a prime stimulus was the expanded commercial exchange between the Near East and Italian trading cities such as Venice, which had survived the Dark Ages because of their connection with the powerful Byzantine Empire, Rome's heir to the east. The merchants who participated in this commercial revival became the builders and rulers of the medieval cities.

The trading cities were dominated first by merchant and craft guilds—trade associations of dealers in or makers of particular products, from cloth to goldsmith work. In time cities acquired independent political authorities—magistrates and city councils elected by this oligarchy of business people. Around the leading merchants and the master craftsmen, a colorful urban population soon gathered. The craft guilds included journeymen assistants and apprentices to the trade as well as masters. Merchants required stevedores, porters, muleteers, and other adjuncts. Priests, students, lawyers, runaway serfs, and other masterless men sought the protection of the city's walls.

In this stimulating environment—a world within the walls once more—what is sometimes called the commercial revolution of the High Middle Ages took place. The robed and ermined merchants of the twelfth and thirteenth centuries revived the use of coins after long centuries of barter and payment in kind. They began once more to lend money at interest and to develop such important modern business practices as double-entry bookkeeping and letters of credit. They began the pooling of capital for large-scale economic investments through the joint-stock company—an institution pointing ahead to all the stock markets of the modern world. Modern Western capitalism was thus born well before modern history began, in the cathedral-dominated cities of the age of faith.

The Feudal Monarchs

This burgeoning economic revival was accompanied and encouraged by the equally striking resurgence of centralized political power in the hands of medieval kings.

They were a varied lot. William the Conqueror of England still signed his name with an X; Frederick II, the German emperor, spoke half a dozen languages fluently. France's Philip Augustus was bald, one-eyed, and crafty. Nor were their lives textbook models of selfless statesmanship. They hunted, wenched, squeezed their subjects for funds, and fought endless wars. They feuded with each other, with the popes, with their own barons, and embarked on futile crusades and extremely successful programs of state-building with indiscriminate enthusiasm. In the end it was this last mentioned effort that has earned most of them their places in history.

Not all even of these famous names succeeded. None of the so-called Holy Roman Emperors of the Germans—not even the redoubtable Frederick Barbarossa—were able to impose genuine unity on the many German-speaking states of central Europe over which they held feudal suzerainty. Throughout most of its history the Holy Roman Empire would remain a ramshackle collection of separate principalities giving only minimal allegiance to its emperor. England and France, by contrast, were among the best examples of the centralized monarchy in medieval Europe.

Duke William the Bastard of Normandy overwhelmed Anglo-Saxon England in 1066, thus earning the more dignified sobriquet of William the Conqueror (1066–1087). He brought developed Norman-French feudalism with him to backward Britain. By asserting his position as king of England at the top of the feudal pyramid of power, he gave the country stronger centralized rule than it had ever had. His successors, including Henry I and Henry II, developed such governmental institutions as the royal council, the exchequer (treasury), and a system of royal justice based on English common law. By the end of the twelfth century—less than a century and a half after the conquest—England had the strongest monarchical government in Europe.

Close behind was the thirteenth-century French monarchy of Philip Augustus (1180–1223) and Saint Louis—Louis IX (1226–1270). Personally unprepossessing, Philip emerged as France's most successful medieval monarch. Like the English kings, he used his place at the apex of the feudal system to increase his power over the nobility. Like English rulers also, he developed an independent royal administrative system, including a more effective chamber of accounts, or treasury, and a stronger legal system. He did not conquer a new country for himself, like William of Normandy, but he did launch a calculated crusade against the heretical barons of southern France that tripled the size of the royal domain, and he took from the heirs of Henry II some important English holdings in France.

Under Philip Augustus thirteenth-century France replaced the Holy Roman Empire as the most powerful nation on the European continent. Under Louis IX the French monarchy acquired the prestige of having a duly canonized saint in its roster of kings. Louis was no weakling: He increased royal power over French towns, dared to issue royal edicts without consulting his baronial vassals, and strengthened the French system of law courts, or *parlements*. But he was also a paragon of medieval Christian and chivalric virtues, washing the feet of lepers, meting out justice under an oak tree, and earning such a reputation for fairness and piety that he was known as Louis the Just in his own time and was canonized only thirty years after his death. In the age of faith, a saintly life was no small contribution to the power of the French monarchy over its people.

It was a long step up from the "do-nothing" Merovingian kings of the Dark Ages to the power and vitality of William the Conqueror or Philip Augustus. And even the conflicts and competitiveness of Europe's kings helped to generate a dynamism that would prove in later centuries more than a match for the great empires of other parts of the globe.

The Feudal Monarchies

Undergirding the achievements of individual feudal monarchs, medieval government itself was evolving. The *feudal monarchy* as a set of political institutions and relationships would survive the Middle Ages and continue to develop through early modern times. In the end, modern bureaucratic government is a distant descendant of the monarchical institutions of the Middle Ages.

Basic problems for medieval rulers who truly wished to rule their lands included the need to impose the royal will on powerful vassals, the necessity of replacing a ragbag of feudal law with some sort of royal law, and perhaps most important, the need to get the right to tax the nation. Where these goals were met, as they were to a considerable degree in England and France, monarchs had to pay for their growing power by recognizing the rights of representatives bodies speaking for the chief estates or classes of medieval society—the nobility, the church, and the wealthy new towns.

The Norman feudalism that William the Conqueror imposed on England was the most developed in Europe. William claimed all the land in England for his own after the conquest: What he distributed as fiefs to his followers came with stringent feudal obligations. All the new vassals were actually required to gather on Salisbury Plain and take a mass oath of allegiance to their king. The legal reforms of William's successors began the process of replacing feudal law with the traditional English common law, which had been evolving for centuries before the Norman Conquest.

The right of English kings to tax their people, finally, was acquired with much more difficulty and in return for significant concessions. During the later Middle Ages, the English Parliament claimed the right to have the nation's grievances redressed before voting the monarch customs duties, taxes, or other sources of government revenue. Granted, Parliament met only when the monarch summoned it and represented only the elites of medieval society—ecclesiastical institutions, the nobility and country gentry, and the urban middle classes—not the masses of the people. But Parliament would in later centuries challenge royal authority and finally bring modern democracy to Britain.

The royal rulers of France had to deal with nobles whose claims went back many centuries and who saw the monarch as merely "first among equals" in the feudal structure. Great landed magnates whose holdings were sometimes larger than the king's would prove very hard to bring under royal control. The royal law the French kings strove to impose was Roman law, which had reached the West from the Byzantine Empire in the eleventh century. This strongly centralized code of laws, with its origins outside feudalism altogether, did significantly strengthen royal claims to overarching authority.

In France as in England, finally, the royal right to collect revenues outside the ruler's own lands was challenged. Again, a body representing the three estates emerged and demanded to be consulted. The French estates general would not prove as successful as the English Parliament in limiting royal power; indeed, in early modern times it would become moribund for the better part of two centuries. But it would be revived in time to trigger the great French Revolution, which would turn that nation toward democracy.

The Popes and the Power of the Keys

The power of barons in the countryside, business oligarchies in the cities, and the stronger kings in the nation as a whole could be great. But in some ways the power of the Catholic church—the power of the keys of heaven—was greater still. And the wielders of that vast power were the popes of Rome, the heads of the Roman Catholic church.

Because Saint Peter, the "rock" on whom Christ had said he would build his church, had been martyred in Rome, the popes, as bishops of Rome, claimed to be Peter's heirs. As successors to Peter, to whom the keys to heaven's gate had traditionally been confided, the popes wielded the vast power of spiritual life and death over Western Christians.

Some Roman popes even asserted a double legacy of authority, declaring themselves to be the custodians of the "two swords" of spiritual and secular sovereignty. They thus claimed supremacy not only in the Church but also over any earthly sovereign—a claim hotly contested, of course, by earthly sovereigns. On the basis of this religious supremacy, the papacy over the centuries built the most impressive of all medieval European institutions: the Roman Catholic church.

The papal administration of the High and later Middle Ages was larger and more sophisticated than that of any king or emperor. The wealth of the Church, which had been collecting tithes, fees, and contributions and receiving gifts and bequests from the faithful for centuries, was greater than that of any landed magnate, merchant prince, or monarch. The Church owned a good percentage of the land of western Europe, and cathedral spires dominated the skylines of medieval cities. Indeed, a significant proportion of the population of medieval Europe held holy orders or otherwise worked for the Church.

Popes contended on roughly equal terms with kings and emperors. Their weapons were the spiritual powers of excommunication and interdict—exclusion from membership in the Church and prohibition of the performance of essential religious ceremonies. Powerful popes such as Gregory VII in the eleventh century and Innocent III in the thirteenth could bring sovereigns as powerful as Philip Augustus to their knees by threatening to excommunicate them or by absolving their vassals of their feudal oaths of loyalty.

Not every hamlet and manor village had its priest, but most probably did. There were also thousands of monasteries and convents scattered over Europe, to which brotherhoods of monks and groups of nuns had withdrawn from worldly temptation to give their lives wholly to prayer and good works. Beginning in the High Middle Ages, Franciscan and Dominican friars wandered the roads begging their bread and helping with the Church's mission of saving souls.

The priests were frequently illiterate, the monasteries sometimes wealthy, and the Church's rule of celibacy not always obeyed. Yet despite endless satire and sermons aimed at Church abuses, the people of the Middle Ages valued their religion as no other Western society has. The most prominent architectural feature of any medieval city, after all, was neither the battlements of its baronial citadel nor its Gothic guildhall, but the towers and soaring spires of its cathedral.

Women in the Later Middle Ages

In later medieval society as a whole, some scholars believe, women lost many of the independent opportunities and positions of authority that had earlier been theirs. This seems to have been so despite the presence of some immensely celebrated individual women in the annals of the High Middle Ages.

Some noblewomen still administered and defended large feudal holdings in later medieval times. Such queens as Eleanor of Aquitaine might accompany their royal husbands on crusades or govern their own realms. And aristocratic and royal ladies played a central role in the emergence of the elaborate code of chivalry that was supposed to govern the conduct of the knightly classes.

In its earliest formulation, chivalry meant mostly such warrior virtues as courage, skill with weapons, fairness to one's foes, and loyalty to one's feudal superior. Church leaders urged protection of noncombatants, including women and of course the Church. Medieval ladies, however, guided the development of the most striking element of the chivalric code—the cult of courtly love. The truly chivalrous knight was thus encouraged, not only to protect women, but to love, serve, and revere a particular lady, usually from a distance. Troubadours and minstrels, medieval entertainers whose reward came from the lady who ran the noble household, were responsive to the tastes of their patronesses, singing songs of love and praising knights who served their ladies well.

At a less elevated level, middle-class women shared in the works and profits of the evolving urban guilds. Indeed, some guilds, including some devoted to the cloth and clothing industries, were actually run by women. In other guilds, women sometimes inherited and continued to operate their husbands' handicraft workshops. At the same time, in the agricultural villages where most people lived, women continued to bear their share of the burden of feeding the medieval world.

Some historians, however, have detected a decline in the independent power of women in later medieval times. As the Church strove to assert its authority over religious appointments and institutions, for instance, wealthy noblewomen lost their right to run the monastic institutions they founded or supported. In the realm of high politics, modifications in feudal practice required even queens and noblewomen to surrender control of their landed property to husbands or male guardians. Among the middle classes, dowries, which had once given women of the burgher class some leverage in a marriage, were increasingly turned over entirely to their husbands.

The image of women in the Middle Ages, finally, was strikingly ambiguous. Eve and Mary, two women from the Bible, were seen as embodying women's extravagant potential for both good and evil. Thus theologians, preachers, and composers of crude popular tales endlessly described women as lustful and treacherous, prone to betray their husbands as Eve had betrayed Adam. Yet church leaders and preachers never tired of extolling the piety of saintly, virginal women like Mary—convents multiplied across the land—and the vast majority of medieval cathedrals were dedicated to the Mother of God.

EASTERN EUROPE AND BEYOND

The Byzantine Empire

All this time, of course, there was another side of Christendom. In Western Europe Christianity spoke Latin, and Christians looked for spiritual guidance to the pope of Rome. But in Eastern Europe during the Middle Ages the language of the Church was Greek, and the fount of Christian consolation was the patriarch of Constantinople. To the eastern half of Christendom and the Byzantine Empire that was its heart we must now turn.

In many ways, medieval Byzantium and Western Christendom were historically opposite and complementary. Western Europe in the Middle Ages was comparatively practical, noisily disunited, and increasingly dynamic. The Byzantine Empire—or Eastern Roman Empire, as it was officially called—was more mystical, united by a rigid autocracy, and intensely conservative. Western Europe began the medieval period in the depths of a dark age and slowly evolved to a twelfth-century apogee. Byzantium's greatest age came at the beginning of the medieval period, during the sixth-century reign of the Emperor Justinian, and the later medieval centuries saw its greatest misfortunes.

The high point of Byzantine power and cultural creativity came under Emperor Justinian (527–565) and his formidable empress, Theodora, a former courtesan who put steel into the emperor's backbone when he needed it. Justinian's greatest effort went into a massive drive to reclaim the West from the barbarian. After decades of campaigning, his generals succeeded in overthrowing the Ostrogothic kingdom in Italy, the Visigoths in southern Spain, and the Vandals in North Africa. For a short time a "Roman" empire—this one ruled from Constantinople—almost girdled the Mediterranean once more.

Justinian is probably best known, however, for his sponsorship of an immense collection, abridgment, and codification of Roman law. Justinian's Code, as it is commonly called, passed Roman law on to medieval and modern Europe, where it proved extremely influential in shaping the law codes of many modern nations.

Justinian's greatest passion after the reconquest of the empire in the West was the Eastern Orthodox church. He built the largest church in Christendom in its honor—Hagia Sophia, the Church of the Holy Wisdom. With its marble and mosaics and its great dome, Hagia Sophia has for fourteen centuries been an awesome symbol of the splendor of Byzantium in the days of Justinian and Theodora.

For the next five hundred years, the Byzantine Empire remained proverbial for wealth, power, and military strength. Its emperor, served by a large and efficient bureaucracy, dominated his church, his nobility, and his people. So great was the power of the Byzantine emperors that one of their titles, *autokrator,* has come into modern languages as a synonym for absolute power—*autocrat.* The Byzantine army and navy, well trained and organized and equipped with such technological innovations as "Greek fire" (a flammable chemical substance sprayed on enemy ships) threw back wave after wave of would-be conquerors—Persians, Arabs, Turks, and many others. In so doing, Byzantium incidentally protected Western Europe from foreign invasion during its weakest centuries.

Constantinople, controlling the bottleneck of east-west trade across Eurasia, became perhaps the richest city in the world during those centuries. From its famous harbor, the Golden Horn, Byzantine goldsmith work, Chinese silks, and Persian carpets reached Europe through the Italian trading cities. The Byzantine capital teemed with shrewd Greek and Levantine merchants and skilled artisans—a profit-hungry business community whose most popular leaders were monks!

With its palaces and churches rich with mosaic and gold leaf, Constantinople flourished down the medieval centuries, while Western Europe was slowly pulling itself out of mud huts and manor villages. Byzantines called their capital, located on a narrow peninsula protected by water and heavy walls, "the city protected by God." For many centuries it seemed that it was so.

Then in the early 1200s, an army of Norman Crusaders, encouraged by Venetians envious of the city's wealth, captured and looted Constantinople. And in 1453 the Ottoman Turkish sultan, Muhammad II, breached the ancient walls, killed the last emperor, and turned the Church of the Holy Wisdom into a mosque. The Eastern Roman Empire had finally fallen—a thousand years after the fall of the Empire of the West.

From Kiev to Muscovy

The history of Eastern Europe is commonly neglected by European historians—a serious mistake, especially in a world that was divided for much of the twentieth century along a line that split Europe precisely into eastern and western halves. A few words, then, about Eastern Europe in these earliest centuries will be in order here.

Even in medieval times, Eastern Europe was never the land of cossacks, gypsies, and Transylvanian vampires of the popular Western imagination. Yet there were distinctive differences between the two halves of Europe long before the Cold War divided the continent. A primary source of these differences was the influence of Byzantine and later of

Mongol culture on the Slavic population of Russia in particular. Slavic origins and Byzantine influences will be glanced at here, and Mongol influences deferred to Chapter 14.

The Slavs settled much of the eastern half of the continent from the Balkans to the Baltic, from predominantly German-speaking central Europe to what became European Russia. These Slavic herders and farmers soon came to be ruled by more warlike minorities—Bulgars and Avars from Asia and Vikings coming down the Russian rivers from the fjords of Scandinavia. The East Slavs, who had settled in what became Russia, were governed by a loose confederation of Viking princes known as Varangians. From their metropolis at Kiev, Varangians and Slavs voyaged down the Dnieper to the Black Sea and on to Byzantium to trade their wheat and honey, furs and amber for the luxury goods to be had in the bazaars of Constantinople.

From Constantinople, then, Eastern Europe in general and Russia in particular received the first impress of a more complex civilization toward the end of the early Middle Ages. But it was a set of cultural influences very different from those Rome had imprinted on Western Europe.

Byzantine missionaries carried Christianity to pagan Slavs, Varangians, and other East European peoples. Thus, the faith to which Russia was converted was the mystical, liturgical Greek Orthodox form of Christianity, with its particular reverence for monks and the lovely little sacred images called *ikons,* and its Byzantine sense of the emperor as head of the church as well as the state. Russia learned to write in the Greek-based Cyrillic alphabet devised by Byzantine missionaries rather than the Roman alphabet used in Western Europe, and Russian art echoed that of the Byzantines. And when the czarist Russian state began to take shape centuries later around Moscow, far to the north, the czars took upon themselves all the autocratic claims of Byzantine emperors in their prime.

The shift in the center of Russian power from Kiev in the southern grasslands to Moscow in the darkly forested north was precipitated by one of Russia's greatest historic catastrophes—the Mongol conquest of the thirteenth and fourteenth centuries. The impact of the Golden Horde on Russian development will be dealt with presently. One key consequence, however, should be stressed here. The primacy of Kiev, already weakened by feuds among the princes, was ended with its destruction by the Mongols. Leadership passed from the open steppes to the more defensible northern woodlands, and finally to the palisaded river city of Moscow. And Moscow, far from a now rapidly declining Constantinople, oriented its policy toward the Baltic and Western Europe, rather than the Black Sea and Byzantium, in centuries to come.

Yet the Byzantine influence lingered on. The Russian Orthodox church continued in the Byzantine pattern: Monasteries owned huge tracts of land; the church supported the evolving monarchy (instead of feuding with it, as the popes did in Western Europe); and the people prayed devoutly before their ikons. The grand dukes—later czars—of Muscovy shaped their new nation on a hazily conceived model of Byzantine autocracy—with a dash of Mongol rigor. And when Constantinople fell to the Turks in 1453, the Moscow rulers took for their own state the title of "third Rome," the heir to both Byzantine civilization and the imperial tradition of the ancient Caesars.

The Crusades: Rehearsal for Empire

Medieval Christian civilization was in general a more dynamic, expansive culture than is often realized. Its growth was by no means as spectacular as that of Islam—whose story will begin in the next chapter—yet Christendom also spread outward from its Mediter-

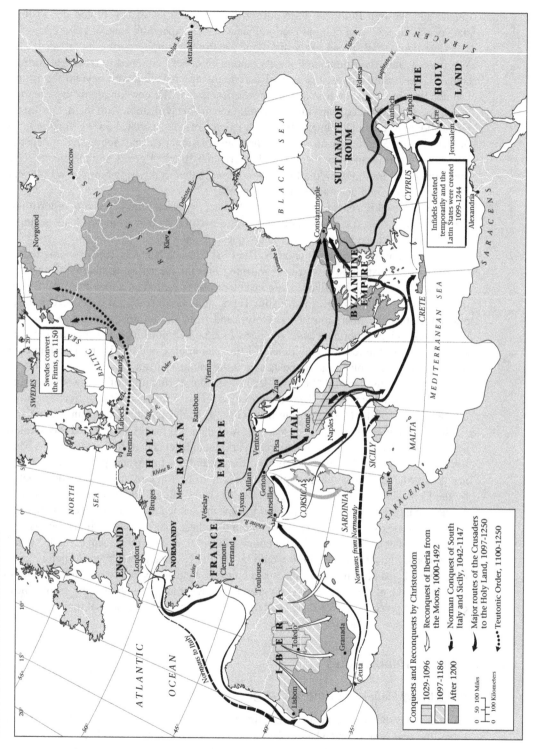

MEDIEVAL EUROPEAN EXPANSION

Swedes convert the Finns, ca. 1150

Infidels defeated temporarily and the Latin States were created 1099–1244

Conquests and Reconquests by Christendom

1029–1096		Reconquest of Iberia from the Moors, 1000–1492
1097–1186		Norman Conquest of South Italy and Sicily, 1042–1147
After 1200		Major routes of the Crusaders to the Holy Land, 1097–1250
		Teutonic Order, 1100–1250

0   50   100 Miles
0   100 Kilometers

SWEDES · RUSSIA · Novgorod · Moscow · Kiev · Astrakhan · Volga R. · Dnieper R. · BLACK SEA · SULTANATE OF ROUM · SARACENS · Tigris R. · Euphrates R. · THE HOLY LAND · Edessa · Antioch · Tripoli · Acre · Jerusalem · CYPRUS · Alexandria · SARACENS · MEDITERRANEAN SEA · CRETE · BYZANTINE EMPIRE · Constantinople · Danube R. · Vienna · Zara · BALTIC SEA · Danzig · Lübeck · Bremen · Oder R. · Elbe R. · Ratisbon · HOLY ROMAN EMPIRE · Rhine R. · Metz · Vézelay · Lyons · Milan · Venice · Genoa · Pisa · ITALY · Rome · Naples · Malta · SICILY · Tunis · SARACENS · SARDINIA · CORSICA · Marseilles · Rhône R. · Loire R. · FRANCE · Clermont-Ferrand · Toulouse · NORMANDY · ENGLAND · London · Bruges · NORTH SEA · ATLANTIC OCEAN · IBERIA · Toledo · Granada · Lisbon · Ceuta · Normans from Normandy · Normans to Italy

239

ranean and Western European base during the Middle Ages. It constituted not a single state or a static region of cultural predominance but an expanding zone of culture.

Christianity had spread to the limits of the Roman Empire during its last centuries. When Rome fell, the Roman and the Byzantine churches continued to reach out for new souls to save, converting new waves of barbarians and reaching well beyond the Rhine-Danube line into areas the Romans had never penetrated. The new kingdoms that emerged in Europe also expanded, carrying developing medieval civilization with them. During the High Middle Ages, finally, international Christian Crusades marched on the Muslim lands of the eastern Mediterranean. Pious Christian missionaries and aggressive monarchs, land-hungry barons and peasants, Crusaders driven by piety or greed, and merchants seeking commercial footholds in the Levant—all contributed to the beginnings of a European expansion that would one day astonish the world.

The medieval European Crusades actually accomplished little in the way of territorial expansion. But they did set in motion a Western outreach that would in later centuries swell into the greatest wave of imperial conquest in history.

The beginnings were small enough. The First Crusade began in 1095, sending tens of thousands of Christian holy warriors swarming into the Near East to liberate from Islam the lands where Christ had lived. The movement was triggered by a plea from the Byzantine emperor for help against the Muslim Turks, and was encouraged by Pope Urban II's assurances that the liberation of the Holy Land from the infidels was a good work in God's eyes. Other important causes included such nonreligious factors as population pressures in Europe, the restless ambitions of European nobles, and the desire of Italian commercial cities to establish trading posts across the Mediterranean.

The First Crusaders did "liberate" Jerusalem, massacring most of its Jewish and Muslim population in the process. They then set up a series of Crusader States stretching along the eastern end of the Mediterranean from Gaza through Lebanon. European pilgrim traffic, Italian trading colonies, and a steady flow of men and money maintained this Western toehold in the Near East for two hundred years (though Jerusalem fell to the famous Muslim leader Saladin in less than a century). European taste for Asian spices and other luxury goods and Christian zeal for spreading the faith by force of arms were both whetted by the Crusades. The Western money economy of the High Middle Ages was stimulated by the expanded trade with the East, and Europeans learned to tax themselves and to organize large-scale overseas ventures while mounting these international military campaigns.

All the later Crusades were costly failures, however, and the movement dwindled to talk and minor skirmishes after 1250. It would be another two and a half centuries before Europeans would again reach out for spices and converts, land and booty, beyond the confines of their own end of Eurasia. But the dynamism, the organizing ability, the ruthlessness, courage, and greed of the West had been demonstrated in this first rehearsal for empire.

THE END OF THE MIDDLE AGES

God's Heavy Flail—or a Time of Change?

After the splendid achievements of the High Middle Ages in the twelfth and thirteenth centuries, the next century and a half looked to medieval people like "God's heavy flail," a terrible divine punishment. Disaster struck all major segments of society, decimated the population, plunged the economy into a long depression. It was, in many important ways the end of an era, and the modern age that emerged from its ashes would be a different world.

Yet in dealing with the end of the Middle Ages, as with its beginnings, recent scholarship has come to see this period as a time of transition rather than one of cataclysm. Between 1300 and 1500, important medieval institutions suffered massive setbacks, often accompanied by traumatic experiences for large segments of the population. Plagues, wars, popular rebellions, economic turmoil, and struggles between rival claimants to the papacy itself scarred the lives of generations of Europeans. But there was a revival too, a recovery from these disasters that was well under way by 1500, when the modern world was clearly emerging. What must have felt like divine punishment to many also stimulated a surge of creative restructuring that produced the modern age.

Schism and War

The papacy fell into the deepest decline of its history during this period. The linked crises of the Babylonian Captivity and the Great Schism filled the century from 1305 to 1415.

The Babylonian Captivity—the name deriving from a fancied parallel with the Hebrews' ancient captivity in Babylon—was the Avignon papacy of the fourteenth century. During this period the popes, once so powerfully independent, fell under the influence of French kings, lived at Avignon in southern France, and became a byword in Christendom for extortionate greed. The Schism followed soon after. For several decades around 1400, there were two and even three claimants at a time to the throne of St. Peter, each excommunicating his rivals, and further degrading the Church in the eyes of bewildered and increasingly cynical Christians.

There were other disasters during this long season of Europe's discontent.

For more than a century England and France, the most successful of the medieval monarchies, mired themselves in the long agony of the Hundred Years War (1337–1453). The great early victories won by the English longbow—Crécy, Poitiers, Agincourt—go into every English schoolchild's notebook, as Joan of Arc's later heroism does on the French side of the Channel. In fact, the protracted conflict devastated France in the fourteenth century and drained England in the fifteenth. In the end, the English kings' efforts to retain control of large parts of the French kings' lands failed. The success of the longbow—which could pierce a knight's chain mail at a hundred yards—marked the beginning of the end of the baronial cavalry as masters of European battlefields. The marauding of mercenary companies and of rebellious peasants added to the havoc of this worst of medieval wars.

Plague and Depression

In the middle of the fourteenth century, meanwhile, an even more terrible calamity befell Europe as a whole. It came with the shiny little fleas that infested a species of black ship rat brought up the Mediterranean from Byzantium or the Black Sea. It was the Black Death.

The Black Death was an excruciatingly painful, almost inevitably fatal, and extremely contagious disease, technically known as bubonic plague. After ravaging the cities of China and traveling west along the caravan routes, the plague struck Europe first in 1348 and ravaged its populations repeatedly for three centuries thereafter. During this first horrifying visitation at the end of the Middle Ages, the plague may have killed a quarter of Europe's people. The population growth of the preceding centuries ended with a crash.

Add to all these catastrophes the deep Europe-wide depression that began in the middle of the fourteenth century, in part as a result of the wars and the plague. The economic hard times shattered the boom of the high-medieval commercial revolution and plunged the European economy into turmoil for a hundred years.

Drastic reduction in the size of the population raised the cost of labor, cut production, and thus inflated the prices of the goods that were produced. Landowners suffered from the high cost of labor, consumers from rising prices. In response, landholders often turned from farming to less labor-intensive sheep raising, while governments at all levels tried to fix both wages and prices. Another expression of this conservative reaction was the organization of protective associations of cities like the German Hanseatic League, dedicated to defending their own economic interests in a shrunken economic arena.

There was a more positive response to the economic upheaval as well, however. The workers who survived the plagues and famines, for example, earned much higher wages than before; merchants profited from rising prices; and sheep raising proved quite lucrative for many landowners. Some alert entrepreneurs, furthermore, adapted to changing times with more flexible business organization and with real technological innovations. In mining, metallurgy, printing, and ship building, lost labor was replaced with labor-saving devices that made these industries considerably more efficient. A new economic order would thus take shape in early modern times. But the upheaval itself must have been enormously painful for most who experienced it.

MEDIEVAL CHRISTIAN CULTURE

The Daughter of God

The Christian religion was the pulsing heart of medieval European culture. And there is no better illustration of the power of religious belief in medieval life than the briefly glorious but tragic career of Jeanne d'Arc—Joan of Arc—one of the most amazing of medieval saints.

The familiar story can be retold in a couple of paragraphs. Born in a small village in northeastern France early in the fifteenth century, Saint Joan grew up illiterate and pious in the middle of the Hundred Years War. In 1429, at the age of seventeen, she began to hear the voices of angels telling her to go forth and save her country from the unending ravages of the wars. With the simplicity of total belief, she thereupon set off for the court of Charles VII, where she miraculously picked that unimpressive—and as yet uncrowned—monarch out of a crowd of his own courtiers. Even more astonishing, she then convinced the unhappy French king that she should be allowed to ride off with the troops currently gathering for a major confrontation with the English.

Inspired by the Maid, as she was universally called, the disheartened French rallied. Joan's soldiers lifted the siege of Orleans—a key French bastion—defeated the English repeatedly, and swept triumphantly through to Reims. There, in the heart of English-held territory, in July of 1429, Charles VII was at last formally crowned King of France in a traditional ceremony in Reims cathedral.

Thus anointed with holy oil by the Church, Charles could look forward to a new loyalty from his people, who everywhere began to flock to the king's support against the English. Joan deemed her mission accomplished and wanted to return home, but she was too potent a symbol to be let go. And not long after her triumph, she was captured, tried for witchcraft by a subservient ecclesiastical court, and burned at the stake in Rouen in 1431.

Joan of Arc's brief, meteoric career did not include time out to sit for portraits. This modern rendering, however, tries to give a sense of the youth, vigor, and naïve piety of this most beloved of medieval French saints. Can you imagine this Joan as an athlete today, or an officer in a modern army? (Powell Gulick/Bettmann)

Joan of Arc believed completely in her voices—Saint Catherine and the archangel Michael—and in the unheard-of task they called her to perform. In this, at least, she was completely typical of her time. The English called her "a disciple and limb of the Fiend"; she insisted that her voices called her a "daughter of God."[3] But no one in that far distant century questioned the reality of the supernatural presences that urged her on.

Faith and Fanaticism

The mind of the Middle Ages was as thoroughly dominated by religion as were the minds of ancient Egyptians, Hindu Indians, or Europe's own Muslim neighbors.

The doctrines of the developed medieval church went far beyond the simple teachings of Jesus of Nazareth. Jesus's basic message remained central: Christ the Son of God still offered eternal life to those who believed. The Pauline virtues of faith in Christ, hope of salvation, and charity toward one's neighbor were still preached. But there was much more now.

Medieval priests catechized Christians on more elaborate creeds established by Church councils over the centuries. God was the Three-in-One—Father, Son, and Holy Ghost. There were seven deadly sins—pride, greed, envy, sexual self-indulgence, violence, laziness, and gluttony. Heaven, hell, and purgatory (a halfway house for purging away modest quantities of sin) were minutely anatomized, with all their angelic and demonic caretakers.

Religious duties were central to every human life. The seven sacraments brought religion into the lives of Christians at crucial points in the life cycle, sanctifying birth with

---

[3]Joseph R. Strayer and Dana C. Munro, *The Middle Ages: 395–1500* (New York: Appleton-Century-Crofts, 1959), p. 486.

baptism, coming-of-age with confirmation, marriage with matrimony, and death with extreme unction. The sacraments also provided penance and absolution for sins freely confessed, conferred spiritual powers on priests through ordination, and celebrated the communion of believers with their Savior in the central Christian mystery of the Mass.

But there was another side to the age of faith. There was the fanaticism that produced popular persecution of Jews, heretics, witches, and others believed to be in league with Satan. The Holy Office of the Inquisition, which was charged with maintaining the purity of Christian thought, used the most unscrupulous methods, including torture, to get confessions from those accused of heresy. Incorrigible enemies of Christ were turned over to the secular authorities to be burned alive in public marketplaces.

A faith founded on the love of God thus sponsored the cruel persecution of all who rejected its tenets. It was a feature of many creeds, past and yet to come, which claimed to offer universal truths to humankind.

The Twelfth-Century Renaissance

It is evident that medieval religion was far from a simple matter. The Christian leaders of the High Middle Ages, in fact, devoted their most intense intellectual efforts to making sense out of their immense and complex religious heritage. And they produced one of the major intellectual triumphs of Western history: the scholastic synthesis of the Twelfth-Century Renaissance.

Dubbed a *renaissance,* or "rebirth," by historians after the more famous cultural revival of the fifteenth century, this medieval cultural flowering was actually a remarkably original synthesis. It took ancient materials—Greek philosophy and science, Roman law, and above all the revealed truths of the Judeo-Christian religious tradition—and wove them into something original and profound.

Paradoxically, this first recovery of Greco-Roman ideas came to Christian Europeans mostly by way of their archenemies, the Muslims. The culture of Islam had flowered several centuries before that of Christendom and had absorbed the wisdom of the restless Greek mind during the Muslim conquest of Byzantine territories in the Near East. Greek books had then traveled across North Africa to Muslim Spain at the other end of the Mediterranean. Here, in the flourishing cultural centers of Córdoba and Toledo, Christian scholars from Western Europe had come to study the pre-Christian philosophy of Aristotle at the feet of learned followers of the non-Christian Prophet Muhammad!

European scholars thus recovered the mathematics, astronomy, and medical ideas of the ancient Greeks and—from Byzantium directly—Justinian's Code of Roman law. Most important, they immersed themselves in the encyclopedic writings of Aristotle, "the master of those who know" in medieval times. From these varied sources St. Anselm drew arguments for the primacy of Christian faith, while Abelard raised probing questions that strengthened the structure of belief it subjected to challenge. The beloved St. Bernard condemned the immoralities of the times, and St. Thomas Aquinas summed up the knowledge of his age in a vast structure of Christian thought.

To study and spread this newly acquired knowledge, medieval scholars invented the Western university. Other cultures had developed their own centers of higher learning, from the informal Greek "schools" of philosophy to such religious institutions as the Buddhist school at Nolanda in India and the Sankore mosque in Timbuktu. In the twelfth and

thirteenth centuries, similar associations of teachers and students, operating in rented halls or in churches, sprang up in many cities in Western Europe.

These medieval universities taught undergraduates rhetoric, law, and above all Aristotle's logic, while graduate faculties gave professional training in law, medicine, and the queen of the sciences, theology. For it was in theological speculation, explored with the help of Aristotelian logic, that medieval thinkers made their greatest contributions to the history of Western thought.

By applying Aristotelian rigor to their inherited Christian insights, these Christian theologians achieved a remarkable synthesis of faith and reason. Even more impressive, they produced a coherent view of the world that was rationally and emotionally acceptable—indeed inspiring—to the simplest peasant and the deepest doctor of theology. They anatomized in convincing detail a world made by God's fiat, guided by God's providence, yet comprehensible by human minds and deeply moving to the human heart.

Chartres Cathedral was one of the most beautiful of the hundreds of great churches built to the glory of Mary the Mother of God during the later medieval centuries. It is seen here as it must have looked then, towering above the cobbled streets and peaked roofs of a medieval town. The two towers flanking the portals in front, built at different times, are very different in design. (Bernard P. Wolff/Photo Researchers, Inc.)

The Art of the Cathedrals

Between 1050 and 1350 no less than eighty cathedrals and hundreds of churches of comparable size and grandeur were built in France alone. They were not built by the people themselves, exalted mobs of true believers with kings and commoners pulling together on the ropes, as romantic historiography once believed. The cathedrals were raised over long, slow decades by master builders, skilled architects who called themselves masons and who hired the best medieval artists to make God's house a thing of beauty. These towering Christian temples, dedicated to the Virgin Mary, still constitute the finest expression we have of the religious spirit of the age of faith.

The image of Paris's Notre Dame leaps quickly to mind, of course. But it is well to remember that not all the great churches of the Middle Ages were gothic, like Notre Dame de Paris. There were many lovely romanesque cathedrals in the earlier medieval centuries, built with round instead of pointed arches, mural paintings instead of stained-glass windows. There were also Eastern Orthodox churches, from Constantinople to Kiev and Moscow, built with wide domes instead of spires, gold leaf and mosaic decorating their labyrinthine interiors. And there is as much beauty and spirituality in Constantinople's Church of the Holy Wisdom as there is in Paris's more familiar Church of Our Lady.

Nevertheless, the great gothic churches built in Western Europe in the High Middle Ages remain the most celebrated artistic achievements of the age. Rising hundreds of feet above the rooftops and the cobblestoned streets of the medieval city below, gothic cathedrals such as those of Paris or Chartres, Salisbury or Cologne (not completed until the nineteenth century) were marvels of architectural skill and daring.

Lofty verticality was the keynote of the gothic style. Pointed gothic arches, clustered pillars, and ribbed vaulting support a thin fabric of stone and glass many stories high. This immense height and the weight of the roof was supported by graceful external braces called flying buttresses. All of it, finally—towers and buttresses, inside and out—was thick with restless gothic decoration: statuary, carved wood, stained glass, finials and spires, kings, saints, and gargoyles. This too was a hallmark of the gothic—abhorence of empty space, so that every inch is filled with intricately interwoven shapes.

The other arts of the medieval period clustered about the churches. Stone figures flanking the deepset portals combine convincingly real faces with robes whose folds blend into the verticality of the surrounding pillars. Along the walls, high arched windows ablaze with stained glass trace scenes from the Bible or the lives of the saints. Under the seats in the choir, animals and humans, bunches of grapes and leering demons show what the art of the wood-carver could do. Even the great handmade Bible in the lectern was bright with illuminated capitals and glowing illustrations of events that happened long ago and far away in fairy-tale places with names such as Jerusalem and Bethlehem, Golgotha and Galilee.

Medieval Literature: Roland's Horn, Dante's Hell, and the Canterbury Pilgrims

Most of the serious religious literature of the Middle Ages, in Western Europe at least, was written in Latin and thus inaccessible to most medieval people. But in the High and later Middle Ages, some impressive popular literature began to appear in the vernaculars—the living languages of modern Europe. Most of this writing was in verse, and the religious element was often powerfully present (two strikes against it for many modern readers). Nevertheless, there is a life to the work of Chaucer or Dante or the unknown author(s) of *The Song of Roland* that is hard to find in the staider, more respectable writing of the time.

The Song of Roland is one of many French "songs of deeds," long epic war poems sung in the halls of medieval barons, much as Homeric bards sang of the deeds of Greek and Trojan heroes to the warlords of an earlier age. It is the story of the heroic death of Roland, one of Charlemagne's mythic paladins, the French equivalent of King Arthur's knights of the round table. Almost to the last moment the chivalrous Roland, though surrounded by enemies, refuses to blow his great horn Olifant, whose high clear note would bring Charlemagne and the French host galloping to the rescue. When Roland's horn is blown at last, it summons the Christian cavalry only to bury their dead—and guarantee chivalric immortality for Roland and his horn.

With the Italian poet Dante Alighieri, we follow the medieval spirit to the other side of death, into the Christian other-worlds beyond the grave. Dante's *Divine Comedy,* an epic poem on the afterlife, traces the poet's imaginary descent into hell, the inferno at the center of the earth, up the steep slopes of purgatory on the other side of the world, and on beyond the stars into the radiance of paradise. It is a journey thick with history and symbol, told in musical Italian verse. Yet it is Dante's inferno, that "nation of the lost," that has always fascinated modern readers.[4] It is a lurid vision of living souls wrapped in agony, punctuated with vivid flashbacks to the world above and the sins that have doomed these men and women to their eternal torment. Even in our calloused age, this plunge into the nightmare geography of the pit, the deepest netherworld of the medieval imagination, is not to be undertaken lightly.

But there was a world above, birdsong and spring flowers glittering with dew along the road to Canterbury—the world of the English poet Geoffrey Chaucer's *Canterbury Tales.* Among the company that assemble at the Tabard Inn in the London suburb of Southwark for the short spring pilgrimage to the cathedral at Canterbury are representatives of all walks of medieval life. The merchant, the friar, and the Oxford university stu-

---

[4]Dante Alighieri, *The Divine Comedy,* trans. Thomas G. Bergin (New York: Appleton-Century-Crofts, 1955), p. 8.

dent, the nun and the much-married wife of Bath, the earthy miller and the "gentle, perfect knight" all have their characteristic tales to tell to help pass the journey. The wit, variety, and high good humor of the whole remind us finally that there was more in the medieval mind than crusades and hellfire. There were bawdy tales, high ideals, and busy worldly lives to be led, even in the shadow of cathedral spires.

SUMMARY

The European Dark Age that followed immediately upon the Fall of Rome was admittedly a hard time of political and social disintegration, poverty, and violence. To deal with waves of invasion, Europeans developed the feudal system, a loose structure of political power based on military service in return for land. To survive after the collapse of Western trade, Europeans evolved the manor system of subsistence agriculture. Rude empires even emerged from time to time, the most famous being the Carolingian Empire of Charlemagne, who was crowned on Christmas Day, 800.

During the High Middle Ages—the eleventh, twelfth, and thirteenth centuries—European society and culture experienced a brilliant revival. Thanks in large part to the reemergence of trade by land and sea, great cities appeared in Europe once more. Kings, by imposing their will on the feudal barons, began the building of modern nation-states in France, England, Spain, and elsewhere. And the Roman Catholic church, led by powerful popes and fueled by the passionate belief of many medieval people, became the most impressive single institution in Western Christendom.

In East Europe and on the fringes of the Middle East, both autocratic imperial government and Greek Orthodox Christianity were centered in Constantinople. This strongly centralized Byzantine Empire spread Christianity and civilization in East Europe, provided economic stimulation, and survived for a thousand years, from the fifth to the fifteenth century. Muscovy, the core of the future Russian state, emerged at the end of the Middle Ages, modeling its political and religious institutions on those of fallen Byzantium.

The Crusades of the High Middle Ages represented Europe's first rehearsal for the great overseas imperial expansion of modern times. But in the fourteenth and fifteenth centuries, medieval society collapsed in a welter of economic disaster, plague, wars, and religious schism.

At its peak, however, medieval Christendom was an impressive cultural achievement in its own right. Built on a mixture of ardent faith and sometimes savage fanaticism, the culture of the Middle Ages was as intensely religious as any the world has seen. The Twelfth-Century Renaissance provided rigorous intellectual underpinnings for medieval Christianity in the scholastic philosophy of Thomas Aquinas. The great church builders of the age raised cathedral spires over hundreds of European cities. The poetry of Dante, Chaucer, and other medieval writers reflected a culture in which this world and the Christian "other world" met and mingled in the minds of western people.

SUGGESTED READING

Allmand, C. *The Hundred Years War: England and France at War, ca. 1300–ca. 1450.* New York: Cambridge University Press, 1988. Concise topical treatment, including a clear and brief summary of the military campaigns.

Bartlett, R. *The Making of Europe: Conquest, Colonization, and Cultural Change 950–1350.* Princeton: Princeton University Press, 1993. Impressive social and cultural overview of the High Middle Ages.

Cohen, M. R. *Under Crescent and Cross: The Jews in the Middle Ages.* Princeton: Princeton University Press, 1994. Student-oriented survey.

Cowdrey, H. E. J. *Pope Gregory VII: 1073–1085.* New York: Clarendon Press, 1998. Stresses the inspirational role of Pope Gregory in the growth of papal power.

Duby, G. *A History of Private Life,* Vol. 2: *Revelation of the Medieval World.* trans. A. Goldhammer. Cambridge, Mass.: Belknap Press, 1988. Social and cultural aspects of the private lives of French and Italian people, lavishly illustrated.

Duggan, A. J., ed. *Queens and Queenship in Medieval Europe.* Rochester, N.Y.: Boydell, 1997. Papers tending to see women's political power as rooted in family connections. But see studies in T. Evergates, ed., *Aristocratic Women in Medieval France* (Philadelphia: University of Pennsylvania Press, 1999), stressing independent power of these women in the High Middle Ages.

Fletcher, R. *The Barbarian Conversion: From Paganism to Christianity.* New York: Holt, 1998. Medieval Christianization of Europe, emphasizing the causes and process of conversion.

France, J. *Victory in the East: A Military History of the First Crusade.* New York: Cambridge University Press, 1994. Sees disorganized early Crusader forces evolving into an effective fighting force. See also his *Western Warfare in the Age of the Crusades 1000–1300* (Ithaca: Cornell University Press, 1999), on all aspects, from recruitment and logistics to castle design and combat tactics, and P. Partner, *God of Battles: Holy Wars of Christianity and Islam* (Princeton: Princeton University Press, 1998), which sees crusading as a key feature of both religious communities.

Franklin, S., and J. Shepard. *The Emergence of Rus 750–1200.* New York: Longman, 1996. Broader socioeconomic interpretation of Russian origins.

Freedman, P. *Images of the Medieval Peasant.* Stanford: Stanford University Press, 1999. Social theory and social reality of life among European peasantry.

Le Goff, J. *The Medieval Imagination,* trans. A. Goldhammer. Chicago: University of Chicago Press, 1988. Challenging probe of the medieval mind through analysis of changing words and conflicting intellectual structures.

Menuge, N. D., ed. *Medieval Women and the Law.* Rochester, N.Y.: Boydell and Brewer, 2000. Essays on ways in which medieval law defined women's place—and ways women used the law for their own purposes.

Treadgold, W. *A History of the Byzantine State and Society.* Stanford: Stanford University Press, 1997. Sweeping narrative treatment of the history of the medieval Eastern Christian empire.

Wright, N. *Knights and Peasants: The Hundred Years War in the French Countryside.* Rochester, N.Y.: Boydell, 1996. Grim evocation of the ways in which chivalric idealism failed to prevent the ravaging of the French countryside.

 Please refer to the document CD-ROM for primary sources related to this chapter.

CHAPTER 10

DOMES AND MINARETS
The Spread of Islam

(600–1300)

A GLANCE AHEAD: A NEW RELIGION REACHES ACROSS THE OLD WORLD

South and east of medieval Christian Europe, a second great world religion emerged during this age of expanding cultural zones: Islam, the faith of the Prophet Muhammad. Islam would be the last religion with truly global reach. During this period, the Islamic faith would in fact spread much farther than Christianity did.

Born of the visions of the trader Muhammad in the Arabian city of Mecca, the Muslim faith was spread far and wide by the Prophet's successors. Hard-riding true believers burst out of Arabia in a holy war that carried Islam—and Arab rule—up into the Middle East, west across North Africa, and even into southern Europe. And wherever the Islamic faith spread, so did Islamic law and flourishing Islamic trade routes, shared beliefs, and forms of worship.

By the fifteenth century, the Islamic cultural zone thus loomed as a massive rival to the Christian zone. And Islam was on the eve of a new golden age of its own as the modern period began in Europe.

THE PROPHET

Muhammad, the Messenger of God

Muhammad the Messenger of God (570–632) lived six centuries after Jesus Christ, twelve centuries after Gautama Buddha. He became the prophet of Islam, the last of the great world religions to emerge in history thus far.

Muhammad was born in Mecca, an oasis city on the caravan routes of western Arabia about forty miles from the Red Sea. It was a busy town, full of merchants, handicraft artisans, and pilgrims. The caravans came and went, carrying silks and spices, frankincense, and other luxury products to and from Damascus, Byzantium, Basra. But Mecca was also a

The Shah-i-Zinda, a burial place for Muslim saints and rulers outside Samarkand. Built on the site of the old city, it has been a focus for pilgrimage and worship since the Muslim conquest. (Anthony Esler)

religious center. Its central temple, the odd cubical structure called the Kaaba, contained a mysterious black stone that God—*Allah* in Arabic—was believed to have cast down from heaven, as well as idols dedicated to a number of other gods, to *jinn* and desert demons.

Beyond Mecca, with its gardens and bustling markets, the sea of sand began: shifting sand hills, dry *wadis,* and the desolate crags of the Najd, the Exhausted Land. Here roamed restless tribes of bedouin—the desert Arabs, herding their flocks, conducting their blood feuds, swooping down on hapless caravans.

It was a world not much changed from Jesus's time, or the time of the Hebrew prophets. It was about to produce a third great religion, and one integrally related to Judaism and Christianity. Muhammad never claimed to be the first Prophet—only the last.

Muhammad, the son of Abdullah, son of Abdul Muttalib, of the tribe of Qureysh, was orphaned early in life and had to make his own way in the marketplaces of Mecca. He probably traveled with the caravans, perhaps as far as Palestine, and picked up the rudiments of the religions of Moses and Jesus there. At twenty-five he married a wealthy and intelligent woman fifteen years older than himself, who gave him a modest place among the Meccan merchants, to whom he was known as *Al Amin,* the Trustworthy. According to Islamic tradition, he was a husky man with a black beard and fair skin, a hooked nose and black, luminous eyes. An upright, sometimes melancholy man, he was given to long silences.

At the age of forty, meditating in a cave outside the town, he had his first vision. "Read!" a voice thundered. "I cannot read," replied Muhammad, who was apparently illiterate. "Read!" the voice intoned twice more. And then, beyond the cave mouth, the Arab saw standing in the sky an angelic figure who spoke once more: "O Muhammad! Thou art Allah's Messenger, and I am Gabriel."[1] The "reading" of the divine message to the world ("recitation" or even "speaking forth" are perhaps better renderings of the original Arabic) occupied Muhammad for the rest of his life and was preserved for the Islamic world in the verses of the Quran (Koran). For countless millions of Muslims, the visions of Muhammad would constitute God's final Message to humankind.

He was at first a prophet without honor in his own country, ridiculed and dismissed as mad or possessed. Some of the poor listened to his revelations, and his wife, Khadijah, stood staunchly behind her husband. He also won the support of a wealthy merchant named Abu Bakr, and Omar, a leading citizen of Mecca. A persecutor of Muhammad in the early days, Omar was to become his most effective successor as leader of Arabic Islam.

The *Hijrah* and the Return

For the time being, however, his enemies prevailed. In 622 Muhammad left Mecca, taking his prophecies north to the oasis city known today as Medina. He was then a man in his fifties, and the black beard must have been at least flecked with gray.

The *Hijrah,* as the move from Mecca to Medina is called, was a great success. At Medina, Muhammad won many converts to his doctrines of *Islam,* "submission" to the will of Allah as it had been revealed to him. He preached an end to idolatry, monotheistic worship of Allah, prayer five times a day, fasting from dawn to dusk through the month of Ramadan, paradise for the faithful, and hellfire for the wicked. He recognized Moses and Jesus as earlier prophets and seems to have expected Jews and Christians to accept him as

---

[1]Mohammed Marmaduke Pickthall, *The Meaning of the Glorious Koran* (New York: New American Library, 1953), p. x.

God's Messenger too. When the Jews of Medina refused to do so, he exercised his new-found ascendancy by expelling them from the city.

There were external enemies of the new faith to deal with as well. Whereas Jesus's three-year ministry was strewn with miracles, Muhammad's career was punctuated with battles. The aging merchant turned holy man personally led some two dozen campaigns during his last ten years. His struggles with his most obdurate foes, the Meccans, climaxed in 630 with his victorious return to his birthplace. There the Prophet cleansed the Kaaba of its idols, prayed before the Black Stone, and forgave his enemies.

He died two years later, the founder of a new religion whose phenomenal spread over the coming centuries would perhaps have awed even Muhammad, the Trustworthy, the Prophet, the Messenger of God.

The Social Message of the Prophet

Like other prophets before him, Muhammad also had a social message for his followers. Like Confucius and the Buddha, like the Hebrew prophets and Christian preachers, the Prophet of Islam urged believers to seek the path of virtue in this world.

Poverty Muhammad saw as a great social evil. To improve the economic lot of Muslims, he urged such reforms as charitable alms-giving and the sharing of inheritances rather than conferring all on the first-born son. In at least one place, he condemned the unearned profit that comes from interest on loans, saying that all income should be earned by honest toil. Some Muslim communities, like some medieval Christian theologians, therefore tried to exclude banking as we know it from economic life.

On the condition of women, Muhammad also urged significant changes. In a society where women were often treated like property, where the birth of a daughter was widely regarded as a disaster, and where female infanticide was not uncommon, the Prophet's teachings substantially improved women's lot. Muslim women, he declared, were to share rights with men, to enjoy a portion of any inheritance, to be married only with their consent, and to be able to initiate divorce proceedings if the marriage failed.

Muhammad also supported the right of a man to as many as four wives if he could support them. And he did encourage the harem system, confining wives and children to the private sphere of the home. These changes, however, could be regarded as a considerable improvement in a world where women had often been treated with promiscuous contempt in times past.

Muhammad also sought to end the curse of blood feuds among Arabs and to improve treatment of slaves. He showed his openness to all peoples by taking Hagar, a black African woman, as his second wife. He even urged more humane conduct of the inevitably brutal business of warfare. Both he and his successors would have plenty of experience of this widespread social practice.

The Islamic World

The force unleashed by the Arab prophet dreaming in the marketplace in Mecca was to have a genuinely seismic impact on history. Yet this militant faith, spreading over substantial portions of all three continents of the Old World, was less focused and considerably more complex than some of those we have examined thus far.

We are not dealing here with a single empire, a territorial polity like ancient Egypt or the Roman Empire. Islam was a living, growing organism, dividing into separate and sometimes antagonistic states, spreading ever farther across Eurasia and beyond. Its extent became in time so vast that it is quite unlikely that the Muslim kings of Sokoto in West Africa, for instance, were even aware of the existence of the Islamic coastal states of Borneo. Yet there are fundamental historical patterns to be detected in this vast intercontinental sprawl that we call Islam.

Islam was above all a religious community, bound together in the first instance by the Holy Quran, the "reading" that Gabriel had enjoined upon Muhammad and that Allah had inspired in his Messenger. This volume of sacred verses, read and memorized in Arabic all across the Muslim world, served as a powerful cultural cement. So did the Muslim Law, a detailed body of religious strictures and traditions professed by holy men sitting in dusty market squares from Spain to Samarkand. Paradoxically, finally, the religious unity of Islam was actually strengthened by the sectarian upheavals that swept through it from time to time. Initially divisive, such challenges to orthodoxy as the mystic Sufi movement or the Sunni–Shiite split—to be examined in a later section—stirred new fervor in the faithful and sometimes, as in the case of the Sufis, contributed significantly to the further expansion of Islam.

Submission to Allah was thus a religious submission first of all. But Islam was also a human dominion, and its bearers, while a diverse lot, fitted a pattern nonetheless. Typically, the ruling peoples of the Muslim world began their rise to predominance as rude converts—hard-fighting, comparatively barbarous warriors of Allah. They ended as cultivated Oriental princes, more worldly and more sophisticated than the founder of their

MUSLIM EXPANSION TO 750

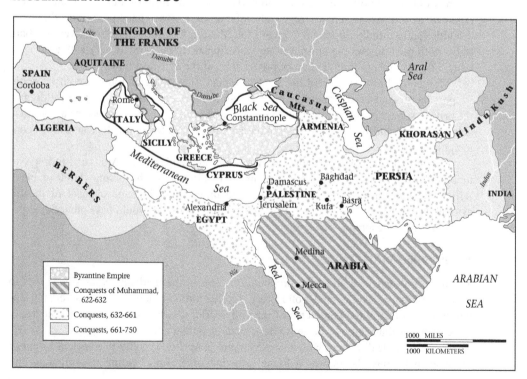

faith had ever been. The Arabs first, then Turks, Mongols, Africans, and others followed this historic cycle, rejuvenating Islam and reaching out for new converts and new dominions each in turn.

Islam is, finally, a variegated and brilliant civilization, a pattern of culture as distinctive in its way as those of China or the Greco-Roman Mediterranean. Mosque and minaret and the Arabic script of the Quran flourished all across this broad swath of Africa, Europe, and Asia. Men of Muslim beliefs and ways of life traded on all the caravan routes across Eurasia and rode the monsoon winds across the Indian Ocean. Their rulers lived cultivated court lives in Damascus or Baghdad, Córdoba or Constantinople, Samarkand or Timbuktu.

A complex entity, Islam was thus not only a religion but also a succession of political hegemonies and a variety of linked cultures. For a thousand years, from the seventh century to the seventeenth, Muslim power reached out, winning converts from the Russian steppes to the African savannas, thrusting into Christian Europe, conquering most of Hindu India, and reshaping the lives of millions of human beings. But there was order beneath the tumult. Islam bound all its millions to a religion, a civilization, and a pattern of history.

THE HOLY WAR

Jihad: The Holy Struggle

When Muhammad died, he had left his mark upon most of the oasis towns and primitive bedouin of northern Arabia. In the centuries that followed the Prophet's death in 632, his followers were to seize with the sword an area larger than the Roman Empire, all in the name of Allah and his Messenger. A survey of Arab Islamic expansion during the first few centuries after Muhammad will give us some idea of the realm with which we will be dealing in subsequent pages and chapters, and of the general pattern of Islamic expansion across the Old World.

The ragged bedouin from the Exhausted Land of Arabia were a proud, tough people, but they had little of this world's goods. They wore clothing and lived in tents made of the hides of their beasts, milked and slaughtered them for food, and warmed themselves around small fires of dried camel dung under the brilliant stars. The simple pressure of overpopulation in their arid land has often been seen as a spur that drove the Arabs on to conquest of other lands.

A key concept from the new religion of Muhammad, however, also contributed significantly to the great wave of Arab conquests of the seventh and eighth centuries. This was the complex Islamic concept of *jihad,* or religious struggle.

The term is often presented as the Muslim equivalent of the Christian crusade, or religious war. In fact, both terms have had wider applications down the centuries, and *jihad* was a more complicated idea from the beginning. It refers to sacred struggle on more than one level. On the individual or personal level, *jihad* is the intense spiritual effort of the believer to live by his or her Islamic beliefs. It is the inner struggle to be worthy of salvation. On the larger, communal level, however, *jihad* has traditionally meant "holy war," struggle to defend or expand the realm where the Prophet is honored, his teachings available to guide people—as Muslims believe—on the path that leads to salvation.

Historically, the religion of Muhammad had been a crusading faith from the beginning. Struggle against ungodly forces, both within themselves and in the outside world, early became a central Islamic duty. And the communal form of *jihad*—holy war against the unbeliever—became the most important form of struggle. It was in a sense a deal the Arabs couldn't refuse. If they won, they came home laden with more booty than any caravan raid provided. If they died in the attempt, they would come home to Paradise: "What though ye be slain or die," the glorious Quran declared, "when unto Allah ye are gathered?" (*The Quran,* III, 158).

The Arab Conquests

When the Prophet died in 632, his old companion Abu Bakr was hailed as *caliph* ("successor") in the cities of Arabia. Some of the desert sheiks resisted, but Abu Bakr brought them around, sometimes by force, before he died, two years after Muhammad.

Omar, the Prophet's earlier persecutor and first official patron, became the second caliph. A man of vision and organizing skill and the best general among the Muslims, Omar fused the desert tribes into an army and turned their first tentative probes into the great *jihad.*

The Arabs were not vastly numerous or well equipped. But by sticking to the barren wilderness they knew, and to their camel cavalry and hit-and-run tactics, they proved quite effective. Their fierce traditional pride and their new faith gave a sharp edge to their swords. As with true believers in other times and lands, their strength would sometimes seem the strength of ten because their hearts were, if not purer than other men's, at least more passionate.

The neighboring lands turned out to be plums ripe for the plucking. The Persian and Byzantine empires northeast and northwest of Arabia were old and worn out with fighting each other. The Berbers of North Africa, otherwise much like their Arab assailants, had no *jihad* to unify them. And once the holy war was well begun, the warriors of Allah developed a momentum that would take some stopping, even by more formidable rivals.

Under Omar (634–644), the ragtag army took the provinces of Syria and Palestine from the Byzantine Empire, occupied most of Sassanid Persia, and conquered Egypt. Under the Umayyad dynasty that followed, despite internal divisions and civil strife, the Arabs swept on westward across North Africa, crossed the Straits of Gibraltar, overwhelmed the Visigothic kingdom in Spain, and swarmed over the Pyrenees into western France. There they were finally stopped by a Frankish army under Charles Martel at the Battle of Poitiers (Tours) in 732. In the eastern Mediterranean, meanwhile, Arab warriors had built themselves ships, destroyed the fleet of the Byzantines, and mounted a massive siege of Constantinople. Here again they met with a substantial check, and in 718 they abandoned the assault on the impregnable walls of the Byzantine capital.

But these reverses at Constantinople and Poitiers did not stop the far-ranging soldiers of the Prophet. In the early eighth century, roving bands were already pushing northeast into the Caucasus and Central Asia and east beyond Persia into the valley of the Indus.

The Long Reach of Islam

The scale of the Islamic zone a century after the Prophet's death was truly amazing. On a map of Muslim lands in the early 700s C.E., you can see a cultural zone that combines most of the Mediterranean core of the former Roman Empire with the Middle eastern sweep of the Persian Empire. Western Asia, North Africa, and significant portions of southern Europe had been overrun in a couple of lifetimes.

During this period, furthermore, the cultural zones on either side of Islam—Europe and the Indian subcontinent—were fragmented. Only Tang China, at the far end of Eurasia, could match the scale of the Islamic achievement. And only the first stage of Muslim expansion was ended. Indeed, the Arab conquest had laid the foundation for a predominance that would fill the center of Eurasia with Islamic power by the beginning of the modern period.

The victorious Arabs tended to be less fanatical then Christian legend long believed. Christians and Jews in particular, as followers of earlier prophets in Muhammad's line, were usually allowed the freedom of their religion, though they paid a special tax for the privilege. Persians and Byzantines, with their long experience of government, were soon managing conquered territories for the victorious but administratively unsophisticated Arabs.

Yet the legend of that first eruption out of Arabia lived on—above all, perhaps, for their most persistent enemies, the Christian peoples still sunk in the depths of the early Middle Ages on the other side of the Mediterranean. Muhammad became Mahound, the Devil himself, to medieval Christians, and "Lord, save us from the Saracens" their most fervent prayer.

THE ARAB EMPIRE

The Caliphs: Successors to the Prophet

The Arab Empire founded by Omar would flourish for some three centuries. Thereafter Islam would march on under other banners than those of its Arab founders. But the development of the two Arab caliphates, the Umayyads (661–750) and the Abbasids (750–1258), was typical of much that was to come.

Under Muhammad's early successors—the "rightly guided" caliphs who immediately followed him and the Umayyad dynasty thereafter—Arabs came to rule vast tracts of the Near East, North Africa, and parts of southern Europe. In attempting to govern their new conquests, they found that their ancient desert heritage of tribal life and their new power in the world interacted to produce unforeseen social and economic problems and some sanguinary political history. However, the Arab Empire also fashioned an integrated society and a brilliant flowering of Islamic culture. These aspects of their history deserve as much attention as the dazzling conquests that carried the Arabs with such rapidity to the mastery of their substantial corner of the globe.

The problems began at the heart of Islam, with the religious leadership of the faithful, which was vested from the beginning in the caliphs.

The institution of the caliphate was intended to be at least partially theocratic. The *caliphs,* as successors to the Prophet, were initially the religious as well as the political heads of Islam, as Muhammad had been. In Islamic thinking there was no difference between these two spheres of activity, secular and ecclesiastical, sacred and profane. As the caliphs became more worldly and luxury-loving, however, their spiritual leadership was harder and harder to reconcile with the style of life their political ascendancy brought them. Under these circumstances they allowed their spiritual authority to pass largely into the hands of the *ulama*—the experts on the life and teachings of the Prophet, the shapers and masters of the Muslim Law. While retaining their nominal headship of the faithful in religious matters, the caliphs thus became concerned more and more exclusively with politics.

Abu Bakr, the first caliph, was chosen by the acclaim of the believers, at least in the Arabian cities. After the first four caliphs, however, the dynastic principle came into play. During both of the two main Arab caliphates, family succession determined the leadership of Islam. The dynastic succession was punctuated, however, by some of the bloodiest high politics since third-century Rome.

The Umayyads

Of the four "rightly guided" caliphs, only Abu Bakr died peacefully in bed. Omar was assassinated in 644; so was his successor, in 656; and so was the next in line, Muhammad's son-in-law Ali, in 661. Nor did the establishment of the Umayyad clan that year put an end to fratricide among the Arab rulers. There was civil strife again in the last decades of the seventh century, and the Umayyad dynasty expired finally in a massacre that all but wiped out their house.

The sources of this sanguinary political history lay in a number of unresolved problems that plagued the Umayyads throughout that first century of Islam. There was the traditional bedouin penchant for clan vendettas that a century of common victories did not abolish. There was the inevitable tendency of recently conquered peoples to revolt, producing recurring civil wars in the Arab Empire. And there was the appearance of the sectarian spirit within the body of the Muslim faithful as early as the death of Ali, whose dissident Shiite followers constitute to this day a sometimes violent minority in the Islamic world.

We have already noticed the emergence of new interpretations and doctrines—often declared heretical by mainstream believers—in Hinduism, Buddhism, and Christianity. Among Muslims, the Shiites remain the largest dissident faction today.

Shiites were originally "the party of Ali," militant supporters of the third of the Rightly Guided Caliphs who followed Muhammad. Personally a man of great piety, Ali was also married to the prophet's daughter Fatima and—Shiites believed—Muhammad's chosen successor. His assassination in 661 should in their view have brought one of Ali's own sons to the caliphate. When the Umayyad dynasty succeeded instead, Shiites refused to recognize the political or religious authority of these new leaders. Over the centuries, the ten or fifteen percent of Muslims who still comprise the party of Ali have developed distinctive religious beliefs and have been bitterly persecuted. The Islamic world, like Christendom, had its fanatics in this age of the temple builders.

A Changing Style of Life

Other transformations, less violent but more far-reaching, were also going on beneath the surface of victorious conquest and self-destructive civil conflict that characterized the rule of the Umayyads.

In the first place, there were transformations in the conquered peoples. The Arabs did not give much attention to conversion of unbelievers during the early years. They collected taxes and tribute regularly, making effective use of the existing Persian or Byzantine bureaucratic structures for these purposes, and otherwise asking—and offering—little more. Before the end of the Umayyad century, however, this policy began to change. The defeated peoples, impressed with the theology and military success of Islam, slowly began to seek conversion to the religion of the victors. This process was no doubt encouraged by the fact that by converting to Islam non-Muslims escaped the taxes levied on infidels. At the same time, the Arabs began to fraternize more with the natives, so that the Arabic language came into increasingly common use all across the Muslim world. The spread of Arabic was also hastened by the spread of the faith, since the Quran could be read and prayers addressed properly to Allah only in the language in which he had spoken to the Prophet.

The spread of the Islamic religion and the Arabic language provided the basis for a slow but extensive change in the peoples the Arabs had overwhelmed during the century after the Prophet's death. It was a process that would continue under later dynasties and other regimes, imposing a far-reaching cultural unity on the Islamic world.

Changes also came about in the Arab conquerors themselves during this early period. Once they had abandoned their isolated garrisons and mingled with the peoples they ruled, Arabs everywhere gradually became part of the indigenous ruling classes. Some of them turned into wealthy landowners, adopted the luxurious lifestyles of their former enemies, and increasingly left the fighting to new, non-Arab converts to Islam. Arab viceroys and governors built themselves palaces and even whole new cities, where they lived in opulence, cut off from the people they ruled. The Umayyad caliphs transferred the capital of Islam from its old center of Mecca to the rich city of Damascus, where a more imperial style of life might be lived more easily. In their new capital, they created a court to rival the most luxurious of earlier Near Eastern emperors.

By the end of its first century, then, the Arab Empire had produced a style of life very different from the desert wandering of Muhammad's day. Under the Abbasid dynasty, which seized the caliphate in 750, Arab rule was to reach its apogee of grandeur. It was also to undergo one final metamorphosis before slipping slowly and lingeringly out of the pages of history.

The Abbasids

The founder of the new dynasty was a powerful and ruthless man named Abu al-Abbas. He had himself proclaimed the true caliph in Persia in 749 and marched at once on Damascus. With him marched the disaffected of the Arab Empire. There were, as always, poor men hoping to better their lot under the new regime. There were Shiites who, believing that only blood ties with Muhammad could confer legitimacy on a caliph, were duly impressed by Abu al-Abbas's assertion of kinship with the Prophet. There was, finally, a group with a powerful future in Islam: the new, non-Arab converts to the faith who had been relegated to second-class status among the faithful.

The new dynasty would not make poor men rich, nor would it turn the Shiite heresy into orthodoxy. But over the two centuries of their actual supremacy—and the five centuries of their nominal rule—the Abbasids would preside over a complete transformation of the ruling class of Islam. The Arab conquerors would merge with the ancient aristocracy of Persia, and with Turks and even Mongols, vigorous new converts from the nomadic northern steppes.

With this support from the disaffected, Abu al-Abbas seized Damascus in 750. He invited all the princes of the defeated Umayyad clan to a conciliatory banquet—and sent the executioners in. Afterwards, according to legend, the victorious Abbasids enjoyed the meal themselves.

Among the Abbasids there were names more famous than that of the founder. The most celebrated was the legendary Harun al-Rashid, the wealthy, sophisticated caliph immortalized in *The Arabian Nights,* who ruled in the decades around 800. The most beneficent was perhaps his cultivated son, Mamun the Great. There were still fighters among them too—the pleasure-loving Harun fought many military campaigns. But the political history of the dynasty during its first two centuries—the period of its real power—was dominated by three new trends: centralization, secession, and the gradual decline of Arab supremacy at the center of the web.

Some sort of centralization of government power was clearly necessary if the Abbasids were to rule so vast a realm at all. By the time of Abu al-Abbas, the Arabs nominally governed territories that stretched from Spain to Afghanistan. Building on Umayyad beginnings and drawing as their predecessors had on the long experience of the Persians in particular, the Abbasid dynasty constructed an elaborate system of administration.

Persian influence became crucially important to the emerging Arab Empire. Persian aristocrats converted to Islam and continued to form an important part of Baghdad's Islamic elite. Besides staffing the emerging administration of the Arab Empire, Persians also helped reorganize a guerrilla Arab army into a more tightly structured military machine.

Baghdad, the new Abbasid capital, thus became the center of an impressive bureaucratic structure. At its head, just beneath the caliph himself, stood the grand vizier (chief counselor), a position that might also have become hereditary if Harun al-Rashid had not shrewdly decided to root out the family that had come to dominate the office in his reign. Beneath the vizier, the will of the caliph was to be carried out by provincial governors all across the empire. Governorships did become hereditary, and the central authority did not always reach effectively into distant provinces dominated by local dynasties. Yet there was a structure of authority, which in the person of the *qadi,* the judge and authority on Muslim law in almost every town and city, reached even to the local level. It was a governmental system far superior to that of contemporary Europe, then struggling out of the earliest Middle Ages into the uncertain light of the Carolingian Renaissance.

A structure of power thus grew up under the Abbasids. But not all the caliph's far-flung realms accepted his authority. Secession also spread, fragmenting the western portions of the empire in particular. Only one of the Umayyad princes escaped Abu's executioners in 750; five years later he founded an independent Umayyad caliphate in Spain. Other secessionist regimes established themselves across North Africa: in Morocco in 788, in Tunis in 800, and the Fatimid dynasty, which traced its lineage back to Muhammad's daughter Fatima, in Egypt in 868. A separatist movement even succeeded in eastern Persia in 820. All these remained part of the great body of Islamic religion, civilization, and commerce, but politically they were lost to the Arab government in Baghdad.

An even more dangerous threat to the Arab predominance, finally, was nourished within the empire itself. As the descendants of the Arab conquerors settled into splendor in Baghdad, other peoples came to the fore. Persian power predominated increasingly in council and among the cadres of lesser officials. At the same time, a new wave of hardy nomads infiltrated the empire from the Eurasian steppes. Among them the Seljuk and Ottoman Turks and the Mongols were to be the most important for the future of Islam.

The Turks infiltrated the frontier cities first, often coming as mercenary soldiers. Sometimes whole tribes of them accepted conversion. By the middle of the ninth century, less than a hundred years after the Abbasids had seized power, Turkish guards were providing the caliph with the heart of his standing army. They proved their value as willing repressers of disorders among the native peoples of the caliphate. In time they became as powerful in Arab affairs as the Praetorian Guard had been in Rome.

The Persians, however, were the first to profit from the decline of Arab vitality and power. In 946 a Persian general unmade one caliph and made another a puppet, content to live in Persia and rule as his masters willed. The Abbasids would reign in name only for three more centuries, till 1258. But Persians and Turks dominated the empire in the east, and secessionist regimes still flourished in the west. Abbasid splendor was not diminished, but Abbasid power was a shadow of what the Arabs had once wielded. The peoples of the northern steppe soon replaced the people of the southern desert as the masters and builders of Islam.

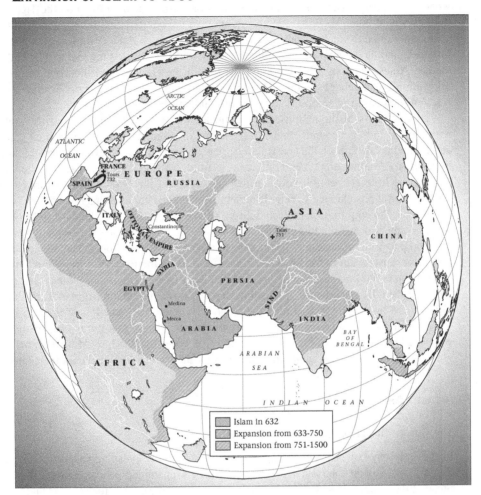

Islam in 632
Expansion from 633-750
Expansion from 751-1500

The Splendors of Baghdad

Through all the conflicts and transformations outlined above, the Arab Empire in general and the Abbasid caliphate in particular did much to advance the welfare of their subjects. The Arab peace fostered agriculture in Egypt and Persia, in Muslim Sicily and Spain. Most important, the spread of a common culture across a wide swath of the Old World encouraged trade, by caravan and swift Arab dhow, from Spain to India.

A common language and religion, a Muslim law code based on the life of the merchant and the caravan town all encourage commercial development. And commerce in turn contributed to the development of handicraft industry; Damascus steel, Córdoba leather, and silks and cottons from the East were all internationally known. The tales of *The Arabian Nights* include mouthwatering descriptions of Baghdad bazaars heaped with good things, from Syrian apples and Arabian peaches to perfumes and incense, aloewood, musk, and candles of Alexandria wax.

Baghdad itself—"City of Peace, Gift of God, Paradise on Earth"—was one of the wonders of the age. Built up by the Abbasids from a small market town on the Tigris, the third capital of Islam (after Mecca and Damascus) grew into a city that rivaled even Constantinople in size, wealth, and beauty. Palaces and gardens, the domes and minarets of mosques, and the endless bustle and color of the bazaars dazzled the eye and bewildered the ear. Arabs, Persians, Turks, and all the rest of the empire's kaleidoscope of peoples mingled in the streets of the city. There were many libraries, a House of Wisdom for the study of theology, and an observatory for the study of the stars.

At the courts of the caliphs, poetry, music, and the other arts all flourished, along with the self-indulgence indigenous to the courts of princes. There were fragrant gardens and fountains, alabaster halls and Kabul carpets, robes of silk and jeweled turbans enough to outfit any Arabian night's entertainment in fitting splendor. At first glance there would seem to be little connection between that paradise and the lives of the majority of the faithful the caliphs claimed to rule. But there were crucial connections nonetheless.

Across the empire, in a thousand dusty villages set among the slender trunks of date palms, farmers drove plodding beasts that turned their water wheels, or squatted around the food pots as their ancestors had done and their descendants would continue to do. But now there was a *Qadi* in the town to enforce the Law of the Prophet. From time to time a caravan came tinkling past and stopped to display unlikely wares from far away. At times, a black-robed, black-turbaned Abbasid prince might ride by with a troop of Turkish mercenaries, on his way east to defend the frontier. Whether they knew it or not, the life of those silent farmers tending their immemorial water wheels was the better for the men who ruled in Baghdad, for the commerce, the protection, and the Law of the Prophet—the good things that Baghdad symbolized and in varying degrees provided over the centuries.

THE FAITH AND ART OF ISLAM

The Quran, the Law, and the Five Pillars of Islam

In the early days of Islam, the simplicity of the religion of Allah appealed to Christians, Zoroastrians, pagans, and other potential converts. Muhammad had fixed upon the Black Stone of the Kaaba, allegedly cast down from heaven, as the earthly focus of his faith. In the beginning any enclosed area with a clearly designated side facing Mecca seems to have done for a mosque. Beyond that there was only the Book, the Law, and the worship they enjoined.

The Quran, the sacred book of Islam, was spoken aloud by Muhammad in oracular, poetic verse in a series of revelations over a period of more than twenty years. These prophecies and injunctions, taken down by disciples, were assembled within a few years of the Prophet's death into a book about the size of the Christian New Testament. Its 114 *suras*, or chapters, are composed in Arabic poetry so moving that Muslims regard this alone as evidence of its divine origin. Small boys memorize its thousands of verses entire, and grown men weep when it is chanted in the mosque.

The faith whose essence is Submission (*Islam*) to the will of God (Allah) begins with a *sura* often described as the Lord's Prayer of Islam:

In the name of Allah, the Beneficent, the Merciful.
Praise be to Allah, Lord of the Worlds,
The Beneficent, the Merciful.

Ibn al-Hajj, the author of this description of public education in Muslim Egypt, composed a number of tracts on religion and morals. By the "private parts of the body" he means anything except the face and hands of the young women students. Have you heard of Islamic societies that require women to conceal even these? Note, however, that whatever Ibn al-Hajj thought about it, these women evidently felt no hesitation about getting involved in the educational process.

[Consider] what some women do when people [that is, men] gather with a shaikh to hear [the recitation of] books. At that point women come, too, to hear the readings; the men sit in one place, the women facing them. It even happens at such times that some of the women are carried away by the situation; one will stand up, and sit down, and shout in a loud voice. [Moreover,] private parts of her body will appear; in her house, their exposure would be forbidden—how can it be allowed in a mosque, in the presence of men?

J. P. Berkey, "Women and Islamic Education in the Mamluk Period," in Nikki R. Keddie and Beth Baron, eds., *Women in Middle Eastern History* (New Haven: Yale University Press, 1991), p. 103.

> Owner of the Day of Judgment,
> Thee (alone) we worship; Thee (alone) we ask
>   for help. (*The Quran*, I, 1–5)

The briefest summary of the faith, offered daily in the mosque, goes simply: "There is no God but Allah, and Muhammad is his prophet."

The most obvious differences between Islam and the Christian tradition lies in the part played by Muhammad himself in the Islamic revelation. The Muslim Prophet claimed no divinity, performed no miracles save the one great miracle of bringing God's will to humanity. The Quran was thus believed to embody God's final revelation, and to be superior to any other holy book.

But the Quran was the beginning, not the end, of the development of the Islamic faith. Theology came to Islam a century after Muhammad's death. Muslims argued like theologians of other religions over such abstruse points as predestination, major and minor sins, the role of reason in expounding the faith. But it was in the Muslim Law that the theological genius of Islam was expressed most strikingly.

The Islamic Law is an attempt to bring the Islamic faith to bear on every aspect of the life of the believer. The Arab compilers of the Law sought to explicate God's will toward people in such detail that the faithful need never be in doubt about how a good Muslim ought to act in any situation. Experts in the Law—the *qadis*—sat in the market squares of all Muslim towns, adjudicating civil disputes and ruling in criminal cases on the basis of their detailed knowledge of the words of the Prophet and the traditions of his faith.

The compilation of Islamic Law was a monumental effort undertaken in the earlier Muslim centuries by the *ulama*, the body of Muslim scholars. These learned men drew upon four sources of divine truth: the Quran, the traditions, consensus, and analogy.

The Quran itself stood first in authority, of course. When the Quran provided no clear direction, the *ulama* turned to the *hadith*, the traditional accounts of the Prophet's deeds and opinions expressed outside the Quran. The scholarly study of these traditions occupied generations of Islamic scholarship.

Where neither the *hadith* nor the Quran offered sufficient insight, the Law was based on the consensus of the Islamic community, on the theory that God would not allow the faithful to be in error about any important matter down the centuries. Finally, where all else failed, the makers of the Islamic Law undertook to reason by analogy; if the Prophet forbade wine, for instance, this prohibition might be extended to other intoxicants as well.

The result was an immense body of *Sunna,* or traditional requirements and prohibitions concerning religion, personal morality, social conduct, and political behavior. Business and marital relations, criminal law, ritual practices, and much more were covered in this vast system. Even where central government broke down, Islamic Law provided an effective framework for living for peoples all across the Islamic world.

Besides the Quran and the Law, lifelong routines of worship welded Islam into a cultural unity. From the earliest centuries the Islamic faith had five essential practices, the Five Pillars of Islam: witnessing to one's belief that there is no God but God, and Muhammad is his Prophet; praying in the mosque five times each day; alms-giving and other forms of charity for the less fortunate; fasting from dawn to dusk during the holy month of Ramadan; and pilgrimage, particularly the great pilgrimage to Mecca that every Muslim dreams of making at least once in a lifetime.

The Book, the Law, and the life of Islam thus blended to produce one of the most successful of all the major religions of humankind. But like all religions, the Muslim faith had its divisions and revisions. And these too are part of the story of the intercontinental reach of Islam.

Shiites and Sufis

Sectarian divisions broke out early in Islamic history. Theology, history, and the mystical impulses to which all religions are liable all helped to divide the faith of the Prophet.

The most historically important sectarian outbreaks, however, were rooted in the political realities of the early Muslim centuries. The most long-lived and devastating of these Muslim religious schisms was the Shiite revolt, which began in the first century after

The ninth-century mosque of Ibn Tulun in Cairo shows the open Abbasid form, with minarets and an arcade around the central court. Like the cathedral shown in the preceding chapter and the temples in the next chapter, this thousand-year-old mosque is still in use today. (Carolyn Brown/Photo Researchers, Inc.)

Muhammad's death and has persisted to the present. It began with the murder of the fourth caliph, Ali, son-in-law to the Prophet, and the accession of the Umayyad dynasty. The Shiites were those Muslims who objected to the Umayyad succession on the grounds that only descendants of Ali and Muhammad's daughter Fatima—Ali's wife—could be legitimate successors to the Prophet. In time the Shiites became opponents of the whole orthodox, traditional approach taken by the Sunni majority. Habituated to martyrdom at the hands of the orthodox, Shiite Muslims remain today a powerful movement, particularly in that part of ancient Persia that is now Iran.

The most successful new direction in the Islamic religion, however, was the Sufi movement. The Sufis were Muslim mystics, seekers after Islamic truth through direct spiritual experience. Like Buddhist or Christian monks, Sufis reacted to the increasing worldliness of the caliphate by stressing self-denial. They saw asceticism as the beginning of the arduous road to mystical union with Allah.

They began their preaching in the seventh century, the first century of Islam. For some time the oddness and immediacy of Sufi religious experience brought them into conflict with the keepers of the Book and the Law. One of the most famous of all Sufi seekers, al-Hallaj, was crucified in the tenth century for asserting, "I am the Absolute Truth."[2] In time, however, Sufism found its place and became an immense influence in Islam. By the twelfth century there were orders of Sufis all across the Muslim world, each with its revered masters and saints, its diverse practices and doctrines, its own version of the mystic way to union with Allah.

These ceremonies included chanting, rhythmic motion, and sometimes the singing of Sufi poems to musical accompaniment. In a murky atmosphere of incense and ritual, prayers, incantations, and invocations of angelic beings, these Sufi performance could bring the adept into a state of religious exaltation.

The Sufis were among the most effective propagators of the faith to unbelievers. Their direct, emotional approach could touch the hearts of potential converts. Later would come Arabic and the Quran, the *qadi* and the Law. But simple faith, a call to the heart, ecstasies and trances were a quicker way to win new converts to the teachings of a Prophet who had himself been summoned to his task by angelic voices.

Islamic Art: Mosques and Minarets

In the Arab Empire, as wherever the faith of the Prophet spread, religious experience and theological prescriptions profoundly influenced the practice of the arts. The most obvious example of this influence is the Muslim ban on the depiction of the human figure in art. This prohibition, honored particularly in the broad spectrum of religious art, all but abolished sculpture and severely limited the figurative element in painting. This rejection of the representational also contributed to the highly abstract nature of Islamic design. Muslim art thus stressed geometric shapes, arabesque curvilinear patterns abstracted from floral designs, and religious maxims in angular or flowing Arabic scripts used as decorative motifs.

The overwhelming influence of religion also made itself felt in more positive ways. Like the cathedral in medieval Christendom, the mosque became the most characteristic artistic achievement of the Muslim peoples, and architecture generally their central art.

---

[2]Annemarie Schimmel, *Mystical Dimensions of Islam* (Chapel Hill: University of North Carolina Press, 1975), p. 72.

A muezzin calls the faithful to prayer from the minaret that is part of every mosque complex. A recorded call has replaced the muezzin in many modern mosques, but the call still goes out five times every day. (Getty Images, Inc.)

The mosque was the center of any Arab town. Its essential features as a place of worship include a large court with a fountain for ceremonial ablutions; a prayer hall with a wall facing Mecca; a decorated niche in that wall providing a focus for the devotions of the faithful; and a pulpit near this niche for readings from the Quran and for sermons. The most readily recognizable element, however, is the tall, often slender tower called a minaret, from which the faithful are called to prayer five times daily.

This simple pattern of court and hall, with inner and outer adjuncts, proved capable of immense elaboration. Typical Arab extrapolations included the addition of an impressive facade flanked by towering minarets, roofed galleries around the courtyard, and forests of pillars in the prayer hall itself. The Great Mosque of Córdoba, built by the Umayyad caliphs of Spain, and the Fatimid Mosque of El-Hakim in Cairo follow this elaborated model.

Other characteristic types of Muslim architecture include the *madrasah,* or Muslim seminary, the mausoleums of sultans and saints, bazaars, and royal palaces. Of the few palaces that survive, the late medieval Alhambra with its famous Lion Court, located in the Spanish city of Granada, is by far the best known. The immense "desert castles," such as that of Ukhaydir in the sea of sand south of Baghdad, give us only the roughest idea of what Abbasid Baghdad itself must have been like in its glory.

Muslims were masters of all the decorative arts—ceramics and tiles, metalwork and textiles, calligraphy, the art of miniature, and many more. A gilded and illuminated copy of the Quran is a thing of beauty to set beside any medieval Christian Bible. But nowhere did the decorative artistry of the Muslim peoples stand out more clearly than in their efforts to express "the experience of the infinite" in the Muslim house of prayer, the mosques that are the glory of Islam.

Arab Literature: Poems and Tales

The mosque is a luminous artistic achievement accessible in some degree, at least, even to the non-Muslim. The same cannot be said for the literature and thought of Islam. Poetry, fiction, history and biography, philosophy, and the sciences all seem to date more rapidly than the direct formal statements of architectural design and decorative motif. Between the modern Western reader and the words and ideas of the medieval Arab Empire lies a gap as great in time as that which separates us from our own Middle Ages—and an even greater cultural divide. Nevertheless, a glimpse must be attempted, particularly into Arab literature, which is one of the great literatures of the world.

Arabic literature began as verse, the oral poetry of the desert Arabs. Arab bards celebrated the greatness of their clans and the perfidy of their enemies; they described the harsh beauty of their desert world and the joys of fighting and fast riding. By the time Muhammad came, Arabic poetry was a highly developed art, and it was the poetic language of the desert Arabs that the Prophet used in speaking the revelations of the Quran.

Arab experience of the world changed drastically after Muhammad, however, and in the centuries that followed, both the subjects and the forms of Arabic literature expanded dramatically. Wine songs, love songs, and poems of a markedly mystical tone replaced the older verses devoted to horses and camels and the pride of the clan. Verse forms became more complex still, and poets reached for more ingenious metaphors, more complicated tropes and figures than before. From the celebration of a hard ride over the desert, they moved to al Masudi's famous ode to the banquet table or Ibn Hazm's frequently erotic *Ring of the Dove:*

> Her body was a jasmine rare,
> Her perfume sweet as amber scent
> Her face a pearl beyond compare,
> Her all, pure light's embodiment. . . .[3]

Arabic prose was as varied and ingenious as Arabic poetry. This was the golden age of the professional Arab storyteller, whose repertoire of popular romantic tales was often arranged in cycles like that of *The Arabian Nights.* Collections of brief anecdotes were also popular, ranging in content from the most pious to downright bawdy tales. Styles varied from the easy flow of the teller of tales to the most elaborate rhetorical devices. The Arabs appreciated a flow of literary eloquence, whether it was the simple tale of the desert bard or the ornate literary construct of a court poet.

Philosophy and Science: Knowledge Lights the Way to Heaven

More substantial genres flourished during the centuries of Arab greatness. Biographies of Muhammad and of Muslim saints and scholars, histories of the caliphs and their wars, of the great cities of the Islamic world—Mecca, Damascus, Baghdad—and general accounts of the history of the Arabs and the civilization of Islam all appeared from the eighth century on. Travel books and geographies surveyed the Mediterranean world and took readers as far afield as central Europe and East Asia. Collections and encyclopedias multiplied on the bookshelves of Arabic scholars.

In all this array of learning, Arabic philosophy and science were perhaps the fields known and admired the most widely.

Arab philosophy, like medieval European theology, drew upon translations of the works of ancient Greek thinkers. Aristotle, Plato, and the Neoplatonists were all still readily available in the Greek-speaking Byzantine region when the Arabs swept in. Much of

---

[3]Ibn Hazm, *The Ring of the Dove,* in A. J. Arberry, *Aspects of Islamic Civilization* (Ann Arbor: University of Michigan Press, 1967), p. 186.

the Arabs' own philosophizing, therefore, took the form of commentaries on the ancients. Avicenna's vast encyclopedias of philosophic knowledge and Averroes's commentaries on Aristotle, both monuments to Arab scholarship, were clearly rooted in the thinking of the ancient Greeks.

Arab philosophers of the ninth and tenth centuries, however, embarked upon some daring speculative paths of their own. Muslim philosophers meditate more boldly than medieval Christian thinkers on such matters as the creation and nature of the universe, divine providence, and even the relative value of rational philosophy and revealed religion as roads to an understanding of the world. From the end of the eleventh century on, however, such speculations came under fire from religious fundamentalists, and philosophical originality and daring declined in the Arab world thereafter.

The sciences bloomed among the Arabs as they had nowhere else in the western half of Eurasia since Hellenistic times. Arab scientists excelled particularly in astronomy and mathematics, where they made important contributions to algebra and trigonometry. They added significantly to the world's store of knowledge in optics, pharmacology, and other branches of natural science. Arab alchemy and astrology—recognized sciences everywhere in those days—were considered authoritative in Europe. The reputation of Arab medical expertise was so high in the West that Christian kings preferred Saracen physicians to Christian doctors.

"Knowledge," the Prophet had said, "enables its possessor to distinguish what is forbidden from what is not; it lights the way to Heaven."[4] It led at least some of its devotees to other sources than the revelations of the Arab merchant of Mecca. During the Arab golden age, however, the faith of Muhammad and the ideas of ancient Greeks and Hindu Indians were able to coexist within Islam, a striking testimony to the flexibility of this world religion.

SUMMARY

The first half-dozen centuries after the coming of the Prophet Muhammad—the period of the Arab predominance in the Muslim world—was one of the great ages of Islamic history.

Muhammad preached his gospel in Arabia in the seventh century of the Christian calendar—the first century of the Muslim one. Muhammad's inspiration turned a rabble of desert bedouin and a scattering of oasis traders into an Arab army embarked upon a holy war. This first great *jihad* carried Muslim power across North Africa, up into Europe, and back across the Middle East in less than a century.

The Arab Empire that resulted was ruled by two successive dynasties of caliphs ("successors to the Prophet"), the Umayyads (661–750) and the Abbasids (750–1258). From the seventh through the tenth century, this first Muslim empire brought a degree of political order, real commercial prosperity, and unparalleled spiritual unity to this broad central swath of the Old World. Baghdad was one of the world's great metropolises, and even humble villagers benefited from Islamic Law and Arab protection.

The history of the Arab Empire after 1000 saw a decline in its material strength. Western provinces from Egypt to Spain seceded. In the east, Persians and Turks became

---

[4]Syed Ameer Ali, *The Spirit of Islam* (London: Chatto & Windus, 1964), p. 360.

the real political powers under the later Abbasids. The rise of medieval Christian power raised the possibility of a serious challenge to Islam in western Eurasia. The faith of the Prophet, however, continued to generate one of the greatest of world cultures.

Islam, built on the Quran, Islamic tradition, and the Islamic Law, provided a framework for living throughout the Arab domains. Sects of Sufi mystics offered a more emotional expression of Islam and were particularly effective as missionaries for the faith.

Muslim art produced beautiful mosques, while Arab scholarship explored and expanded Islamic theology as well as Greek philosophy and science. Arab literature, building on a poetry that predated the Prophet and was incarnated in the verse of the Quran itself, found expression in a glittering spectrum of sophisticated poetry and prose.

The cultivated and worldly court of Harun al-Rashid in ninth-century Baghdad was a far cry from the marketplace at Mecca where Muhammad had preached. But Islam, like medieval Christendom, remained a profoundly religious hegemony.

SUGGESTED READING

Armstrong, K. *Muhammad: A Biography of the Prophet.* San Francisco: Harper, 1992. Useful account of a life too unfamiliar in the West. See also W. E. Phipps, *Muhammad and Jesus: A Comparison of the Prophets and Their Teachings* (New York: Continuum, 1996).

Bonner M. *Aristocratic Violence and Holy War: Studies in the Jihad and the Arab-Byzantine Frontier.* New Haven, Conn.: American Oriental Society, 1996. Political and theoretical forces within the Islamic world forge the concept of holy war.

Crone, P., and M. Hinds. *God's Caliph: Religious Authority in the First Centuries of Islam.* New York: Cambridge University Press, 1986. Challenges the view that the caliphs early abandoned their religious role in Islam for purely political functions.

Dunn, R. E. *The Adventures of Ibn Battuta: A Muslim Traveler of the Fourteenth Century.* Berkeley and Los Angeles: University of California Press, 1986. Scholarly, thoroughly readable account of the life and voyages of the great Muslim traveler.

Ettinghausen, R. *Islamic Art and Architecture, 650–1250.* New Haven: Yale University Press, 2001. New edition of a valuable survey. See also R. Hillenbrand, *Islamic Architecture: Form, Function, and Meaning* (New York: Columbia University Press, 1994), in which Islamic architecture is described, particularly in terms of religious function.

Ghazzali, A. H. M. *The Alchemy of Happiness,* trans. C. Field. New York: Sharpe, 1991. Eleventh-century Arab summary of Islamic values, with emphasis on the Sufi way.

Grube, Ernest J. *The World of Islam.* New York: McGraw-Hill, n.d. Clearly written, very well-illustrated coverage of Islamic arts and architecture by region and period.

Gutas, D. *Greek Thought, Arabic Culture: The Graeco-Arabic Translation Movement in Baghdad and Early Àbbasid Society.* London and New York: Routledge, 1998. The rescue of ancient Greek thought by medieval Arab scholars.

Guthrie, S. *Arab Social Life in the Middle Ages.* London: Saqi Books, 1995. Brief, broad, and scholarly.

Hawting, G. R. *The First Dynasty of Islam: The Umayyad Caliphate* A.D. *661–750.* London: Routledge, 2000. Brief introduction to the caliphs who succeeded the Prophet's own contemporaries and relatives.

Hill, D. R. *Studies in Medieval Islamic Technology.* Brookfield, Vt.: Ashgate, 1998. A grabbag of studies, including many on Arabs and early machinery.

Hodgson, M. G. S. *The Venture of Islam: Conscience and History in a World Civilization* (3 vols.), Chicago: University of Chicago Press, 1974. An impressive interpretive study of Islamic history, beliefs, and values.

Keddie, N. R., and B. Baron, eds. *Women in Middle Eastern History*. New Haven, Conn.: Yale University Press, 1991. Scholarly papers on Muslim women in various times and places, including the Arab Empire.

Kennedy, H. *The Armies of the Caliphs: Military and Society in the Early Islamic State*. London and New York: Routledge, 2001. Part of a valuable series on warfare and history, a subject too often neglected by historians.

Lassner, J. *The Shaping of Abbasid Rule*. Princeton, N.J.: Princeton University Press, 1980. Scholarly recent account of the Baghdad caliphate.

Mernissi, F. *The Veil and the Male Elite: A Feminist Interpretation of Women's Rights in Islam*. Reading, Mass.: Addison Wesley, 1991. A less positive interpretation than many of the status of women in Islamic societies. But see also Mernissi's *The Forgotten Queens of Islam* (Minneapolis: University of Minnesota Press, 1993), which sees women playing an important part in the politics of the Islamic world.

Peters, F. E. *Allah's Commonwealth: A History of Islam in the Near East A.D. 600–1100*. New York: Simon and Schuster, 1973. A good overview of the subject.

Rahman, F. *Islam*. 2nd ed. Chicago: University of Chicago Press, 1979. Excellent concise summary of Islamic ideas and institutions: a good place to begin.

 Please refer to the document CD-ROM for primary sources related to this chapter.

CHAPTER 11

MERCHANTS AND MISSIONARIES OF THE INDIES
India and Southeast Asia
(600–1500)

A Glance Ahead: India's Domination of Southern Asia

Like Christian Europe and the Islamic zone, "India" was a culturally defined region rather than a single country during this period of its history. The Gupta Empire had crumbled, and the Mughal Empire would not reunify India until after 1500. The many Indian states, however, shared a religious culture based on Hinduism, Buddhism, or, toward the end of this period, Islam. Much of India also accepted the ancient caste system, rule by hereditary rajas, and roads and harbors full of energetic traders.

Indian merchants and missionaries had already spread this culture to South Asian neighbors from the Himalayas to Ceylon. Now they moved on to the next great southward bulge of land to the east—the enormous peninsula and thousands of islands we call Southeast Asia today.

You can still find Hindu temples, Buddhist monasteries, and countless Muslim mosques across that zone today. And much of the money that paid for these pious works came from the network of regional trade developed by Indian merchants in this age of expanding cultural zones.

India Between the Guptas and the Mughals

Attempts at Unity: Harsha and the Delhi Sultanate

The political history of India for much of the thousand years between the decline of Gupta rule in the fifth century and the coming of the Mughal dynasty not long after 1500 is a tangle of short-lived states, foreign invasions, and power struggles leading nowhere. Some of the peoples of this millennium, such as the chivalric Rajput princes in the north and the ambitious Cholas in the south, left a mark on India's history. There were also two significant attempts at national conquest: the empire of King Harsha and the Turkish regime called the Delhi Sultanate. But none of these matched the political achievements of the Mauryas and Guptas before them or the Mughal Empire to come.

The seventh-century reign of King Harsha (607–647) saw a brief futile attempt to impose order on the peoples and kingdoms of the subcontinent. The cultured warrior King Harsha conquered all of northern India from the Himalayas to the river Narmada, the traditional divide between northern India and the Deccan. Between campaigns, he—like Charlemagne two centuries later—patronized religion and the arts and gave lavishly to the poor. Considerably more literate than the great Frankish king, Harsha may actually have written the plays and poems that are attributed to him.

He moved his capital from Patna, the traditional center of political unification since the Mauryas, to the city of Kanauj farther up the Ganges valley. But—again like Charlemagne—he controlled his north Indian empire primarily by moving about it at the head of his army. The empire itself was probably no more than a loose collection of kingdoms and principalities, and most Indians could have been little affected by the transitory power at Kanauj. With Harsha's death, his empire crumbled and political division reasserted itself.

The second significant effort to impose order on the subcontinent was the work of foreigners—the Turkish Afghan regime known as the Delhi Sultanate, which dominated much of northern India from the thirteenth into the sixteenth century. It was an impressive span of years, but the size of the realm the newcomers ruled varied drastically from reign to reign. For a few years in the fourteenth century, Sultan Jalal ud-din Khalji held at least feudal suzerainty over most of the kingdoms of the south as well as northern India. But this was exceptional, and during the fifteenth and early sixteenth centuries the Turkish sultans really governed little beyond the immediate environs of the city of Delhi itself.

They did make this city, still farther up the Ganges, into the third political center of northern India—and New Delhi is the nation's capital today. But the Delhi sultans had only a rudimentary system of administration, and their rule was essentially feudal. Provincial governors were really soldiers granted control of villages or larger territories in return for military service. These local rulers governed only as far as their troops could reach. Again, most Indians had little significant contact with those who claimed to govern them.

Challenge from the South: The Cholas

More effective governance may have emerged in southern India, the home of several Tamil-speaking Dravidian kingdoms in this period. The kingdom of the Cholas in particular apparently had a more centralized administrative system based on unions of villages. It

THE DELHI SULTANATE AND ITS NEIGHBORS

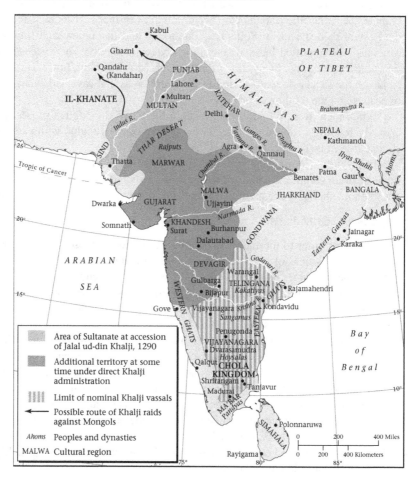

also produced powerful rulers like Rajaraja I (985–1014) and Rajendra I (1014–1042). Great conquerors as well as effective governors, these men extended Chola rule both north and south, from Bengal to Ceylon. For a time it seemed possible that the Cholas would reverse the historic pattern by conquering northern India from a southern base. More striking still in this age of expanding zones of power, Rajendra I dispatched fleets east across the Bay of Bengal to impose temporary Chola rule in parts of Burma, Malaya, and the country-sized island of Sumatra.

Chola dominance in the south lasted the better part of three centuries before its thirteenth-century decline and fall. And despite effective individual rulers and administrative skills, village autonomy remained great. Its major achievements, as we will see, were once again economic and cultural.

Invasions and Divisions

Besides political disunity, another disturbing feature of the history of those centuries of disarray was the unending series of invasions from without and power struggles within the subcontinent.

Among the foreign invaders who took advantage of India's weakness to push down through the passes of the Northwest Frontier were the White Huns who undermined the Guptas, the Arabs, the Rajputs who became India's military aristocracy, the Muslim Turks who established the Delhi Sultanate, Tamerlane and his Tatars, and finally the Muslim Mughals who reunified India at last in the sixteenth century. This succession of nomadic invasions made things lively along the frontier. Most of them, however, made scarcely a ripple on the steady flow of Indian life that went on as it always had beneath the marching of armies and the feuding of princes.

When there were no new hordes swarming down the Afghan passes, there was still princely feuding to contend with. Two major power struggles within the subcontinent should at least be mentioned here.

In the north, during the centuries following the brief meteoric passage of Harsha, three separate kingdoms struggled to dominate his short-lived empire. There was no decisive outcome but only the gradual decline and fragmentation of the contenders.

Rajputs and Dravidians

But there was order to the Indian experience, even during these disordered centuries. Beneath the aimlessness of politics, profound social and cultural changes were taking place. Many of these changes represent continuations of earlier trends. But they reached a climax of sorts during the millennium of political disarray between the Guptas and the Mughals.

The greatest social transformation, a continuation of a much older tradition, was the absorption of new peoples into the already complex fabric of Indian society. This was basically the result of creative compromise by Hindu India's brahman elite, who found room in the ancient caste system for the newcomers. Thus, when nomadic invaders such as the Rajputs actually settled in India, their leaders would be accepted as *kshatriyas* (the ancient Aryan warrior caste), less prominent tribesmen as *sudras* (farmers), and even their priests as brahmans of a sort. Like Mongols in China or Germans in the Roman world, these steppe peoples were typically seduced by life in the host culture's rich cities and princely courts and were glad to be part of it. As caste allegiances grew among the new peoples, old loyalties to tribe and clan decreased, until the newcomers were thoroughly assimilated into the polyglot Indian population.

The patterned movement of Shiva Nataraja, Lord of the Dance, symbolizes the pulsing cosmic energy of the universe. This famous figure of the multiarmed god, grinding the demon of ignorance underfoot as he dances the universe into being, is a product of the Dravidian Hindu imagination of southern India. The god holds an hourglass-shaped drum in one of his four hands, fire in another, symbols of his power to awaken the natural world to life and to destroy it at the end of a cosmic cycle. ("Shiva Nataraja" 13th-Century Scultpure-Bronze-Indian, 34.25 × 27.5 × 13 inches [87 × 69.9 × 33 cm]). (The Nelson–Atkins Museum of Art)

The fiercely proud Rajputs—"Sons of Kings"—in particular provided ruling houses for many north and central Indian kingdoms. They fought chivalric wars with one another, provided the strongest military force India could muster against subsequent invaders, and still compose an important part of the Indian army's officer corps today. As *kshatriyas,* their warlike proclivities were thus channeled into the service of the ancient Indian society that had absorbed them.

A similar process of assimilation went on in south India. The great triangle of peninsular India had been the haven of the Dravidian peoples driven south by the conquering Aryans many centuries before. Dravidians, particularly the Tamil-speaking people of the far south, had built a flourishing city-based society on foreign trade and agriculture during the preceding half-dozen centuries. The absorption of the Dravidian south into a single cultural zone with northern India, however, dates from approximately the year 500.

Again, the vehicle was the spread of Hinduism and the caste system. The worship of the great Hindu divinities Vishnu and Shiva grew in the south, and Sanskrit began to challenge Tamil as the literary language. Above all, a modified caste system—almost excluding the warrior *kshatriyas* but containing many "untouchable" groups—was gradually imposed upon Dravidian society.

Henceforth, the Indian subcontinent would constitute a single zone of culture, though there would continue to be significant regional differences. The north would remain politically dominant; the south would be a center of artistic and intellectual development.

Caste and Sex

Another important change during this period—again a continuation of an older trend—was the rigidification of the caste system. The number of castes continued to grow far beyond the four original divisions generated at the time of the Aryan-Dravidian synthesis. Categories and subcategories multiplied, and the obligations imposed by membership in a given caste grew more elaborate—and more rigorous. Respect for caste grew especially as Buddhism—which had ignored caste distinctions—declined in India. And new recruits, among northern tribesmen or in the Dravidian south, took up the system with the fervor of converts.

There was still some freedom of choice in occupation, and marriages across caste lines could occur, if perhaps uncommonly. But the direction of development toward a caste-bound society was clearly established during these centuries before 1500.

The freedom of women in society, which would come to be curtailed more rigorously in India than in many other places, was considerably less constrained during this millennium. The strict seclusion of respectable women was not common yet. And the cruel practice of self-immolation by widows was still rare; some widows even remarried without losing popular respect. Ladies of the upper classes seem generally to have been educated and cultured during this period. They enjoyed music and dancing and shared freely in the pleasures of life at the courts of the *rajas*.

A FERMENT OF RELIGIONS

Land of Many Faiths

Religion, as we have seen, is one of the great perennials of world history. It would be extremely difficult to find a people in most times and places who did not believe in higher powers and seek supernatural support. Political authority has repeatedly claimed divine sanction, calculating merchants have frequently prayed or consulted their astrologers before setting sail, and both sides in wars have traditionally claimed that God was on their side.

The role of religion in India's long history, however, seems to loom particularly large. Certainly the rich variety of India's religious heritage continued to flourish in this period.

A thousand years ago, while Christians and Muslims burned and crucified famous heretics across their zones of the Old World, there were in the sprawling subcontinent of India separate but generally tolerant communities of Hindus, Buddhists, Jains, animists, Parsis, Muslims, and even some Christians and Jews. But the religious history of the centuries between 500 and 1500 is really concerned with only three of these religions. It is the story of a continued Hindu flowering, of the virtual disappearance of Buddhism in the land of its birth, and of the coming of Islam to India in force.

Hindu Mysticism

Hinduism, as we have seen, played a large part in the assimilation of new peoples into the mainstream of Indian life. In so doing, the Vedic tradition and the dominance of the brahmans were increasingly identified with that Indian mainstream. The brahmans also consecrated new generations of monarchs, conferring the status of *devaraja*, "god-king," and suitably divine ancestors on princes all over India. In the process, the status of the brahmans rose still further, till they were commonly accorded the same sort of spiritual standing and powers that Christian priests enjoyed in Europe. Waves of new converts, royal patrons, and the increasingly exalted spiritual status of the brahmans all helped to advance the cause of India's oldest religion.

Main trends in Hinduism during this period included a variety of mystical paths to salvation. The most important of these mystical schools of religious thought, called Vedanta, was the work of a brahman named Sankaracharya. Seeking to purge traditional Vedic thought of its tangled and sometimes obscure theology, the prophet of Vedanta Hinduism declared the true goal of religion to be quite simple: it was the mystic union of the individual soul of the worshiper with the Absolute Soul of the universe. It was vigorous assertion of an ancient emphasis in Hinduism, and it would be an even more central theme thereafter.

The Decline of Buddhism in India

The decline of Buddhism in the Buddha's own country is perhaps harder to understand. It is sometimes explained by the scarcity of powerful royal patrons to advance the Buddhist cause. Kings in search of sacred support for their right to govern turned increasingly to Hinduism. There were more divine ancestors available in the elaborate pantheon of the brahmans, who had been providing religious sanctions for society and its rulers since Vedic times.

Persecution also undoubtedly played a part, particularly in the Muslim-dominated north. The massacres of Buddhist monks and the burning of monasteries at the time of the establishment of the Delhi Sultanate dealt a fatal blow to Buddhism in the northeast, as well as depriving India as a whole of one of its most vital centers of religious culture.

A more subtle but nonetheless important development was the slow convergence of the Buddhist and Hindu traditions in India. Hinduism became more and more monotheistic in all but name, though the one true god might be Vishnu or Shiva, depending on the cult one belonged to. Since Buddhism was already monotheistic, transferral of allegiance from one faith to the other was made that much easier. Buddha himself was absorbed into some versions of Hinduism as an incarnation of Brahma, like Krishna or Rama in earlier Hindu mythology.

Given the growing prestige of the brahmans, the lack of powerful patrons for Buddhist monks, and the acceptance of Buddhist insights by the older faith, it is not surprising that the number of Buddhist believers dwindled. By 1500 Buddhism was essentially dead in India, while—as we shall see below—it flourished all across Southeast and East Asia.

The Spread of Islam

Islam descended upon northern India in waves during the later centuries of this period. There were Muslim Arabs in the far northwest before 1000, and Muslim Turkish raiders pushed still further into the north in the eleventh century. But it was the Turko-Afghan regime of the Delhi Sultanate in the thirteenth century that made Islam a vital force from the Punjab in the west to the frontiers of Bengal in the east.

In subsequent centuries Islam was to replace Buddhism as India's second religion, until in the first half of the twentieth century a quarter of India's huge population was Muslim. The process began, however, under the Delhi sultans. Some Indians were converted by the sword during the Turkish invasions. More probably accepted Islam as the high road to political advancement, once the sultanate was established. Many, finally, were drawn to the faith of the Prophet by the Sufis, whose mystical approach to religion appealed to the hearts of Indians even when their heads rejected the rigor of Muslim theology and law.

At the upper levels of Indian society, Hindus and Muslims found it quite possible to live in intellectual and religious harmony in these early days. Fifteenth-century Indian religious leaders argued that there were no spiritual differences between Allah and Vishnu. Intellectuals of both faiths sought to understand the Supreme without theological hairsplitting and undue attention to labels. But at the level of worship and ritual, the masses of north Indians had already drawn the line. Music in front of a mosque (where music was forbidden) or a Muslim beef feast (the cow still being sacred to Hindus) could trigger a riot in an Indian town at any time over the past eight centuries.

Tolerance thus had its limits, even in India. To this most religious of peoples, religion has never been a matter of lip service and formal ceremonies. Religious beliefs are woven into their lives. To this day they have remained a source of potentially explosive interaction with other aspects of Indian history.

THE ARTS OF INDIA

The Age of the Temple Builders

The high culture of India during the millennium 500–1500 was thus, as usual, profoundly shaped by religion, and particularly by the renascent Hindu faith. The most striking art forms of this age were religious architecture and sculpture, as combined in the stone temples then beginning to rise all over India. Just as cathedrals and mosques were being built during this period across western Eurasia, this was the age of the temple builders in India.

A Westerner's first impression of an Indian temple is likely to be one of confusion. Here is none of the simplicity of a Greek temple, or even the underlying structure of a gothic cathedral. Buddhist, Jain, and especially Hindu temples of this and later periods, with their beehive-shaped or pyramidal towers and courtyards alive with sculpture, look at first glance rather more like organic growths than human constructs.

In fact, these Indian temples are designed very carefully according to intricate architectural—and metaphysical—principles. The ground plan is a complex of *mandalas,* or squares enclosed in circles, intended to reflect the shape of the world as it was theologically understood at the time. The tower (or *shikara,* meaning "mountain") is the image of the "world mountain," the pillar between heaven and earth, pointing to God. In the north the typical Indo-Aryan *shikara* is shaped rather like a cucumber, or one of the finger-length bananas vendors sell in the streets. In the south, the Dravidian *shikara* is a pyramidal series of terraces of decreasing size, each dedicated to a different god. Over all available surfaces, intricate decorative motifs and the swaying, dancing figures of gods and mortals, animals and plants move round and round the terraces, friezes, bases, and towers.

Whole cities of these great temples—some of them all but deserted now—were built during the centuries between the Guptas and the Mughals across the vast land of India. Perhaps the finest in the Indo-Aryan style is Khajuraho in central India, a score of huge towers (where more than eighty once stood) looming above the plain. Built by Rajput sovereigns a thousand years ago, each mountain of stone, seen closer up, is a mass of detailed, if time-worn, carving.

The Dance of Shiva

This highly developed civilization did produce a complex secular culture over these centuries, ranging from royal biographies and histories of the various Indian kingdoms to popular tales and erotic poetry. Courtly poetry and elaborate critical commentaries on earlier Indian literature also emphasized the sophistication of India's high culture.

Indian culture during this age also combines devotional poems with poems of sexual passion in a wash of sensuality. In the very secular and languorously sexual *Gita Govinda* of Jayadeva, a woman overwhelmed with desire calls upon the god Krishna, manifesting

The <u>Descent of the Ganges</u>. India's sacred river, from heaven to earth is depicted in this celebrated sculpture at Mamallapuram. All earth's teeming life—animal, human, and divine—gathers to give thanks for the divine gift in this awesome life-size granite carving, only a detail of which is shown here. A lush plenitude of figures and detail is as typical of Indian as of European gothic religious art. (New York Public Library Picture Collection)

himself as a very physical lover, as "the joy of her heart," sweet as sugar and mango and wine.[1]

Painters decorated Buddhist manuscripts with vivid illustrations, as medieval European artists illuminated Christian manuscripts. And Indian sculpture continued to bring all the gods and goddesses to vivid life across the subcontinent.

Many different styles developed in the various parts of India, from the elaborate, ornate stone carving of the west to the spare yet elegant bronzes of the south. Yet all projected the sense of burgeoning life characteristic of the art of South Asia. The famous *Descent of the Ganges,* a gigantic bas-relief put from living rock at a temple complex near Madras, shows the sacred river, which once flowed only through heaven, descending at last to earth, to the admiration of all its creatures. Gods and spirits, men and women, graceful deer and lumbering elephants converge upon the holy spot in the great stone panorama.

Even more famous are the widely imitated and worshiped south Indian bronze sculptures of the *Dance of Shiva.* In this vivid pose, the Destroyer is shown dancing the universe back into being. Often wreathed with a ring of fire, trampling the demon of

---

[1]J. D. Yohannan, *A Treasury of Asian Literature* (New York: New American Library, 1956), pp. 298–299.

ignorance, Shiva deploys his four arms gracefully as he moves to the cosmic measure that makes worlds—and destroys them.

Tamil Culture

An outstanding illustration of the minority cultures of divided India during this period is that of the Tamils of southern India. A Dravidian people and the builders of such powerful southern states as that of the Cholas, they also produced a distinctive and brilliant body of literature and art of their own.

Tamil literature is the oldest written literature in India after the classical Sanskrit of the north. Early Tamil poetry evoked heroic deeds going back well before Gupta times. The later Tamil poet Kampan made the ancient *Ramayana* available in the vernacular to Tamil speakers in the southern region where Rama had come to seek his kidnaped bride in the ancient epic. Later Tamil literature also included collections of wise sayings on subjects ranging from love and morality to princely politics.

But religious poetry perhaps flamed more passionately across the Tamil south than any other form. *Bakhti*—emotional personal piety—early challenged more traditional and formal types of worship in the hot south. *Bakhti,* like earlier Buddhism, made religion available to true believers regardless of caste or gender. These Hindu believers, hearts overflowing with love for the god—usually Vishnu, but particularly incarnated as Rama or Krishna—sang ardent hymns and made arduous pilgrimages in his honor. And gifted *bakhti* poets created a vivid literature of devotion.

These songs and hymns often described their religious feelings in terms of such intense human affection as love for a parent, a friend, or a lover. Some of these Tamil poets and musicians expressed their piety so movingly that their hymns were incorporated into the official ceremonies in the temples. Some of them were themselves worshiped as saints in later centuries.

The Indian Sphere of Influence: Southeast Asia

Indian Outreach

This churning center of economic development and religious and cultural ferment inevitably had an impact on neighboring peoples. Even without a single political center, Indian influence on its neighbors was great.

We have seen how Chola rulers from southern India sent naval expeditions to neighboring peoples to the east. The Muslim invasion that established the Delhi Sultanate in the north drove many Buddhist monks out of that part of India, and some of these crossed the Himalayas into Tibet. On that high, desolate plateau, their teachings replaced traditional local shamanism with the distinctive derivative of Buddhism called lamaism, a monkish faith still struggling to survive-and reaching out to a religion—starved world—today.

The most important zone of Indian influence between 600 and 1500, however, was Southeast Asia.

A Pattern of Village Life

We have touched down in Southeast Asia before, usually on our way somewhere else. This collection of islands and peninsulas at the southeastern corner of Asia was the way station for prehistoric immigrants passing on out through the islands toward Australia and Oceania. We have mentioned the beginnings of Chinese imperial penetration into Vietnam and will have more to say about that directly. In the present chapter, we focus on the profound influence of Indian culture on the region as a whole.

Geographically, Southeast Asia juts south between India and China, pointing roughly toward Australia, Mainland Southeast Asia is Myanmar (Burma), Thailand, Cambodia, Laos, Vietnam, and the long curving peninsula of Malasia, with Singapore today at its southern tip. Island Southeast Asia is mostly Indonesia now, including Java where most of the population live, Sumatra, the large central island of Borneo, the heavily touristed island paradise of Bali, and part of New Guinea, just off the Australian coast. Add the Philippines for the eastern flank—and some 13,000 smaller islands scattered between the Indian Ocean and the China seas—and you have a substantial zone of culture indeed.

But the region had its own culture before the foreigner came. The mountains and rain forests, the rich, fertile river valleys, and the waters full of fish have sheltered human life for many centuries. Bamboo villages on stilts, water buffalo, and rice paddies were all in place before the first Chinese soldier or Indian merchant came marching through the jungle or poking up the muddy rivers. Dong-Son culture developed its special combination of agriculture, trading, and piracy with minimal foreign input. If bronze working filtered down from China, the unique bronze drums that symbolize the Dong-Son achievement are a Southeast Asian artifact.

Perhaps most important, the pattern of Southeast Asian village life—the life of most Southeast Asians to this day—was firmly established long before civilized Indians and Chinese, Muslims and Christians came to bring the splendors and miseries of urban-imperial culture to this substantial corner of the world.

It is too easy to slip into the dismissive frame of mind that sees one peasant as much like another, an agricultural village in Java as really no different from one in Nigeria or Peru. But there are differences, some of them extremely important still.

Southeast Asian villagers were still animists, worshiping natural objects and the forces of nature, while Indian peasants were adopting the larger and more complex creeds of Hinduism, Buddhism, and later Islam. Many parts of Southeast Asia built societies around the small nuclear family of parents and children—as most modern societies do—rather than the extended family prevalent in India and China. Perhaps most striking, Southeast Asians from early times accorded a higher degree of equality to women than their neighbors did.

Women in Southeast Asian villages shared more than labor with their men. In ancient times they were often priestesses and even chiefs. Women sometimes chose their husbands (instead of the other way around), and matrilineal descent—inheritance through the wife's rather than the husband's side—was common. Against this ingrained tradition of relative female equality, such later influences as the Indian drift toward seclusion for married women or such Muslim institutions as harem isolation and the veil could make little progress. Today you are considerably more likely to see young women jogging in the streets of Indonesia's capital Jakarta, for instance, than in New Delhi or any Arab city.

Most of what follows concerns the absorption of Southeast Asia into a larger zone of culture whose radiant center was India. But it should be remembered that the glories of Angkor Wat or Borobudur were built by the labor of village people whose hearts and lives were still shaped to a large extent by an older world where such incongruous beliefs as nature worship and female equality lived on in perfect harmony.

INDIA AND ITS SPHERE OF INFLUENCE

PACIFIC OCEAN

BORNEO

JAVA

Prambanan

Borobudur

SUMATRA

MALAYA

CHAMPA KINGDOM

VIET KINGDOM

Angkor

KHMERS

Malacca

THAIS

BURMA

Pagan

PUNDRAVARDHANA

PAVAKA

KAMARUPA

LICCHAVI

Vaisali

Pataliputra

NEPALA

BAY OF BENGAL

NAGAS

Delhi

Ayodhya

Padmavati

Airikina (Eran)

Nandivardhana

Mathura

Vengi

Sanchi

Ajanta

SAKAS

Ujjayini

Dasapura (Mandasor)

Girinagara (Girnar)

CHOLAS

PALLAVAS

PANDYA

LANKA (SIMHALA)

ARABIAN SEA

INDIAN OCEAN

KUSHANS AND SAKAS

SASANIAN EMPIRE

0   500   1000 Miles

0   500   1000 Kilometers

Missionaries and Merchants

Indian influence in Southeast Asia goes back to the classic period, the age of the Guptas and before, but it reached its peak during the thousand years between 500 and 1500. As a source of cultural influence, India substantially outweighed China, whose impact during these centuries seldom reached much further than northern Vietnam. Indian influence, by contrast, spread to most of the mainland peoples, from Burma into southern Vietnam, and to a number of the larger islands, including Sumatra, Java, and Borneo.

This Indian influence differed strikingly from the looming Chinese presence. When the Chinese did come south, it was as conquerors, the organized political and military agents of the world's most populous and powerful nation. Indians, by contrast, filtered into the region primarily as merchants and missionaries. In the end, the cultural impact of Indian civilization, built on mutually beneficial trade and on the emotional and spiritual appeal of India's religions, penetrated Southeast Asian culture as Chinese political influence seldom did.

Indian traders settled into the port towns of Malaya, Java, and Sumatra, even Thailand and south Vietnam, as easily as they did along the coasts of East Africa, far to the west. They gave village chiefs impressive gifts, the products of an Indian handicraft industry that local artisans could only envy. They exchanged textiles, jewels, jars of oil, and perfume for spices and timber, gold and tin. In time they married the daughters of local dignitaries and became influential citizens of communities that grew increasingly prosperous thanks to Indian trade.

Indian missionaries came to spread all three of the greatest Indian religions. Buddhist monks brought a simple, caste-free faith that had a great appeal to ordinary villagers. Brahmans brought a Hinduism that sanctioned *rajas* in Southeast Asia as easily as it did in India and that soon became a common cult among rulers and aristocrats. Islam, when it came, came often in the simple straight-from-the-heart Sufi form. But Indian Muslims came frequently as conquerors too, and some prudent Southeast Asians accepted Islam as a rapid road to success in Muslim-controlled areas.

Sometimes Indians taught techniques of land irrigation and terraced hillside agriculture, though these skills had been developed in many areas before they came. In many places Indians helped Southeast Asian rulers to develop bustling port cities for further trade with India and elsewhere. And Indian monks, brahmans, and Islamic mullahs raised temples to Vishnu and Shiva, to Buddha or to Allah, among the palms and paddies of these lands of the eastern seas.

Climbing over the mountain of terraces, statues, carved gateways, and broken stairs of Borobudur, in Java, one has the odd feeling of exploring a gothic cathedral turned inside out. All the stairs and gates and statues are on the outside; there is no inside. But there is the same careful stonework in a carved Buddha meditating on the Javanese jungle as in any sculptured Christ looking down on a gothic nave. The religious symbols and the religious stories are different, but the Buddhist temple at Borobudur is as much a holy mountain reaching up to God as any Notre Dame.

Lands of a Million Elephants: From Malacca to Angkor Wat

The fusion of traditional ways with Indian influence produced a whole series of kingdoms and empires across Southeast Asia, a number of them comparable in splendor, if not in size, to those of India itself.

Almost every modern Southeast Asian nation can point to some such glorious center of civilization in the past. The islands of today's Indonesia, especially Java and Sumatra, were the sites of briskly feuding Indianized nations between 500 and 1000, a period when Europe was languishing in its Dark Ages. As early as the ninth century, the huge Buddhist temple at Borobudur and the Hindu temple complex at Palambanan had risen over the jungles of central Java. The great Anirudda filled the far-famed Burmese capital of Pagan with temples and shrines dedicated to Buddha in the eleventh century, at about the same time that the gothic cathedrals were beginning to rise in Europe. Laos looks back to the great days of Lan Xang—Land of a Million Elephants.

Malaya remembers the meteoric career of the great port city of Malacca, which under the leadership of Muslim Indian merchants dominated East Indian trade and spread the faith of Muhammad to many parts of Southeast Asia. Dazzled by bazaars heaped with Indian fabrics and Chinese porcelain, spices, aromatic woods, and precious metals, pearls and perfumes and silks, a Portuguese visitor in the 1400s declared that "Men cannot estimate the wealth of Malacca."

In 1511 the Portuguese captured Malacca, and a new era began for Southeast Asia. But the long millennium between the end of the classic age around 500 and the beginning of the modern era around 1500 had produced achievements in civilization second to none. Perhaps the most famous of all was the kingdom of the Khmer in what became Cambodia—the civilization whose most awesome monument is the great lost city of Angkor.

VOICES FROM THE PAST

Even the economic historian who brings us this quote from an early modern observer is impressed by the wonders of medieval Malacca, the commercial crossroads of Asia until the arrival of European imperialists in the sixteenth century. Note that Tomé Pires credits part of the port's prosperity to the local princes, who saw the importance of "favoring" and "not neglecting" it. Would modern economists agree that favorable government policies are essential to economic success?

At the end of the 15th century hundreds of merchants from Arabia, Persia, India, Further India, and China, as well as from the Indonesian regions closer at hand, flocked together every year in Malacca, which was then the centre of inter-Asian trade. Like a rich and colourful pageant under the blazing tropical sun, this busy eastern market made an indelible impression on the first Europeans who visited Malacca. It is worth while turning to the almost lyrical descriptions of people like Duarte Barbosa and Tomé Pires.[1] "There is no doubt" writes the latter "that the affairs of Malacca are of great importance, and of much profit and great honour. It is a land that cannot depreciate, on account of its position, but must always grow. No trading port as large as Malacca is known, nor any where they deal in such fine and highly-prized merchandise. Goods from all over the East are found here; goods from all over the West are sold here. It is at the end of the monsoons, where you find what you want, and sometimes more than you are looking for." But it is as if Pires already foresees the fate that lies in store for Malacca" "Wherefore a thing of such magnitude and of such great wealth, which never in the world could decline, if it were moderately governed and favoured, should be supplied, looked after, praised and favoured, and not neglected."

[1]Tomé Pires, *Complete Treatise on the Orient* (London: Hakluyt Society, 1944), quoted in M. A. P. Meilink-Roelofsz, *Asian Trade and European Influence in the Indonesian Archipelago* (The Hague: Martinus Nijhoff, 1962).

The Cambodian "lost city" of Angkor Thom built in the twelfth century while the gothic cathedrals were rising in Europe has awed many Western visitors. Closely shaped by Indian artistic and religious influences, the towers and walls and endless sculptured galleries of Angkor remain one of the greatest monuments of ancient Southeast Asian civilization. (Anthony Esler)

The Indianized, Hindu-Buddhist state of Kambuja (Cambodia) flourished from the ninth to the fifteenth centuries. The Khmer peoples who ruled it extended their sovereignty into parts of southern Vietnam and Thailand. Over its half-dozen centuries of splendor, the Khmer Empire learned Sanskrit, mathematics, architecture, and art from the Indians. Khmer rulers became *devarajas* and pious Hindus, while many of their people accepted the less hierarchical Buddhist faith, the religion of most Cambodians today. The ancient Indian epic poems, the *Mahabharata* and the *Ramayana,* were widely known in southern Indochina. And the great temple of Angkor Wat was built to reproduce on earth the Hindu vision of the shape and structure of the cosmos.

The Khmer Empire was never large in size or population. But the Angkor dynasty channeled the wealth of the land and the labor of their million subjects into huge building projects dedicated to the greater glory of their gods and their god-kings. The temple complex of Angkor Wat is the most splendid evocation of the wealth and dedication of this vanished civilization.

Here the moated city of Angkor once stood, several miles around, surrounded by a green plain criss-crossed by irrigation channels and lush with rice paddies and orchards. Within the city swarmed a population many times as large as that of medieval London. The booming business of the city was dominated—like so much else in Southeast Asia— by women. But the city's great centers, clearly visible over the rooftops of the earth or wooden houses of the people, were the bristling stone towers of the royal city of Angkor Thom and the temple complex of Angkor Wat.

Even the ruins that survive today—much of it still overgrown with jungle, discolored by monsoon rains, pocked by the bullets of more recent Southeast Asian wars—are among the most impressive to be found anywhere. Angkor Wat itself, six hundred feet on a side, has been described as the largest temple in the world. Around its courtyards and galleries and up the sides of its *shikara,* hundreds of carven figures retell Hindu myths and glorify the Khmer King—Suryavarman II—who built it in the twelfth century. The style is distinctly that of this great Southeast Asian people, but the images of Vishnu and Shiva and Buddha, the creation myths, and the cosmological design all reflect the cultural influence of India.

Summary

The thousand years of Indian history between the Guptas and the Mughals were tangled and confused politically, like so much of India's history. But they were also centuries of cultural flowering and of the spread of Indian influence, above all into Southeast Asia.

During this period, from roughly C.E. 500 to 1500, the Northwest Frontier admitted Rajputs, Turks, Tatars, and others to find their place in the polyglot population of India. The Dravidian south merged with the north in a single arena of competitive states. The caste system grew more complex and more rigid, and women's place in society became fixed. Attempts at imposing political unity included the short-lived empire of King Harsha and the longer but no more substantial regime called the Delhi Sultanate.

India's culture, with its roots still deeply planted in the subcontinent's many religions, continued to probe spiritual profundities and to generate artistic splendors.

Hinduism, which had experienced a spiritual revival under the Guptas, still flowered during the following millennium. But Buddhism lost favor in the Buddha's own homeland, expiring finally in the turmoil following the Muslim invasions. The rise of Islam itself, particularly in the north, made the Muslim faith the third main current of Indian religious history during this period, India's second largest religion in later centuries.

As Western Christian art centered on the cathedral and that of Islam on the mosque, so Indian art focused on the countless huge stone temples that were built in all parts of India in this age. Dense with life, myth, and symbol, the temples of Hindu, Buddhist, Jain, and other faiths glorified Indian cities, as churches of Our Lady did the cities of Christendom. Among the many regional cultures of divided India, that of the Tamils glowed with particular brilliance in the south, particularly in the Chola kingdom.

This ancient and complex culture, finally, had an important impact on a large cultural zone comprising almost all of Southeast Asia in this period.

Indian merchants and Buddhist, Hindu, and Muslim missionaries guided the developing cities and empires of these lush islands and peninsulas. Southeast Asian village culture was significantly affected by the new faiths. Kingdoms in Burma, Java, Sumatra, and the famous Angkor Wat of Cambodia all reflected the influence of the timeless culture of India.

Suggested Reading

Chattopadhyaya, B. *The Making of Early Medieval India.* New York: Oxford University Press, 1994. Aspects of Indian social and political development.

Chaudhuri, K. N. *Asia Before Europe: Economy and Civilization of the Indian Ocean from the Rise of Islam to 1750.* Cambridge, England: Cambridge University Press, 1991. Regional study of the ocean and its neighboring peoples. See also K. R. Hall, *Maritime Trade and State Development in Early Southeast Asia* (Honolulu: University of Hawaii Press, 1985).

Jackson, P. *The Delhi Sultanate: A Political and Military History.* New York, Cambridge University Press, 1999. Highly praised recent overview.

Mannikka, E. *Angkor Wat: Time, Space, and Kingship.* Honolulu: University of Hawaii Press, 1996. Inner meanings of the Khmer complex at Angkor.

Michell, G. *The Hindu Temple: An Introduction to Its Meaning and Form.* Chicago: University of Chicago Press, 1988. Religious symbolism in architecture.

Pearson, M. N., ed. *Spices in the Indian Ocean World.* London: Variorum, 1996. Impact of a small but vital commodity on South Asian trade.

Ramusack, B. N., and S. L. Sievers. *Women in Asia: Restoring Women to History.* Bloomington and Indianapolis: Indiana University Press, 1999. Women playing active roles in both South and East Asian history.

Wriggens, S. H. *Xuanzang: A Buddhist Pilgrim on the Silk Road.* Boulder, Colo.: Westview Press, 1996. Highly readable account of the Chinese pilgrim's epic journey in quest of Indian Buddhist texts.

Zimmer, H. *The Art of Indian Asia* (2 vols). New York: Pantheon Books, 1960. Outstanding study, beautifully illustrated, of the art of the Indian zone of culture.

Please refer to the document CD-ROM for primary sources related to this chapter.

CHAPTER 12

THE MIDDLE KINGDOM
China and East Asia

(600–1250)

A Glance Ahead: China's Supremacy in Eastern Asia

Towering over the eastern end of Eurasia, China was still the world's largest country in this period of world history. It passed through two of its certified golden ages during this era, the Tang and the Song dynasties. And its traditional cultural zone continued to include all of East Asia, while Tang armies pushed still farther west across the steppes of Eurasia.

China's main influence, however, continued to be on its nearer neighbors, including Vietnam, Korea, and Japan. Across this vast zone, the ancient "middle kingdom" continued to radiate its cultural imperatives, a mix of Confucian principles and commercial know-how, military power, Buddhist faith, and the sheer weight of its ancient civilization.

A crisis lay in wait toward the end of this period—the catastrophic Mongol conquest. But China would shrug off this disaster too and enter the modern age with an enormous potential to impress its neighbors and resist encroachment from beyond its zone.

The Tang Dynasty

The Six Dynasties

There are sober businessmen in Singapore or Hong Kong or Tokyo—and even soberer scholars in America—who will tell you that the twenty-first century will be the century of the Pacific rim. The Atlantic powers have had their day, they will say. The nations that border the Pacific will be the arbiters of the planet's destiny in the new century and East, South, and Southeast Asian nations will lead all the rest.

A traditional Chinese scholar would tell you that the Asian rim of the Pacific has actually been the center of world history for a couple of thousand years already. Since the Qin and Han dynasties united China in the third century B.C.E., creating at a stroke the largest and most populous nation on earth, Chinese primacy has been an article of faith in the land they call the Middle Kingdom.

Basic geography—and basic history—certainly seemed to support the Chinese sense of being the center of human civilization during most of the millennium between the end of the classic age and the beginning of the modern era.

China sprawls massively across the eastward bulge of Asia. For most of its history it has been a large, powerful, centralized state with a proud and ancient culture. During much of the period under consideration here, China basked in the renewed glories of two of its greatest ages, the Tang and Song dynasties.

Over these centuries, which saw the rise of Islam and the climax of the Christian age of faith at the other end of Eurasia, another major zone of civilization thus developed and produced great things along the far Pacific rim.

The four hundred years that elapsed between the collapse of the Han dynasty in 220 and the accession of the Tang in 618 are a hopeless tangle politically. The epoch may be subdivided into the sometimes overlapping periods of the Three Kingdoms, the Six Dynasties, and the brief pre-Tang unification under the Sui dynasty. But the essential elements of this age—which we may refer to for convenience simply as the Six Dynasties—lay not in its political confusion but in other areas of Chinese history and culture.

Perhaps the decisive event was not political but military. It was not so much the third-century collapse of the Han monarchy that shattered Chinese unity but the fourth-century

Li Shimin, known to history as Tang Taizong, the reunifier of China and founder of the great Tang dynasty, looks pardonably self-satisfied in this drawing based on a rubbing from Shensi. Notice the elaborately embroidered robe, the carefully trimmed and curled beard, and the traditional full sleeves. (Courtesy of the Library of Congress)

overrunning of northeastern China by a chaotic flood of preurban nomadic peoples from beyond the Great Wall. The result of this barbarian conquest of the old Chinese heartland was to leave China culturally as well as politically divided between north and south for most of the next three hundred years.

But the impulse toward complete political unification was always there. Toward the end of the sixth century, finally, the brief Sui dynasty (589–618) reunited most of China and began the great unifying works that the Tang emperors were to bring to a triumphant climax.

The two Sui emperors, Yang Jian and his brilliant, unscrupulous son Yang Guang, were northerners with the blood of the Xiongnu in their veins. The armies of the militant Sui broke through the Yangzi demarcation line to conquer the south. Then this vigorous father and son labored successively to rebuild an administrative system for all China. They worked also to extend the Grand Canal system begun by the Han and the Great Wall built by the Qin emperor Huangdi. They strove with considerable success to keep out the barbarians and to impose Chinese rule once more upon the Vietnamese and Chinese influence on the Koreans.

The Sui emperors, like Huangdi, exhausted the country with extravagant building projects at home and costly military campaigns abroad. A nation strained beyond the breaking point rebelled, and the dynasty fell after less than thirty tumultuous years. But like the Qin, the Sui had paved the way for something more long lasting.

The Founder: Tang Taizong

For some Chinese historians, the Tang dynasty (618–907) was the greatest of dynasties and the three hundred years of Tang rule the most lustrous of China's several golden ages. For others, the Han and Tang stand roughly on a par, twin peaks in China's history.

Like the Han, the Tang combined political and economic strength, imperial expansion, and cultural brilliance in a uniquely successful way. The earlier Tang, like the former Han, was an era of powerful personalities and glittering accomplishment, a period when China's preeminence and influence were unquestioned throughout East Asia. The latter half of the Tang period, like the Later Han, was a time of retrenchment and decline. In both cases, however, a long-reigning dynasty and frequently competent leadership gave China a considerable spell of domestic tranquility and international power.

The first two Tang emperors, like the two Sui, were father and son. But in the case of the Tang founders, the son was so clearly the dominant personality that it is common to see him as the true establisher of the dynasty, though he was its second emperor. This hard-driving second son is in fact often considered the greatest of all China's many emperors.

The father, Li Yuan, was the scion of an ancient northwestern Chinese family who married a daughter of the northern steppes, sired three sons, and became a leading general under the Sui. He seems, however, to have fallen strongly under the influence of his second son, an ambitious young war hero named Li Shimin. When the brief Sui restoration of imperial unity began to crumble, Li Shimin urged his father step by step along the road to power.

The older man was still at the fore when a key alliance was forged with the northern Turks against the crumbling Chinese regime. Father and son took the Sui capital of Chang'an (modern Xi'an) together, and soon thereafter Li Yuan was installed with all due solemnity as the new Son of Heaven, emperor of China. In the eight years of his reign, the new emperor firmly established the Tang regime at Chang'an, crushed several drawn-out rebellions in South China, and repelled an invasion by the new dynasty's former allies, the Turks.

In the end, however, the stronger personality of Li Shimin thrust its way forward. Returning from the wars, where he had spent his youth fighting for his country and his clan, the second son confronted a conspiracy hatched against him by the crown prince and by the third Li brother, both envious of Shimin's fame. The border warrior reacted with the directness of the military commander he was. He took a squad, ambushed his brothers and their retainers outside the palace gates, and shot both the plotters down with bows and arrows. He then compelled his aging father to step down and mounted the throne himself—emperor at the age of twenty-six.

Li Shimin would be listed in the history books as Tang Taizong (629–649), Grand Ancestor of the Tang. Brilliant general, governmental reformer, famous historian, and master of the calligraphy brush, he would be one of the most admired of all Chinese emperors.

Taizong's governmental reforms were in part a restoration of the Han system already partially revived by the Sui, in part a long step beyond these traditional ways. This real founder of the Tang put government in the hands of an administrative system of six central ministries (for state revenues and public works, defense and justice, personnel and religious rites), ten provinces, and hundreds of prefectures and lesser administrative units. He expanded the Confucian examination system for civil servants and established a structure of schools, including a central university at Chang'an that would prepare students for the exams. He promulgated a flexible new law code and a new state-supported court aristocracy in nine graduated ranks. He laid the groundwork, in short, for the whole Tang system of imperial government.

Taizong also launched the reunited Chinese nation on the road to renewed imperial preeminence in East Asia. He led his armies himself, following the trail of westward expansion already blazed by the Han. Taizong's armies pushed the Turks back out of the Tarim Basin and carried Chinese power all the way to the Pamirs and into the valley of the Oxus River beyond. South of the Tarim Basin he imposed Chinese authority on the newly unified mountain kingdom of Tibet. He thus opened the doors to trade with western Eurasia once more—though in the seventh century there was no developed civilization in Europe with which to trade.

Tang Taizong ruled for more than twenty years, building palaces for himself and public granaries for his people, exalting Buddha at his court and establishing temples to the honor of Confucius across the land. He died at the comparatively young age of forty-nine, his health destroyed by a hard military campaign in Korea.

In the end, Taizong's one great failure was that he produced no heir strong enough to hold and build upon this heritage. But even this turned out to be for the best, for weakness at the top allowed his true successor to fight her way up through the cauldron of court politics—his former concubine who became the formidable Empress Wu.

The Greatest Empress: Wu Zetian

Like the Han empress Lü, Empress Wu Zetian (649–705) of the Tang period owed her initial power to male connections. Concubine of the second Tang emperor, wife of the third, and mother of the next two, Wu finally dispensed with surrogates and ruled in her own right and name. Beautiful and cruel in her early years, she displayed in later life the intelligence, good judgment, and foresight that make a great ruler.

In her climb to the throne of China, Wu Zetian struck down her rivals ruthlessly, exalted her own family, and even tried to establish a new dynasty of her own. She fostered the Buddhist faith as her predecessors had, fell temporarily in love with a Buddhist monk, and even had herself proclaimed a new incarnation of the Enlightened One. In her later years she declared herself emperor, performed the rites, and received the homage due the Son of Heaven. Though other women governed China—from the Han empress Lü to imperial China's last great ruler, Ci Xi in the nineteenth century—Empress Wu was the only woman to hold the titles as well as the power in her strong hands.

This later representation of the Empress Wu Zetian probably does not do justice to the powerful preserver of the Tang order even in her later years. Can you detect winged dragon motifs—symbolic of imperial power—in the empress's headdress? (New York Public Library Picture Collection)

Tang China

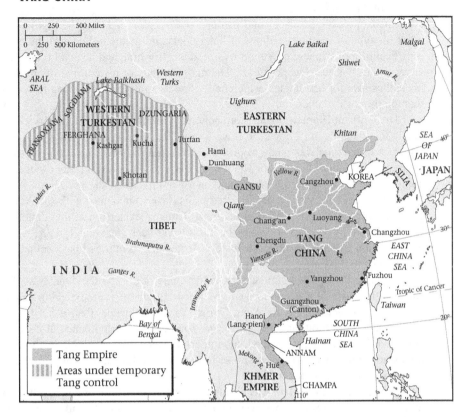

Beneath the gaudy surface of her long tenure of power, however, Wu Zetian governed capably and well. Her chief ministers tended to be men of talent, the provincial officials stayed loyal, and the state prospered. In foreign affairs, she shrewdly supported the unification of Korea—which the Chinese had been trying and failing to conquer for generations—and thus enjoyed cordial relations with the new state throughout her life. In the west, she sent Chinese armies out as her predecessors had to chastise Turks and Tibetans and keep open China's trade routes across the Tarim Basin into western Asia and beyond. She was "perspicacious, and rapid and sure in decision" and enjoyed an international reputation for astuteness and success.[1]

Empress Wu's efforts to establish a new dynasty—her own—finally brought her down. She was deposed at last in her eighties, after more than half a century of ruling China. She left the nation more firmly united, wealthier, and more powerful than it had ever been before. What Tang Taizong had begun, Wu Zetian finished, and she was as much the architect of Tang greatness as he.

The Brilliant Emperor: Tang Xuanzong

The last in this colorful line of great early Tang rulers was Empress Wu's grandson Tang Xuanzong (713–756). The long reign of Xuanzong, known to history as the Brilliant Em-

---

[1]C. P. Fitzgerald, *The Empress Wu* (Vancouver: University of British Columbia Press, 1968), p. 146.

peror, covered most of the first half of the eighth century and is often seen as the cultural apogee of the Tang period.

Xuanzong's huge palaces and gardens at Chang'an and elsewhere glittered with the work of some of the most famous of Tang poets and painters. Some of the most exquisitely beautiful of Chinese porcelain was produced for him, and he and his courtiers ate off silver dishes that were works of art. The magnificence of his court is often illustrated by his enthusiasm for fine horses, which he reportedly gratified by keeping forty thousand of them in the royal stables.

The Brilliant Emperor made more concrete contributions to the history of China than just living magnificently, however. It was during his reign that the fertile Yangzi River valley of central China was made to produce agriculturally on a scale that substantially increased the wealth of the nation. The imperial armies pushed still farther to the west under Tang Xuanzong, down into Kashmir and on toward the Caspian once more.

But it was here in central Asia that a disastrous encounter with the Arabs, driving eastward as the Chinese pushed west, ended Chinese expansion in that direction forever. China's defeat by Muslim armies at the Talas River near Samarkand in 751 was, in fact, a turning point in Chinese imperial history. It began a centuries-long decline of Chinese power in central Asia.

At home there was a similar turn in the emperor's—and the dynasty's—fortunes. It came in the guise of a September-and-May love affair between the aging Xuanzong and an attractive concubine named Yang Guifei. Yang's influence, that of her family, and finally that of her ambitious young protégé, An Lushan, predominated at court thereafter. When An Lushan openly revolted, the imperial troops demanded the death of the concubine whose influence had raised him so high. Yang Guifei was executed, and the Brilliant Emperor abdicated, a broken king.

The revolt of An Lushan was ultimately suppressed. But there were other revolts and other palace intrigues to come over the next century and a half. And there were no more Taizongs, no more Empress Wus, in the second half of the Tang era. The road, if not downhill all the way, was distinctly bumpier.

The World's Largest Country

From the administrative capital at Chang'an, a nation as large as all Europe was governed by a handful of courtier-politicans and an army of scholarly civil servants. There were too many bureaucrats, as is frequently the case—secretariats and chancelleries to check every piece of paper the emperor saw. But the six ministries for revenue and public works, justice and defense, personnel and rites and ceremonies did their jobs with relative efficiency. There was a board of censors, who kept tabs on the whole elaborate system and reported inefficiency, malfeasance, and treason directly to the palace. The nation beyond the walls of the capital was administered at three levels, including ten provinces, 360 prefectures, and hundreds of subprefectures or districts.

Office seekers were trained in the unique Chinese educational system of local schools, provincial colleges, and a national university at Chang'an where one could study not only the Confucian classics but science, mathematics, and law. This system of education, keyed to examinations for civil-service jobs, in time perfected the ancient Han system of scholar bureaucrats. Most officeholders henceforth came not from the ranks of the aristocratic large landowners but from the literate gentry class of lesser landholders whose sons qualified for office by study and high marks. It was a system based substantially on merit, awarding the highest posts in government to those most qualified.

The power of this centralized administration was, for the seventh or eighth century C.E., very great indeed. Every ward in the great planned city of Chang'an was locked at midnight, and no one moved around thereafter. Every peasant belonged to a "collective-guarantee" group of neighbors, all of whom were responsible for one another's taxes and general good behavior—and all of whom thus kept an eye on one another for the government. Military service and corvée labor were rigorously imposed and could fall heavily on whole villages.

Responsibility, not freedom, was the keynote of a system of government that became traditional in China—and may sound oppressive to a Western ear. On the other hand, at a time when emperors like Charlemagne in Europe and Harsha in India had to mount many military campaigns to maintain their empires intact, China was ruled in a rather more modern way—by a steady flow of paper from the capital out across the provinces of the world's largest nation.

Equal Fields and Wide Empire

Tang officialdom developed further the "equal-field" system originated by earlier dynasties, a form of land nationalization that assigned most of China's agricultural land on an equal basis to free peasants. The practice was intended to regularize—and maximize—the land tax. It also had the effect of limiting the amount of land held by wealthy landowners and hence of further undermining their power.

The government, like the governments of many developed nations, involved itself vigorously in the economy. A hundred mints produced strings of copper cash, and government-issued paper money was widely used. Royal roads radiating from Chang'an were equipped with hostels every ten miles and an impressive system of royal posts. Both the roads and the canal system were thronged with domestic traders.

Government incentives also helped turn the huge Yangzi valley into China's rice bowl. The emperor built ten shipyards in central China alone to give China a merchant marine, and entertained foreign merchants in growing numbers at Canton and other southern ports. Tang China was a great deal richer than Han China, and the imperial government played a significant part in this development.

Empire-building and foreign trade, finally, were carried to new highs under the Tang.

At the height of their power, the Tang emperors dominated Asia. Their writ ran more or less effectively from the southern margins of Siberia down to Southeast Asia and west from the Pacific to somewhere beyond Ferghana—sometimes even to the neighborhood of the Caspian Sea. Chinese armies intervened in the affairs of northern India and Afghanistan, and China established a temporary protectorate over eastern Persia.

China's network of foreign trade reached out to the whole of Asia, from Japan to Syria. Foreign influences played more freely on Chinese culture than ever before. And China's manifest superiority was admired and imitated by a larger proportion of the human race than ever previously. If it was not China's greatest age, it was certainly a strong candidate for this highly competitive honor.

THE SONG DYNASTY

The Five Dynasties

The last years of the Tang seem to have been typical of that cyclic dynastic end game that recurs so frequently in Chinese history. There were fractious governors in the provinces, feuding bureaucrats and eunuchs at court, and underage or ailing emperors trying to hold it all together. Unpaid armies revolted, provinces seceded, short-lived emperors became tools in the hands of scheming subjects. In the 880s the nation slid helplessly into anarchy. In the early 900s the last Tang emperor and all his family were slaughtered, the magnificent capital at Chang'an pillaged and burned.

The period of the Five Dynasties that separates the Tang from the Song lasted only a little more than fifty years (907–960)—a striking contrast with the several hundred years of the Six Dynasties between the Han and the Tang. The five dynasties in question—all in the north—were necessarily brief, usually no longer than the life of the founder. There were at least ten other secession states in the south, all feuding, conniving, dreaming of unity, and destroying any of their number who strove to impose it. Rebellion was endemic, and invaders from beyond the Great Wall once more overran the north. A famous poem of the time, "The Lament of Lady Qi," describes fountains running with blood, palaces in ashes, feet crunching through the calcined bones of court officials.

Yet it ended. In 960 a group of loyal and no doubt ambitious officers threw an embroidered dragon robe around the shoulders of a general named Zhao Kuangyin and told him he should be their emperor or die on the spot. General Zhao, who commanded the armies of one of the northern dynasties, chose to live and reign. He became the founder of the Song.

The Song dynasty (960–1279) would not achieve the universality, the range of achievement of the Han or the Tang; in some areas, however, it would exceed these predecessors. When it came to governing, to getting and spending, and to art and poetry, the Song have seldom been excelled.

Northern Song, Southern Song

General Zhao Kuangyin (960–976) seems to have been the only one of the twenty Song emperors whose personality stands out in the traditional historiography. He was a scholar as well as a general, an autocrat—and a man who saw that unity had become China's destiny.

As a general, Zhao Kuangyin first unified as much as he could of the north, leaving a wedge of territory still in barbarian hands, and then reconquered the fragmentary kingdoms of central and southern China. As a scholar, he revived the traditional Confucian education and examination system, which had fallen into abeyance during the Five Dynasties period, and fostered culture at his court. As an autocrat by nature, he revived and strengthened the Tang system of provinces and prefectures and strove to concentrate as many functions of government as possible in his own hands. And as a man with a sense of Chinese unity, Zhao Kuangyin benefited from the fact that many educated Chinese had come to believe that the secret of peace, prosperity, and order lay in unity and centralized authority. Many cities opened their gates to Zhao simply on the assurance that unity, not loot, was his object. The Song thus became in a sense the first dynasty established as much by consensus as by conquest.

The Song dynasty lasted about the same length of time as the Tang—three centuries. Like the Han and the Zhou before it, the Song was a clearly divided dynasty. The Northern Song (960–1127) governed from Kaifeng in the northern Yellow River valley; the Southern Song (1127–1279) fell back to the great city of Hangzhou in the valley of the Yangzi, China's great waterway. The whole era, contemporary with the High Middle Ages at the other end of Eurasia, was another high point in Chinese history.

In domestic affairs, the Song period was one of China's golden ages. Song emperors further improved on the Tang administrative structure. They controlled the military more effectively than their predecessors had, and they tried to tax large and small landowners alike. Song China was freer from popular discontent and rebellion than China had ever been before.

The dynasty even produced a great reforming minister of state in Wang Anshi, who in the eleventh century, a hundred years after Zhao Kuangyin, tried to revitalize the Northern Song with innovations in agriculture, trade, education, and the army and navy. Wang's Legalist rigor and his attack on wealth alienated Confucian bureaucrats and wealthy landowners and led to the frustration of many of his reforms. Nevertheless, Wang Anshi was one of a long line of reforming spirits who periodically shook up and infused new vigor into the Confucian system, which otherwise tended to become set in its ways.

China's problems under the Song dynasty—and the nation had serious ones—were rather foreign than domestic in origin. Most of these difficulties were with China's northern neighbors, the external peoples of the steppe. These conflicts climaxed with the loss of North China to the barbarians in the twelfth century.

Throughout the Song period parts of northwestern China were occupied by the Tibetans, and a slice of territory south of the Great Wall in the northeast was controlled by semiagricultural peoples from Mongolia. The Northern Song emperors were never able to dislodge these northern barbarians, who had established themselves during the anarchy of the Five Dynasties. In the first half of the twelfth century, finally, the Ruzhen (Jürchen) people descended from the Manchurian steppes in the far northeast, helped the Song overpower the rulers of the northeast, and then rampaged on south, conquering all of North China and carrying off the last emperor of the Northern Song to live out his life as a prisoner beyond the Great Wall.

The Southern Song, established by a son of that unhappy exile, set up a new capital at Hangzhou and ruled a truncated empire for the next century and a half. China under the Southern Song was vastly wealthy, immensely cultured, peaceful, and well governed. But the Chinese failed in all efforts to expel the Ruzhen and were actually forced to pay them tribute and to recognize China's status as vassal to the northern barbarians.

The Song emperors' deemphasis of the military, while it minimized the risk of warlordism and civil war, thus cost them dearly in the international arena. It was the middle passage of a long decline in China's power in East Asia. That decline, which began with the Brilliant Emperor's defeat on the Talas River in central Asia in 751, would climax in the thirteenth century with the overthrow of the Song and the conquest of the entire nation by the Mongols of Genghis Khan—to be dealt with in the following chapter. Through it all, however, China's wealth, its remarkable administrative institutions, and its cultural brilliance would continue to dominate the life of East Asia—even when Chinese armies could not.

The First Meritocracy

Despite foreign-policy setbacks and the catastrophic loss of North China, the Song period saw material achievements that deserve further notice. These include the perfection of the scholar bureaucracy and its examination system and the immense wealth of the nation.

China's civil-service examinations and the resulting governmental meritocracy are as uniquely Chinese as the caste system is Indian or the Muslim law and its powerful local judges is Islamic. The examination system, originated by the Han dynasty and developed under the Tang, reached what was essentially its final form under the Song. For the next ten centuries it was to give China a stable administration that for most of that time was the envy of all who observed it.

The people who took the exams were for the most part children of China's gentry class—not aristocrats or holders of large estates, but men whose families were well enough off to spare them from agricultural labor while they devoted their lives to study. They typically spent many years reading the Chinese classics—Confucius above all—memorizing and analyzing every line. The tests required them to write passages from memory, to discuss and explain them, to compose a poem or other literary work in the style of particular masters, and to discuss theoretical problems of government having contemporary relevance.

Examinations were prepared with scrupulous attention to fairness. Papers were identified by number rather than name, and were even recopied before being graded so that the calligraphy might not be recognized by a grader. Exams were taken at several levels, beginning locally, where between 1 and 10 percent passed, and climaxing with the palace examinations, which passed perhaps a couple of hundred men a year into high governmental posts. The average "presented scholar" at this top level was in his middle thirties, well off but not wealthy, immensely learned, and one of a handful chosen out of China's millions to govern.

Economic Growth—and Problems

The Chinese were also more numerous and wealthier than they had ever been. And two thirds of the population and wealth were for the first time concentrated in central and south China, rather than in the old northeastern heartland.

In Song times, China's population passed the hundred-million mark, twice the number counted in the Han period. This growing population created a huge economic demand, which in turn generated what is sometimes called an economic revolution in the Middle Kingdom.

Agriculture grew rapidly, and its center shifted with the center of population from the millet- and wheat-growing north to the rice paddies of the Yangzi and the southeast, where two crops a year of special strains of rice could be grown. Agricultural reforms included increasing use of fertilizer, improved irrigation, and better iron farming tools.

The iron and related coal industries developed rapidly under the Song, and there was widespread production of fine steel for tools, weapons, stoves, nails, and much more. Other growth industries included shipbuilding, the manufacture of ceramics, silk, and paper, and tea and salt processing. Many of these manufacturing enterprises were small craft-shop operations, but some were much larger in scale, employing hundreds of workers.

Trade flourished in Song China. Domestic traders frequently organized themselves in guilds and set up shops dealing in the same articles in the same streets, as in medieval Europe. Inland trade was carried out more commonly on the nation's elaborate network of waterways, both rivers and canals, than by road. It was a larger country, and water was the cheapest form of transport.

Southern Song cities such as Guangzhou (Canton) carried on long-distance foreign trade, both through foreign merchants—whom the Chinese government, for once in its history, eagerly encouraged to come to China—and its Chinese vessels plying foreign waters. Chinese ships were among the most impressive in the world, large enough to carry hundreds of men and large cargoes. They were equipped with such up-to-the-minute technology as watertight bulkheads, sea anchors, rudders (instead of steering oars), depth-sounding lines, compasses, and gunpowder-powered rockets for use in war or against pirates.

China imported drugs, textiles, and some luxury goods. The nation also exported silk in large quantities, metals, and especially ceramics, an export encouraged by the government. Song Chinese porcelain has been found not only in Southeast Asia and India but in the Middle East and East Africa.

There are, however, no paradises on this earth, and Song China was no exception to this melancholy rule.

There were economic problems even under the Song. Growing population, increasing taxation, and played-out land drove peasants into pauperism even in so wealthy a time. The government's paper money encouraged trade—until too much paper currency was put in circulation, leading to inflation. Government spending grew beyond the capacity of even so wealthy a land to support—especially military expenses, which devoured 80 percent of the budget, supported an unheard-of army of a million men, and still could not defeat the northern barbarians.

SOCIETY AND CULTURE UNDER THE TANG AND SONG

The Condition of Women

In some ways, upper-class women at least enjoyed increased freedom during the Tang and Song periods. But there were disturbing trends, particularly in Song times.

Urbanization brought women as well as men into the liberating, often tempting atmosphere of the cities. Only men could immerse themselves freely in the urban pleasures of teahouse and wine shop, theater and brothel, but some wealthy women did take discreet lovers. Imperial wives and concubines indulged in the political pleasures of conspiracy and cabal, seeking to advance their own interests and those of their relatives and political factions. Simpler and healthier pleasures were also apparently open to them: We even have ceramic images of Tang women on horseback, playing polo!

On the other hand, the power of male heads of households seems to have been ever greater during these centuries. From a woman's point of view, a limiting aspect of the neo-Confucian revival (dicussed below) was its emphasis on women's place in the home as a producer of male heirs. The retreat of Buddhism also undercut the place that liberating faith had offered for women as nuns or even scholars. And while men had their pick of multiple wives and—increasingly—concubines too, Song women in particular were confined to the home and forbidden to remarry even after their husbands' deaths.

Most disturbing, however, was the introduction of footbinding among the women of China's elites during Song times. This involved wrapping the feet of young girls with long strips of cloth, which produced a "lily foot" about half normal size. This made women useless for work—hence advertised their husbands' wealth—and gave them an odd, stilted walk that men found intensely attractive. The footbinding itself was also an extremely painful process for the daughters of the aristocracy.

VOICES FROM THE PAST

This speech is part of the famous legend of the Chinese Princess Miaoshan, whose dedication to the spiritual life in the end revealed her own Buddhahood as an incarnation of Guanyin, the Chinese Buddha of Compassion. The three conditions she sets for abandoning her religious commitment for a "normal" married life closely echo the experience of the original Buddha, Prince Siddartha, who discovered his vocation when he encountered old age, sickness, and death for the first time.

The king told his wife, "Our daughter does not (want to marry. Please talk to her and make her change her mind." The mother then tries to persuade Miaoshan, who answered,) "I will obey Mother's command only if it will prevent three misfortunes." The mother asked, "What are the three misfortunes?" she answered, "The first is this: when people are young, their faces are as fair as the jade-like moon, but when they grow old, their hair turns white, their faces are wrinkled; in walking, resting, sitting, or lying down they are in every way worse off than when they were young. The second is this: one's limbs may be strong and vigorous, one may walk as briskly as if flying through the air, but when one suddenly becomes sick, one lies in a bed (without a single pleasure in life. The third is this: a person may have a large group of relatives and) be surrounded by his flesh and blood, but when death comes, even such close kin as father and son cannot take the person's place. If a husband can prevent these three misfortunes, I will marry him. But if he cannot do so, I vow never to marry. People of the world are all mired in these kinds of suffering. If one desires to be free from these sufferings, one must leave the secular world and pass through the gate of Buddhism. Only when one practices religion and obtains its fruit can one deliver all people from suffering. This is why I have undertaken my quest (for enlightenment . . ."

Susan Mann and Yü-Yin Cheng, *Under Confucian Eyes: Writings on Gender in Chinese History* (Berkeley: University of California Press, 2001), p. 35.

Missionary Buddhism and the New Confucianism

The great intellectual currents of Tang and Song times were the spread of Buddhism in the earlier period and the resurgence of Confucianism in the latter. Buddhism was brought by missionary monks from northern India to western China over the caravan routes of the great Silk Road. As early as the first century C.E., it was the faith of many foreign merchants resident in China. It appealed to Chinese and other East Asians through its direct dealing with human suffering, from which Buddhist enlightenment promised escape. In addition, evolving Mahayana Buddhism soon offered ritual and music, magic, art, and a variety of heavens and hells for people who couldn't grasp the nonbeing of Nirvana. During the Six Dynasties, Chinese Buddhist monks spread their faith all over China.

There were problems with translating abstract Indian concepts—like Nirvana—into Chinese. And the celibacy of Buddhist monks and nuns clashed jarringly with the Chinese emphasis on continuing the family line. But adaptable Buddhist missionaries in North China outdid the barbarian shamans at magic tricks, while Buddhists in the sophisticated south adroitly mixed religious propaganda with witty worldly conversation. Monasteries blossomed in many places, royal patrons were won, and the poor and unfortunate of the divided land found solace in the new faith.

But the real flowering of Chinese Buddhism came after the nation was reunited in Tang times. Despite the status of Confucianism as China's official philosophy and the penchant of a number of emperors for Daoism, Buddhism enjoyed its golden noon in Tang China. There was a proliferation of sects, providing a form of Buddhist belief for any Chinese. The *Tiantai* (Heavenly Terrace) sect tried to synthesize the conflicting doctrines of northern and southern Chinese Buddhism on various levels of truth, while claiming that all truth could actually be found in a single sermon—Buddha's famous Lotus Sutra. *Qingtu* (Pure Land) Buddhism, widely followed by ordinary Chinese with no head for theology, worshiped Buddha as ruler of a paradise in the west called the Pure Land and offered salvation simply through calling upon his name with a pure and sincere heart. *Chan* Buddhism, better known by its Japanese name of *Zen,* rejected all theology, scripture, and ceremony in favor of pure meditation, which alone would provide a true mystical understanding of the path to enlightenment.

In Tang times Buddhism thus channeled China's spiritual and intellectual impulses in an untypically religious direction. Under the Song, however, the Neo-Confucian revival—like the Hindu renaissance in Gupta India—drew China's educated classes back to an older faith. In China's case, it was a turn from an other-worldly religion back to a more typically Chinese secular philosophy.

Neo-Confucianism produced many commentaries on the Confucian classics. It established the Four Books of Confucian wisdom that were to be China's core curriculum for the next millennium. Confucian scholars and philosophers reinvigorated historical study and revived public and private education. Perhaps most striking, however, they tried to answer the sort of question about the ultimate nature of things that Master Kong himself had always avoided—to provide a metaphysical foundation for Confucian social and ethical thought.

The most famous instance of Neo-Confucian metaphysical theorizing was the work of the philosopher Zhu Xi, a twelfth-century thinker who was to the Confucian revival what his contemporary Thomas Aquinas was to the scholastic theology of the Christian Middle Ages. The best-known philosophical explorations of Zhu Xi involved a Platonic-sounding effort to explain the world in terms of *li* and *qi.* The *li* of anything was its basic form or fundamental principle, its *qi* the substance or stuff of which it is made. The most celebrated application of this doctrine had to do with the ancient dispute as to whether human nature was basically good, as Mencius had asserted, or evil, as the Legalists had always insisted. For the Neo-Confucianists, we are in a sense both. Our *li,* or basic principles are good, but the substance of which we are made, our *qi,* is gross, corruptible, and bound to lead us into evildoing. Self-improvement, the cultivation of our human essence of *li,* is, of course, best accomplished through study of the Confucian classics.

Science and Technology: From Gunpowder to the Printing Press

The physical sciences were an area in which there was striking progress from the third to the thirteenth centuries. In this as in so many things, the Chinese tended to be practical, to make contributions to technology rather than to pure science.

Thus, the famous trio of inventions of which Europeans would boast during their own Renaissance—the compass, the printing press, and gunpowder—were all discovered many centuries earlier in China. Gunpowder was used more commonly for fireworks than for military purposes by the Chinese, but they did have forms of military rockets, hand grenades, and even explosive shells by Song times. The printing press was used most commonly for wood-block printing—whole sheets reprinted from single blocks—rather than printing with movable type, Gutenberg's great contribution. But this was simply because movable type was impractical where thousands of characters, instead of twenty-six letters, were involved. The compass was a clear advantage; it opened all the eastern seas to Chinese junks.

The Chinese of these centuries studied acoustics, optics, astronomy, and mathematics. Chinese cartographers made elaborate maps of Asia, some with a superimposed grid indicating elevations and trade routes across the Far East. They compiled botanical studies classifying many sorts of plants, from garden herbs to trees. Even such apparently superstitious exercises as alchemical experimentation taught the Chinese a good deal about genuine chemical reactions.

Chinese medical studies included treatises on drugs, diagnosis, and other aspects of disease and its treatment. Tea and hot baths were recommended for many ailments, but quite convincing drug treatments were urged in other cases. Chinese doctors took the pulse as an aid to diagnosis and inoculated people against smallpox. Acupuncture, the famous Chinese practice of sticking needles into patients to anesthetize them for surgery, still puzzles Western doctors, who are unsure whether it impedes the flow of pain signals through the nerves or stimulates the body to secrete its own anesthetic substances. Whatever it does, it apparently often works.

The list of practical Chinese inventions goes on and on, well beyond the celebrated trio of compass, gunpowder, and printing press. Sedan chairs for the wealthy and wheelbarrows for the peasants, water mills and suspension bridges, paper and porcelain, ships' rudders and sea anchors, and many other handy devices were produced by the pragmatic Chinese intellect.

Poetry: Moon in the Water

Besides Buddhist religious writing, Neo-Confucianist scholarship and philosophy, and China's pace-setting performance in science, the Tang and Song periods produced a flood of literary prose and poetry of all kinds. The literary legacy of these centuries is as rich as any in the history of this immensely literate civilization.

Poetry appeared in massive quantities. We have the names of more than two thousand Tang poets and almost four thousand from the Song period, as well as tens of thousands of surviving poems. Poetry, calligraphy, and painting were the gentlemanly arts, and every gentleman, scholar, or official seemed to feel a social if not an aesthetic compulsion to grind out a few verses at least.

Some of the best-known of these poets are still read today. China's most famous poets, in fact, are the Tang masters Du Fu and Li Bo.

Du Fu, perhaps the most admired of all Chinese poets, was an eighth-century writer who wrote in elaborate verse forms. Yet he expressed a deep involvement with ordinary Chinese people, particularly with the oppressed and exploited. His "A Song of War Chariots," for instance, opens with a stirring call to battle:

The war-chariots rattle,
The war-horses whinny.
Each man of you has a bow and a quiver at his belt.

But it soon moves on to a grimmer assessment of the famous wars of the Tang:

> We remember others at fifteen sent forth to guard
>   the river. . . .
> The mayor wound their turbans for them when they
>   started out.
> With their turbaned hair white now, they are still at
>   the border,
> At the border where the blood of men spills like the
>   sea—
> And still the heart of Emperor Wu is beating for war.[2]

Du Fu wrote with grave Confucian concern of the misfortunes that have afflicted humankind from that day to this.

Du Fu's friend and contemporary Li Bo was as bohemian a poet as ever drank himself under a table or declaimed his verses at the moon. Like Du Fu a minor official, Li was a footloose wanderer, a lover of wine, good company, and nature—all of which he celebrated in his poetry. Actually, he seemed quite capable of conjuring up his own company, given the wine and a suitably romantic slice of nature. According to a famous legend, Li Bo drowned during a drunken boating party when he reached over the side to scoop up the moon from the water.

The poets of the Song period wrote masses of verse on such traditional topics as country life, oppressive officials, friendship, and unhappiness. The most famous of them was probably the eleventh-century writer Su Shi. He and his artistic coterie often combined all three of the gentlemanly arts by writing their poems in elegant calligraphy as part of a painting. Su Shi was also a thoughtful critic of both literature and art. Poems, he once said, are "pictures without form," and paintings "unspoken poems."[3]

Art: Mountains in the Mist

The arts of the thousand years encompassing the Six Dynasties, the Tang, the Five Dynasties, and the Song created beautiful things in many forms. Of them all, Tang architecture was perhaps the most admired in its day, Song painting today. Of the other arts, the two most distinctively Chinese were probably calligraphy and ceramics.

Song pottery is particularly sought after. The simple, graceful vases and jars, sometimes porcelain and sometimes stoneware, manage to blend the strength of earlier pottery with the elegance and delicacy of later ceramics. One style of decoration popular even in the imperial palace was the crackle design, an array of thin cracks produced by a glaze that cooled and broke over the surface of the vessel as it did so.

Calligraphy is one of the hardest of Chinese arts for a foreigner to understand. Chinese characters, executed with brush and ink on paper or silk have, however, a striking beauty to the cultured Chinese eye. The abstract pattern of the character itself, the strength, dash, fluidity, or grace of the brush stroke, the revelation of the personality behind any particular calligraphic style—all have an endless fascination.

Most of the surviving sculpture of the period is Buddhist in origin and includes Buddhas and bodhisattvas, especially Guanyin, the bodhisattva of mercy. The fullness and

---

[2]"A Song of War Chariots," in Cyril Birch, ed., *Anthology of Chinese Literature from Early Times to the Fourteenth Century* (New York: Grove Press, 1965), pp. 240–241.

[3]Susan Bush, *The Chinese Literati on Painting: Su Shih (1037–1101) to Tung Ch'i-ch'ang (1156–1636)* (Cambridge, Mass.: Harvard University Press, 1971), p. 25.

swaying poses of Indian sculpture frequently merge here with the linear quality of much Chinese art, usually in the folds of clothing. There is some awesome stone statuary, notably the huge figures in the seventh-century Longmen cave temples centering on an immense fifty-foot Buddha. There are many smaller, extremely realistic figures in wood, bronze, or china, including graceful Guanyins seated at ease, one hand extended in gentle blessing. In Song times vivid portrait figures of *lohans,* mountain hermits adept in both Buddhist and Daoist mysticism, give us a close look at the faces of these saints of other faiths.

The most massive and sometimes extravagant architecture of these centuries was that produced during the Sui and the earlier Tang. This age of empire builders was built on an imperial scale that was still admired in Song days. Huge palaces, pavilions, pagodas, and other structures are described in surviving literature, and some surviving pagodas give at least a flavor of the age. Pagoda towers, with their multiple, gracefully sloping eaves curving up at the corners, were built in connection with Buddhist temples or tombs.

Palaces also called for monumental building. Empress Wu Zetian, a great builder, once erected a royal hall three hundred feet on a side and almost three hundred feet high. An earlier ruler caused a pavilion to be constructed in which hundreds of guests could dine, and which could be rotated by machinery while they did so.

Not much remains of these great works except a few pagoda towers. But Song painting survives to delight us still. Painting on wall hangings or hand scrolls (to be unrolled horizontally, giving a gradual exposure to the work) was common from the Six Dynasties on. The most common Chinese word for painting is *hua,* meaning "to define by line," and Chinese painting has always been strongly linear.[4] Done with brush and ink, like calligraphy, it frequently looks more like drawing than painting to Western eyes. By whatever name, it is a major achievement.

Tang painting tended to use more color than was usual later. It also concentrated on the human figure, including some thoroughly convincing portraits and many figures of monks and other religious personages, elegant ladies, and other stock subjects. Other painters specialized in particular genre subjects, such as horses, birds, or flowers.

There was some Tang landscape painting, but this form really came into its own under the Song. Here, landscape painters largely abandoned color to concentrate on poetic line and on the famous Chinese composition that makes empty space an important part of the picture. The subjects define the face of the Chinese land as it looked a thousand years ago: bamboo and water, naked tree branches against snow, and again and again mountains in the mist.

Unrolling a hand scroll such as Gao Keming's eleventh-century *Streams and Hills Under Fresh Snow* is like taking a walk along the wintry river, with here a laden coolie, there a barge, gnarled trees close up, and further off a cozy house along the snowy bank, the master and mistress just glimpsed through an open door as they are served their dinner. Fan Guan's magnificently vertical *Travelers Among Streams and Mountains* shows the travelers in their carriages dwarfed by the pine-crowned hills just behind them, rendered utterly insignificant by the gigantic mountains that rise out of a veil of mist to dominate the picture.

---

[4]Wan go Weng, *Chinese Painting and Calligraphy: A Pictorial Survey* (New York: Dover Publications, 1979), p. xvi.

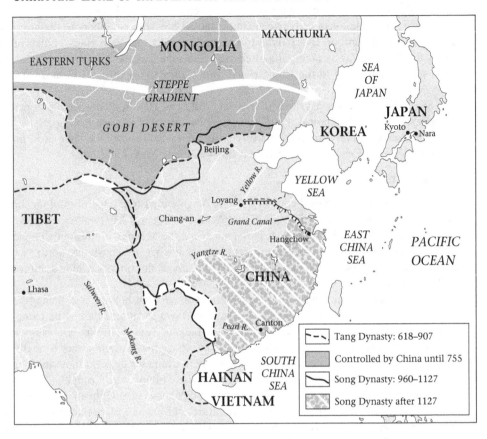

Tang building is gone, Song painting survives. Both make it only too clear why Chinese civilization dominated the East a thousand years ago.

CHINA'S SPHERE OF INFLUENCE: EAST ASIA

The Borderlands

The Chinese sphere of influence consisted of a ring of states and peoples around the Middle Kingdom. All these cultures were less developed than China's during the ten centuries from the fall of the Han to the fall of the Song. Two distinct regions—and relationships—may, however, be distinguished among these peoples of China's borderlands.

Most of China's inner frontier, facing north and west upon Eurasia, opened onto relatively barren and thinly peopled terrain. The dusty deserts, the thin grass of the steppes, the high cold plateaus of Manchuria, Mongolia, Tibet, and the Tarim Basin encouraged a pastoral nomadic style of life very different from China's intensive agriculture and developed urban society. The languages of the Turko-Mongol peoples beyond the Great Wall were so different that they could not even be written in Chinese characters.

The normal relationships between China and its nomadic neighbors to the north and west was one of conflict. Every dynasty had to deal with "the barbarians," either defensively like the Song or by taking the offensive against them as the Tang emperors did. But large-scale assimilation to the Chinese way would prove very difficult in most of these inner Asian borderlands.

South and east, however, the case was very different. Here settled agricultural peoples had already made a beginning at a more developed culture. And here the impressive Chinese achievement in civilization decisively influenced what became the three most important East Asian nations outside of China itself—Vietnam, Korea, and Japan.

Vietnam: The Lesser Dragon

Vietnam is a narrow S-shaped country running down the eastern edge of the Indochinese peninsula from South China into Southeast Asia. The country has two "rice bowls," the broad, fertile deltas of the Red River in the north and the Mekong in the south, connected by a long, curving mountain spine. Intruders from China began to push into north Vietnam toward the end of the first millennium B.C.E., just about the time of China's unification under the Qin.

They found a Bronze Age people, recently evolved from hunting and fishing yet already shaping an urban, seafaring society on a narrow agricultural base—the Dong-Son culture whose remains were to be found in many parts of Southeast Asia. Vietnam was no match for its huge neighbor. Shortly before 100 B.C.E., the Han emperors formally annexed the country, which would remain part of South China for the next thousand years.

Particularly under the aggressive Tang dynasty, Chinese rule brought Chinese administration and language, Confucian classics, and Mahayana Buddhism. Chinese influence also brought intensified wet-rice agriculture and a more elaborate urban culture. The Chinese presence, however, also generated a growing sense of national identity and resentment of foreign rule on the part of north Vietnamese officials and aristocrats in particular.

North Vietnam was never simply another Chinese province. The Vietnamese felt the cultural pull of their Indianized Southeast Asian neighbors. They were frequently preoccupied with the beginnings of their own long, slow conquest of southern Vietnam, which was then dominated by the Indianized kingdom of Champa. And resentment of their powerful neighbor to the north grew with every passing generation.

When the Tang dynasty collapsed into anarchy in the tenth century, the Vietnamese seized the chance to secede. After a long millennium as part of China, Vietnam was an independent—and growing—nation.

And yet before that century of independence was out, Vietnam's leaders had prudently accepted a tributary relationship with Song China. The cultural ties—and political enmities—that existed between the two nations would continue down the centuries, even to the present one. The troubled relationship between China and Vietnam, sometimes called the Greater and Lesser Dragons, remains a fact of East Asian life today.

Korea and Chinese Cultural Hegemony

Korea is a broad, slightly hooked peninsula thrusting down between North China's Yellow Sea and the Sea of Japan. The country is broken up by mountain ranges extending throughout much of its length. The western and southern coasts, however, smooth down into level plains and finally break up into many harbors and islands. The population at the time of the first Chinese intrusion was sparse and not long removed from dependence on hunting and fishing, though the western coastal plains particularly were already under cultivation. The Koreans still lived in tribal societies dominated by hereditary chiefs and female shamans called *mudang*. Their major monuments were stone-walled tombs, or dolmens, of the sort found in many parts of Eurasia, from western Europe to Japan, in earlier centuries.

The expansionist Han Chinese pushed into northern Korea in the last centuries before Christ. Empress Lü temporarily annexed part of the northern peninsula around 100 B.C.E. But Korea itself was moving rapidly ahead with state formation by then, and Chinese political control soon evaporated. Nevertheless, an influential colony of Chinese remained in the northern part of the peninsula for several hundred years.

From about the fourth century C.E. on, the Three Kingdoms divided Korea among them. These three rival Korean powers competed for Chinese skills and cultural innovations to strengthen them in their endless feuds. When the Sui and Tang dynasties reunited China in the seventh century, massive Chinese expeditions were launched against Korea. Once more, the attempt at conquest failed. But Empress Wu's shrewd alliance with the Korean kingdom of Silla, which soon established control over most of the peninsula, enhanced the continuing Chinese influence.

Under Silla in Tang times and under the kingdom of Koryo in the days of the Song, Korea's own rulers set out to turn their recently unified nation into a carbon copy of their huge neighbor. What remained of the old tribal culture was replaced as far as possible by a structure of central bureaus and provincial officials. The Korean economy—particularly the commercial sector—remained comparatively backward by Chinese standards. But the Chinese written language and culture, and most especially Chinese Mahayana Buddhism, were widespread.

Like the Vietnamese, the Koreans traditionally paid tribute to China. But the Korean debt to the Middle Kingdom went far deeper than annual payments. The development of Korean civilization illustrates perfectly the pattern of cultural hegemony that underlay the phenomenon of growing zones of culture around the world.

The Island Kingdom of Japan

The offshore-island kingdom of Japan provides a variant and even more important example of the impact of Chinese culture. Japan was dramatically affected by its encounters with Chinese civilization, yet a distinctive Japanese form of East Asian culture, contrasting sharply with China's in some ways, evolved in the end.

The reason for China's limited impact on Japan was probably primarily geographic. Japan lies more than a hundred miles east of the Asian mainland—five times as far from Asia as Britain is from Europe. At such a distance China's armed forces, which were spearheads of Chinese influence in Vietnam and even Korea, had no impact on Japan. The Japanese were thus much freer to accept or reject Chinese influences, to seek contact with the giant power to the west or to cut themselves off from it for generations at a time. From this unique circumstance evolved the strikingly selective pattern of China's influence on Japan.

The four main Japanese islands run some 1,300 miles, from jagged Hokkaido in the northeast through the long, indented curve of Honshu to the smaller islands of Kyushu and Shikoku in the southwest.

Four fifths of the island country is too mountainous for agriculture, but intensive rice cultivation in the narrow river valleys and coastal plains has made it possible for today's Japan to support the sixth largest population in the world. The mountains contribute to the nation's picture-postcard beauty and have given it a national symbol, the sacred snow-capped cone of Mount Fuji.

The center of Japan's early history was not in the heart of the large central island of Honshu, where Tokyo sprawls today, but in western Japan, around the narrow Inland Sea framed by Kyushu and Shikoku and the southwesternmost tip of Honshu. Here prehistoric hunting, fishing, and farming bands and settlements developed, matriarchal in social organization, worshiping nature spirits, working bronze and then iron.

During the early centuries of the Christian era, a simple clan-based society evolved around the Inland Sea, each small clan, or *uji,* having its hereditary chief and its ancestral god, often a totemic animal or other nature spirit. By the fifth century a loosely feudal state had appeared, dominated by the powerful Yamato clan; other *uji* were ranked in a rough hierarchy. By this time too, the collection of cults and religious practices called *Shinto* had emerged, along with its simple rites and local shrines dedicated to mountains, waterfalls, ancient trees, and a few sanctified individuals.

Japan and the Chinese Model

In the sixth century Chinese Buddhism reached Japan through Korea, bringing Chinese culture with it. In the seventh and eighth centuries, reforming Japanese regimes sent repeated embassies, including many students and monks, to Tang China to acquire the skills and learn the ways of the East Asian colossus. Powerful Japanese statesmen encouraged this procedure. The famous Prince Shotoku, in particular, preached centralized government and court hierarchy and even imported the Chinese calendar.

The resulting changes seemed likely to turn Japan into another small version of the Tang state. Japanese rulers and *uji* chiefs, some of whom were more powerful than their sovereign, nevertheless preached centralized rule by an absolute emperor and urged a Confucian sense of duty and Buddhist reverence. Centralized bureaus were established, a Chinese-style law code was promulgated, and attempts were made to establish the equal-field system and centralized taxation of Tang China. A capital city called Nara was built at the eastern end of the Inland Sea, modeled on Changian, with royal palaces and massive monasteries. The Japanese elite learned Chinese and used Chinese script, borrowed Chinese court ceremonials, Chinese styles and entertainments.

Beneath these transformations at the top of Nara society, however, Japan remained in many ways the Japan of old. The *uji* aristocracy preserved much of its former feudal independence despite the emperor's exalted claims. The economy remained comparatively simple; money, for example, was still rare, barter far more common. And the great Chinese invention of an educated civil service based on merit was never adopted at all beyond the Sea of Japan.

Then, as Tang China declined and crumbled into chaos in the ninth century, Japan turned away from its great model and began to develop its own distinctive style of civilization. The Heian period (roughly 800–1200), when the Japanese capital was at Heian (present-day Kyoto) was the period when this return to older ways was strongest. In three dynamic centuries Japan's ruling elite had absorbed all they could learn from China. The following four hundred years were given over to digesting and modifying these cultural acquisitions in terms of Japan's older native heritage.

The core of that heritage was *uji* feudalism, and the Heian period saw a significant resurgence of the power of the landed magnates in the *shoen* (estates) system. The *shoen* typically consisted not of a single estate but a dispersed collection of tracts owned by a single aristocratic proprietor. This proprietor looked up to a patron, usually a powerful figure at the royal court or in the Buddhist establishment. Below the proprietor were his estate managers, the farmers they managed, and the farm laborers the farmers hired. The result was a structure much like the feudal and manorial systems of Europe at that time— and very different from the centralized economy of China.

The chief patrons of the *shoen* system were wealthy court families, such as the Fujiwara, or religious institutions, commonly rich Buddhist monasteries. The great families in particular became the real rulers of Japan, using the royal court as an arena for their endless intrigues. The Fujiwara soon became the most powerful of these great clans, supplying the royal house with most of its empresses, monopolizing high government posts, and holding more *shoen* estates than any other family.

Occasionally feisty emperors challenged Fujiwara dominance, and there were damaging splits in the Fujiwara clan itself. But the real problem was that the authority of the government declined so drastically as to be a prize hardly worth controlling. As the power behind a powerless throne, the Fujiwara slowly went down with the monarchy they had themselves undermined.

The Culture of Court and Monastery

The Japanese cultural accomplishment during the seven centuries from the Yamoto state to the Heian period reflected even more strikingly the unique Japanese amalgamation of indigenous elements and foreign influences. This mixture is clear whichever of the twin centers of Japan's emergent culture we look at—the Buddhist monasteries or the imperial court.

The imported Buddhist faith comprised a variety of Chinese sects, from the ecclectic *Tendai* (Chinese: *Tiantai*) with its emphasis on the Lotus Sutra, through the popular

A Kyoto temple today, with its curving pagoda roof line, reflecting pool, and setting of trees and flowers beautifully embodies both the Chinese Buddhist influence and the grace and elegance of Heian Japan. Lightness, graceful lines, and the integration of buildings with the natural world around were features of Japanese architecture. (Japan National Tourist Organization)

Pure Land school, to the mystic withdrawal of meditative Zen (*Chan*). Pure Land Buddhism, offering hope of rebirth in the Buddhist paradise, had a particular appeal during the later Heian period, when the decay of central government and accompanying domestic violence made many fear that a Buddhist version of the end of the world was nigh.

Buddhist temples and Buddhist sculpture survive in considerable quantities, and Chinese influences are clear. The graceful lines of multiple pagoda roofs rose above the worldly capitals of Nara and Heian and among the forested mountains where some monks sought refuge from the world. Statues of Buddha, of various bodhisattvas, and of famous monks in meditation were crafted in stone, bronze, wood, and other materials. One of the most famous is the *Portrait of Ganjin*, a Chinese monk who tried six times to reach Japan, survived pirates, storms, and shipwreck to do so, and finally arrived—blind, having lost his vision in the course of his tribulations. There is more than realism in this simple figure seated in the Buddhist posture of meditation; the gentle face, shaved head, and closed eyes blend with the curving folds of the robe to project a feeling of benevolence and great peace.

The secular culture of the Heian period especially was immensely sophisticated for a people only a few centuries removed from the rude life of feudal clans. The court life of that period of intrigue and conspiracy was elegant in the extreme. Fashion, aesthetics, and the most delicate sensibilities governed the dress and decorum, the love life and artistic creativity of these courtiers of old Japan.

Poetry and exquisite prose were produced in substantial quantities, much of it by highly cultured court ladies. The greatest subject was love, the medium a mix of prose and poetry. An unusual literary form was the poetic diary, a first-person account of a journey, a love affair, or simply the daily life of the court, much of it written in verse. Though a core of autobiographical fact was necessary, artistic requirements seem to have determined the shapely contours of the finished work.

The novel also appeared this early in Japanese literary history. The most famous Heian novel—indeed, the most famous and influential of all Japanese novels—was Lady Murasaki's eleventh-century *The Tale of Genji*. Often described as the first psychological novel, this lengthy account of the life and love affairs of Prince Genji gives as much attention to nuances of feeling as to complex plotting and court life. Overlying it all, there is a romantic melancholy, a sense of the fragility of all things human, and of the heightened intensity this sense of transitory humanity gives to life, love, and beauty.

Among the rude barons of the back country, however, devotees of the warrior code of *bushido*, the builders of the next age, were already gathering their forces. The reign of the samurai was fast approaching.

SUMMARY

Between the third and the thirteenth centuries, many dynasties ruled China, but two loom gigantic in the history books: the empire-building Tang and the brilliant Song.

The Tang dynasty (618–907) was founded by Emperor Tang Taizong—"Grand Ancestor," victorious general, political reformer, scholar, artist, and perhaps the greatest of all Chinese rulers. The greatest of Chinese empresses, the Dowager Empress Wu, left the land richer and more powerful than it had ever been. Overall, China's political centralization, foreign trade, domestic wealth, and conquests beyond its own borders had never been greater than they were during the Tang.

The Song dynasty (960–1279) produced fewer great emperors, no foreign conquest, and diminished commercial exchange with the outside world. Yet the Middle Kingdom was never more brilliant. A population of one hundred million Chinese fed itself and was governed by the world's first meritocracy, the Confucian scholar bureaucrats.

Chinese culture during this millennium from the fall of the Han to that of the Song was varied and colorful. Chinese learning probed the nation's lengthening past and analyzed the classics of Confucius. Buddhist monks carried that Indian religion far across China and beyond. The printing press, the compass, gunpowder, and acupuncture all enriched Chinese culture.

Poetry blossomed in unparalleled quantities, including the lyrics of China's most admired poet, Du Fu, who wrote with Confucian concern for the Chinese underdog. Song ceramics and landscape painting established Chinese traditions that have been admired around the world since.

Under the Tang, furthermore, China's zone of influence among neighboring peoples exceeded even that of the Han. China ruled Vietnam as a loosely held province and exercised a decisive cultural influence on Korea. But Tang China's most important impact was felt by the still undeveloped islands of Japan.

Under Chinese influence, the island nation of Japan evolved from a culture of feuding clans into a Tang-style monarchy. China's impact declined during the inward-looking Song era, when Japan's emperors lost most of their power to its great noble families. Yet Japan remained a sophisticated new nation, where Buddhist monks, court poets, and novels like the famous *The Tale of Genji* reflected the seminal influences of the ancient empire more than a hundred miles away across the Sea of Japan.

SUGGESTED READING

Bol, P. K. *'This Culture of Ours': Intellectual Transitions in T'ang and Song China.* Stanford: Stanford University Press, 1992. Leading Chinese scholars defend and develop their culture.

Chaffee, J. W. *The Thorny Gate of Learning in Sung China: A Social History of Examinations.* New York: Cambridge University Press, 1985. Widely admired study of the development of China's scholarly elite during a period of rapid growth.

Deng, G. *Chinese Maritime Activities and Socioeconomic Development, c. 2100 B.C.–1900 A.D.* Westport, Conn.: Greenwood Press, 1997. Brief overview of Chinese maritime history, including major achievements in earlier centuries.

Dudbridge, G. *Religious Experience and Lay Society in T'ang China: A Reading of Tai Fu's* Kuang-i chi. New York: Cambridge University Press, 1995. Presents supernatural stories as records of spiritual life in "this-worldly" China.

Ebrey, P. B. *The Inner Quarters: Marriage and the Lives of Chinese Women in the Sung Period.* Berkeley and Los Angeles: University of California Press, 1993. Emphasizes women's initiatives in the limiting context of a patriarchal society.

Fitzgerald, C. P. *The Empress Wu.* Vancouver: University of British Columbia Press, 1968. Readable and scholarly life of the great Chinese empress.

Heng, C. K. *Cities of Aristocrats and Bureaucrats: The Development of Medieval Chinese Cityscapes.* Honolulu: University of Hawaii Press, 1999. Changing urban structures in Tang and Song times.

Lo, W. W. *An Introduction to the Civil Service of Sung China.* Honolulu: University of Hawaii Press, 1987. Personnel and organization.

Murasaki, S. *The Tale of Genji,* trans. E. G. Seidensticker. New York: Knopf, 1976. Accurate translation of this most famous of Japanese novels; Arthur Waley's older translation (London: Allen and Unwin, 1935) still has great literary appeal.

Pollack, D. *The Fracture of Meaning: Japan's Synthesis of China from the Eighth Through the Eighteenth Century.* Princeton: Princeton University Press, 1986. Complex interaction of borrowed ideas from China and indigenous Japanese concepts to produce Japan's own unique traditional culture.

Waley-Cohen, J. *The Sextants of Beijing: Global Currents in Chinese History.* New York and London: W. W. Norton, 1999. Survey of cultural contacts, challenging traditional view of Chinese isolation.

Wechsler, H. J. *Mirror to the Son of Heaven: Wei Cheng at the Court of T'ang T'ai-tsung.* New Haven, Conn.: Yale University Press, 1974. The founder of the Tang and his China.

Weinstein, S. *Buddhism Under the T'ang* (New York: Cambridge University Press, 1987), an examination of shifting government policies toward the spread of Buddhism in China.

Weng, W. *Chinese Painting and Calligraphy: A Pictorial Survey.* New York: Dover, 1978. Beautifully reproduced examples from a famous American collection, including many samples from the Northern and Southern Song.

 Please refer to the document CD-ROM for primary sources related to this chapter.

CHAPTER 13

KINGS AND CONQUERING PEOPLES
Empires of Africa and the Americas
(600–1450)

A Glance Ahead: Africa and the Americas

Large cultural zones took shape in Africa and the Americas during this period, too. From the grasslands of the Western Sudan to the Swahili coast of East Africa, from the peaks of the Andes to the banks of the Mississippi, neighboring peoples tended to share common cultural patterns.

Similarly intricate patterns of exchange linked peoples across North America as they did the cities of East Africa's Swahili coast. Toltec conquerors in Mexico, Christian kings in Ethiopia, and South American empire builders all raised cities and temples over broad swathes of the Old and New Worlds.

From common building styles or carvings, from the memories of visitors, and from their own heroic legends, we can reconstruct the common cultures that united each of these regions. We will see the peoples of East and West Africa and of North, Middle, and South America following distinctive styles of life shared with their neighbors, defining ever broader subdivisions of the earth.

West Africa: Ghana and Mali

The *Bilad al Sudan*

A number of interrelated factors contributed to the emergence of a distinctively West African civilization on the great westward bulge of Africa well before the year 1000. These linked causal factors included geography, trade, and religion.

While North and East Africa were geographically oriented outward toward the developing civilizations of the Mediterranean and the Indian Ocean, West Africa faced inward. Owing to a lack of natural harbors on the coast of West Africa, transport and trade were largely internal. And since commercial exchange was an essential ingredient in the development of kingdoms in West Africa, these new states emerged primarily in the interior, rather than along the coasts.

The interior of Africa, it will be remembered, is divided into a series of horizontal belts of land and climate. These belts are nowhere more clearly marked than in West Africa, and they are crucial to the emergence of trade in that region. In the north there is the thin strip of fertile land along the Mediterranean—the Maghreb, site of ancient Carthage, home in the year 1000 of Muslim Berber and Arab kingdoms, from Tunisia to Morocco. South of this coastal strip the Sahara Desert stretches the width of Africa, with its scattering of oases and caravan trails. Farther to the south lies the Western Sudan, the western end of the belt of lightly wooded savanna that also runs the width of the continent. Still farther south, finally, the dense rain forest of the Guinea coast extends eastward around the internal angle of Africa into the jungles of the Congo basin.

Trade in West Africa flowed predominantly north and south across these belts of climate and terrain. From the Maghreb in the north, camel caravans crossed the desert southward to the savannas to trade in the cities of the *Bilad al Sudan,* the "Land of the Black People," as the Western Sudan was then called. The goods and products these traders took back with them, including the famous gold of Africa, came mostly not from the Sudan itself but from the forests beyond. It was by building their power in this strategic location

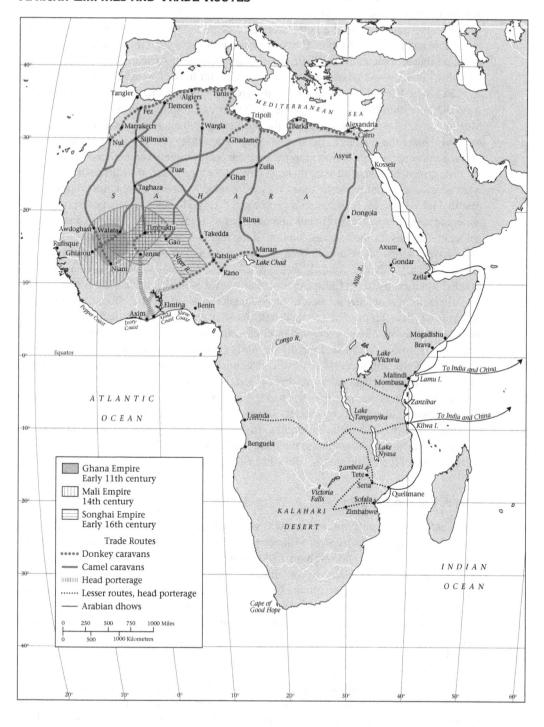

between the Sahara and the forest peoples of the Guinea coast that the Sudanic kingdoms waxed rich and famous as centers of trade.

With the traders from the north there also came the new religion of Islam. Muslim merchants and teachers, Arab or Berber, settled in the growing cities south of the Sahara and contributed their faith and their skills to the new West African states. They brought with them literacy and administrative experience, and they often held high offices under African kings. They also brought one of the great world religions, a faith which, while always that of a minority, helped to integrate the African kingdoms into the larger world of Muslim trade, Islamic pilgrimage, and the hospitality of their coreligionists wherever they traveled. Under these stimuli, the ironworking agricultural villages of the Western Sudan evolved into impressive African empires over the centuries between 600 and 1600.

The typical Sudanese state could be as large as, or larger than, the European nations that were developing about the same time. They were ruled by divine-right kings who served as essential intermediaries between their people and their gods. These rulers governed through a combination of appointed officials and alliances with lesser kings. They also maintained substantial armies for the constant warfare of the region. For long stretches of time the peoples of West Africa seem to have been well governed and prosperous. European as well as North African goods were on sale in the cities of the Sudan, and West African gold contributed significantly to the European economic revival of the High Middle Ages.

There were problems in the Sudanese kingdoms, as in all the efforts at civilization-building we have chronicled so far. These African empires seldom had clearly defined boundaries; they are often represented by circles on maps. And as in their medieval European counterparts, royal power faded rapidly the further one moved from the capital. There were serious problems with succession as well, since succession in West Africa was based not on direct patrilineal hereditary descent, but on a more generalized lineage concept that often produced more than one possible heir to a throne. As in most early civilizations, finally, rebellious generals and revolts by recently conquered peoples were common problems.

All such difficulties notwithstanding, the empires of the Western Sudan did represent a major expansion of urban imperial culture, and as such will be examined here. We shall focus on two of the most famous: Old Ghana and Mali.

Ghana: The Land of Gold

The Western Sudan before the year 1000 was open grassland dotted with scattered trees and groves. The people lived in villages of round, thatch-roofed earthen huts and granaries, cultivated millet and sorghum, and worked iron. The oldest male in a particular village normally ruled the village or sometimes a collection of villages, often with the strong advice and consent of a queen mother or a council of elders. Spirits dwelt nearby in sacred pools and groves of giant baobab trees, and carefully carved fetishes were kept in a special hut and consulted on all serious problems. It was a life, in short, much like that of other peoples outside the walls of urban culture.

Then, perhaps as early as 600, the walls of cities began to go up in West Africa too.

Ghana, the older of the two medieval West African kingdoms to be discussed here, flourished from the eighth through the eleventh centuries, and Mali, its successor, from the twelfth through the fourteenth. Both Ghana and Mali were dominated and most frequently ruled by Mande-speaking peoples: the Soninke, or northern Mande, and the Mandinke, or southern Mande, the latter the famous Mandingo of later history.

Ghana set the pattern of wealth and power built on trade that its successors would follow. As early as 800, while Charlemagne was being crowned in Rome and most of Europe was sunk in feudal chaos and subsistence agriculture, Ghana was already being described by Arab chroniclers as "the land of gold."

The origins of Old Ghana are lost in the mists of time and scholarly dispute.[1] By the eighth and ninth centuries, however, the Soninke kings of Ghana ruled all the lands bounded by the shallow V formed by the upper Niger and Senegal rivers. They governed many villages and clans through a centralized administrative structure and a powerful army. They claimed divine sanction for their governance; like rulers everywhere, they were the chief link between their subjects and the gods. In fact, however, it was commercial exchange that made them great.

From the north came Tuareg camel caravans down across the desert, navigating from oasis to oasis by sun, stars, and wind patterns on the dunes. The Arab and Berber merchants in these caravans brought cloth, brass, glass, and above all, blocks of salt—essential to life in the tropics—to the metropolises of Ghana. From the south, Ghanaian traders brought back agricultural products, slaves, and most important, gold from the mines of Wangara, just south of the Ghanaian frontier. Both Africa and Arab profited from the exchange. And the kings of Ghana collected heavy customs duties on all the gold and all the salt that crossed their borders. So great was the northward flow of gold that medieval Arab travelers and historians thought the king of Ghana must be the richest ruler in the world.

In the end, it was apparently excessive ambition and the slow southward advance of the Sahara that brought Ghana down.

The ambition of the Soninke kings led them to try to extend their authority northward along the trade routes into the Berber lands on the southern edge of the Sahara. The disunited Berbers fell easy victims at first. But in the eleventh century, unified and filled with crusading zeal by the puritanical Almoravid sect of Islam, they swept north as far as Morocco and on into Spain—and south to overwhelm Old Ghana.

The southward creep of the Sahara completed what the Almoravids had begun. The continuing drying-out of northern Africa parched the former heartland of Ghana. Before the slowly advancing sands, black power retreated farther to the south.

Mali: Where the King Dwells

The Almoravids broke the back of Ghanaian power, but they were not strong enough to rule for long. The result was to create a power vacuum in the Western Sudan where a number of African kingdoms fought for mastery. Another branch of the Mande-speaking people, the Mandinke, emerged victorious by the early thirteenth century from this anarchic period. They became the builders and rulers of an even larger realm than Old Ghana had been: the Empire of Mali.

Mali is an Arab corruption of a southern Mande word meaning simply "Where the King Dwells"—and the Mandinke rulers of Mali were kings indeed. They governed in conscious emulation of their Ghanaian predecessors, with appointed officials—including departments of defense, foreign relations, and finance—and with an effective army to enforce the royal will. They revitalized the trans-Saharan trade in gold and salt and grew

---

[1]"Old Ghana" is sometimes so called to distinguish it from the modern nation of Ghana, which is located some hundreds of miles southeast of the empire discussed here.

VOICES FROM THE PAST

This famous eleventh-century description of the capital of Ghana clearly reflects both the impact of Islam and the persistence of older African traditions. The Arab chronicler Al-Bakri records that the capital was really two "cities"—or city centers, since houses filled all the space between them. The Arab quarter is dominated by its mosques, while the "king's town," or political center, has its sacred grove consecrated to older gods.

According to this Arab account, the king received visitors in state in his royal pavilion, surrounded by the sons of subordinate chiefs, leading advisors, and governors. Guards with swords and shields stood behind him. The royal turban and robes, the shields of the sentries, and even the collars of guard dogs stationed at the door were all of gold.

What does this description tell you about the economy and political structure of Ghana? What do you deduce about the importance of the Arab traders from the fact that, while his majesty's African subjects were required to prostrate themselves on the ground before him and throw dust on their heads, Muslims were allowed to greet him simply by clapping their hands?

"The city of Ghana consists of two towns situated on a plain. One of these towns, which is inhabited by Muslims, is large and possesses twelve mosques, in one of which they assemble for the Friday prayer. There are salaried imams and muezzins, as well as jurists and scholars. In the environs are wells with sweet water, from which they drink and with which they grow vegetables.

The king's town is six miles [about 10 km] distant from this one and bears the name of al-Ghāba. Between these two towns there are continuous habitations. The houses of the inhabitants are of stone and acacia wood. The king has a palace and a number of domed dwellings all surrounded with an enclosure like a city wall.

In the king's town, and not far from his court of justice, is a mosque where pray such Muslims as pay him formal visits.

Around the king's town are domed buildings and groves and thickets where the sorcerers of these people, men in charge of the religious cult, live. In them are their idols and the tombs of their kings. These woods are guarded and none may enter them and know what is there."

Al-Bakri, *Kitab al-masalik wa'l mamalik,* in Nehemia Levtzion, "The Sahara and the Sudan from the Arab Conquest . . . to the Rise of the Almoravids," in J. D. Fage, ed., *The Cambridge History of Africa* (Cambridge: Cambridge University Press, 1986), Vol. 2, p. 668.

richer than the Soninke Mande of Ghana. They turned caravan-route cities like Timbuktu into famous emporiums of trade and centers of culture.

Mali reached its highest point in the fourteenth century under its most famous ruler, Mansa (King) Musa (ca. 1307–1332). Musa expanded the empire to its greatest territorial extent, to the big bend of the Niger. He was celebrated not only in Arab lands to the north but as far away as Europe.

The famous Arab traveler and historian Ibn Batuta, who visited Mali around the middle of the fourteenth century, was impressed with what he saw. He received good medical attention there when he fell ill, and he had respectful words for the scholars he met. Above all, he was struck by the strong sense of justice and the rigorous enforcement of it that he found in Mali. The roads of Mali were safe for travelers, he wrote, as they were in few other parts of the world.

This picture of a well-governed, wealthy, and powerful state has its darker side. There were frequent disputes over the succession to the throne, and factions feuded at the courts of the kings of Mali, as they did in royal courts from China to Britain. Conquered peoples were often restless and ready to rebel. Religion became an important divisive factor too, with Mandinke rulers turning to Islam while their peasant subjects and the neighboring peoples with whom Mali traded remained faithful to the old gods and the spirits of the land.

Like all great nations, the kingdom of Mali had its enemies, rivals awaiting only the opportunity to pull the greatest of West African powers down. In the fifteenth century, as we will see, one of them took advantage of internal weakness to do just that.

Mansa Musa's Pilgrimage

Like all the kings and increasing numbers of the ruling classes of Mali, Mansa Musa was a Muslim, and his most renowned exploit was a pilgrimage to Mecca. His royal progress across Africa astonished the peoples through whose lands he passed. On this long journey to the north and east across Africa, Musa was accompanied by his wife, his chief officials, thousands of servants, and a hundred camels laden with gold. He was given a palace in Cairo by the Egyptian sultan and spent three months there before continuing on to the holy city. He and his retinue had spent so much gold in Cairo that the price of that precious metal declined because there was so much of it in circulation. As an Egyptian official reported,

> This man spread upon Cairo the flood of his generosity: there was no person, officer of the court, or holder of any office of the Sultanate who did not receive a sum of gold from him. The people of Cairo earned incalculable sums from him, whether by buying and selling or by gifts. So much gold was current in Cairo that it ruined the value of money.[2]

On his return, Mansa Musa glorified his capital city. From his pilgrimage, he brought back artists, scholars, and a famous architect to build him palaces and mosques. He established diplomatic ties with African states as far away as Egypt and Morocco. It was from this time on that European map-makers began to put Musa's picture on their maps of West Africa with a lump of gold in his hand.

East Africa: Ethiopia and the Swahili Coast

The Christian States of Nubia

The influence of Islam was profound across North Africa, West Africa, and—as we will see—down the eastern coast of the continent as well. In one area, however, another great world religion exercised a determining influence. In the northeastern corner of Africa, several Christian kingdoms flourished, including the states of Christian Nubia and the Christian kingdom of Ethiopia.

Nubian civilization already had a long history when Christianity reached the Upper Nile in the sixth century. Nubia had been the home of a flourishing culture in the days of ancient Egypt. Kush and Meroe had flowered there, and Axum had overrun the southern core of the region. But great changes came over Nubia when Greek Orthodox preachers from the north converted first the kings and then the upper classes of the Nubian zone.

---

[2]ál-Omari, in E. Jefferson Murphy, *History of African Civilization* (New York: Crowell, 1972), p. 120.

The political history of Christian Nubia covered eight hundred years, from the sixth to the fourteenth centuries. The most powerful of the Christian kingdoms of Nubia was Makouria, whose chief cities were the royal capital at Old Dongola and the chief religious center at Faras.

At the height of its power, Makouria's King Kyriakos could march up the Nile into Muslim Egypt to force the sultan to release the imprisoned head of Egypt's Christian minority. In its heyday around 800, Makouria was ruled by a hereditary monarch who dictated to a dozen subsidiary kings and commanded a large number of officials.

Converted to Christianity by missionaries from the Greek-speaking Byzantine Empire, the Christian Nubian elite also spoke Greek, used Greek titles for officials, and used Greek as the official language of the church. Pictures of Nubian kings show them wearing golden crowns encrusted with jewels and clad in sumptuously embroidered robes like those worn by Byzantine rulers in Constantinople.

In its best days, Christian Nubia was a lovely land of cities and villages, churches and monasteries. A tenth-century Arab visitor recalled "villages with beautiful buildings, churches, monasteries and many palm trees, vines, gardens, fields and large pastures in which graze handsome and well-bred camels."[3]

By the 1300s, however, royal power had declined, and bloody coups were frequent. A feudal aristocracy with castles scattered across the land divided real power between them. Then Arab tribesmen broke through the frontiers, and Egypt's new rulers, the military aristocracy known as the Mamelukes, interfered repeatedly in Nubian royal politics. Cut off from the main body of medieval Christendom in Europe, Christian Nubia held out as long as it could against the growing power of Islam in Africa. By 1400, however, a Muslim dynasty ruled Makouria, and almost all of Nubia was in Islamic hands.

The Kingdom of Ethiopia

Southeast of Nubia, the Christian survivors of ancient Axum had withdrawn ever deeper into the mountainous regions of their corner of Africa in the latter part of the first mellennium C.E. A one-time trading people, they were now cut off from their former trading partners in the eastern Mediterranean and the Red Sea. Christian converts from the fourth century, they were surrounded by pagans and, from the seventh century on, by Muslim Arabs. Forgotten by their fellow Christians and by those whose ancient civilization they had shared, the people who would come to be known as Ethiopians struggled to survive in their isolated upland home.

Only in the twelfth century did a fusion of Ethiopian peoples under the Christian Zagwe dynasty bring a new flowering of this African kingdom. Under the Zagwe kings, a uniquely Ethiopian form of Christianity took shape. Heavily imbued with both local pagan and ancient Judaic elements, the Ethiopian church also forged a close alliance with the monarchy, a cooperation that strengthened both. The most striking relics of this era still remaining are the dozen rock-carved churches hacked out of the volcanic stone of the Ethiopian mountains at Roha during the reign of King Lalibela (ca. 1181–1221). According to a later medieval account, the king's stone carvers labored on the churches by day, while angels carried on the work at night.

---

[3]Ibn Selim, quoted in William Y. Adams, *Nubia: Corridor to Africa* (Princeton, NJ.: Princeton University Press, 1984), p. 461.

The Solomonid dynasty succeeded the Zagwe kings in 1270 and at least nominally ruled the land for the next seven centuries. Claiming direct descent from Israel's King Solomon and the Queen of Sheba, the Solomonids reached their apogee under King Zara Jacob (1434–1468). Still depending heavily on religion as a social cement, these Ethiopian rulers suppressed heresy at home and crusaded vigorously against neighboring Muslim peoples. From the fourteenth century, priests and monks generated a literary renaissance that produced hymns, royal chronicles, and biographies of kings and saints. By the beginning of modern times, sixteenth-century Ethiopia was an extensive if still isolated kingdom.

Medieval Europeans told legends of the golden realm of Prester John, a fabulously rich Christian king lost somewhere in the unknown southern lands of Africa. A hardy Portuguese traveler even reached Ethiopia in 1494, two years after Columbus reached the New World. But this and other early contacts came to nothing. Muslim military pressure was renewed in the later sixteenth century, and Ethiopian Christians themselves fell into a bloody schism. By 1600, the Solomonid monarchs were little more than figureheads, the kingdom itself a loose confederation of princes.

A Capital on the Move, A Mountain of Kings

Medieval Ethiopia's political system, at its apogee under the Solomonids, evolved some unique features all its own. Ruling over a large, geographically fragmented realm, over Christians, Muslims, Jews, and traditional animists, over Africans, Arabs, and other peoples, Ethiopia's kings devised a governmental system combining flexibility with strength. A loose feudal regime of vassal kings and nobles meant that the king of Ethiopia delegated a good deal of authority to regional powers. A large military force, ready to move at the first threat of serious disorder, gave the ruler the final say.

Two other institutions emphasized the flexibility of the Ethiopian system. One was the traveling royal court, the other Ethiopia's unique Mountain of Kings.

The court of the Ethiopian king was not settled in a single capital city but was always on the move. In some ways it resembled the restless monarchies of medieval Europe, moving from one castle or province to the next to keep an eye on feudal vassals whose loyalty was often fickle. In Ethiopia, however, the kings seem to have had no favorite seat. The royal court was a movable camp, ever ready to pull up stakes and move on to the next valley, to march against a rebellious prince or an aggressive neighboring people.

The royal caravan brought all the upper classes, ethnic groups, and religious sects together, while moving majestically from one part of the kingdom to another. Thus, the traveling court of Ethiopia performed a vital integrative function for this extremely heterogeneous society.

Ethiopia's legendary Mountain of Kings combined stability with flexibility in a very different way. King Yikunno-Amlak, who established the Solomonid dynasty in 1270, was determined to avoid future palace coups or revolutions. He therefore sent all his relatives except his designated heirs up to the heights of Mount Geshen, an inaccessible retreat guarded by picked troops garrisoning all the passes below. On Mount Geshen, all the princes of the realm who could be rivals for the throne lived in luxurious isolation. They were free to enjoy all the pleasures that went with their high birth—but cut off from political ties to the world below.

As the years passed, many of these royal exiles turned to religious study, took up poetry or music, became wise or creative spirits. And if ever the direct royal line failed in the kingdom, the wisest of all the denizens of the Mountain of Kings could be summoned down to take his place on the throne of Ethiopia.

The City-States of Zanj

Down the east coast of Africa, along the shores of the Indian Ocean, a process of commercial growth, Islamicization, and cultural synthesis similar to that in West Africa was taking place. The result was the flourishing string of East African ports and city-states the Arabs called the Land of Zanj—mostly Kenya and Tanzania today.

Wave after wave of migrants had settled along this edge of the continent. The Bantu-speaking Africans were migrants across central Africa to these coasts, bringing iron and agriculture. Other peoples had come by sea. Southeast Asians had been coming for centuries, populating the huge southern island of Madagascar and introducing the ubiquitous banana to Africa. Shirazi Persians, probably moving south from earlier settlements on the Horn of Africa, came as traders. But the most successful immigrants, merchants, builders, and sometimes rulers were the Muslim Arabs we have already met in so many places.

The history of evolving relationships between African animists and agriculturists on the one hand and Arab Muslim traders on the other must be worked out largely from archaeological remains and oral tradition. Arabs, by that time masters of most of the Indian Ocean trade, seem to have settled in East Africa in growing numbers from the twelfth century on. They may have established trading posts alongside African towns, as they did in the Western Sudan, accepting the protection of African kings. Or they may have imposed Arab overlordship, as they would do along these coasts in later centuries.

Swahili Society

In either case, the Muslim faith spread here as well as in West Africa. A mixed Afro-Islamic Swahili culture developed. A Bantu language, Swahili, continued as the lingua franca of the coast, and African customs persisted even among the rulers of the new city-states that emerged. But there were Arab influences in Swahili too—the word itself means "people of the coast" in Arabic—and the architecture of the new towns was more likely to be Arabic or Persian than African in design.

The wealth of East Africa, like that of the Western Sudan, was based on commerce. Here the trade routes of inner Africa met the sea lanes of the Indian Ocean, linking Africa with the Mediterranean, Arabia, India, Southeast Asia, and China. Ivory, gold, iron, copper, pearl, coral, and slaves left African shores; Indian beads, Chinese porcelain, and silks flowed into Africa from overseas.

The East African cities of Kilwa, south of Zanzibar, and Sofala, still farther to the south beyond the Zambesi, dominated the region. The first Portuguese intruders around 1500 reported a number of such cities, with fine stone buildings, women wearing imported silks and beads, and rich agriculture produce. The houses of Mogadishu in the north were multistory structures, and the palace at Kilwa covered two acres, with courtyards and vaulted chambers on a cliff overlooking the sea.

The quality of life in these coastal cities would later be testified to by the Portuguese. The narrow stone-walled city streets were similar to their own. Doors were elegantly carved, beds sometimes inlaid with ivory, walls inset with Chinese porcelain or Persian ceramics, like the dishes on which the wealthy ate. Early European visitors also noticed the luxurious silk and cotton garments of wealthy Swahili women, their gold and silver bangles and earrings set with precious stones.

Foreigners seldom penetrated the inner courtyards of the homes of the well-to-do. But baked clay lamps lit interior rooms, and one Arab author reported that the elites of these East African towns "take spiritual delight in the study of philosophy."[4]

A stroll down the streets of the island town of Lamu off the coast of Kenya today may give a general impression of that lost world. Close-pressing walls of whitewashed stone, intricately carved doorways, cool courtyards and tangled gardens frame the life of what is now a quiet backwater. The muezzin still wakes you before dawn each morning with his call to prayer. And the old stone pier where you land and leave still shelters Arab dhows in from the Red Sea or the Persian Gulf.

African Society and Culture

Urban and Rural Africa

Across the continent, outside influences took root much more rapidly in urban than in rural environments. In both East and West Africa, Muslim traders settled in cities. As we have seen, kings sometimes converted to Islam, built mosques, and invited in Muslim artists, holy men, and scholars. Even where they remained pagan, as in Ghana or a number of trading cities in East Africa, African rulers encouraged the development of a wealthy, literate, and skilled Muslim community.

The countryside, by contrast, preserved old ways of life. Most villagers' religious beliefs remained animistic, with strong emphasis on the cults of their own ancestors. The natural world still spoke to them, and their lives were shaped by communal traditions and the legends and memories of their heroic past. Not infrequently, these traditional Africans resented the innovations that took root in the cities. As we will see, it was a social division that could shake the stability of even the great empires of the Western Sudan.

Women East and West

Family structures varied significantly across the continent. Though a common African pattern of matrilineal control of property may be detected in early times, it was fading by this period of African history. The spread of Islam, furthermore, strengthened patriarchal authority and patrilineal lines of descent. Islam also brought religious sanction for polygyny, allowing up to four wives for a single man.

The spread of Islam, on the other hand, could have a positive impact on the lives of some African women. Women in some places learned to read Arabic and studied the religious documents of their new faith. Others gained materially from conversion, acquiring rights to property and to inheritance prescribed by Islamic law.

As in most societies, of course, women's lives also differed up and down the social scale. In many parts of Africa, women enjoyed both material wealth and real power. As mothers or chief wives of kings, and as officials and independent local magnates, women could hold places at the top of African society. Especially in West Africa, they were a powerful force in the marketplace. Everywhere, they could raise children, feed and clothe families, and do most of the farm work too.

---

[4]Abu 'l-Kasim al-Andalusi, quoted in V. V. Matviev, "The Development of Swahili Civilization," in D. T. Niane, ed., *General History of Africa* (London: Heinemann, 1984), Vol. 4, p. 457.

Visitors also frequently commented on a generally easy pattern of socializing between the sexes. African women did not traditionally live in harems or *purdah*. They seem to have had more power to choose their own friends, their own activities, and the way they lived their lives than in many other parts of the world.

Muslim and Christian Cultures

As noted previously, Muslim visitors to West Africa were impressed by the building programs of rulers like Mansa Musa. They saw mosques built of brick as well as traditional "mud mosques" made of traditional pounded earth. They saw Arabic scholars supported by African kings and books for sale in the local bazaars. They heard imams preach the faith of the Prophet and other holy men reciting the Quran for the edification of the multitudes. Cities like Timbuktu and Gao struck such visitors as admirable centers of Islamic culture.

Physical remains from East Africa leave the same impression of a rich, sometimes Christian, heritage. Among these are the beautiful frescos rescued from the Nubian cathedral at Faras and the rock-cut churches built by Lalibela.

In the most famous of the Faras frescos, the three youths cast into the fiery furnace in the Old Testament are shielded from harm by the towering Archangel Michael. The figures, garbed in blue and gold, stand out vividly against a wall of leaping scarlet flames.

The eleven churches of the Lalibela complex were named after structures in Jerusalem. A stream flowing through the center was called after the river Jordan, and a high spot overlooking the churches was labeled "Calvary" after the site of Christ's execution. According to legend, King Lalibela had been mystically transported to Jerusalem, where Christ himself showed him the holy places as they were later duplicated in the king's rock-cut church center. There each year Christ's baptism, crucifixion, and resurrection were reenacted in a passion play at this sacred site high in the mountains of Ethiopia.

Traditional Culture: Dancing the Mask

Recent studies of the traditional religious life of Africa tend to focus on a profound sense of unity in African life. They stress the continuity of nature and humanity, land and people, the individual and the group, the living and the dead. More commonly than not, this faith is called *animism*—a religion that sees a common *life* in all things.

There is, African animists seem to feel, a spiritual vitality in everything around them. Mountains, streams, wells, trees, the animals they kill, and the plants they grow all live as people do, and many communicate with them as people do with each other. Africans and the world they inhabit are thus, in a deep spiritual sense, one.

The individual is also one with the group, or groups, of which he or she is a part. The family and the clan, the age group into which one is born, the village community as a whole form a living network of relationships. This network absorbs people at birth, nurtures them all their lives, and determines their destinies. The individual is part of the community, as he or she is of nature.

There are, finally, fundamental ties binding the generations, living and dead. The spirits of ancestors are with the living still, to guide, warn, or haunt them as their actions warrant. Past and present, life and death thus merge in the mind of the African animist into a seamless web of spirituality surrounding us all.

The African mask, perhaps the most successful African sculptured form, expresses these spiritual themes with unsurpassed intensity. African masks clearly illustrate the con-

Traditional African dancers embody the powers of nature and celebrate key transitions in human life. These Dogon dancers from West Africa perform the same spectacular steps recorded on film by anthropologists early in the last century. (Anthony Esler)

tinuity of the clan and the people. They are made according to strict tribal traditions, and every West African can tell a Senufo from a Mande mask, the shaman's mask from that of a men's secret society. Carved in wood, painted, decorated with raffia, cowrie shells, and colorful beads, these masks have a life of their own—the vivid, sometimes fearful life of the spirit they personify.

It may look like a finished art product, strikingly carved and intricately decorated, hanging on the wall of a museum. But an African mask is never really experienced until it is seen in motion—in performance—worn by an African dancer as part of the ceremonial activity it was made for.

Dancing the mask still expresses the deep African feeling of oneness, of identity among the dancer, the mask he wears, and its indwelling spirit. It is this spiritual presence that possesses the dancer when he presses the wood against his face, feels the leather thongs behind his head and the raffia mane spreading over his shoulders. And it is this spiritual presence that possesses him as he sees through narrow eye slits the familiar village faces, the hard-packed earth of the dancing place, as they appear in the distorting and exalting vision of the spirit of the mask.

NORTH AMERICA: THE PUEBLOS AND THE GREAT MOUNDS

Expanding Zones Beyond the Seas

Africa has been closely linked to other cultures of the Old World for thousands of years—hundreds of thousands if we go back to the first great migrations of early hominids north out of Africa. Trade, religious influences, and other connections are thus not surprising. But the peoples of the Americas—the New World, as Europeans would soon be calling it—continued to develop in isolation from Old World peoples and often from each other. Nevertheless, they too evolved expanding zones of common culture during this period of their development.

Pueblo Culture

Pueblo means "town" in Spanish, and we still apply this label to the unique collections of adobe or masonry houses under the red cliffs of the American southwest that the conquistadores recognized with astonishment as "real towns" in that otherwise barren land. In fact, the Pueblo culture is only one phase of a general regional flowering that made Arizona, New Mexico, and the northern provinces of today's Mexico one of the two most impressive zones of preurban development in North America.

This transition was brought about by the arrival from Mexico of the three basic Amerindian crops—corn, beans, and forms of squash—and by their gradual adaptation to the arid southwest. This was accomplished about the time of the Fall of Rome. As we saw, Indians of several cultures were thus transformed into village agriculturalists. Finally, between 900 and 1300—a period roughly contemporary with the High Middle Ages in Europe—the later "pueblo" phases of what archaeologists call the Anasazi culture produced the most remarkable flowering of this impressive preurban society.

The pueblo culture of the Anasazi—"Ancient Ones" in Navaho—left impressive remains and has been studied thoroughly, perhaps more intensively than any other Native American society. Archaeologists note their dikes and dams for collecting precious water, their woven cotton blankets, their feather robes, their bows and many specialized arrows, and their tiny cult figurines, perhaps related to fertility. Collectors treasure their black-and-white Mesa Verde pottery. But it is the pueblos themselves that impress the more casual visitor.

Constructed originally of mud and sticks, these clustered apartment buildings of the southwest were soon being built of stone instead. They were sometimes erected against cliffs or even under rocky overhangs. Others were laid out in rectangular, L-shaped, or semicircular blocks that were several stories high and contained an enclosed court. There were sometimes towers and usually storage pits for the grain that was the mainstay of the economy. There was almost always a *kiva,* or underground ceremonial chamber. With the passing centuries these residential complexes grew larger, till some had more than a hundred units and scores of families living together.

These remarkable structures were usually built on ledges across steep cliffs or on the flat tops of mesas. The builders cultivated their carefully irrigated fields in the valleys below. When attacked by less settled neighboring peoples, they could retreat to their precipitous cliff or mountain-top dwellings and hold their foes at bay.

Among the most famous of these pueblo settlements were those at Chaco Canyon, probably built as early as the eleventh or twelfth century. Those at Mesa Verde were elaborate multistoried cliff dwellings that flourished during the next couple of centuries. Thereafter, changes in southwestern climatic conditions drove the builders to move to the Hopi mesas and the Rio Grande valley, where their descendants still live today.

The Mississippi Culture

Another impressive Native American society in North America flourished not in the southwest but in the southeast. The major remains of the Mississippi culture are to be found along the rivers of the Mississippi valley, and its cultural roots lie less in Mexico than in the classic Hopewell culture of the eastern woodlands of the future United States.

Mississippian sites, located usually on river banks, feature flat-topped mounds, a particular sort of pottery made with eggshell, and a collection of exquisite artifacts—jewelry and even metalwork—found in graves and associated with what used to be called a death cult. These remains are found across a wide tract of well-watered, temperate, originally thickly forested land that includes the east coast of the United States, the southern Appalachians, and the whole length of the Mississippi River valley.

During the period between 750 or so and the appearance of the first Europeans in 1540, Native Americans in the southeast shifted slowly from hunting and gathering toward dependence on agriculture. Ceremonial religious centers point to a powerful priestly cult among them. But fortifying walls become more common at later Mississippian sites too, indicating warfare and war leaders. These leaders may even have been hereditary, which would have made the societies that built the great mounds true chiefdoms, only half a step from the bureaucratic political state.

Mississippian societies traded widely on the rivers of North America. They practiced some specialized crafts, whole villages manufacturing stone hoes or mining salt. Their ceremonial pottery included exotic human and animal shapes, and their graves have yielded copper and shell ornaments and flat copper representations of winged human beings.

The famous mounds actually took a number of forms and served a variety of purposes. Some are cone shaped, some pyramidal in form. Some were raised in the shape of animals of various types, including birds and serpents. Most were magnificent burial mounds for local notables. The "effigy" mounds—those shaped like living creatures—were probably intended for religious purposes. But some were used like similar earthen mounds in Mexico—or on the hills of ancient Greece—as foundations for important buildings.

The largest such center so far excavated was at Cahokia, a site near the modern city of St. Louis. Here a string of some 85 mounds stretches for six miles along a river bank. In the 1200s, most of the people of Cahokia worked the hundreds of acres of corn that surrounded the complex, feeding a population of perhaps 30,000 people.

The largest of Cahokia's impressive earthworks was the huge Monks Mound, a hundred feet high and built on a base seventeen acres in area. Constructed entirely by Indian labor equipped with baskets to carry the earth, this mound must have dominated Cahokia as an acropolis did an ancient Greek city-state. Like the mounded temple bases of Mexico, this man-made hill was almost certainly the location of temples and the rude palaces of chiefs. Religious ceremonies on the high mound would feature chiefs and priests in elaborate costumes and dazzling headdresses made of brightly colored feathers.

The Ritual Ball Game

Ancient peoples of many lands, from classical Greece and Rome to Celtic Britain, engaged in rough competitive team sports involving balls. In the urban-imperial parts of the pre-Columbian Americas, a Great Ball Court was a common feature of both Toltec and later Aztec towns. The ball court at Chichén Itzá was huge, a walled enclosure 270 feet long and 25 feet high. In these Mexican versions of the great game, hard rubber balls were hurled through stone rings in a violent competition, which may have climaxed with the ritual sacrifice of the losers.

Among the preurban peoples of North America, the game was played without a ball court or human sacrifice. But a winning strategy could involve knocking rival players out of the game by breaking limbs or even by killing them. The North American ball game was thus often seen as good training for warfare: The Cherokee called it "the little brother of war." At the same time, there was clearly a religious dimension to the game, which was often surrounded by mystic rites and ritual dancing.

The ball game as played by the Cherokee of the southeastern part of the future United States well illustrates these religious elements. Amerindian peoples, like the African village peoples already discussed, saw themselves as part of the natural world and strove consciously to live in harmony with other natural creatures—animals, plants, and earth itself. Training for the game thus involved not only physical exercise but also invoking the spirits of the natural world. Instead of an athletic coach, the village shaman presided: praying to the spirits of powerful or swift animals (the eagle, the deer) and forbidding tabu foods such as the timorous rabbit. The game itself was preceded by a full night of dancing, invocations, and the ritual "scratching" of the competitors with turkey claws until their legs, arms, and bodies ran with blood. There followed an early morning hike of several miles to the playing field, final prayers to all the forces of the living world, and the game began. Needless to say, the losers immediately demanded a rematch!

MIDDLE AND SOUTH AMERICA: FROM THE TOLTECS TO CHIMU

Mexico and Peru: Continuing Centers of American Civilization

Major centers of civilization in the pre-Columbian Americas continued to lie south of the Rio Grande, in Mexico and Peru. By C.E. 1000 both these zones of developed and intermittently urban imperial culture were well established in the Americas.

The complex societies of both regions were built primarily on agriculture.

Mesoamerican culture was built on the traditional agricultural base of maize, beans, chilies, and squash, which supported a comparatively dense population of several million people. Mesoamerican societies were as hierarchical as any in the Old World. Amerindians in this part of the New World were learning the art of effectively governing large empires. They also suffered periodic influxes of skin-clad Indians from the north, attracted as Goths were to Roman Europe or Mongols to China by the seductive charms of civilization.

Agriculture was widely practiced in South America also, but the range of products was greater. Corn, beans, and various kinds of squashes were common in Peru as in Mexico. In addition, potatoes were the upland staple of the Andes, and coca and other tropical products came from the Amazonian interior. Huge flocks of llamas and alpacas were herded in the high country. Hillsides were terraced for agriculture, and irrigation canals and ditches spread water over lowland valleys.

In various parts of Peru, large ceremonial centers and even some true cities featured huge stone buildings, especially temples and palaces. Many crafts were practiced, including the ancient ceramics and textile industries and more working in metal than in Middle America.

The Toltecs: A Race of Legendary Heroes

The decline of the Mesoamerican civilizations of the classic age—of Teotihuacán and the cities of the Mayans—was apparently accompanied by widespread violence. Preurban, sometimes even preagricultural peoples, particularly from the north, overran central Mexico and the southeastern lowlands. Many of these invaders, like the ancient Aryans in India, did not occupy the cities they conquered but shied away, regarding them as supernatural places. Some used deserted cities as burial places for their dead.

A Toltec pyramid at the Mayan sacred city of Chichén Itzá, in modern Mexico, shows how much the conquerors had absorbed from the subtle minds of the Mayans. The pyramid, for example, has 365 steps, one for each day in the Mayan—and the modern—solar calendar. Its nine levels correspond to the nine levels of the Mayan underworld, while the temple on top is dedicated to the god Kukulcan, the Mayan version of Quetzalcoatl, the Feathered Serpent whose cult went back to ancient Teotihuacán. (Hugh Rogers/Monkmeyer Press)

One famous race of conquerors, however, surged down from the north not to destroy but to reinvigorate the crumbling urban culture of Mesoamerica. These were the legendary Toltecs, the most celebrated of all the precursors of the Aztecs in Middle America.

Like the Aztecs who came after them, the Toltecs were apparently a Nahuatl-speaking, warlike, less developed people from the north. They descended into central Mexico around 900. They may have participated in the destruction of Teotihuacán; they certainly imposed their will on the surviving Mayans of Yucatán—and learned from them. Toltec power extended even into Guatemala.

Everywhere the central feature of their culture was the predominance of a warrior ruling class. Grim-faced soldiers of the orders of the eagle and the jaguar march across the walls of temples in their metropolis of Tula. Priests, who were the highest caste in most Mesoamerican cultures, yielded pride of place to soldiers under the Toltec hegemony.

These invaders were not barbarians, however. They had lived on the northern fringes of Middle American urban culture long enough to be at least partially civilized themselves. And some of their vigor went into other than warlike pursuits.

Far from destroying or abandoning cities, the Toltecs built new ones, like their capital at Tula, or expanded old ones, like Chichén Itzá in Yucatán. Tula included a number of typical Mesoamerican features, such as a central plaza with temples, palaces, and other large buildings around it, as well as such innovations as long roofed colonnades around the square.

Metalworking also developed among the Toltecs, though more commonly for jewelry than for useful objects. Most important, the Toltecs substantially expanded commercial relations within and perhaps beyond Middle America, linking the Mexican highlands with the tropical lowlands and conceivably even with South America.

Especially important trade goods were tropical products with a great appeal to the people of Mexico's central plateau: cocoa, feathers, and cotton. Cocoa was both a favorite drink in Middle America and a common medium of exchange, used as money for buying, selling, and paying debts. Feathers from tropical birds, used as a chief form of personal adornment, became a major medium of artistic expression. Cotton cloth grew in importance during this period and could even be worked into the armor of the warrior elite who dominated the era.

The famous semimythical Toltec ruler Topiltzin, identified with Quetzalcoatl as sage, founder of civilized arts, and spiritual leader, embodied the virtues the Toltecs most admired.

Topiltzin was even alleged to have tried to keep his people from practicing the bloody religious rituals of human sacrifice. In the end, the living embodiment of Quetzalcoatl "went away," promising to return at some distant future time. With his passing, prosperity departed from the Toltecs. After a century of achievement, drought and famine spread over the land, and new waves of more barbarous invaders came down from the north.

Tiahuanaco and Huari: Cities of the Andes

The postclassical period in the Andean region saw several substantial regional hegemonies emerge. One among them, the Chimu state, was the most impressive political structure erected anywhere in South America before the coming of the Incas. Two other names, however, also help to fill the centuries between the decline of the Mochica and other classical cultures and the rise of the Inca Empire: the linked names of Tiahuanaco and Huari.

Tiahuanaco, on the high Bolivian plateau south of Lake Titicaca, has left behind some huge stone temple ruins and some rare statues of human beings. Huari, in Peru, had dwelling places as well as public buildings and was evidently a true city, rather than a ceremonial center only. The surviving ceramics, textiles, and carvings of these two peoples bear enough resemblance to indicate some relationship between them. But as is usual where written records are lacking, the political history of Tiahuanaco and Huari—and any political ties between them—can only be conjectured.

The two may have been separate conquest empires, one ruling northern Peru, the other southern Peru and parts of Chile and Bolivia, between C.E. 600 and 1000. Or people from Tiahuanaco may have spread north to the Huari area, mixed with coastal peoples to build Huari itself, and then spread a modified Tiahuanaco-Huari culture by conquest over much of pre-Incan Peru.

Under such joint or divided Tiahuanaco-Huari hegemony, in any case, the Andean area saw some changes. The breeding of llamas, for instance, spread down into the valleys, bringing meat, wool, and other advantages. Bronze began to be worked on a modest scale. Most important, a number of small cities sprang up. Many of these were walled and included no temples at all, leading some archaeologists to suggest that here, as in Mexico, a military aristocracy was shouldering the priesthood aside.

It was in the coastal state of Chimu, however, that these tendencies reached their climax.

Chimu: People of the Coast

According to local legend, the founder of the royal house of Chimu and his entourage came on balsa rafts across the ocean—a story that has led some scholars to postulate an Asiatic origin for this remarkable society with its highly autocratic government. Others point to the elaborate irrigation system that was central to Chimu culture and see in it a typical example of a hydraulic empire requiring strong central authority to regulate the crucial water supply. Whatever its origins, this was a rigorously centralized and militaristic state, and one of the most culturally advanced of pre-Columbian times.

Located in northern coastal Peru, Chimu in the fourteenth century controlled some five hundred miles of coastal valleys along the Pacific. Its geographical and cultural core was the old Mochica region, its economic basis the much expanded irrigation systems of those valleys. The scope of these works, sometimes uniting several valleys in a single hydraulic network, was unprecedented across the region.

This enigmatic statue from Tiahuanaco has some of the "Atlantean" feel of being totally unlike the work of any other culture. The roughly rectilinear decoration generally resembles other pre-Columbian carving, and the figure is no more naturalistic than most early American art. Nevertheless, an overall feeling of strangeness seems to hover over this robot-like survivor of a ruined city on the shores of Lake Titicaca in the stark Andean uplands. (Carolyn Kerson/ D. Donnie Bryant Stock Photography)

The cities of Chimu, particularly the capital, Chanchan, were large and rich, with houses and gardens for the warrior nobles, pyramid temples, and administrative centers. Chanchan's walls were thirty feet high and several miles around. The population may have run as high as 100,000. Unlike Mesoamerican cities with their central plazas, however, the Chimu capital was built in ten separate walled wards or precincts, perhaps to house different clans or social classes. Chimu cities were built of adobe brick rather than of stone, but brick so good that surviving examples sell for ten times what a modern brick will bring in Peru today.

The Power of the Chimu State

It is the government of the Chimu state, however, that arouses the most interest. The scale of irrigation projects and urban construction would have required a central authority with power over large numbers of laborers. The increasing proportion of palaces, fortresses, and other secular structures, as against temple architecture, indicates that here too a warrior elite was replacing a priestly one.

According to Inca evidence, the Chimu state was a kingdom, founded early in the fourteenth century by conquest. The king of Chimu—wherever he came from—was believed to be divine and had immense authority. Each separate valley had its own appointed governor, and a regular structure of government existed in which village headmen, or *curacas,* reported to *curacas* at higher levels up through the governors to the king.

The presence of large buildings, which apparently served as both administrative and religious centers of cities and wards, strengthens our sense of centralized authority. State power also extended to the frontiers, where large fortresses anchored a system of defense against the smaller states of the Peruvian coasts.

Chimu was in fact the most powerful centralized state in South American history before the coming of the Incas, who, like the Aztecs in the north, would put empire-building on a whole new level in the Americas.

Summary

From West Africa to East Africa, from North to South America, societies and civilizations outside Eurasia continued to evolve during this age of expanding zones of culture around the world.

In Africa, commerce and religion were at the heart of the new zones of urban imperial culture that took shape between C.E. 600 and 1450. The kings of the Western Sudan, located between the Sahara and the deep forests, became middlemen in the lucrative trade between the Arab states of the Maghreb and the forest peoples of the Guinea coast. The kings built powerful states on the grasslands, and Arab merchants brought Islam, literacy, and other innovations to their urban elites.

The most famous of these Sudanic kingdom was Ghana (eighth to eleventh centuries), known to Arab travelers as "the land of gold." Mali (twelfth to fourteenth centuries) emulated earlier Ghanaian practices with even greater success, building such commercial metropolises as Timbuktu and producing one of the most famous of West African rulers in Mansa Musa.

The spread of early Christianity up the Nile strongly influenced the new civilizations that emerged in Nubia and Ethiopia (ancient Axum) between 500 and 1500. Powerful monarchs ruled these countries while churches and monasteries generated new schools of art, architecture, and religious literature. Christian Ethiopia, though declining politically, survived as an independent state on into modern times.

On the East African coasts a number of city-states played an important part in trade on the Indian Ocean between the seventh and the fifteenth centuries. Cities like Kilwa or Sofala had Muslim Arab commercial communities and they traded with Arabia, India, and countries even farther east.

In the New World, new societies continued to emerge north and south of the Rio Grande. In North America, the Pueblo and Mississippi cultures evolved steadily toward the urban economies and centralized governments already developed by their southern neighbors. The Cahokia Mound Builders were closing rapidly on the developed civilizations of Middle and South America when the first Europeans reached the western hemisphere.

Developed civilizations continued to flourish in Mexico and Peru and their neighbors. In both areas warrior elites seem to have been more prominent, priestly predominance less central, than in earlier times.

The Toltecs in Mexico were the most important conquerors before the coming of the Aztecs. Arriving in the ninth century, at the time of the passing of the Classic Maya and Teotihuacán cultures, the Toltecs created several regional states and encouraged trade and city-building in many parts of Middle America.

Among the regional hegemonies of South America, the Tiahuanaco and Huari cultures emerged as early as the seventh century. The most politically integrated was the fourteenth-century Chimu culture of the coast of Peru. With their elaborate cities and huge irrigation works, the Chimu dotted the land with fortresses and created the most impressive centralized government in South America before the coming of the Incas.

SUGGESTED READING

Adams, R. E. W. *Ancient Civilizations of the New World.* Boulder, Colo.: Westview Press, 1997. Brief but up-to-date account.

Brooks, G. E. *Landlords and Strangers: Ecology, Society, and Trade in Western Africa, 1000–1630.* Boulder, Colo.: Westview Press, 1993. Ecologically rooted study of social and commercial patterns among West African peoples during the period of the great West African empires.

Brose, D. S., J. A. BROWN, and D. W. PENNEY. *Ancient Art of the American Woodland Indians.* New York: Abrams, 1985. Good account of the artistic achievements of these North American peoples.

Coe, M. D. *Mexico: From the Olmecs to the Aztecs,* 4th ed. New York: Thames and Hudson, 1994. Expert overview for the general reader.

Connah, G. *African Civilizations: Precolonial Cities and States in Tropical Africa: An Archaeological Perspective.* Cambridge, England: Cambridge University Press, 1987. Geographical and archaeological analysis of centers of civilization from the Nile to the West African Sudan.

Feidel, S. J. *Prehistory of the Americas,* 2nd ed. New York: Cambridge University Press, 1992. Chronological survey, from the first comers to the emergence of complex societies.

Hassig, R. *War and Society in Ancient Mesoamerica.* Berkeley and Los Angeles: University of California Press, 1992. Theoretically informed study of war and empire-building.

Ibn Battuta, M. *Travels in Asia and Africa, 1324–1354,* trans. H. A. R. Gibb. New York: McBride, 1929. Vivid descriptions of the kingdom of Mali are among the selections translated here.

Josephy, A. M., ed. *America in 1492: The World of the Indian Peoples Before the Arrival of Columbus.* New York: Knopf, 1992. Regional and topical studies of Native American cultures.

Levtzion, N., and J. F. P. HOPKINS. *Corpus of Early Arab Sources for West African History.* New York: Cambridge University Press, 1981. Valuable primary sources.

Marcus, H. G. *A History of Ethiopia.* Berkeley and Los Angeles: University of California Press, 1994. Concise overview of Ethiopian history.

Middleton, J. *The World of the Swahili: An African Mercantile Civilization.* New Haven, Conn.: Yale University Press, 1992. Economic and social history of East African trading communities.

Niane, D. T., ed. *UNESCO General History of Africa,* Vol. 2: *Africa from the Twelfth to the Sixteenth Century.* Berkeley and Los Angeles: University of California Press, 1984. African perspectives on the history of the continent during the centuries before major Western penetration.

Nurse, D., and T. SPEAR. *The Swahili: Reconstructing the History and Language of an African Society, 800–1500.* Philadelphia: University of Pennsylvania Press, 1985. Swahili interaction with Arabs and Persians in the shaping of East African society.

Pearson, M. N. *Port Cities and Intruders: The Swahili Coast, India, and Portugal in the Early Modern Era.* Baltimore: Johns Hopkins University Press, 1998. Explores the African end of the Indian Ocean trade routes.

Smith, R. S. *Warfare and Diplomacy in Pre-Colonial West Africa,* 2nd ed. Madison: University of Wisconsin Press, 1989. The art of war as practiced among the West African kingdoms.

Young, B. W., and M. L. Fowler. *Cahokia: The Great Native American Metropolis.* Champaign: University of Illinois Press, 2000. Outline of archaeological and historical work at the Illinois site.

Please refer to the document CD-ROM for primary sources related to this chapter.

CHAPTER 14

TOWARD A LARGER WORLD
From the Bantu Migrations
to the Mongol Empire

500 B.C.E.–C.E. 1500

A Glance Ahead: Beyond the Cultural Zone

Over the course of this volume, we have seen cities, nations, and empires rise, expand to classic scale, and give rise to even vaster regional cultural zones. By 1500, there was only one more step to take: the clumsy, cruel, and uncertain lurch toward a global cultural zone.

The second volume of this book will be centrally concerned with the slowly growing rumble of globalization in the modern period. But before moving on to that enormous struggle—in which we are still involved today—we should pause for a look at peoples who pressed against regional barriers in earlier times.

It is a kaleidoscopic story, full of camel caravans and sailing ships, pastoral nomads, migrating peoples, and the astonishing explosion of the Mongol Empire. These early efforts to break through the boundaries of existing cultural zones laid down no lasting boundaries of their own. But their spirit—venturesome, often violent, and sometimes consciously expansionist—will become familiar as we forge ahead into a globalizing future.

Trade, Migration, Conquest

Pressing against the Boundaries

In the chapters of Part III, we have seen centers of civilization, new and old, expand and grow. We have seen how these core powers could shape large sections of the inhabited earth in their image, forging impressive cultural zones in many parts of the world. In this final chapter, we will encounter some restless peoples who pressed against these regional barriers—and some who broke through them.

Settled peoples, city-dwellers and empire builders, often seem to dominate history. Yet many historians today would say that real world history is the history of the margins of such cultural zones, of contacts between them, and of the impact of such contacts on the lives of peoples. In the period that emerged in the centuries around 1500, cultural outreach and interaction would certainly play an important role in the global story. Indeed, you can make a good case that the Western empire-builders who set sail with Columbus at the end of the fifteenth century and dominated most of the world by the beginning of the twentieth were the most successful of all these restlessly expansive peoples.

But they were not the first. This chapter will conclude our survey of expanding cultural zones with a look at transregional expansion beyond these spheres of regional influence.

Forms of Transregional Outreach

We have already seen a number of individual instances of such expansive outreach. Alexander the Great, born in the Greek zone, marched all across western Asia and died in Babylon. The Islamic faith and culture bound impressive slices of three continents into a vast transregional cultural zone. In this and earlier times, however, there were three particular forms of outreach that regularly carried peoples beyond the frontiers of the lands of their birth.

Long-distance traders were among the first to travel the seas and caravan trails of the world. Migrating peoples moved, slowly but inexorable, far beyond the familiar fields of home. And no people had a greater impact on distant populations than history's great conquerors, carrying their cultures on their spears and transforming the regions they overran.

We will look below at half a dozen of these peoples from the two thousand years before 1500. We will survey traders on the Silk Road and the Indian Ocean, at the slow but
enormously influential Bantu migrations across Africa and Polynesian reach across the
Pacific, and at the stunning impact of the Mongol Empire from one end of Eurasia to the
other.

EURASIAN TRADE ROUTES

The Horse-Trading Impulse

Commercial exchange has motivated merchants to reach out for many centuries. This
horse-trading impulse, originating often in ritual gift-giving and evolving into the classic
exchange-for-profit of historic times, seems to be widespread among peoples at all stages
of social evolution. Exchange of goods between urban societies and less developed neighboring peoples goes back as far as the city itself. There had been some culturally stimulating exchange between the major early civilizations of western Asia and Africa—the
cultures of Mesopotamia, Egypt, and Harappan India. Still, most of the trade in early
times was *within* the major civilized areas—back and forth across the Mediterranean, for
example, or up and down the Maurya Indian empire.

It was not till the first two centuries C.E.—the heart of the classic age—that the three
continents of Asia, Europe, and Africa were linked by highly developed regular trade
routes. And even that late, trade between North and South America is hard to prove, and
any trade at all between the Americas and the Old World very unlikely indeed.

Western European merchants return from the far end of Eurasia along the
Great Silk Road, reopened by the Mongols during the later Middle Ages. What
sort of animals are being ridden and used as beasts of burden here? What
features seem to be typical of the stylized cities shown on the map below the
travelers? (The Bettmann Archive)

Caravans on the Great Silk Road

The Old World was linked by two great lines of trade during the early centuries C.E. The northern road was the clopping hooves of horses and mules, the tinkle of camel bells, the dust and heat and babble of caravansaries—the land route across Asia. The southern route was the ruffle of lateen sails, the strumming of the monsoon wind in the cordage, gulls calling, and the smell of tar and spices in a foreign port—the sea route from Asia to Africa and the Near East.

The two great empires of the eastern and western ends of Eurasia—Han China and Rome under the heirs of Augustus—were the anchors of the land route. The middlemen were the peoples of the Persian Empire and the Kushans, whose empire included part of northern India but also stretched far up into Central Asia. Particularly when the Romans were not at war with the Persians and when the Chinese controlled the Tarim Basin north of Tibet, goods could flow in an uninterrupted stream from the banks of the Tiber to the Yellow River of North China.

Trade goods were normally carried across China's half-civilized far-west region of Xinjiang to the eastern end of the Takla Maklan Desert in the Tarim Basin, the beginning of the fabled Silk Road linking China and the Middle East across Central Asia. There the route divided, following strings of oases either north or south of the Takla Maklan, north of the Himalayas into the Pamirs. From the western end of the desert, the road wound up through the passes north of the Pamir Knot, where all the great ranges of Eurasia seem to come together, and down into the rich horse country of Ferghana.

From here, the route ran southwest across the Kushan Empire, across the Oxus and into Persia, and then west the length of the Persian Empire. South of the Caspian, south of the Black Sea, the road wound on over the Anatolian plateau and down at last to the warm shores of the Aegean, at the eastern end of the Mediterranean Sea.

Riding the Monsoon Winds to India

The sea route in the south hinged on India and Southeast Asia and included Africa in the complex equation. Chinese goods entered the flow of international sea trade in the far southeast of the Middle Kingdom, perhaps from Canton, perhaps from Haiphong, in what is today northern Vietnam. Merchandise flowed from there around the southern end of Indochina and through the Indonesian archipelago to Malaya. Goods were either transported by land through the jungles of the Malay Peninsula or carried by ship around the southern tip and northwest again between Malaya and Sumatra. Thence the sea lanes lay west to the southern end of India, or perhaps northwest across the Bay of Bengal to the muddy delta of the Ganges.

From the other side of India, one could follow the shore northwest around to the mouth of the Persian Gulf, up the gulf, and across western Persia to the Mediterranean. Or one could sail due west, riding the seasonal monsoon winds to the mouth of the Red Sea, and thence to the Axumite port of Adulis in East Africa or to one of several Egyptian ports for transshipment to Alexandria and the blue Mediterranean.

Still another flow of goods by sea began in Southeast Asia or in India and crossed directly on the steady monsoon winds to East Africa, perhaps with an intermediate break in the nation-sized island of Madagascar, early settled by Southeast Asian migrants. From East Africa, cargoes were carried by sea up to Axumite or Egyptian Red Sea ports, and from there overland to the Mediterranean.

A reconstruction of one of the ancient lateen-rigged trading vessels that once plied the Indian Ocean, carrying goods from South Asia to East Africa or the Near East. These triangular sails, borrowed by European shipbuilders, would add greatly to the maneuverability of Western ships during Europe's "age of discovery" around the time of Columbus. Arab dhows similarly rigged still make the shorter runs up to the Red Sea or the Persian Gulf today. (G. A. Ballard)

The most popular of all the goods that circulated on this interregional trade system was silk from China. Indian muslin and precious stones, spices from Southeast Asia, incense and drugs from Arabia, metals, glass, and pottery from Rome, and many other luxury items, light in proportion to their market value, were exchanged over the caravan trails and sea lanes of the classic age.

A great deal of coin of the realm also traveled from the West to Asia at this time. Europeans prized Asian goods much more highly than Asians valued European products. The Romans, therefore, had to pay cash for the silks and spices of the East. But while it lasted, this long-range commerce at least began the process of drawing the peoples of Eurasia together economically.

MIGRATION ACROSS AFRICA AND THE PACIFIC

Whole Peoples on the March

Perhaps the oldest of all forms of linkage among the widely dispersed peoples of the globe has been the continuing human urge to pack up and move on, to see if the grass is really greener on the other side of the fence, the pasture better on the other side of the hill. Such migration from one part of the world to another brings whole peoples together. It may result in war, as so frequently happened with the Eurasian steppe peoples. It may also lead to trade or even a fruitful exchange of ideas. Or it may even result in a merging of peoples and cultures into a new people, a new culture altogether.

EURASIAN TRADE ROUTES

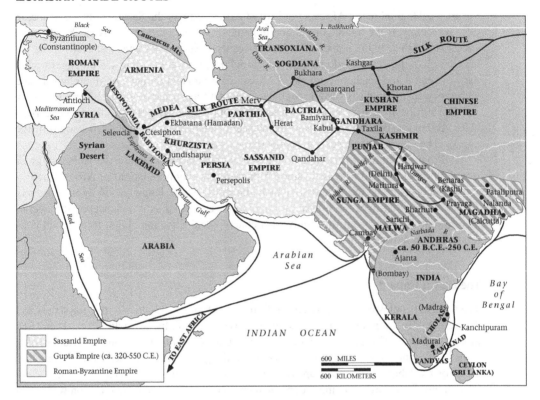

The great migrations of our prehistoric ancestors had peopled almost the entire globe with *Homo sapiens*, the most adaptable of all creatures. In the earliest age of urban culture, nomadic migrations had sometimes destroyed entire civilizations, as we have seen. Migrations had also, however, forged new peoples and new cultures, including those of ancient Sumeria, Gangetic India, and Greece. From the beginning of history, then, migration produced a yeasty mixing and melding of populations and ways of life.

This process continued in the classic age. Migrations and resulting mixtures of bloodlines and basic skills, folk-ways and mythologies, forged most of the great civilizations of this period in Europe, Asia, and Africa. An original mixing of Latin and Etruscan peoples produced the Romans, whose empire was as polyglot a mix as the world has seen. Indian culture was enriched during the classic age by the influx of new peoples—Greeks, Arabs, Kushans, and others—across the Northwest Frontier. Even China, in the most homogeneous end of Eurasia, felt the external pressure of nomadic steppe peoples such as the Xiongnu, and would be overrun by such peoples in the next stage of its history.

We will look in more detail now at two such instances of productive mass migrations: the great Bantu trek across Africa and the seaborne migrations of the island peoples of the Pacific.

The Bantu Migrations

We are used to thinking of Africa, or at least of Africa south of the Sahara, as black Africa. In fact, as recently as the middle of the first millennium B.C.E., black Africans inhabited only a small slice of their future homeland—the tree-scattered Sudanic savanna just south of the Sahara. North of the desert predominantly caucasoid peoples were herding and trading. Over all the vast central and southern portions of Africa, Khoi-San and diminutive Mbuti hunters and gatherers were thinly distributed through the great rain forests and over the southern savannas.

During the fifteen or more centuries after 500 B.C.E., the Bantu migrations carried black, Bantu-speaking peoples from the Western Sudan over most of Africa south of the Sahara. The secret of their success seems to have been iron.

All that we know of this great southward expansion must come from archaeology or from anthropological or linguistic study of the present-day populations of Africa. There is serious debate about the extent to which the culture and language of Bantu speakers spread independently of the migrating population. Unsettled as it is, however, the overall picture that emerges from this study of archaeological digs and Bantu root words is as dramatic as any written history.

The Bantu Impact

The African peoples who had moved south from the desiccated Sahara to the grasslands and the fringes of the rain forests farther south were typical Neolithic agriculturalists. They lived in small villages of wattle-and-daub huts, grew grains such as millet and dry rice, herded goats, sheep, and cattle. They made tools of carefully ground and polished stone. Apparently much of the labor was divided up by gender, women having traditional chores that were only slightly less heavy than those done by men. Social and political organization was based on family and clan, as it was in most of the world outside the walls of cities. Some of these peoples, especially in the West African end of the sudanic belt, spoke a language ancestral to the family of Bantu languages that are to be found in many parts of Africa today.

As indicated in an earlier chapter, we do not know for certain how these people learned to smelt and forge hard iron. But whether the new skill was developed independently in West Africa or acquired across the savanna from ancient Meroe, it proved an invaluable aid to the Bantu migrations. Equipped with iron tools and iron weapons, the peoples of the sub-Saharan grasslands pushed through or around the equatorial rain forests into central and southern Africa in a few centuries.

With iron tools came agriculture and a slow but certain withering away of the old hunting-and-gathering life. Cereals from the northern savannas came south with the Bantu cultivators. Another whole range of tropical crops—bananas, coconuts, and yams—were acquired by black settlers in East Africa from Indonesian immigrants. From northeastern Africa cattle and other domesticated animals spread into the south. With all these new peoples came distinctive styles of pottery, distinctive patterns of village life. And with these new things came the Bantu words for them—words that, like Indo-European roots in modern Eurasian languages, tell us much of what we know today about the spread of the culture that produced them.

By C.E. 500 or 1000 at the latest, Bantu-speaking ironworking agriculturalists were almost everywhere south of the Sahara. They still lived in small villages and organized themselves by family and clan. They were probably animists, believers in a multiplicity of nature spirits and in their own close relationship to gods, ghosts, and the rest of the natural world. Little remains of their art, but the famous Nok figurines show what they could do. These terra-cotta figures of animals and human beings, produced by the Nok people of northern Nigeria around the time of Christ, are relatively naturalistic by contrast with the normally nonrealistic traditions of most African art. The human figures are sometimes depicted wearing bracelets, beads, and other indications of a gracious style of life.

Seaborne Migrations Across the Pacific

We have dealt thus far with the precivilized peoples of the great continental landmasses— Eurasia, Africa, and the Americas. With Oceania we enter a very different world. For Oceania, though it includes the continent of Australia, is largely a world of water.

A remarkably wide variety of environments is encompassed in this fragmented collection of empty landmass, scattered archipelagoes, and open sea. The desiccated Australian Outback contrasts sharply with the steamy rain forests of interior New Guinea; countless barren atolls broiling in the sun differ from such tropical paradises as Tahiti and Hawaii. But the wide Pacific washes all their shores.

The ocean did not completely isolate Oceania from the rest of the world; there was probably considerable communication at least with the islands of Southeast Asia. But the surrounding waters did help shape the distinctive cultures of the region, affecting everything from their economies to their relations with one another. Above all, the Pacific became the pathway for the great Oceanian adventure—the long seaborne migration that is the heart of Oceania's history.

Australia and New Guinea had been reached by human beings during the great prehistoric migrations. The inhabiting of the rest of the jungle-clad volcanoes and coral reefs of the South Pacific would occupy the peoples of Oceania throughout most of their history.

The chronology of these immense seaborne migrations is much disputed by scholars. There seems to be a rough consensus among archaeologists and anthropologists, however, that Melanesia and Micronesia, closer to Southeast Asia, were settled first, during the period of civilization's beginnings. Most of Polynesia would not be explored and occupied by South Sea islanders till much later, during the first dozen centuries C.E.

From the Outback to Easter Island

The aborigines who had settled Australia thousands of years before had come as Paleolithic hunters and gatherers. The new migrants to the islands of Melanesia and Micronesia were Neolithic agriculturalists, though they hunted and fished as well. Like most of North and South America, then, western Oceania filled up with very successful Stone Age peoples.

The first South Sea islanders hunted animals and birds or speared fish in the rivers of Australia or the lagoons of the islands. They cultivated root crops such as taro and yams and tree fruit such as the coconut. They made tools and weapons tipped with smoothly ground stone or shell, and the remains of their famous Lapita ceramic ware are found today on many widely separated islands.

The Hawaiian Islands, the Society Islands (especially Tahiti), and the original Polynesians of Tonga developed strong chiefdoms, elaborate structures of class and rank, and a material culture that stands out today in museums of indigenous art. The large island of New Zealand fostered the inward-looking society of the Maori, whose carved war canoes were things of beauty. Far-off Easter Island—much closer to South America than to Australia—produced the unique Easter Island statues. These huge heads, probably of former chiefs, make the hearts of true believers in the mythical lands of Atlantis and Mu beat faster to this day.

But the most amazing accomplishment of these long voyagers, these Vikings of the Pacific, as Europeans would call them, was surely the long voyages themselves.

They sailed in outriggers or—for longer inter–island voyages—double canoes, lashed together with braces and a platform. Some of these vessels were reportedly a hundred feet long and could carry food, plants, and livestock for colonizing new islands, as well as a hundred or more Polynesians. They navigated by the stars, by the sun and moon, by the direction of the sea swells and the trade winds, and by the formations of the clouds. Their long double canoes were liable to break apart in heavy seas and were almost impossible to bail when they took in water. But they were "sea-kindly craft," normally stable, and their single triangular sail could carry them a hundred miles in a day of good wind.[1]

They set out in search of new homelands for many reasons. Famine in the home islands, defeat in war, frustrated ambition for political leadership could all impel Polynesians to take to the sea and head east, where experience taught them there were always more islands.

Cross-fertilizing each other's cultures as they voyaged routinely among the islands, hundreds and even thousands of miles between landfalls, theirs is certainly one of the most remarkable achievements of peoples on the move.

THE MONGOL CONQUESTS

Herders of the Steppes

While China shaped the societies and destinies of neighboring peoples, some of its most despised neighbors were poised to impact China itself—and the rest of Eurasia—more powerfully than any people ever had. These were the latest wave of steppe-dwelling nomads from the north—the Mongols—and their greatest leader, Genghis Khan.

The nomadic lifestyle adopted by the Mongol tribes had been determined from earliest times by dependence on moving herds of animals. These included goats, sheep, cattle, and even reindeer. The essential animals for riding and for transport were the horse, the ass, and the camel.

Among the Mongols, men traditionally dominated society, but women had a central place as well. Mongol warriors learned to live almost entirely off the milk, blood, and meat, the hides and the wool, of the animals they herded. But girls learned to ride as early as boys did—about the time they learned to walk! Women exercised primary control over

---

[1]Ben R. Finney, "Voyaging," in Jesse D. Jennings, ed., *The Prehistory of Polynesia* (Cambridge, Mass: Harvard University Press, 1979), p. 331.

the camp, and they could at least express opinions in tribal councils, though they apparently had no voice in final decisions.

Three clear patterns of migration guided the ponderous but purposeful progress of the nomads of northern Eurasia in particular.

As a pastoral people, first of all, they followed an established annual round, back and forth across a predefined territory where they knew they would find water and pasturage at each season of the year. As warrior peoples defending—or deliberately invading—unmarked grazing grounds, nomads also frequently clashed with other peoples. If they were defeated, they necessarily retreated from their familiar pasturage and set out in search of new territories—quite often clashing with still other pastoral folk. This jostling tended to flow from east to west, as uprooted nomads turned their horses' heads toward the warmer and moister grasslands of the western steppes.

There were, finally, the predatory southward drives of nomadic peoples into the fat lands of the city-based civilizations. Tempted by the wealth or weakness of the developed societies that stretched from one end of Eurasia to the other, these mobile armies, whole peoples on the move, could have a devastating impact.

Powerful leadership, military skills, and elan, combined with unparalleled mobility and the toughness that went with their rigorous style of life, made nomads formidable opponents for the cities and empires of the civilized zones. Pastoral nomads—as we have seen—left more than one island of urban culture in ruins.

Over the centuries their impact was heaviest on the sedentary populations of western Eurasia. The reason for this nomadic pressure on the West was what is sometimes called the *steppe gradient*—the warmer weather and superior pasturelands of the more southerly western steppes. By 2000 B.C.E., the steppe gradient had already drawn Indo-European nomads into Europe, where they became the ancestors of the Greeks and Romans, the Slavs, Celts, and Germans of later centuries. Other Indo-Europeans in the second and first millennia B.C.E. and Turko-Mongols in the first and early second millennia C.E. followed this historic drift from eastern Asia toward Europe. But they were masters of the eastern steppes as well—and imperial China's most unrelenting foe down the centuries.

Genghis Khan, Lord of All Men

Genghis Khan (1167?–1227) was born plain Temujin (Ironsmith), son of a minor Mongol chieftain on the chilly steppes northwest of China. While he was still a boy, his father was poisoned by enemies. The heir apparent had to flee from the tents of his own people to wander with a few followers, an outcast among the drifting clans.

He had tremendous physical strength and the physical courage expected of his people. He was also a natural political intriguer and a born military strategist—in both areas patient, cunning, and ruthless when the time to strike finally came. He was a religious man, a believer in the nature gods of the steppe, yet tolerant and eager to have priests of all faiths around him, lest he give offense to any powerful divinity. Perhaps strangest of all in a wandering child of the steppes, he had a remarkable head for organization. He organized his armies and his empire with a rigor that would have done a Chinese or Byzantine bureaucrat proud.

The motives that drove Genghis Khan have been variously represented. To some degree, certainly, it was the simple imperative of many nomadic conquerors before him. He

Joveyni (1226–1283) was a cultivated Muslim man of letters; he was also a Persian official in the employ of the Mongol conquerors of Persia. The desecration of the mosque of Bokhara by Genghis Khan and his pagan Mongols described here should be read with an awareness of the author's difficult position as a pious Muslim who served in the government of one of Genghis Khan's descendants.

Does Joveyni try to disguise the blasphemous behavior of the Mongols? How does the remark of the wise imam quoted here try to explain the desecration of Allah's house in terms of Allah's power? Does this explanation seem to mitigate the shocking behavior of the "World Conqueror" Genghis Khan?

"On the following day when from the reflection of the sun the plain seemed to be a tray filled with blood, the people of Bokhara opened their gates and closed the door of strife and battle. . . . Chingiz-Khan rode into the Friday mosque and pulled up before the maqsura, *[where he] asked those present whether this was the palace of the Sultan; they replied that it was the house of God. Then he too got down from his horse, and mounting two or three steps of the pulpit he exclaimed: "The countryside is empty of fodder; fill our horses' bellies." Whereupon [Chingiz-Khan's men] opened all the magazines in the town and began carrying off the grain. And they brought the cases in which the Korans were kept out into the courtyard of the mosque, where they cast the Korans right and left and turned the cases into mangers for their horses. After which they circulated cups of wine and sent for the singing-girls of the town to sing and dance for them; while the Mongols raised their voices to the tunes of their own songs. . . . After an hour or two Chingiz-Khan arose to return to his camp, and as the multitude that had been gathered there moved away the leaves of the Koran were trampled in the dirt beneath their own feet and their horses' hoofs. In that moment, the Emir . . . famous for his piety and asceticism, turned to the learned imam Rukn-ad-Din Imamzada . . . and said: "Maulana, what . . . is this? That which I see do I see it in wakefulness or in sleep, O Lord?"* Maulana *Imamzada answered: "Be silent: it is the wind of God's omnipotence that bloweth, and we have no power to speak."*

'Ala al-Din 'Ata Malek Joveyni, *The History of the World Conqueror,* trans. John Andrew Boyle (Manchester, England: Manchester University Press, 1958), pp. 103–104.

led his soldiers into battle, he once said, for the sheer exaltation of winning, the joy of seeing other men break and run before him, of taking their horses, looting their tents and cities. But there was a deeper motive at work as well behind that wind-darkened forehead, those enigmatic eyes—a religious motive. The Eternal Sky—chief of the Mongol gods—had ordered him to take the field against the world.

Drying pasturage and greed for the material luxuries of the cities, common motives for movements of steppe nomads, may also account in part for this greatest onslaught of the steppes against the softer, richer southern lands. But without the uniquely inspired leadership and genius for organization of this most remarkable of nomads, the long ride of the Mongols could never have happened.

In combat the Mongols would circle their enemies, discharging flight after flight of arrows. They might also pretend to flee, drawing their antagonists into yet more devastating barrages. But when enough enemy mounts and men had fallen, they would turn and charge, screaming columns of leather and fur and flashing swords, with always that relentless cloud of armor-piercing arrows driving on before them. That was the last sight many a more civilized soldier ever saw—the charge of the Mongol cavalry—before the dust and blood engulfed him.

In 1206, at a tribal conclave on the Kerulen River in the wastes of Mongolia, the clan chiefs of these Mongol warriors chose Temujin to be their paramount leader. He was neither a boy nor an outcast by then, but a seasoned warrior and a skilled political tactician who had outmaneuvered and destroyed all his rivals among the Mongol tribes. They made him their great khan—Genghis Khan, Lord of All Men.

The Mongol March Across Eurasia

The Mongol conquests, which began in Genghis Khan's time and lasted through most of the thirteenth century, astonished and horrified all the zones of civilization across Eurasia. Three major centers of urban culture were primary targets of Mongol raids, conquest, and eventual subjugation: Confucian China, the Muslim Middle East, and the eastern part of Christian Europe. Most of the world's largest landmass was thus shaken for a century by the pounding hoofbeats of the Mongol hordes.

Genghis Khan drove first down into North China, where he crushed the Tibetan and Jürched states that shared a divided China with the Song emperors in the south. The Great Wall had been breached and Beijing left a smoldering ruin by 1215, opening the way to the subsequent conquest of all North China and Korea.

After this first assault on China, Temujin turned his horses westward and advanced against the Muslim Middle East. Ancient trading cities like Samarkand and Bokhara were pillaged, their inhabitants slaughtered. By 1220 Afghanistan and Persia lay helpless before the Mongols.

The armies of Genghis Khan pushed on into European Russia, riding through the rich pasturelands of the Ukraine. There a flying column of Mongol horsemen met and overthrew a coalition of Russian princes in 1223. It was only a foreshadowing of what was to come.

To accomplish these feats, Genghis Khan had disciplined his troops as no Mongol horde had been before. He had added military experts from conquered peoples, such as the Turks and Chinese, and more elaborate military technology, such as the catapults and battering rams that now rumbled along in the baggage train. He had developed the process of preliminary intelligence-gathering into a fine art. He had turned the casual terrorism of any nomad campaign into calculated psychological warfare. And his unbeaten cavalrymen were still there, tough, ever-victorious, eager to conquer and loot the rest of the world for his successors.

Mongol armies rode west once more in the 1230s and 1240s. They captured and devastated Kiev, the old southern capital of Russia, and overran a number of northern Russian cities as well, including the still modest town of Moscow. From a base on the Volga, they sent massive raids into Eastern Europe. They ravaged Hungary and Poland and probed Austria before swinging back toward the northern grasslands.

In the 1250s powerful Mongol formations poured into Muslim Persia once more in a campaign that climaxed with the capture of Baghdad. The Abbasid capital was sacked and much of the population put to the sword. The last Abbasid caliph was trampled to death by Mongol ponies.

The conquest of the rest of Song China took the better part of half a century, but that too was accomplished—the first time all of China had ever been overrun by the nomads from beyond the Great Wall. In 1279 Genghis Khan's renowned grandson Kublai Khan overwhelmed the last Song emperor.

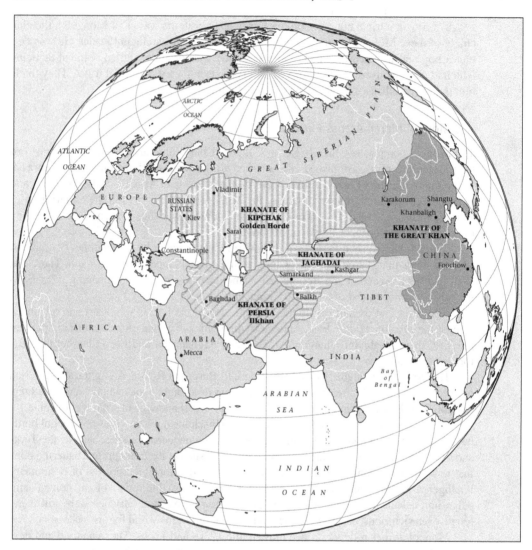

THE MONGOL EMPIRE

Mongol Mastery of the Eurasian Heartland

The empire the Mongols put together was the largest the world had yet seen. It included both the largest and the most populous of modern nations, China and Russia, as well as much of the Middle East and portions of Southeast Asia. It stretched all across Eurasia, from European Russia to the Far East.

This vast expanse was divided into four khanates, with a splendid capital at Karakorum in the ancestral grasslands of Mongolia. The premier khanate, the realm of the Great Khan, was East Asia, centering in China but including Korea, Tibet, and Mongolia itself. The Jagatai Khanate dominated a vast slice of central Asia. The Ilkhanate ruled the Muslim Middle East. And the Khanate of the Golden Horde governed the rolling expanse of Russia.

The imperial order imposed upon this heartland of the world island was a free-form combination of ancestral ways, military discipline, and borrowed bureaucratic techniques.

The government at Karakorum included administrators from a number of conquered peoples, organized in rough imitation of the developed bureaucracy of China. There were ministries of justice, of the treasury, and of war, and officials were trained by a government academy. Records were kept in a system of Mongolian writing that used Arabic script. A famous system of couriers and post houses carried the word of the Great Khan out across his far-flung realms.

Out in the khanates, however, native officials were generally allowed to continue governing as they had before the Mongols came. They had to pay their tribute regularly and obey all decrees from the khans. Beyond that, the rough feudalism of the nomadic tribes and clans seems to have prevailed.

The final source of Mongol strength, however, remained neither borrowed bureaucracy nor traditional clan structure, but the army. Efficiently organized in groups of tens, hundreds, and thousands, and led by officers promoted on merit, Mongol troops remained ready to ride on the shortest notice. And it was terror of the return of that host that kept the tribute coming and secured obedience to all decrees.

For a time, in the thirteenth and fourteenth centuries, Mongol predominance guaranteed order across northern Eurasia. It certainly opened the road to trade from one end of the world island to the other. Once more, as in the classic age, goods, ideas, and travelers could pass back and forth from Europe to China.

Marco Polo was the most famous merchant traveler to take that long road east and back again. The mere outlining of his route gives some sense of the magnitude of the Mongol achievement.

From Venice the Polos—Marco, his father, and his uncle—sailed to Acre (still a Muslim sultanate) and then plunged into the Ilkhanate, crossing today's Turkey, Iraq, and Iran to the Persian Gulf. They then turned up through Afghanistan and on across the Hindu Kush into the Jagatai Khanate of central Asia. They continued east across the Tarim Basin north of Tibet and on into the Great Khanate, crossed the Great Wall of China, and swung south at last to Beijing.

Later travels took Marco to Burma, to South China, and home by sea via India, the Middle East, Constantinople, and the Adriatic to Venice. The journey, which included much time spent in the service of the Great Khan, took him seventeen years. It was a journey that could not even have been undertaken a hundred years before.

Or a hundred years later. For the precarious Mongol imperium came soon to its end.

China Under the Mongol Khans

The Mongol Yuan dynasty that reigned in China for a century (1260–1368) was in many ways an interlude rather than a major period in Chinese history. Yet this was the China of the Great Khan Kublai, the "Cathay" that roused the awe and wonder of Western visitors such as Marco Polo, and it should be noticed here.

The conquest itself was a long and bloody business. The Song emperors of South China resisted for decades, depending on rivers and broken country to slow the Mongols and falling back at last on the port cities and their navy. The last Song emperor was killed in a naval battle off Hong Kong in 1279, ending a struggle that had lasted for forty-five years.

Marco Polo's arrival in the palace of the Mongol Khan Kublai is here imaginatively portrayed by a later illustrator. Marco and his older kin do not seem to be kowtowing as they may be presumed to have done before the most powerful ruler in the world, and the architecture and some of the accoutrements make little claim to authenticity. Nevertheless, some sense of pomp and opulence, and of alien cultures encountering each other, does seem to come across. (The National Palace Museum. Kublai Khan (1215–1294) ruled lands stretching from the Pacific Ocean to the Black Sea and founded the Yuan Dynasty in China (1279–1368))

Kublai Khan, the victor in the long war with the Southern Song, was the most remarkable Mongol after Genghis Khan. Grandson of the founder, he was also Great Khan, or Khan of Khans, nominal head of the whole sprawling Mongol Empire—though after he moved his capital south of the Great Wall to Beijing, his concerns were largely with his vast Chinese realm.

A Chinese portrait shows a well-padded face with a small, pointed beard and a moustache narrowing to carefully cared-for points. The eyes, under heavy lids, look small, clear, and thoughtful. Marco Polo eulogized him as a giver of alms, builder of public granaries, maintainer of roads, and so on, while allowing him the usual royal vices—overindulgence in food, concubines, and hunting.

Polo found the royal city of Cambaluc, as Beijing was then called, a vast twelve-gated metropolis several miles on each side, laid out foursquare with wide, straight avenues, splendid palaces, gardens, and courts. The royal palace stood in walled parklands a mile square. The central complex was a lofty building on a high platform decorated with gold, silver, and dragons. According to Marco Polo, as many as six thousand people could sit down to dine in the great hall—off gold plate.

The Mongols retained much of the Chinese political system, especially the six central bureaus established by the Tang dynasty and the general division of government into the civil service, the military, and the censors. They even strengthened the system—one of their few lasting innovations—by tightening the links between the central government and the provincial authorities. The result was probably a harsher autocracy than China had seen before.

As elsewhere, the Mongols retained as many natives in power on the local level as possible—here, the large numbers of Chinese clerks and bureaucrats. The new government also paid lip service to Confucian principles of government. But in practice the Mongol Yuan dynasty suspended the civil-service examinations, promoted few Confucian scholars to high positions, and turned most of the top spots in government over to a new, non-Chinese elite of Mongols and hired foreign officials, including Muslims from the Middle East and Christians such as the Polos.

Russia Under the Golden Horde

But the empire the Yuan dynasty ruled was the dominant component of a Eurasian realm much larger than China. A brief look at the far European edge of the Mongol Empire will emphasize this remarkable period of East Asian power in western Eurasia.

The Mongols who burst into Russia for the second time in 1236 were a whole horde on the move, with wagons, families, and herds, come to stay on the steppes of southern Russia. The Russian princes and city-states, organized in only the loosest of federations, were no match for the Mongols. City after city was sacked and burned, including the old southern capital of Kiev and the new one at Vladimir in the north. By 1240 the Mongols were effectively the masters of European Russia. They would remain so for the next two and a half centuries (1240–1480).

The khans of the Golden Horde—so called from the color of their tents—settled at a new city called Sarai on the lower Volga. Once the initial carnage was ended, the Tatar Yoke, as the Russians call the period of Mongol rule, was less onerous than it might have been. The khans retained control over princely successions and exercised a veto over all major policy decisions. Taxes had to be paid on time and recruits for the Mongol armies sent as ordered. Beyond this, the Russian cities, once they had dug out of their ruins, ordered their affairs pretty much as they wished. A senior Russian prince was even put in charge of tax collection for the Golden Horde, and Mongol officials rigorously punished any profanation of the Orthodox church.

The two and a half centuries of Mongol rule that followed left their mark on Russia. Russian economic growth suffered—from heavy tributes and from a number of punitive expeditions, the Mongol method of maintaining order in Russia. Politically, budding city assemblies that had had some power in the Kieven period withered under the Mongols. Thus, Russia lost the urban merchant oligarchies, the "rising middle classes" that appeared in Western Europe about this time.

A Mongol element may be detected in the Russian population, and some Mongol influence on Russian coinage, military organization, and early administrative practices. But the most significant consequence of the centuries of Russian subservience to the Golden Horde was the impetus it gave to authoritarian rule in czarist Russia.

The Russian people learned to accept harsh discipline under the Mongols. They carried over these habits of obedience into later centuries, making them excellent subjects for future czars. Some have even traced to these early models the seeds of a Russian style of autocracy that would be echoed in the hardfisted regimes of such later Russian rulers as Ivan the Terrible, Peter the Great, and Joseph Stalin.

The End of the Mongol Adventure

Like the expansion of the Islamic zone eastward across southern Eurasia, the Mongol conquest of most of northern Eurasia was unprecedented. Both would be precursors of the global wave of western imperialism to come. But the Mongol Empire would not last as long as either of these other surges of interzonal expansion.

The Mongol Empire, as indicated previously, depended in the last analysis on the unbeatable Mongol army. When Mongol armies began to fail of their objectives—as inevitably they did—the Mongol predominance was instantly in jeopardy.

Before the thirteenth century was out, a diminished Mongol horde was beaten by the Egyptian Mamelukes in Palestine. Mongol expeditions dispatched to conquer Japan discovered that a lifetime of cavalry warfare on the steppes was no advantage in facing the perils of a seaborne invasion. And thrusts into the dank heat of Southeast Asia, toward Burma, Vietnam, and Sumatra, fell afoul of climate and terrain as well as the tropic seas. There were limits, in short, to what even the Mongol military could do.

The political unity of the Mongol Empire also began to disintegrate within two generations of the death of Genghis Khan. There were too few Mongols to manage so vast a domain, even if they had developed the administrative skills to do so. There were inevitable quarrels among the khans themselves, and they tended to forget their redoubtable founder's warning that due recognition of the primacy of the Great Khan was essential for continued unity. When the Great Khan Kublai moved his capital from Karakorum to Beijing, he turned his attention more and more to Chinese affairs, and the lesser khans went their own ways in their own domains.

Most destructive of unity, finally, was the tendency of the victorious Mongols, like victorious barbarians in many other times, to adopt the culture of the more developed societies they had conquered. But since the Mongols had conquered peoples of so many different cultures, this process of acculturation soon divided the Mongols among themselves.

The fall of the Mongol Yuan dynasty in China followed the ancient Chinese pattern. Mongol rule was never popular there, and Mongols were never socially acceptable to cultivated Chinese. The conquerors dressed in leather and fur instead of silk, ate mutton and mare's milk instead of Chinese cuisine, frequently could not read and write, and had no surnames. Mongol women refused to bind their feet in Chinese fashion, went hunting on horseback with or without their husbands, and sometimes shaped the policies of even the Mongol emperor. Only shrewd leadership and brute force could keep these aliens in power, and after Kublai Khan there were no more great leaders shrewd or strong enough to accomplish this.

In the first half of the fourteenth century, eight lesser Mongol rulers tried to maintain the regime intact. But unbacked paper money led to inflation. The gods indicated their displeasure through repeated destructive flooding of the Yellow River and famine across North China. Secret societies such as the White Lotus proliferated, as in the last days of many dynasties, and rebellion flared in many provinces. During this prolonged crisis the Mongol leaders once more fell to fighting among themselves.

In 1368 a Chinese rebel leader expelled the Mongols from Beijing and declared a new dynasty—the Ming. The Yuan and their followers retreated northward to Mongolia, whence their famous founder had led their ancestors one hundred fifty years before.

Elsewhere, Mongol rule lasted longer. In Russia, a grand duke of newly prominent Moscow finally expelled the Golden Horde more than a century after China had overthrown its Mongol rulers. By 1500, the Mongol adventure was history across most of Eurasia.

In China, the Mongols left only a scattered legacy. They had strengthened the government, as they did elsewhere. They had encouraged further economic growth. They had developed craftwork by fostering the establishment of hereditary crafts within families. They had unintentionally encouraged the arts by driving classically educated people out of government to seek their fortunes where they could find them—even in the arts.

But like the Muslims at the other end of Eurasia, the Mongols had demonstrated the possibility of larger conquests than the world had seen before. Like restless traders on the Great Silk Road or the Indian Ocean, like Bantus drifting across Africa or Polynesians across the Pacific, the Mongols pressed against the traditional regional barriers of their time.

Other restless peoples would follow their example in the age just beginning as the Mongols drifted back to Mongolia. The centuries after 1500 would see vaster intercontinental empires, a genuinely world market emerging, and migrations that would dwarf all earlier such movements of peoples. But the world had confronted new faces in strange lands ever since the first hominids—probably already trading, certainly already fighting—had migrated north out of Africa.

SUMMARY

Through much of human history, some peoples have pushed restlessly beyond their own lands, beyond familiar boundaries, even beyond the broadest cultural zones. Such restless movement out into a larger world paved the way for the five centuries of genuinely global encounters we call the modern period.

Some of these earlier traveling peoples were long-distance traders, some migrants in search of new places to live, some conquerors of strange and distant peoples. Over the two thousand years between 500 B.C.E. and C.E. 1500, these peoples on the move voyaged, migrated, or imposed their rule on many peoples across a sizable slice of the globe.

Some of the oldest of long-distance trade routes were those across or around Eurasia. The most important or these were the Silk Road from China to Europe and the sea routes from China and India to the Middle East and Africa. Major long-term movements of peoples included the Bantu migrations across Africa and the Polynesian peopling of countless Pacific islands.

The largest land area ever conquered by any people was the stunning if short-lived Mongol conquest of much of Eurasia. Genghis Khan, the founder of the Mongol Empire, welded the nomadic tribes of the eastern steppes into an unstoppable cavalry army. Imposing centralized authority for the first time on the discordant whole, Genghis and successive khans made themselves masters of much of the world island.

In the end, like other conquerors before them, the Mongols reached their limits too. They penetrated only a short distance into Europe and failed to conquer Japan, India, or Southeast Asia. But Russia, China, Persia, and other substantial chunks of the heartland of human civilization fell under the rule of the Mongol hordes for the better part of two centuries.

The Mongols governed as much as possible through local agents and already established institutions. Yet Russia never forgot the Tatar period in its history, which even more than the Byzantine influence shaped the autocratic regime that emerged in Muscovy. And the Chinese Empire, despite much initial devastation, in the end achieved new levels of centralization under Marco Polo's much admired master Kublai Khan.

SUGGESTED READING

Allsen, T. *Commodity and Exchange in the Mongol Empire: A Cultural History of Islamic Textiles*. Cambridge: Cambridge University Press, 1997. The role of a key trade item in the empire.

Amitai-Preiss, R., and D. O. Morgan, eds. *The Mongol Empire and Its Legacy*. Leiden: Brill, 1999. Essays on the impact of Mongol rule, especially in the Middle East and China.

Bently, J. *Old World Encounters: Cross-Cultural Contacts and Exchanges in Pre-Modern Times*. New York: Oxford University Press, 1993. Excellent brief summary.

Christian, D. *Inner Eurasia from Prehistory to the Mongol Empire*. Oxford: Blackwell, 1998. Struggle between nomads and more settled peoples dominate volume 1 of Christian's *History of Russia, Central Asia, and Mongolia*.

Coleman, S., and J. ELSNER. *Pilgrimage: Past and Present in the World Religions*. Cambridge, Mass.: Harvard University Press, 1995. Multidisciplinary study of the meanings of pilgrimage in major world religions.

Curtin, P. D. *Cross-Cultural Trade in World History*. Cambridge: Cambridge University Press, 1984. Insightful overview of the part played by trade in binding distant cultures together.

Foltz, R. C. *The Religions of the Silk Road: Overland Trade and Cultural Exchange from Antiquity to the Fifteenth Century*. New York: St. Martin's Press, 1999. Spread of major religions, including Buddhism, Islam, and Christianity, along the great inner Asian trade route.

Halperin, C. J. *Russia and the Golden Horde*. Bloomington: Indiana University Press, 1985. The impact of the Mongol conquest on Russian history.

Kirch, P. V. *The Lapita Peoples: Ancestors of the Oceanic World*. Cambridge, Mass.: Blackwell, 1997. Pacific migration and the traces it left.

Langlois. J. D., ed. *China Under Mongol Rule*. Princeton, N.J.: Princeton University Press, 1981. Scholarly essays.

McPherson, K. *The Indian Ocean: A History of People and the Sea*. New York: Oxford University Press, 1993. Commercial and cultural exchanges in a context of international relations.

Ostrowski, D. *Muscovy and the Mongols: Cross-Cultural Influences on the Steppe Frontier, 1304–1589*. Sees the oppressive "Tatar yoke" of traditional Russian historiography as largely mythical.

Polo, M. *Travels of Marco Polo*, trans. R. Latham. New York: Abaris, 1982. Report of the celebrated merchant traveler to Kublai Khan's China.

Rossabi, M. *Khubilai Khan: His Life and Times*. Berkeley: University of California Press, 1988. Authoritative biography of the greatest of the Mongol emperors of China.

Ruysbroeck. *The Mission of Friar William of Rubruck . . . to the Court of the Great Khan Mongke, 1253–1255*, trans. P. Jackson. London: Hakluyt Society, 1990. Classic account of a visit to the Mongol Empire by a Western contemporary.

Severin, T. *In Search of Genghis Khan*. New York: Atheneum, 1992. Illustrated by good photographs.

Please refer to the document CD-ROM for primary sources related to this chapter.

Index

America. *See also* North America
  1960s, turbulence of, 713–714
  blacks, post-slavery lack of growth or self-government, 516
  Civil War, 512–514
  colonies, 467, 506–507
  conservatism, return of (post 1960s), 714–715
  critique of culture, literary, 754
  cultural exchange, 759
  cultural influences, 1600–1900, 528–530
  democracy, development of, 509–510
  Depression (*see* Depression, Great)
  diseases, 468
  economic growth at start of nation, 510, 512
  economic power, 763–764
  Epoch, 712
  farmers, problems of, latter nineteenth century, 516
  global foreign policy, current, 769
  immigrants, victimization of, nineteenth-century, 516
  Jazz Age, 615
  overseas expansion, 1900s, 518
  Panama invasion, 769–770
  Persian Gulf War, 770
  post-Civil War economic growth, 514–515
  power, post Iraq war, 778–780
  provincialism, 527–528
  Revolution, 507–509
  Roaring Twenties, 612–613
  slaves, impact on agriculture, 466–467
  slaves, lack of input in political process, 510
  superpower, establishment as, 680–681
  technological advances, 1920s, 615–616
  westward expansion, 582–583
  women, role of, 1800–1900, 515–516
Anabaptists, 380
Andes, 138, 139–140. *See also* Peru
Angkor, 4
Angola, 728
angst, 746
animism, in Africa, 324
anti-globalization sentiment, 771–773
Antoinette, Marie, 486
apartheid, 700
appeasement, 655
Arab Empire, 257, 259. *See also* Islam
Arab nationalism, growth of, 726–727
Arab-Israeli conflict, 702–703
Arafat, Yaser, 727
architecture. *See also* specific nations
  globalism, 750
  modernism, 748
Argentina, 526, 729
Aristarchus, 90
Aristotle, 87
  morality, 88–89
  politics, view of, 88
arms race, 691–692. *See also* Cold War
Arouet, Francois-Marie, 482
art. *See also* specific artists; specific nations' art
  Achaemenids, depicting, 157
  Appalachian, 757
  as propoganda tool, 750–752
  baroque, 497
  cubism, 748
  folk, 756–757
  French modernist, 753
  futurism, 748
  in Alexandria, 203
  modernism, 748
  Renaissance, during, 372–374
  Stone Age, 18–20
  traditional African, 560–561
Arthasastra, 103
as-Rashid, Harun, 259
Ashantis, 553, 554
Asia. *See also* specific nations

attempts to exploit, by outsiders, 573, 575
  cultural change in arts, 755–756
  East Rim, 717–718
  economics of 1990s, 2000s, 765–766
  filmmakers, 760
  trade with, seventeenth century, 464, 466
Assur, 43
Assurbanipal, 39
Assyrians, 43–44
atomic bomb, 672, 744
atomic theory, 742–743
Aum Shinrikyo cult, 747
Aurelius, Marcus, 163, 164–165
Austen, Jane, 494, 500
Australia, 718
  aborigines, 341
  prehistoric migrations, 341
Australopithecines, 12–13
Austria, 477–478
automobiles
  congestion, in Japan, 717
  rise in use, 612, 614–615
Axis of Evil, 778
Axum, 143
  agriculture, 204
  Christian survivors of, 320
  culture, 204–206
  location, 204
  rise of, 204
  temples, 206
  trade, 204
Aztecs, 133–134
  children, training of, 438
  development of civilization, 432
  gender roles, 438
  human sacrifice, 439
  luxuries, 433–434
  market economy, 433–434
  priests, 433
  pyramids, 135
  religion, 439
  rise, 433
  rulers, 434
  warriors, 433
  women, role of, 434

Babur the Great, 12, 393–394
Babylonian Captivity, 241, 375
Babylonian Empire, New, 44–45
Bagdhad. *See also* Iraq
  bazars, 260
  bureaucratic structure, 260
  history, ancient, 261–262
Bakr, Abu, 256, 257
ballet, 748
Bang, Liu, 186
barbarians, reign of, 225–226
Barbarossa, Frederick, 233
Battle of Poitiers, 256
Battle of Stalingrad, 665–666
Batuta, Ibn, 318
Bay of Pigs, 689
Beatles, 758
Benin, 427–428
Benin bronzes, 431–432
Berlin Wall, 684, 692, 715. *See also* Germany
Bess, Good Queen, 370, 371
Bhagavadgita, 104
Bharatiya Janata Party, 773
Bhutto, Benazir, 747
Big Brother, 753
Bilbao, Francisco, 530
bin Laden, Osama, 774
Black Death, 241, 744
Black Hand, 599

Black Shirts, 647
Blair, Tony, 764, 777
Blok, Aleksandr, 751
blues, 758
Boers, 571
Bohr, Niels, 742
Bolivar, Simon, 521–522
Bolsheviks, 627–628
Bonaparte, Napoleon, 486–487, 490
Borges, Jorge Luis, 749, 754
Bosnia, 721, 770
Boulton, Matthew, 489
Brahma, 104, 105, 182
Brazil, 526–527. See also Latin America
    economics, 729
    poverty, 729
Brezhnev, Leonid, 719
British East India Company, 462, 575
Brittain, Vera, 608
Bronte, Emily, 500
Bronze Age, 37, 306
Browning, Elizabeth Barrett, 494
bubonic plague, 241
Buddha, 4, 107. See also Buddhism
Buddhism
    calligraphy, 303
    decline, in India, 277
    dharma, 101
    doctrines, 107
    Hinayana, 182, 183
    Japan, introduction to, 308
    lamaism, 280
    Mahayana, 176, 182–183
    missionaries in China, 300–301
    missionaries in India, 283
    Siddhartha (see Siddhartha)
    suffering, cause of, 107
    temples, 107
    twentieth-century spread of, 747
Buonarotti, Michelangelo, 373–374
Burroughs, Edgar Rice, 125
Bush, George W., 775, 777, 778, 780
Byzantine Empire, 236–237, 256

Caesar, Augustus, 162–164
Caesar, Julius
    assassination, 161
    complexity of personality, 161
    political ambition, 160
caliphs, 257
    Abbasid, 261, 386
    control, 260
Calvin, John, 375–376, 378
Calvino, Italo, 752
Cambyses, 150
Canada, 718
Canterbury, 247
Canterbury Tales, 247–248
capitalism vs. communism. See also specific nations;
        Cold War
    economic strategies, 710–711
Cardenas, Lazaro, 636
Carlos the Jackel, 776
cartels, 494
Carter, Jimmy, 714
Carthage
    government, 132
    human sacrifice, 132
    rise of, 129, 130
    Roman emorie, as part of, 202
    sea power, 130, 131
    trade, 130, 131
Castro, Fidel, 686, 689, 729, 778
cathedrals, building of great, 246–247
Catherine the Great, 478

Catholic Church (see Roman Catholic Church)
caudillos, reign of, in Latin America, 523–524
cave paintings, 19
    Cro-Magnon, 19
    Les Eyzies, 20
Ceausecu, Nicolae, 721
Cellini, Benvenuto, 431
Chaco Canyon, 326
Chandra Gupta I, 179
Chandra Gupta II, 179–180
Chandragupta palace, 102–103
Chao, Ban, 191
Chao, Pan, 196
Charlemagne
    description, 227–228
    feudal lords beneath, 228–229
    heirs, 228
Charles VII, 242
Chaucer, Geoffrey, 247
Chavin culture, 138–141
Chavin de Huantar, 139
Cherokees
    ball games, 327, 328
Chichen Itza, 329
Chile, 527
Chimu
    geography/location, 330
    government, 331–332
    houses, 331
    legend of, 330
China. See also Asia
    agriculture, 543
    ancestors, veneration, 111
    art, ancient, 116–117
    art, during Manchu dynasty, 549–550
    borderlands during Song and Tang dynasties, 306
    Britain, war with, 577
    Bronze Age, 113
    Buddhism, growth in, 300–301
    calligraphy, 303–304
    city walls, Shang dynasty during, 111
    civil servants during Tang dynasty, 294
    Communist Party, 723
    Confucius (see Confucius)
    cultural supremacy, 108
    development, modern, 723–724
    economic development, 500 B.C.E., 113
    family, role of, 110
    filial piety, 110
    footbinding (see footbinding)
    Great Leap Forward, 723
    Great Wall of (see Great Wall of China)
    Han dynasty (see Han dynasty)
    horse-trading routes, 337. See also horse-trading
    hundred flowers period, 119–200
    imperialism, fight against, 577–179
    influence, 1500, 405
    Iron Age, 113
    isolation, 108
    Japan, threat of, 633–634, 635
    Legalism, 114, 116, 196
    literature, ancient, 117–118
    Long March, 634
    Manchu conquest, 541–542, 543–544, 549
    Mandate of Heaven, 112
    Ming dynasty (see Ming dynasty)
    neolithic era, 108
    Qing dynasty, 542–543
    regions, 108
    revolution, 625, 630–635, 723
    Shang dynasty, 110
    size, 108, 404–405
    Song dynasty (see Song dynasty)
    Tang dynasty (see Tang dynasty)
    Three Principles, 631

modernization, 554–555
mummification, 60–61
New Kingdom, 48, 50
Old Kingdom, 47
pharoahs (see pharoahs)
pyramid age, 45–46 (see pyramids)
religion, ancient, 58–60
temples, ancient, 57
women, rights of, 154
writings, ancient, 54–56
Einstein, Albert, 743
Eisenhower, Dwight, 686, 713
El Dorado, 459
Eliot, George, 494
Eliot, T. S., 749
Elissa, 130
Elizabeth I, 371
Ellison, Ralph, 754
Emerson, Ralph Waldo, 529
England. See Great Britain
Enlai, Zhou, 634, 724
Enlightenment, 482–484
Ethiopia
    Christianity, 319–320, 321
    Italian invasion, 656
    modernization, 555
    political system, medieval, 321
    Prester John, legend of, 321
Etruscans, 157–158. See also Rome
Euclid, 89
Europe. See also specific nations
    cities, role of, 365
    Dark Ages, 367–368
    debt after WWI, 610
    Eastern, recovery from revolutions, 720–721
    economic revival of 1500, 364–365
    nineteenth-century political change, 495
    population explosion, seventeenth century, 479–480
    rising middle class, seventeenth century, 479–480
    unity, moves toward, modern, 764–765
Eve, African, 11
Eve, view of during Middle Ages, 236
evolution, 12–13
existentialism, 745–746

Fatim (Muhammad's daughter), 260
Faulkner, William, 754
feminism, 714
Ferdinand of Aragon, 369, 456
Ferdinand, Archduke Francis, 600
feudal monarchy, 232–234
feudalism, 228–229
film, 758, 760
Fitzgerald, Scott, 615
Fitzgerald, Zelda, 615
folk art, 756–757
footbinding, 299, 411
Forbidden City, 408, 411
Ford, Gerald, 714
Ford, Henry, 617
Fourier, Charles, 493
Fourteen Points, 611
Fracis I, 368
France
    classical drama/novels, 497–498
    colonies, relationship between, 572
    economy, post WWI, 618
    empire building, seventeenth century, 461–462
    French Revolution (see French Revolution)
    reform following the revolution, 495–496
    religious wars, 368
    Revolution (see French Revolution)
    royal absolutism under Louis XIV, 475, 476
    royalty, rise of, 368
    women, role of, seventeenth century, 480–481

Franklin, Benjamin, 507–508, 529
Frederick II (Germany), 232
Frederick II the Great, 477
French Revolution
    Bastille, storming of, 485
    causes, 484–485
    hunger, 484
    ideological revolution, 485–486
    Reign of Terror, 486
    slums, 484
    third estate, 485
Freud, Sigmund, 744–745
Fu, Du, 302
Fuentes, Carlos, 754

Galilei, Galileo, 481
Gama, Vasco de, 458
Gandhi, Indira, 725, 726
Gandhi, Rajiv, 725
Ganges, 94
Gaozu, Han, 186
Garvey, Marcus, 638
geishas, 550
General Agreement on Tariffs and Trade (GATT), 663
George, David Lloyd, 603
Germany. See also World War I
    economic recovery after Soviet Bloc collapse, 715
    economy, post WWI, 618
    Nazism, origins of (see Nazism)
    post-WWI economy, 613
    rearmament, 657
    reunification, 715–716
    rivalry with Great Britain, prior to WWI, 600, 601–602
    war guilt, forced to acknowledge after WWI, 609–610
Ghana
    capital, 316
    description, 316
    historical overview, 316–317
    liberation, 696
    size/power, circa 1500, 423
    trade, 317
    war, 728
Ghandi, Mohandas K., 637–638
Ghazi princes, 387–389
Ghost Dance, 583
Gibbon, Edward, 165–166
Gita Govinda, 278
Gladstone, William, 495, 571
global village, 736
globalization, 355–356
Golden Horde, 350
Gomulka, Wladyslav, 684
Good Neighbor Policy, 617
Gorbachev, Mikhail, 682, 720
Gordimer, Nadine, 755
Gordon, General "Chinese," 584
Graham, Martha, 748
Grant, Ulysses S., 513
Gray, Tom, 9
Great Ball Court, 327
Great Britain
    African holdings, 571–572
    Age of Steam, 489
    colonies, liberation of, 594
    economy, post WWI, 618
    empire-building, early attempts at, 462–463
    Glorious Revolution, 479
    novels, moddle-class, emergence of, 498
    reform, age of, 495
    rivalry with German Empire, 600, 601–602
    Scottish Stuart dynasty, 478–479
    textile manufacturing, during Industrial Revolution, 489
    Tudor rule, 370–371
    war on terrorism, 773–778
    WWII defense, 662

arts, 102–103, 183–184
Aryan invasions, 97, 98
Asoka, reign of, 100–102
Babur, rule of, 393–394
Bharatiya Janata Party, 773
British presence, 575–576
caste system, 98–99, 106, 181, 275–276
Chandra Gupta I, 179
Chandra Gupta II, 179–180
Chola rulers, 280
Cholas, 273–274
climate, 94
crops in Gupta era, 180
dance, 278–280
Deccan (*see* Deccan)
Delhi sultanate, 272–273
democracy, move to, 724–726
Dravidians, 274–275, 280
Ganges (*see* Ganges)
geographical subdivisions, 94
Ghandi's nonviolent revolution, 637–638
Gupta rule, 393
Harappa (*see* Harappa)
harems, 394
Harsha, King, 272–273
Hinduism (*see* Hinduism)
influence in distant lands, 283–286
Kushans (*see* Kushans)
Land of a Million Elephants, 284
literature, in Gupta era, 184–185
marriages/sex, across castes, 276
mathematic achievements, in Gupta era, 185
Maurya dynasty, 100, 393
Mauryan carvings, 103
medicine, achievements in, in Gupta era, 185
monarchy, 99
Mughal rule and decline, 540–541
paintings, 279
Pakistan, conflict with, 704–705
poetry, epic, 103–104
rajputs, 274–275
raw materials, 178
religions other than Hindu, growth in, 276
scientific achievements, in Gupta era, 185
sculpture, 279–280
sea lanes, 337–338
sexuality, 278–280
Tamil culutre, 280
trade, 178–179
village life, 280–281
women, role of, 394–395, 551
women, role of in Gupta era, 181
indigenous peoples, demand for rights, 772. *See also* specific
    nations and peoples; Native Americans
Industrial Revolution
    Age of Steam, 489
    causes, 488–489
    energy output, role of, 487–488
    spread of, 493–494
    women, role of during, 494
influenza, 744
Information Age, 730
international commerce, 588–589
Iran
    ally of America, 703
    American embassy seizure, 703
    Khmomeini, Ayatollah Ruhollah, put into power,
        703, 704
    Revolution, 696
    shah, exile of, 703
Iraq, war on, 777. *See also* Hussein, Saddam
Iron Age, 65
Isabella of Castile, 369, 456
Isaiah, 72, 73
Isis, 60

Islam
    architecture, 399–401
    art, 265–267, 399
    city/village, in Muslim life, 395–396
    conquests, first, 256
    conversion, 384–385
    differences between worshippers, 254–255
    divisions, 253–254
    divisions, after Muhammad's death, 386–387
    fundamentalism, 766
    hadith, 263–264
    history, impact on, 253
    impact, fifteenth century, 384–385
    India, spread in, 277–278
    jihad (*see* jihad)
    Law of, 263
    literature, 397–399
    mosques, 266–267
    mullahs, 766
    philosophy, 267–268
    polygamy, 396
    prose, 267
    science, 267–268
    sectarian divisions, 264–265
    shiites (*see* shiites)
    simplicity, in early days of, 262
    spread of, 256–257, 258–259, 747, 759
    submission to, 262–263
    sufis (*see* sufis)
    vs. Christianity, 263, 324
    women, role of, 396–397
Israel. *See also* Middle East
    British mandate, 702
    creation of (ancient), 69
    economic growth, 718
    suicide bombers, 773
    technology advancements, 718
Italy
    Ethiopia, invasion of, 656
    facism, 646–647
    unification, 1850s, 497

Jains, 105, 106, 276
James, Henry, 529
James, William, 529
Japan
    agriculture, 415–416
    anarchy, 1500, 416
    art, circa 1500, 418, 419
    automobile crowding, 717
    Buddhism, introduction via Japan via Korea, 308
    bushi culture, 415, 416
    China, attack on, 1931, 655–656
    China, impact of culture, 307–308, 414
    China-Burma-India war theater, WWII, 666, 668
    Chinese-style laws (7th and 8th centuries), 308–309
    Christmas, celebration of, without Christianity, 747
    cultural accomplishments (Yamoto to Heian period), 310
    economic boon of 1900–1940, 585, 586
    economic downturn, recent, 766
    economic recovery following WWII, 674
    economic superpower, emergence as, 717
    Fujiwara, 309
    geography, 308
    Heian period, 309
    imperial ambitions, post WWI, 610–611
    imperial government, year 1200, 414–415
    Kabuki theater, 757
    literature, circa 1500, 419
    Meji Restoration, 576
    military limits, WWII, 666, 668
    novel, introduction of, 310
    Pearl Harbor, 664
    pollution problems, 717
    religion, circa 1500, 418, 419

MacArthur, Douglas, 687
Machi Picchu, 4
Machiavelli, Niccolo, 372
Machu Picchu, 441
Macmillan, Harold, 700
Magellan, Ferdinand, 2
Mahabharata, 103, 104
Mahavira, 106
Mahayana Buddhism (*see under* Buddhism)
Mahfouz, Naguib, 750
Maji-Maji Revolt, 584
Malaysia, 766
Mali, 316, 317–319, 423
Mamun the Great, 259
Manchuria, 414
Mandate of Heaven, 192, 197
Mandela, Nelson, 701
Manetho, 49
Manifest Destiny, 512
Maoris, 772
Maria Theresa, Empress of Austria, 477–478
Marlowe, Christopher, 374–375
Marques, Gabriel Garcia, 754
Martel, Charles, 256
Marx, Karl, 492, 493
Marxism, 624. *See also* Russia; socialism
Mary (mother of Christ), view of during Middle Ages, 236
Masaryk, Jan, 683
materialism, 498, 499
Mau Maus, 699
Mauraya Indian empire, 336
Mayans. *See also* Peru
  art, 216
  astronomy, 216–217
  calendar, 216–217
  classical, 143
  decline, 328
  development, 432
  economy, 215
  language, 217
  living standards, 215
  marriage, 215
  mathematics, 216
  political structure, 215
  pyramids, 135, 215–216
  religion, 215–216
  social structure, 215
  violence, 328
  writing, 217
McCarthy, Joseph, 712
McLuhan, Marshall, 736
Mecca, as birthplace of Muhammad (prophet), 251–252
Medici, Lorenzo de,' 366
Medicis, 365–366, 366
meditation, 759
Mei-Ling, Soong, 633
Melville, Herman, 529
Menelik II, 555
Mesoamerica
  agriculture, 328, 432
  Aztecs (*see* Aztecs)
  geography, 135–136
  Mayan city-states (*see* Mayans)
  Peru (*see* Peru)
  pyramids, 214
  Toltecs (*see* Toltecs)
Mesopotamia
  art, 56–57
  Assyrian rule, 43–44
  Babylonian Empire, New, 44–45
  city-state, 38
  crafts, 37, 38
  crops, 37
  deities, 39
  domesticated animals, 37

  dynasty of Sargon, 40–41
  irrigation, 37, 38
  law, system of, 42
  region, description of, 29, 35–37
  religion, 58–60
  temples, 56
  unification, impediments to, 40–41
  women, role of, 39
  writings, ancient, 54, 55
Mexico. *See also* Latin America
  desert Southwest, 208–209
  dictatorship at turn of 20th century, 525–526
  geography, 135–136
  Olmec culture, 135–138
  Revolution of 1910, 635–636
Miaoshan, Princess, 300
Michelangelo, 7, 373–374
Middle Ages
  Babylonian Captivity, 241
  barbarian rule, 225–226
  cathedrals, building of, 246–247
  Charlemagne (*see* Charlemagne)
  chivalry (*see* chivalry)
  Church life, 230
  cities, rebirth of, 231–232
  Crusades (*see* Crusades)
  depression at end of, 240–241, 242
  feudalism (*see* feudalism)
  literature, 247–248
  manors, 229
  monarchs, feudal, 232–234
  nobility, 231
  peasants, 229–230
  plague, bubonic, 241
  religion, role of, 243–244
  serfs, life and role of, 229–230
  urban sprawl, 231–232
  village life, 230
  women, role of, 230–231, 235–236
Middle East. *See also* Israel
  colonies, 575
  complexity of situation, 702
  Cyrus (*see* Cyrus the Great)
  geography, 149
  rainfall, 149
  Western view of, 149
Middle Kingdom, 48
migration
  as human desire/urge, 338–339
  by conquerors, 335–336
  transregional, 335
Mile High Center, 750
militarism leading to WWII, 600–601
Miller, Arthur, 754
Millet, Jean-Francois, 500
Milosevich, Slobodan, 721
Ming dynasty
  agricultural accomplishments, 409
  art, 417
  economics, 410
  governmental organization, 409–410
  Korea, influence on, 413
  maritime exploits, 409
  overview, 405, 407
  provinces, 410
  tributary system, 412–413
  vs. Manchu invaders, 411–412
  women, role of, 410–411
  Yongle emperor, 408–409
  Yuanzhang, Zhu, rule of, 407
Minoan Crete, 76
Mitterant, Pierre, 764
Mobuto, Joseph, 699
Mochica culture, 212
modern dance, 748

Omar (Muhammad's patron), 256
Opium War, 577
Orozco, Jose, 750
Orwell, George, 753
Osiris, 47, 60
Osman, 387
Ottoman Empire
   administrative operations, 390
   corruption, 538
   decline, after Suleiman's death, 537–539
   Ghazi princes, 387–389
   origins, 387–388
   Suleiman the Magnificent (*see* Suleiman the Magnificent)
Oyo, 554

Pacific islands
   geography, 339
   migrations, 339
   prehistoric migrations, 341–342
Pakistan, India, conflict with, 704–705
paladins, 247
Paleolithic period, 16–20
Palestine Liberation Organization, 703, 782
Panama invasion, 769–770
Pasha, Muhammad Ali, 554
patriarchy, description of, 26
Pavlov, Ivan, 745
Pax Americana, 712, 782
Pearl Harbor, 664
Pei, I. M., 750
Peloponnesian War, 84–85
Pelstinian issue, 702–703
Pentateuch, 67
Pericles, 82–84
Peron, Eva, 729
Peron, Juan, 729
Perry, Matthew, 576
Persia
   Achaemenids (*see* Achaemenids)
   art of imperial age, 156–157
   classes, 154
   decline following Shah Abbas's death, 539–540
   diversity, 154
   dynasty of Cyrus (*see* Cyrus the Great)
   dynasty of Darius (*see* Darius the Great)
   empires vs. small politics, 152–153
   gender relations, 154
   Safavids, rise of, 390–392
   Sassanids rule, 153–154
   Zoroaster faith (*see* Zoroaster)
Persian Empire, 80–82
Persian Gulf war, 770
Persian Gulf, tensions in, 727
Peru
   Andean ruins, 139–140
   art, 140–141
   Chavin culture, 138–139, 140–141, 211–212
   Chimu (*see* Chimu)
   civilizations, vanished, 212–213
   geography, 138–139
   Mochica culture, 212 (*see* Mochica culture)
   postclassical period, 330
   religion, 140–141
   stone terraces, 139, 140
   worship centers, 328
Peter the Great, 478
Peter, Saint (*See* Saint Peter)
Petrarch, Francesco, 374
pharoahs, 47
   Akhenaton, 52–53
   god powers (people's belief in), 47, 48
   Hatshepsut, 50–51
   hereditary lineages, 46
   power of, 53
   pyramid tombs, 48

Ramses II, 53
   Thutmose III, 51–52
Philip Augustus, 232, 233
Philip II, 369
Philip of Macedon, 85
Phoenicians, 65–66, 66
phonograms, 55
physics, Newtonian, 743
Picasso, Pablo, 748
pictograms, 54–55
Pilgrimage of Grace, 379
Pitt, William, 463
Pizan, Christina de, 367
Pizan, Christine de, 367, 374
Pizzaro, Francisco, 459
plague, the, 241
Plath, Sylvia, 754
Plato, 87
   ethical teachings, 88
   morality, 88–89
   universe, view of, 88
PLO (*see* Palestine Liberation Organization)
Poe, Edgar Allen, 529
Poland, 721
polio, 744
polis, 78–79, 83. *See also* Greek Civilization
Polish Solidarity, 685
Polo, Marco, 347, 348, 752
Pompey, 161
popes, power of, 234, 235. *See also* Roman Catholic Church
Populist reform, 1890s America, 517–518
Portugal
   Asian exploration, 458
   treaty with Spain, 1494, 460
postmodernism, 752–753
poststructuralism, 745, 746–747
poverty, Third World issues, 723. *See also* economics; shantytowns; Third World
prehistoric world
   human development (*see* human development)
   Old Testament version of, 7
   origins of earth, scientific, 8
Princip, Gavrilo, 599
Progressivism, 517–519
Prussia
   German unification, 496–497
   Hohenzollern dynasty, 476, 477
Ptolemy, 90
Pueblos
   at Chaco Canyon, 326
   culture, of the Anasazi, 326
   description, 326
Puig, Manuel, 753
Putin, Vladimir, 765
pyramids
   age of, in Egypt, 45–46
   Aztecs, 135
   Chavin, 139
   Mayan, 135, 215–216
   size, 57
   Teotihuacan, 214
Pythagoras, 89

Qaddafi, Colonel, 726
Qian, Sima, 197
Qianlong, 542
Qing, Jiang, 724
Quran, 262, 263, 264. *See also* Islam

Rabelais, Francois Shakespeare, William, 374374
racial diversity, 15–16
Rajputs, 548
Rama, Prince, 103, 104
Ramadan, 252
Ramayana, 103